# The Women of Mexico City
## 1790-1857

# The Women of
# Mexico City, 1790-1857

SILVIA MARINA ARROM

STANFORD UNIVERSITY PRESS

STANFORD, CALIFORNIA

Stanford University Press, Stanford, California

© 1985 by the Board of Trustees of the
Leland Stanford Junior University

Printed in the United States of America

Original printing 1985
Last figure below indicates year of this printing:
01  00  99  98  97  96  95  94  93  92

Published with the assistance of the Andrew W. Mellon Foundation

Library of Congress Cataloging in Publication Data

Arrom, Silvia Marina, 1949–
  The women of Mexico City, 1790–1857.

  Bibliography: p.
  Includes index.
  1. Women—Mexico—Mexico City—History—19th century.
I. Title.
HQ1465.M6A77  1985    305.4'2'097253    83-51324
ISBN 0-8047-1233-6 (cl.): ISBN 0-8047-2095-9 (pbk.)

∞ This book is printed on acid-free paper.

*To David Robert Oran*

# Acknowledgments

THERE ARE MANY who have helped with this book over the years since it began as a doctoral dissertation at Stanford University. I am particularly grateful to my dissertation adviser, John J. Johnson, for his encouragement, advice, and editorial assistance at every stage of the research and writing. I have also benefited from the suggestions of many colleagues who read all or part of the manuscript and answered specific questions. I especially wish to thank José J. Arrom, J. G. Bell, Beatriz Bernal, William Christian Jr., John Coatsworth, Edith Couturier, Mary L. Felstiner, Estelle Freedman, Tamara Hareven, Doris Ladd, Asunción Lavrin, Peggy Liss, Celia Maldonado, Barbara E. Mnookin, María Dolores Morales, Alejandra Moreno Toscano, Robert Potash, Silvia Ravelo de Arrom, Beatriz Schmuckler, Peter H. Smith, Barbara Tenenbaum, Emilia Viotti da Costa, and John Wirth. My greatest debt is to my husband, David Oran, whose constant support, criticism of each draft, and expertise with computers and word processors improved this book in countless ways.

In Mexico, the Seminario de Historia Urbana of the Departamento de Investigaciones Históricas, Instituto Nacional de Antropología e Historia, accepted me as a member in 1971 and 1975, shared their research with me, and generously allowed me to use their data bank of the 1811 census and the base map of Mexico City that appears herein. The task of investigation was facilitated by the kind staffs of the Archivo General de la Nación, the Archivo Judicial del Tribunal Superior de Justicia del D.F., the Archivo General de Notarías, the Archivo del ex-Ayuntamiento de la Ciudad de México, the Colección Lafragua at the Biblioteca Nacional, and the Hemeroteca Nacional. I am also thankful to

Guillermo Floris Margadant for allowing me to use the library of the Seminario de Derecho Romano e Historia del Derecho Mexicano at the Facultad de Derecho of the Universidad Nacional Autónoma de México.

Financial support for this book came from many sources. The dissertation research and writing was funded by a Foreign Area Fellowship from the Joint Committee on Latin American Studies of the Social Science Research Council and the American Council of Learned Societies, a pre-dissertation travel grant from the Stanford University Latin American Studies Program, and a Weter Memorial Fellowship from the Stanford University History Department. Subsequent research expenses have been funded by two grants from the A. Whitney Griswold Fund and the Concilium on International Studies at Yale University.

Some of the material in Chapters Two and Three first appeared in my articles "Cambios en la condición jurídica de la mujer mexicana en el siglo XIX," *Memoria del II Congreso de Derecho Mexicano* (Mexico City, 1981), and "Marriage Patterns in Mexico City, 1811," *Journal of Family History 3, 4* (Winter 1978), copyrighted (1978) by the National Council on Family Relations, 1219 University Ave. Southeast, Minneapolis, Minnesota 55414, and used with their permission. Parts of Chapter Five appeared in *La mujer mexicana ante el divorcio eclesiástico (1800–1857)* (Mexico City, 1976).

The shortcomings of this book are, of course, entirely mine. Since it is in many ways an exploratory study, I hope that others will come after me, explore new data, and revise the interpretations I have offered.

S.M.A.

# Contents

# Tables

## Text Tables

## Appendix Tables

# Figures and Illustrations

## Figures

## Illustrations

# The Women of Mexico City
## 1790-1857

# Introduction

## The Problem

On Christmas day 1839 doña Frances Inglis Calderón de la Barca, the Scottish wife of Spain's first minister to independent Mexico, arrived in the Mexican capital. Soon afterwards she wondered in her journal: "How do the Mexican ladies occupy their time? They do not read—they do not write—they do not go into society. For the most part they do not play—they do not draw—they do not go to the theatre—nor have they balls, or parties, or concerts—nor do they lounge in the shops of a morning, or promenade in the streets—nor do they ride on horseback. What they do not do is clear, but what do they do?" Two years later Fanny, as she was usually called, answered her earlier query: "With the time which they devote to . . . charitable offices, together with their numerous devotional exercises, and the care which their houses and families require, it cannot be said that the life of a Mexican señora is an idle one—nor, in such cases, can it be considered a useless one."[1] So completely had Fanny changed her opinion after being accepted into Mexican society and becoming acquainted with her friends' activities (which included nearly everything she once thought they did not do) that she deleted the original entry from the published edition of her journal.

Fanny's initial impression is lent weight by much of the historical literature. In the rare instances when women are mentioned at all, they are usually portrayed as passive, powerless beings, absorbed in familial duties, confined to the home, and totally subordinated to men. There were exceptions, to be sure: some lower-class women forced to work by desperate poverty, occasional strong-willed widows, a few vicereines, saints, writers, and heroines of the independence wars. The literature strongly implies, however, that beyond chronicling the celebrities, there was little worth saying about Latin American women until the twentieth century, when their position began slowly to improve.

Apart from a very few dissident voices, Mexican writers agreed that marriage and motherhood were "the duties to which nature solely destined" women.[2] The division of roles and spheres should be complete, with men "governing States, cultivating the Sciences, and bestowing splendor on Nations" and women "limiting themselves to the interior of the family home."[3] The perfect wife knew her place: in the words of the liberal thinker José Joaquín Fernández de Lizardi, "she dedicated herself entirely to pleasing her husband, . . . recognizing at the same time his superiority and her necessary dependence on him; thus she never asked where he was going or whence he came; neither did she attempt to discover his secrets or keep track of the money he earned; even less did she oppose his wishes in anything, or dissipate in luxury and fashion the sweat of his brow."[4]

Later generations accepted this prescriptive literature or the superficial impressions of travelers as accurate descriptions of nineteenth-century women's lives. Depending on their own perspectives on women's proper roles, these authors either praised the "domestic angels" of the past or decried their oppression. Liberal humanists bemoaned the "emptiness" and "monotony" of a life consisting solely of matrimony and motherhood, where women were "not allowed" to work outside the home and were "condemned to an existence of ignorance and triviality."[5] Marxists characterized Latin American women as "owned, privatized, ensconced in the home, isolated from each other, from the means of production, and from the mainstream of society."[6] Traditionalists yearned for the tranquil days when women were content with a life devoted to Family and Church, before the foundations of civilized society began disintegrating.[7] But all agreed on the basic outlines of what has become the stereotype of Latin American women.

Women's actual behavior was another matter. Thus don Celestino Porras, a Spanish merchant testifying at his sister-in-law's divorce trial in 1816, stated that "she has excellent qualities . . . and is very much devoted to her home, virtues difficult to find among women in the Kingdom of New Spain." The conservative historian and statesman Lucas Alamán distinguished between the exemplary women of rural Mexico—"loving wives, good mothers, retiring, assiduous, and kind"—and those of "the capital and certain other large cities where the corruption of morals is common." Another writer complained that Mexican women shunned their destiny by avoiding marriage: "Spinsterhood, cancer of the very fabric of morality, gangrene of the population, . . . is making rapid, surprising, and devastating progress."[8]

Clearly, then, the stereotype is not a reliable guide to actual behavior, but I found it a useful starting point for organizing my research. My initial questions fell into three general areas. First, I sought to discover if adult women's roles and spheres were as narrowly defined as the literature suggests. This line of inquiry raised numerous subsidiary questions. What proportion of women married or entered consensual unions, and for what portion of their lives? Did they marry young, to be reduced to "mere shreds" by constant childbearing?[9] Was the cloister the only viable alternative to matrimony? Which women deviated from these norms and under what conditions? Was it primarily widows and single women who engaged in economic and legal transactions, because they could not depend on men? Did the participation of married women in public activities reflect support for wives to enter the public sphere, or were they primarily substituting for absent or incapacitated husbands? If it was mostly lower-class women who engaged in public activities, was this because behavioral norms were class-specific, or were they shared by women of all social backgrounds?

Second, I sought to discover the extent to which women were dominated by men. Was Mexico a classic patriarchy, with women denied authority in both public and private matters, or were there certain areas they controlled, such as childrearing, the allocation of household resources, or personal property? In what ways could a woman appeal to community pressure or formal institutions to limit her husband's or father's power? Did women often make such appeals, and how did society view those who did? How many women in fact lived in male-headed households where they could be subject to male rule?

Third, I wondered whether significant differences might be found between younger and older women, married and single, upper class and lower class, Spanish and Indian. The stereotype makes no such distinctions, reflecting the universality typical of myth. Neither did educated women of the time, who identified with "the sex to which I belong" and professed their concern "for the betterment of my sex."[10] Yet in an era when women were said to *tomar estado*, or fix their place, by marrying or entering a convent, it is likely that their experiences varied considerably once they took such a step. And in a highly stratified society, where divisions were both socioeconomic and ethnic, there may not have been a female experience that transcended the lines of race and class.

In the course of my research, I discovered evidence that women's experiences had changed during the first half of the nineteenth century, and the nature of this change became a fourth concern of mine. What had happened to prompt a prominent writer in 1836 to announce that "the progress of Mexican civilization is especially evident in the Fair Sex"?[11] Had this "progress" led to improvements in women's status in ways that could be measured and evaluated? Was the change initiated by independence, as liberals claimed, or did it begin earlier, as a number of late colonial writers suggested, denouncing an even more distant past when women had been relegated exclusively to domestic roles?[12]

It is customary to begin or end studies of Mexico with 1821, on the assumption that independence was a watershed. It made sense to test this assumption by going back to the 1790's, when important legislation expanded female education and abolished guild restrictions on women's work, and forward to 1857, when the promulgation of the liberal constitution led Mexico directly into the Wars of Reform. These dates do not entirely bind this investigation; since social change occurs slowly and builds on previous trends, the first chapter reviews the principal developments affecting women in the second half of the eighteenth century and the Conclusion hints at the direction of later change.

## The Place

Mexico City is an ideal location to study women during late colonial and early republican times. As the richest and most sophisticated city of Mexico, capital of the viceroyalty of New Spain and then of the independent nation, new ideas and institutions found their way there quickly. As the seat of Church and government offices, center of international commerce, and home of leading intellectuals, it generated a mass of documentation of exceptionally high quality. In a thinly researched field, it has been intensively studied, making it possible to relate findings on women to contemporary historical processes.

Mexico City women were not, in all likelihood, representative of Latin America. In an overwhelmingly rural hemisphere, the Mexican capital was distinctively urban. The marketing and manufacturing hub of a broad agricultural hinterland, it had a diversified economy on the verge of industrializing, and a growing middle class. It was also distinctively Hispanic, for in a country populated mostly by Indians and Castes (as Mexicans designated those of mixed blood), half the capital's inhabitants were of Spanish descent.[13]

As the nineteenth century opened, the residents of this cosmopolitan center fully expected to join the ranks of leading centers of the Western world. Their hopes were dashed as independence brought political instability and recession, the worst experienced by any Latin American country. Although scholars have long acknowledged the potential for social change in these developments, they have not yet focused on women as contributors, victims, or beneficiaries.

Discussions of the late colonial period present it as a time of ferment. The Intellectual Revolution of the Enlightenment reached New Spain in the last half of the eighteenth century, with its doctrine of natural rights, questioning of authority, secular emphasis, and desire for social progress. This revolution coincided with another, which David Brading terms the Revolution in Government. Following the British capture of Havana in 1762, the Bourbon kings embarked on an ambitious campaign of "defensive modernization" to restore the power and glory of the

Spanish empire. Informed by enlightened theories, they enacted sweeping programs to consolidate colonial administration,
strengthen the State at the expense of entrenched corporations,
increase the colony's wealth, improve its education, and stream-
line the system of production and trade.[14]

Less well documented are other alterations in colonial life. An
unprecedented eighteenth-century population boom was the
key to the rapid urbanization of Mexico City. By the end of the
century, the fragile balance of the countryside around the capital
was threatened by the demographic upsurge and simultaneous
expansion of haciendas and ranchos onto Indian lands. Remaining village holdings sustained their growing populations with
difficulty; tribute payments, levied according to the number of
men, became an ever harsher burden. Natural disasters compounded these maladies. As recurring droughts and epidemics
hit central Mexico, villagers were driven off the land and left for
haciendas and cities seeking work, food, and charity.[15] In 1784-
87 alone, when the Valley of Mexico was ravaged by crop failures and disease, some 40,000 unemployed migrants streamed
into Mexico City, a sight so menacing to one colonial administrator that he proposed building a wall around the capital to
keep them out.[16]

Although the rural poor constituted the majority of migrants
arriving in the capital, Mexico's "most distinguished citizens"
were also drawn to urban life. Unlike the unskilled laborers,
who usually came from surrounding towns, artisans and professionals came from the leading provincial cities and from as far
away as Spain. Just as Mexico City's commerce and bureaucracy
provided employment for well-educated men, its social activities, consumer market, medical services, convents, and cultural
life attracted those who could afford them. The concentration of
the well-to-do in turn created a demand for servants, clerks, and
craftsmen, thereby contributing to the city's drawing power.[17]

Mostly as a result of migration, Mexico City's population increased by a third during the second half of the eighteenth century and continued to grow at an even faster pace during the
first two decades of the nineteenth. Annual growth rates, though
imprecise because of the unreliability of population statistics,
suggest that on the eve of independence Mexico City was grow-

ing at an annual rate of 1.4 percent, more than twice the rate for the colony as a whole (see Table D.1). Its 137,000 inhabitants in 1803 made it the largest city in the Western Hemisphere and the fifth most populous in the Western world.[18] Many thousands more migrants flooded into the city during the drought years of 1808–10; in 1811, when refugees swelled its population to 168,846, it may have surpassed the enormous Aztec capital on whose foundations it rested.[19]

With the increasing demand for consumer goods, the capital began to boast thriving—if somewhat primitive—factories producing textiles, cigars, glassware, leather, and other goods processed from agricultural and pastoral products. The Crown directly encouraged some of this economic growth by establishing the Royal Tobacco Factory in Mexico City in 1765, a huge monopolistic enterprise that employed close to 7,000 workers under one roof. The capital's textile industry also expanded dramatically, especially in the 1790's when the Napoleonic Wars cut off European imports and forced native capitalists to find local sources for investment. In addition, the city prospered from a late colonial spurt in mining and agricultural exports that fil tered through its merchant houses.[20]

Mexico City's economy was not as healthy as it looked, however. Praise of the city's majestic avenues, spacious plazas, glittering churches, and palatial residences alternated in travelers' accounts with horror at the vast inequalities of fortune and the miserable condition of the city's poor. Even though Mexico City had more upper- and middle-class inhabitants than the rural areas, they were still only a small part of the population. A breakdown of households in the 1811 census sample by number of servants, perhaps the best single indicator of status in nineteenth-century Mexico, provides a rough idea of the relative size of the capital's socioeconomic groups. By the measure of three or more live-in servants, the upper class—people of independent wealth, prosperous merchants and miners, top-level bureaucrats and clergy, ranking military officers, and the titled nobility—at most accounted for 4 percent of the capital's households. Another 18 percent had one or two servants, and might be considered middle class, though they were in fact closer to the top than the bottom, part of the *gente decente* rather than the *populacho* or *plebe*, the main line of demarcation in this society. This group included the intellectuals, professionals, merchants and businessmen of modest means, government and private clerks, middle-ranked militia officers, and lower clergy. It also included some successful independent artisans and small shop-keepers who, though contemporaries did not label them middle class, lived with some comfort, had a servant, and considered themselves superior to the unskilled workers of the lower class. At the bottom were the masses, those who worked with their hands, if indeed they worked at all. The vast majority of city residents were either wage earners in factories and workshops, manual laborers, peddlers, and household servants—or *léperos*, the ragged poor who lived from hand to mouth as occasional workers, beggars or, if we are to believe contemporary accounts, thieves.[21] In 1803 the Prussian scientist Alexander von Humboldt numbered the unemployed "dregs of the people" at "from twenty to thirty thousand wretches"; by midcentury, observers placed them as high as a quarter of the population. In the capital's most prosperous years, then, at least one-fifth of the residents lived in abject poverty and without work, while many more found it a constant struggle to earn their daily bread.[22]

During the last two decades of Spanish rule, Mexico City's elites increasingly shared in the economic uncertainty that had long been the lot of its poor. Late colonial prosperity was dampened when Spain exacted a series of forced contributions for its European war efforts, notably through the Consolidación de Vales Reales of 1804. With the outbreak of the independence wars in 1810, the economy deteriorated still further. Although the capital was spared the fighting, it endured periodic food shortages and interruptions of commerce and communications. A primate city controlling provincial wealth, it reflected the decline of regional economies. Some agricultural and mining areas received direct war damages during the prolonged struggle; others suffered from the flight or conscription of the labor force and the loss of mules required to transport goods to market. As Doris M. Ladd has argued, the real victim of the war was investment. With public confidence shaken, the wealthy sent their capital abroad. The resulting breakdown in the credit system affected the whole of New Spain and ushered Mexico into nationhood with minimal capital reserves and near bankrupt.[23]

Mexico did not regain its colonial prosperity during the first half century of independence. The country soon became mired in political unrest and economic stagnation, each reinforcing the other with disastrous results. The new nation experienced 44 changes of government and three foreign invasions between 1821 and 1857. Law and order deteriorated as contending factions staged coups, and banditry and smuggling spread. Caste uprisings and secessionist movements threatened to fragment the nation, and half the national territory was lost in the Mexican-American War. Silver mining and smelting, the mainstay of colonial wealth, remained paralyzed in many areas, lacking the necessary infusion of capital and cut off from supplies of cheap mercury previously assured by the Crown. Commercial agriculture stagnated in central Mexico owing to the instability of the countryside and the disruption of trade. Local textile industries collapsed when early republican governments opened Mexican ports to cheap imported cloth, although protective tariffs and a short-lived government development bank spurred a recovery in the 1830's. Meanwhile, high military expenditures and loan repayments drained the national treasury. Bankrupt administrations were often unable to meet the day-to-day expenses of governing, let alone invest in railroads and other badly needed infrastructural improvements. And, as often observed, whenever salaries went unpaid, the military revolted. New loans, taken out at exorbitant rates, extinguished rebellions, but merely postponed the inevitable crises.[24]

Mexico City felt these difficulties keenly. Its leadership challenged by the provinces, its wealth and influence declined. Disappointed visitors to the independent capital contrasted its rundown appearance with the glowing colonial accounts they had read.[25] The city's troubles were reflected in its demographic trends: once the largest metropolis in the hemisphere, by midcentry it had been matched by Rio and Havana and outdistanced by Philadelphia and New York. Although Mexico City remained the country's leading city, it failed to keep up with national population growth. Its average annual increase of approximately 0.3

percent from 1824 to 1857 was less than half that of the nation as a whole. Moreover, this increase was erratic. The city's population fluctuated between 160,000 and 205,000 for four decades, dropping markedly after epidemics like those of 1833 and 1850, then recovering slowly, apparently as much owing to continued migration from depressed mining and agricultural centers as to natural growth.[26]

Faced with these vicissitudes, Mexican leaders heatedly debated the direction the new nation should take. They often divided on how to achieve progress, some espousing federalism or centralism in the early decades, and later liberalism or conservatism. Liberal ideas in particular had the potential to alter gender roles. The emphasis on freedom, equality, and natural rights, the abolition of hereditary political power and ascriptive privilege, and the promotion of private property and liberty of contract logically undermined the inequality of the sexes, just as the changes in city life potentially expanded women's opportunities.

## The Sources

Women's experiences cannot be documented easily, since they rarely appear in the standard sources used by historians. Furthermore, historical records, almost entirely created by an educated elite, emphasize the privileged classes. Their perspectives are important, but I wanted to move beyond them to explore broad patterns of social thought and to understand the daily lives of "ordinary" women. I especially wanted sources that both spanned the first half of the nineteenth century, permitting an analysis of trends over time, and included lower-class women, the vast majority of urban women and a group crucial to an assessment of the impact of change.

Four types of documentation fit these prerequisites to a greater or lesser degree: laws and legal commentaries, censuses, notarial records, and ecclesiastical divorce cases. Because each deserved to be dealt with at some length, the sources largely dictated the structure of this book. Chapter One, based on well-known published material, outlines the changes contemporaries considered important for women. The remaining chapters explore the effect of these changes on four areas of women's lives. Chapter Two examines women's legal status, analyzing the conceptions of their roles in laws and legal commentaries. Chapters Three and Four examine demographic patterns and work as reflected in censuses and notarial records. Chapter Five defines the position of women within marriage as revealed in ecclesiastical divorce cases. The Conclusion draws from a variety of sources to show how developments in these disparate areas led to a readjustment of ideas about women at midcentury.

Each type of document provides different and sometimes contradictory perspectives on women's experiences. Laws, for example, can tell us much about the possibilities for women in Mexico City and the limitations on them. They also express ideas about women's proper activities and relationships to men. Although drafted by elite men, laws are a better source for social norms than scattered writings in newspapers, pamphlets, and books because they were supposed to cover all foreseeable circumstances and apply to women of all classes. Because they regulated existing situations, they are one level closer to describing women's experiences than didactic writings that show how Mexicans wished their society to be. But the laws themselves cannot tell us whether they were obeyed or enforced. In addition, given that most laws in nineteenth-century Mexico were centuries old, they might reflect antiquated views. Legal commentaries and proposals for legal change go far to rectify this drawback, since they demonstrate how Mexicans viewed their laws and how they believed judges interpreted them in most cases. However, such materials do not necessarily show how people actually behaved.

Censuses, notarial records, and court records counteract these biases to some extent. As official sources, not filtered through the minds of writers intending to regulate, entertain, or instruct, they in some respects more accurately document women's daily activities, but do so spottily. Valuable though these records are in providing details unremarkable to contemporary observers— and therefore unremarked by them—we never know how many women are omitted from them, and we are never told enough about the ones who are included. For example, though censuses show the distribution of various features of marriage and employment over the population as a whole, they give us a skeleton without flesh and blood. The same is true for the contracts and wills in notarial records, which provide statistical information on marriage, fertility, and economic transactions for a more limited segment of the population. The unusually rich municipal census of 1811 allows some fleshing out of these patterns, but in the absence of comparable censuses, those data cannot be compared with figures for earlier and later years except at the most general level. Records of litigation between husbands and wives show how laws were applied in practice and provide intimate views of family life. Of these documents, ecclesiastical divorce suits are especially useful for studying marital relations. But even these illustrate social values and points of tension more than behavioral patterns, for there is no way of knowing how representative the couples involved are. And, as with other sources, the person who furnished the information or recorded it might have had reason to be less than honest. Even when truthful, each document, written for a particular purpose, unwittingly gives undue emphasis to one aspect of women's experiences.

Because these sources are partial and imperfect, I have supplemented them with such published materials as city guides, newspaper advertisements, didactic pieces in ladies' magazines, essays on educational reform, and humorous pieces satirizing the mores of the time (available in abundance because of the expansion of the periodical press during this period). Novels and travelers' accounts were particularly valuable for this study, though they too have their weaknesses. Mexico City was the home of two of the earliest Mexican novelists. José Joaquín Fernández de Lizardi's *El Periquillo Sarniento* (1816) and Manuel Payno's *El fistol del diablo* (1845–46) are magnificent *costumbrista* pieces that attempted to depict daily life accurately. Full of details of the material culture, such as clothes and buildings or scenes of work and play, they are less reliable in their description of individual behavior and social norms because they emphasize the unusual and dramatic. Fernández de Lizardi's didactic novel *La Quijotita* (1818–19) is primarily a reformist tract and does not furnish evidence of contemporary Mexican behavior. Payno's *Bandidos de Río Frío*, a colorful evocation of midcentury Mexican life, must be used with caution as a source for the mores of the time because the author wrote it in European exile during 1889–91.

The eyewitness descriptions of foreign travelers are also of decidedly mixed value. Beyond repeated remarks on women's smoking, gambling, and tiny feet, they often tell us less about Mexicans than about the travelers themselves. Students of Mexican history are fortunate, however, in having two outstanding travelers' accounts for this period. Alexander von Humboldt wrote his *Political Essay on the Kingdom of New Spain* after a scientific expedition to Mexico in 1803 and 1804, during which he had access to a wide range of official documents, some of them since lost. Fanny Calderón's *Life in Mexico*, a lively and perceptive narrative of an extended residence in Mexico from 1839 to 1841, illustrates not only her own activities, but those of elite women in the Mexican capital with whom she became intimately acquainted.

Yet some aspects of women's experiences are ignored by all these sources. Mexican women did not keep diaries, and the few surviving letters I located afford only rare glimpses of how they felt and what they believed. Educated women of the time did not even write novels, as so many of their counterparts in Europe and the United States did. Although some published essays on current issues or petitioned government offices on behalf of various causes, these documents were meant for public consumption. Women's innermost thoughts can occasionally be gleaned from depositions in court records, but again, the testimony was meant to appeal to authorities. I have therefore tried to refrain from guessing at women's feelings. I can only hope that in sorting out clues from available evidence, I have portrayed a world they might recognize.

# ONE

# The Mobilization of Women

NINETEENTH-CENTURY liberals, writing in a partisan vein, depicted the colonial era as a Dark Ages for women, from which they began to emerge only after independence. This bleak portrait of ignorant and idle women, living in rigid enclosure, led the historian Mary Wilhemine Williams to argue that until the twentieth century, Latin American "women were not encouraged or permitted to make their contribution toward general social and national development."[1] Yet this view would have been foreign to Mexicans in the late colonial period when, far from being discouraged, women were urged to help bring about social change.

Contemporaries believed that though women had not been integrated into "social and national development" in the past, they should become so in the future. Thus Bourbon officials, desiring to consolidate their power and promote colonial wealth, encouraged women's education and incorporation into the labor force. They included women in their plans, not because they intended to raise women's status, but because they considered female cooperation essential to progress and prosperity. By 1810 their efforts had initiated a subtle transformation of women's experiences in the Mexican capital. The outbreak of the independence wars reinforced this trend, as both royalists and insurgents sought to involve women in the struggle; and after independence Mexican leaders, faced with the misfortunes that befell the young republic, continued to recruit their countrywomen. Because colonial and republican reformers understood that women's mobilization required the modifying of traditional values, laws, and institutions, they set about making the necessary changes. These efforts had effects beyond their immediate aims, gradually altering the way women saw themselves and the way they were seen by others. By the time Mexican liberals took up their pens, there had been a perceptible change in women's lives, although it began much earlier than they cared to admit.

This chapter outlines the attempts to mobilize women for national development, concentrating on changes contemporaries advocated for women as well as changes they believed had taken place. Relying on published essays, newspapers, and legislation, it necessarily presents the perspective of an educated elite. To the extent that women's experiences are documented by the occasional testimony of privileged women or by examples from the lives of celebrated heroines, we only learn the impact of these developments on a few individuals of the upper classes. Taken together, however, the mobilization of women created broad possibilities for the improvement of their status. Later chapters will explore how events of the first half of the nineteenth century affected these possibilities and what they meant for a larger group of women.

## Educated Mothers

Education was the most far-reaching and sustained part of the effort to mobilize women. Touching women of all classes in Mexico City, it was a high priority for Bourbon officials and republican Mexicans alike. This emphasis was the very hallmark of the Enlightenment; at a time when Europeans were increasingly concerned with childrearing, the proper formation of mothers became an essential feature of the new educational programs. Enlightened reformers believed that economic and political development demanded a transformation in values: reason and knowledge must replace superstition; habits of work, saving, and initiative must supplant aristocratic leisure; civic concern must conquer indifference. Because of women's pivotal role in instilling these ideas in future citizens, motherhood took on a civic function, increasingly exalted in the writings of the time. And since mothers could fulfill their responsibilities only if they were themselves first enlightened, reformers vigorously advocated the education of the Fair Sex.

Educating women clashed with traditional attitudes in a society where few women received schooling, where some men believed women incapable of learning and others saw female education as unnecessary—or downright dangerous. Benito Gerónimo Feijóo y Montenegro, the father of the Spanish Enlightenment, attempted to dispel these notions in his *Essay on Woman, or Physiological and Historical Defence of the Fair Sex*, published in 1739. Arguing that both sexes were inherently equal in intellectual ability, he attributed men's apparent superiority to a socialization that allowed them to develop their talents, while forcing women to restrict their thoughts to cooking, dresses, and love. Feijóo maintained that, with proper instruction, women could be equally valuable members of society. In subsequent decades Spanish writers like the count of Campomanes and Josefa Amar y Borbón, expanding these arguments, insisted that women's education was required in order to secure their cooperation with social reform.[2]

Enlightened reformers wanted to educate women in the broadest sense of the term, to prepare responsible mothers, thrifty housewives, and useful companions for men. In addition to providing a solid training in reading, writing, and arithmetic, the curriculum was to cultivate women's spiritual development. Christian doctrine was therefore essential, along with enough of the principles of politics and history to develop a well-informed citizenry. Sewing, cooking, and other housekeeping skills were prescribed even for wealthy women, so they could properly supervise servants and, if need be, adjust to changes in fortune— for contemporaries were well aware of the precarious state of the economy.[3] Among the poor, it was especially important that "the education of women bring to the most miserable hut the habits of order, economy, and work, which daily serve to improve the condition of the worker."[4]

The new ideas about feminine education began to be implemented in cosmopolitan Mexico City soon after they were aired in Spain. The Company of Mary, a Catholic teaching order, arrived in the Mexican capital in 1753 and opened a boarding school in the Convent of Nuestra Señora del Pilar. It soon became known as La Enseñanza (literally, the Place of Teaching). Five years later a separate school, dubbed La Enseñanza Nueva, was established to instruct Indian girls.[5] A third school, the Colegio de San Ignacio de Loyola, opened in 1767. Popularly called Las Vizcaínas after its Biscayan founders, it gave preference in admittance to daughters of men from that province in Spain. Although these schools have yet to be fully investigated, pioneering studies by Josefina Muriel, Gonzalo Obregón Jr., and Dorothy Tanck Estrada give us an idea of the curriculum offered by the end of the colonial period. La Enseñanza and Las Vizcaínas, the most prestigious of the three schools, took girls from the age of seven and gave them what was a complete education for the time. Both taught reading, writing, religious precepts, embroidery, sewing, and music, along with some Latin, arithmetic, science, and history. La Enseñanza Nueva, oriented to the lower status of its Indian students, taught only basic literacy, instead emphasizing household skills like washing and ironing that seemed more suited to the humble destiny of its alumnae.[6]

These differences in curricula show that female education was not intended to facilitate social mobility; on the contrary, it was meant to reinforce the existing social system while serving national goals. As the *Semanario Económico de México* put it, "The comfort and wealth of one class of women may make it convenient for them to become enlightened . . . with certain noble arts that will elevate them in their station." Not so for others, who "because of their destiny should dedicate themselves solely to the care of the home [or] work in servile jobs in order to subsist." Reformers understood that women's education should be adapted to their position in society, for as the editors of the *Semanario* concluded, "it cannot be otherwise."[7]

Enlightened schooling at first reached a restricted number of women in Mexico City. Although surviving documents disagree on the enrollments of the three schools (La Enseñanza and Las Vizcaínas together had anywhere from under 200 to 326 elite pupils in 1790; La Enseñanza Nueva had 55 to 125 Indian pupils), it is evident that they served only a small fraction of the female population in a city with approximately 130,000 inhabitants in 1790. A few wealthy girls were tutored at home, but most Mexican girls received no formal schooling or studied with the *amigas*, schoolteachers known as friends. More like nurseries than primary schools, the amigas' establishments accepted

children from the age of three, offering them rudimentary instruction. According to the amigas' critics, these spectacled old
ladies, who barely knew how to read and write themselves, primarily provided day care for harried mothers and taught girls
little more than to memorize the catechism, pray, and sew.[8]

Female education was given new impetus in 1786, when the
municipal government became directly involved in improving
the public school system. In that year the city council issued a
series of decrees in response to a potentially explosive situation:
as the capital filled with migrants escaping a terrible famine in
the countryside, the council ordered parishes and convents to
establish free primary schools to keep vagrant youths occupied.
The city fathers also encouraged existing institutions to take
non-paying students and proposed the establishment of two
municipally funded schools.[9] These directives met with some resistance but nevertheless produced results: La Enseñanza and
Las Vizcaínas were among the convents founding *escuelas pías*,
as the free day schools were called. Las Vizcaínas opened its
"pious school" in 1793, daily enrolling up to 500 girls, mostly
daughters of artisans.[10] As the demand for women's education
grew, beneficence institutions opened or expanded existing
schools. In fact, two retirement houses originally established to
provide refuge for widows and spinsters, San Miguel de Belen
and Nuestra Señora de Covadonga, were converted into educational institutions in 1787 and 1794.[11] Thus by 1802 approximately 3,100 girls were enrolled in 70 convent, parish, municipal, and private schools.[12]

Women's education was still a controversial issue in Mexico
City newspapers at the turn of the century. In 1807 the *Diario de
México* obliquely attacked opponents of female schooling, refer-
ring to the "fools who see women as creatures destined solely
for pleasure and servitude, as if they were incapable of contributing to the highest goals of the State, once enlightened." Three
years later the *Semanario Económico de México* insisted in a crusad-
ing tone that women were both educable and in need of education. Answering its own "Interesting Question: Should Women
Be Enlightened?" with an emphatic Yes, it assured its readers
that woman "contributes most particularly to the happiness of
the State. . . . In her bosom man begins to exist, in her lap he

grows, is nourished, and acquires his first notions of Good and Evil. [Therefore] women have even more reason to be enlightened than men."[13]

A decade later Fernández de Lizardi conceived his novel *La Quijotita* as a plea for the reform of women's education. In it he contrasted two well-to-do sisters, doña Eufrosina and doña Matilde, and their daughters Pomposa (La Quijotita) and Pudenciana. Doña Eufrosina embodied the female faults that El Pensador Mexicano (as Fernández de Lizardi styled himself) wished to eradicate. She was superstitious, frivolous, and vain. Devoted to luxury, the latest fashion, and the social whirl, she frittered away her husband's money, spoiled her children shamelessly, and turned her home over to unsupervised servants, giving Pomposa to wet nurses in infancy and sending her to the neighborhood school as soon as she was weaned. Doña Matilde, on the other hand, embodied the enlightened domesticity Fernández de Lizardi wished to cultivate in women. As humble and modest "as a retiring novice," she devoted herself personally to the care of husband, child, and home. Unlike her sister, she nursed her daughter, put her in school only at the age of five, and did not overindulge her. Her daughter Pudenciana thrived under this positive influence, became a fine young woman, married well, and lived happily ever after; Pomposa sank to the depths of poverty and prostitution, and met an early death.

Throughout the next half century, as Mexicans called for improved female schooling, they echoed these criticisms of contemporary women. Reformers complained that women's limited and superficial education made them woefully unfit for their historical task. Indeed, female reformers were among the hardest on their own kind. In 1823 the teacher doña Ana Josefa Caballero de Borda condemned women's "barbarous ignorance, mortal enemy of all good and original source of all evil," as the "distinctive characteristic of the women of our land." Their frivolous consumption (especially after independence, when the opening of Mexican ports to foreign goods expanded the demand for luxury articles) prevented the nation from channeling its scant resources into productive investment. Worse still, their failure to take their maternal mission seriously produced children who were "animals as dangerous as they [were] torpid and burdensome to the nation." "The Delicate Sex," she concluded, was "the fatal cause of [Mexico's] misfortunes and present state of decadence." Soon after the crushing defeat in the Mexican-American War, an anonymous female writer similarly blamed women for "our political and moral indifference, our neglect of our duties and interests, the abandonment of our country, our weaknesses, our petty vanity." Yet she held out the hope that "all this would change if our mothers were respectable matrons and strong and virtuous citizens. . . . To improve their education is, in a sense, to happily transform the human race." [14]

By the middle of the century few questioned the need for women's education. Opposition to female schooling had diminished to the point where, in 1841, the editor of the *Semanario de las Señoritas Mejicanas* could pronounce it "antique." [15] The journalist Florencio del Castillo apparently represented an established consensus when, in 1856, he declared, "The most effective way to better the moral condition of the land is to educate women." The proper instruction of women, then, was to be an integral part of the solution to national problems.

Republican governments, following in the footsteps of their colonial predecessors, thus encouraged the expansion of primary education. Tanck Estrada documents how successive administrations established the Office of Public Instruction, held evening classes for adults, insisted anew that parishes and convents run free schools, and attempted to raise the quality of instruction at existing institutions. An 1842 law made education obligatory for girls and boys aged seven to fifteen. Although unenforceable because of the shortage of elementary schools, the adoption of such a law shows what Mexican governments would have liked to accomplish, had it not been for their perennial financial straits.

Although female education did not expand as much as republican governments would have liked, Mexican observers noted a marked improvement after independence. For example, the liberal theoretician José María Luis Mora wrote in his 1836 *Mexico and Its Revolutions* that "the Fair Sex in Mexico" had advanced considerably in the last generation. While conceding that women's schooling still left something to be desired, he claimed it was far superior to that offered under the colonial regime, when their instruction was "reduced to the barest essentials required to fulfill domestic obligations." Mora was optimistic that, as the curriculum expanded and women's "fondness for reading" progressed, the new generation would surpass the last.[16] Indeed, each succeeding decade increased Mexicans' pride in women's schooling, at least in the capital, where educational opportunities were greater than in the provinces.[17]

The scant available evidence suggests that enrollments did not actually exceed colonial ones until the 1840's, for both schools and enrollments had declined during the struggle for independence. By 1838 they had barely recovered, with 3,280 girls registered in 82 convent, parish, municipal, and private institutions in Mexico City. Then, as new primary schools were established in the next two decades, enrollments doubled, with girls attending school in approximately the same numbers as boys. The quality of girls' schools was apparently raised as well, with incompetent teachers increasingly replaced and a more demanding curriculum introduced. Writing and arithmetic were taught in all schools; languages, geometry, geography, drawing, and—in compliance with a government order—civics were added to the instructional program of older girls.[18]

Although universal education remained a mirage, an increase in female literacy can be documented with a variety of sources. As Table 1 shows, the proportion of women who could not sign their names to their wills dropped steadily between 1802–3 and 1853–55. To be sure, the figures may reflect no more than a rise in rudimentary literacy; but in the proliferation of ladies' magazines in the 1840's and 1850's we have more solid evidence of a growing female reading public. Although periodicals "for the entertainment and edification of the Fair Sex" were edited by men, women wrote letters to the editors and sent in musical compositions, poems they composed or translated from the French, and solutions to puzzles appearing in previous issues. Most women preserved their anonymity with pen names like "La Preguntona," "La Crisálida," or "A Sixty-Two-Year-Old Subscriber." A few women ventured to sign their names. One was Margarita Hernández, who proudly acknowledged her authorship of a "Waltz to the Memory of the Unhappy Days of July 15, 1840" (the date of a coup against the government of Anastasio

TABLE 1
Illiteracy Among Mexico City Will-Makers, 1802–1855

| | Females | | Males | |
|---|---|---|---|---|
| Period | Number in sample | Number illiterate | Number in sample | Number illiterate |
| 1802–3 | 100 | 20 | 100 | 0 |
| 1825–27 | 100 | 17 | 100 | 1 |
| 1853–55 | 100 | 13 | 100 | 1 |

SOURCE: Wills sample, Appendix B.
NOTE: Illiteracy is defined as not knowing how to sign one's name. 49 people who stated that they were too infirm to sign have been considered literate.

Bustamante), published in the *Semanario de las Señoritas Mejicanas* in 1841. Another was Carolina Iturria, who in 1852 congratulated the editor of *La Semana de las Señoritas* for his excellent journal "dedicated to the sex to which I have the honor of belonging." [19]

A few women attained a high level of education during this period. For instance, Leona Vicario, a heroine of the struggle for independence, was translating Fénélon's *Télémaque* at the time of her imprisonment in 1813, and admitted in her trial to having read books on the Inquisition's Index of prohibited works. [20] A handful of women entered poems in national contests, occasionally winning first prize with their works. Others, preferring to hide behind the cloak of anonymity, published pamphlets on current issues. And some nuns, as they had throughout the colonial period, wrote chronicles of their convent and its members, as well as of their mystical experiences. These women were, in fact, among the most ardent advocates of improving female education during the first half of the nineteenth century. [21]

Still, the strides in women's schooling should not be over-emphasized. The 3,280 girls enrolled in primary schools in 1838 represent less than one-sixth of those eligible to attend. [22] Furthermore, enrollment figures disclose little about the quality of instruction offered; contemporaries repeatedly complained of incompetent teachers, the neglect of non-paying pupils, the scarcity of textbooks and teaching materials, and the irregular attendance of students in public schools. [23] Visitors from Europe and the United States, comparing the education of Mexican ladies with that of their own countries, were far from impressed

—and at that they were criticizing the best-educated women in the capital. Indeed, though Fanny Calderón noted the improvement of female education in her remark that "it is not long since writing was permitted to form part of a lady's education in Mexico," her airy dismissal of the "mass" of Mexican women, who "never open a book," is what readers of her journal remember most.[24]

Despite the gradual increase of literacy among the women who made wills, fully 13 percent of that privileged group could not even sign their names as late as 1853–55. Nearly one-third of the women in the 81 ecclesiastical divorce suits I examined, who came from a wider social spectrum, had to affix the sign of the cross to their depositions. In addition, these documents demonstrate that women's literacy lagged behind men's, since only 6 percent of the men could not sign their names.[25] The discrepancy between the sexes is even more pronounced among the propertied people who made wills: less than 1 percent of the male will-makers were unable to sign, compared with 17 percent of the women. Literacy thus differentiated the sexes most among the elites, where men had for centuries enjoyed access to education.

Moreover, only elementary schooling was available to Mexican women. At a time when the first women's colleges were founded in the United States and the first woman attended medical school, Mexican women could not obtain a secondary education, let alone enter a university. Fanny Calderón, once a schoolteacher herself, paid special attention to discussions of female education. She found that unlike the United States, with its division "between the advocates for solid learning and those for superficial accomplishments," Mexico had a total consensus on its goals.[26] An 1852 "Discourse on the Influence of Public Instruction on the Happiness of Nations" plainly stated the purpose of female schooling: not meant "to elevate women to the level of competing with men and taking part in their deliberations," it was strictly designed to make women "good daughters, excellent mothers, and the best and most solid support of the goals of Society."[27] Many girls were therefore taken out of school at the age of ten, when a piano teacher and drawing master were brought in "until at fourteen their education is complete."[28] A young lady "filled society with delight" once she spoke French, played the works of Mozart and Rossini, knew how to embroider and cultivate flowers, and could carry on an intelligent conversation based on "edifying and amorous reading."[29]

Yet even as Mexican writers affirmed the mental capacities of women, they ridiculed those with extensive learning. The intellectual woman, the *literata* who spent her day reading to the neglect of her personal appearance and home, the *talentacia* who made a fool of herself with her pedantry (*bachillerías*), was a stock comic character in newspaper satires by the 1840's.[30] The prejudice against learned women might have softened since the seventeenth century, when the celebrated poet Sor Juana Inés de la Cruz was cruelly censured, but scholarliness was still unseemly in women. Thus Juan Wenceslau Barquera, editor of the *Diario de México*, pronounced advanced learning unnecessary, for far from aiding the performance of women's special role, it was "useful only to shine in the salons." And Fernández de Lizardi regarded "erudite and manly women, [who] demonstrate that sex is not an obstacle to being learned, . . . as more to be admired than copied."[31]

Because an elementary education was considered sufficient for women, the editor of the *Semanario de las Señoritas Mejicanas*, the first Mexican ladies' magazine, felt compelled to justify the inclusion of articles on physics, botany, geography, and history in his journal (along with short stories, recipes, fashion engravings, and the like). In the inaugural issue, published in 1841, Isidro Gondra assured his readers that "the more women applied themselves to studying sciences and exercising the fine arts, the less they would be exposed to risks and dangers." Nor would they be "frivolous or dissipated" as long as they dedicated themselves to serious reading.[32] Although he was bent on enriching his subscribers' knowledge, Gondra never proposed to modify the roles of the elite women for whom he wrote; education, in his view, should merely entertain and edify women while simultaneously improving their preparation for domestic tasks.

As women became educated, however, and began to command both respect and self-respect, a few tried to push their horizons beyond the limits envisioned for them by reformers. By 1856 a group of women, no longer content with access to primary education, petitioned the liberal president Ignacio Comon-

SEMANARIO

DE LAS

SEÑORITAS MEJICANAS.

EDUCACION CIENTIFICA, MORAL Y LITERARIA,
DEL BELLO SEXO.

TOMO I.

MEJICO: 1841.

IMPRENTA d. VICENTE G. TORRES.
3ª calle de San Francisco n.º 5.

Lit. calle de la Palma n.º 4.

1. Title page of the first issue of the *Semanario de las Señoritas Mejicanas*. The
launching of a magazine especially for women in 1841 attests to the expansion of
their literacy in the preceding decades, just as its demise a short two years later
attests to the still-limited size of the reading public to which it appealed.

fort to establish a secondary school for girls. And the next generation would demand the right to enter the universities and
practice the professions—a far cry from the kind of education
that women needed to exercise a beneficent maternal influence
on society.[33]

## Productive Workers

Although reformers insisted that women were "born but to be
wives and mothers,"[34] they in fact had an additional role in
mind for the poor. Enlightened motherhood might suffice for
the elites, but it was widely understood (if rarely stated) that
lower-class women should enter the work force, just as, with expanding female schooling, those of the middle classes should
increasingly devote themselves to teaching others of their sex.
The desire to mobilize women for national development therefore went beyond the mere "upgrading" of motherhood, as
Asunción Lavrin has aptly termed it.[35]

In Spain, the enlightened count of Campomanes, adviser to
Charles III, argued that poor women should engage in "all possible industrial arts" because the strengthening of the economy
required all available hands. The employment of women in
"sedentary trades" would have many advantages. Women displayed a natural aptitude for weaving, lacemaking, fan-painting,
baking, and shopkeeping, to name a few. Their entry into these
trades would free men for more complicated and arduous tasks,
such as mining, farming, and military service. It would allow
women to contribute to their family's income, simultaneously
expanding the purchasing power of the populace and increasing
the market for manufactures. And not least, because women's
labor was "incomparably cheaper" than men's, it would reduce
the cost of consumer goods, benefiting the public and making
Spain's products more competitive with those of its European
rivals.[36]

Incorporating women into the labor force required modifications of traditional values that had discouraged women from
working; it required legal changes, because artisan guilds excluded women from most of the controlled trades; and it required changes in the schools called on to prepare the female
labor force. In short, it required active government intervention

to counter the weight of custom or, as Campomanes saw it, to overcome centuries of stultifying Arab influence holding back the Spanish empire. In his *Discourse on the Popular Education of Artisans* of 1775, Campomanes recommended two specific measures to encourage women's economic activity: eliminating legal barriers to women's work and giving them vocational training. The Crown implemented both in the next quarter of a century.

In keeping with the first goal, the Crown abolished guild restrictions against women in 1784. This measure did not at first apply to Spain's New World possessions, for the Crown originally intended to promote Spanish industry exclusively, maintaining the colonies as a market for its manufactured goods. Only 15 years later, after Spain had begun to lose this market because of the British naval blockade of 1796, did the Crown extend the ruling to New Spain. A landmark decree of January 12, 1799, permitted women and girls "to engage in all labors and manufactures compatible with their strength and the decorum of their sex, regardless of Guild Ordinances and governmental regulations to the contrary." In order to ensure women's success in those ventures, the decree further stipulated that "under no circumstances will the Guilds or any other persons prevent women and girls from being taught all those labors appropriate to their sex, nor shall they be kept from freely selling their manufactures in person or through others."[37]

The royal decree contains a detailed account of the events that led to the elimination of legal barriers to women's work in New Spain. On July 22, 1798, doña Josefa de Celis, a widow residing in Mexico City, had approached the viceroy because the Embroiderers' Guild had been preventing her from selling shoe uppers, her only means of earning a livelihood. The guild had lodged a complaint with the *juez de plaza*, charging that she and other women in this trade violated guild ordinances and endangered the public because of the inferior quality of their merchandise. The judge ordered the women to sell their products within the week and refrain from making new ones. Doña Josefa had then appealed to the viceroy so that, as she insisted, she and her many children would not starve.

Reversing the judge's ruling, Viceroy Miguel Joseph de Azanza permitted doña Josefa and all other women to continue in this industry. He based his decision on the 1784 decree, reasoning that if such a step had been desirable on the peninsula, it was even more necessary in New Spain. "Nowhere else," he argued, "are Guild Ordinances excluding women from the occupations and labors appropriate to their sex more prejudicial than in that Province, because in no other are women so idle, especially in the metropolis [Mexico City], where they lack branches of industry for their subsistence and that of their families." The viceroy added that it was "absurd," in fact nearly "indecent," for "a small number of men [to] monopolize jobs and tasks that do not require robust arms," like the embroidery of shoes, which was far more suitable "to the delicate hands of women, and compatible with their sedentary and secluded life." Six months later the king approved the viceroy's ruling, extending it to cover all restricted occupations.

The royal decree cited three reasons for facilitating women's incorporation into the labor force: first, because "it has been observed how prejudicial Guild restrictions are to the development of industry and to the progress of the arts"; second, because those restrictions excluded women from "tasks more suitable . . . to their sex than to men, whose robustness could more conveniently be applied to Agriculture, Arms, and the Marine"; and third, "because of the well-known advantages that would be obtained from the employment of women and girls in tasks proportionate to their strength, and in which they could obtain an income, serving for some as dowries for their marriages, and for others as assistance to maintain their houses and obligations." The order of these justifications is not without significance: it saves for last the benefit that women might obtain from legal access to new sources of employment—a benefit presumably centuries old but never acted on before.

The lifting of guild restrictions against women was part of a larger attack on the monopolistic guild system. By the mid-eighteenth century the Crown realized that Spanish manufactures, produced under the traditional artisanal system, could not compete with French and English factory goods. In an appendix to his *Discourse*, Campomanes argued that guilds were a primary cause of the backwardness of Spanish industry. Ending their unnecessary privileges and regulations would encourage "the free exercise of industry"; open competition, in turn, would increase the efficiency and productivity of the economy.[38] The decree on women's work, along with several other late colonial measures, dealt the guilds a staggering blow. The viceroy's original ruling on female shoe embroiderers had required that they allow guild officials to inspect their manufactures; the king's decree went further, permitting women to enter all trades and circumvent guild regulations entirely. Although guilds apparently continued to function in Mexico until they were definitively abolished (along with other corporations) by the 1857 Constitution, the 1799 decree effectively broke their monopoly on regulated sectors of the economy.[39]

Campomanes had foreseen that women's expansion into traditionally male trades would require more than legislative changes and had consequently proposed vocational education for women. Female schooling was already being advanced for diverse reasons by other reformers; Campomanes insisted that beyond teaching the basic literacy essential to an efficient labor force, schools should inculcate the virtue of work and provide poor women with useful skills. To this end, the Spanish Crown ordered that vocational training be incorporated into the public-school curriculum throughout the kingdom. Repeated directives to that effect bore some fruit in Mexico. For example, Las Vizcaínas taught girls to produce silver and gold braid in its *escuela pía*, and the Mexico City Poor House added a sewing and embroidery workshop to the elementary school opened in 1806.[40]

Fernández de Lizardi took up the call for vocational training of women in 1818, in *La Quijotita*. Lamenting that Mexican women were usually taught only needlework, which commanded low prices, he decried the belief that "the sewing cushion encompasses everything that women need to or can know." In words that echoed Campomanes' *Discourse* of a half century earlier, El Pensador Mexicano argued that all crafts "not requiring physical strength, but only constant application," were ideal for women. He urged parents to prepare their daughters to be musicians, silversmiths, watchmakers, painters, or printers, according to the girls' inclinations. Such training, essential for impoverished women, was even desirable for daughters of the middle classes, who might if orphaned or widowed be reduced to a precarious state.[41] This section of the novel has long confounded scholars because the rest of the book argues so forcefully that women should be responsible wives and mothers. But no real contradiction exists; there were two ways that women could contribute to economic development and social change: through enlightened motherhood, the role of all women, or through participation in the work force, the role of the poor.

The goal of expanding women's work was not adopted as readily as the goal of educating them, in part because of widespread male unemployment. In fact, as the economic situation deteriorated, appeals for women to enter the work force diminished. The only reformer to raise the issue after independence was Estevan de Antuñano, who in 1837 published an essay entitled *Political, Civil, Manufacturing, and Domestic Advantages of Employing Women Also in the Modern Mechanized Factories Beginning to Be Erected in Mexico*. The owner of a Puebla textile mill, Antuñano was troubled by the resistance of his fellow industrialists to hiring women and girls for factory work. He reassured his colleagues that since modern machines simplified production to the point where it no longer required a long apprenticeship or much strength, children as well as women were capable of filling these jobs; boys could start at the age of 10 and girls at 12. Recognizing that some "timorous people" would be shocked by the idea of the sexes mingling in the workplace, Antuñano extolled the moral advantages of family employment: men working alongside their wives would be "more tied to their homes and obligations," young girls under the constant supervision of their elders would be safe from temptations born of idleness. The employment of entire families would also benefit the working classes financially. By pooling their wages they could raise their standard of living and might even afford to live in company towns. Factory work would especially be a blessing for widows otherwise condemned to misery. Behind these arguments lurked the point that working families could live better on several wages at no additional cost to the factory owner; even the expense of constructing company towns would be borne by the workers, impossible as things stood because of the meager sum paid to a single breadwinner. Concluding with statistics on families laboring together happily at his model factory, La Constancia, Antuñano urged that the practice of hiring women and children be adopted throughout Mexico.[42]

These simultaneous attempts to engage women in production and improve their education were related to a broader campaign against corporate privilege, which Bourbon officials initiated tentatively and Mexican liberals carried to its conclusion during the Reforma. Enlightened leaders hoped to reduce those distinctions between individuals that were counterproductive to national development. In the case of women, the counterproductive distinctions were unequal access to education and exclusion from many trades, both of which prevented or at least discouraged them from contributing to the process of social change. In short, freedom and equality were not advocated for their own sake; reformers merely wanted to free women so that they could participate according to their talents and ambitions in the rebuilding of their country. Yet both freedom and equality were potential by-products of these policies, since the barriers beginning to be removed had helped maintain the privileges of men.

The twin developments in female education and work advanced much further in Mexico City than in other areas of Latin America or Mexico itself. Indeed, the decree abolishing restrictions on women's work was promulgated only for New Spain, because of the "inconveniences" that might arise from the "inopportune generalization of this measure"; the order that convents open public schools was extended to the rest of Mexico only in 1817, three decades after being mandated for Mexico City.[43] There were good reasons for Mexico City's singularity. For one thing, since it was the most important city in the Spanish empire, the government lavished special attention on it. For another, it was the home of wealthy and cosmopolitan people who kept up with European trends. Enlightened ideas also took hold there sooner because they responded to local needs. As the city grew, increased female job opportunities and schooling could help fuel the expanding economy and control the influx of migrants—the majority of whom were women. These migrants were a potential problem, but also a potential resource, if they could be properly integrated into urban life. Their schooling would keep them occupied, teach them Spanish, and train them to work in the factories and service sector, where cheap labor was always welcome. It only remained to find them jobs in the city's flourishing industries and businesses or in the homes of the expanding middle classes, and to erode the prejudices against working women.

## Feminine Fighters

The mobilization of women received an additional boost with the outbreak of the independence movement. As often occurs in times of crisis, some women stepped beyond traditional roles, and others gave traditional roles a political significance. It is difficult to determine just how many women participated in the struggle. Whereas the spectacular exploits of a few heroines are widely known, the other contributions women made have on the whole gone unheralded. It is doubtful that a majority of women—or men—were actively involved in the war effort at any one time, and relatively few were consistently involved throughout the 13-year struggle. Nonetheless, existing sources show that thousands of women were mobilized for both the royal and the insurgent cause, mostly in the provinces, where the struggle was largely waged, but a fair number in Mexico City also.[44] Their activities not only influenced the course of the war, but had a subtle impact on contemporary attitudes toward women. In showing themselves a force to be reckoned with, these women contributed to the growing view of women's competence and reinforced the idea that their cooperation was essential to the achievement of national goals.

Women's participation in the independence struggle, sometimes characterized as merely supplementary to the more important role of men, is more accurately viewed as complementary and equally valuable to the war effort. As Janet Kentner shows in her detailed study of women in the Mexican independence movement, many women were in fact able to do what "could not have been done as well, or even at all, by their male counterparts."[45] The prime example was the "seduction of troops," the charge most frequently brought against women by the Spanish government. Not a carnal act in this usage, seduction meant an attempt to persuade soldiers to desert the Royal Army and join the insurgents. The trial proceedings against Carmen Camacho illustrate one way in which women recruited rebel soldiers. Befriending soldiers at a local garrison, she would entice them to join her for an evening in a *pulquería* or *mesón*, then, after a few drinks, would urge them to desert, promising them a plot of land in independent Mexico as a reward.[46]

Viceroy Félix María Calleja recognized the effectiveness of this peculiarly female activity in a report on the different ways in which members of colonial society worked for independence: ecclesiastics preached revolt in the confessionals, magistrates dismissed the guilty, and women seduced the troops, sometimes even prostituting themselves in order to convince the soldiers to change sides. The Spanish government became increasingly alarmed about this "most prejudicial" activity, which often succeeded, according to the then royalist general Agustín de Iturbide, because of "the power of the beautiful sex on the hearts of men." By the fall of 1815 a judge was prompted to declare that women were "one of the greatest evils we have had from the beginning of this war," for "on account of their sex" they were "the instrument of seducing all classes of persons."[47]

On account of their sex also, women could smuggle messages and weapons under full skirts. They met with rebels on the pretext of leaving the capital for a day in the country, accompanied by children and picnic baskets and, in one celebrated instance, concealing a printing press among the delectables. Women were able to obtain information without arousing suspicion through a network of female servants and friends who, because of marriage or employment, were in daily contact with royal officers and soldiers. In their traditional role as men's companions, women accompanied the troops, prepared their food, and nursed them. When apprehended, women were quick to take advantage of the privileges of their sex. Kentner cites instances in which women alleged pregnancy (apparently sometimes feigned) or invoked the plight of their children to obtain release from prison. In desperation, some women claimed to have misunderstood what they had done or pleaded that they had been forced to comply with their husbands' wishes.

Although some insurgent women may have merely followed husbands or lovers in working for independence, for others such a claim was an excuse. Contemporary observers portrayed women as having a highly developed political consciousness. Anastacio Zerecero, Carlos María de Bustamante, and William Robinson alike noted a growing dissension in households where Mexican women married to royalist Spaniards openly sympathized with the rebels.[48] The case of doña Mariana Rodríguez de Toro, though she did not defy her husband, exemplifies the leadership some women furnished within the privacy of their homes. The wife of the wealthy miner don Manuel Lazarín, she hosted a salon in her Mexico City home where politics were a frequent topic of conversation. During one of these *tertulias*, she presented a plan to take Viceroy Francisco Javier de Venegas hostage in order to obtain the release of the revolutionary leader Father Miguel Hidalgo. When the men around her proved reluctant, she supposedly prodded them into action by asking, "Are there no longer any men in America?" Persuading the men to join her, doña Mariana directed the plot until its discovery.[49] Her activities, blurring the boundaries between public and private roles, contradict the view of women following men and being only peripheral to the independence movement.

The Patriotas Marianas, another example of female initiative, shows how wartime activities began to modify women's political behavior. The first known secular female organization in Mexico, this royalist group was established by doña Ana Iraeta de Mier, the widow of a former *audiencia* judge, when Hidalgo's rebels surrounded Mexico City in October 1810. Its initial purpose was to defend the Virgin of Remedios, patroness of the Royal Army. While the city panicked in fear of the insurgents, this association of ladies watched over the Virgin's statue in the Cathedral and sewed her image onto banners as a counter to the insurgents' banners of the Virgin of Guadalupe. The Patriotas helped the Spanish propaganda effort by publishing pamphlets proclaiming their loyalty to Spain and Ferdinand VII. They combined these largely symbolic morale-lifting activities with fund raising, channeling some of the money to the needy families of royalist soldiers by hiring their wives to help guard the Virgin's statue in the Cathedral. Highly visible in Mexico City, the group served as a model for royalist women in other cities of New Spain, allegedly organizing some 2,500 women at its peak. The Patriotas Marianas did not disband immediately after the rebels were defeated in the Battle of Las Cruces; a year later, in 1811, doña Ana formally petitioned the city council to commemorate the battle, and her organization continued to be active during the next few years.[50]

As women's activities became more visible and their effectiveness increasingly evident, colonial authorities began to change their view of insurgent women. If at first some judges gave them light sentences in deference to the "weakness of the sex," the authorities gradually learned that flirtations with soldiers were not as harmless as had at first appeared, that family outings in the country might have more than one purpose, that women understood perfectly well the conversations they overheard, that they were capable of organizing and leading if necessary, and that even married women might act independently on behalf of their political convictions. Kentner documents the increasingly stiff punishments meted out to women, finally including the death penalty, which the government had at first eschewed. Accounts of the independence movement show that numerous women were executed, imprisoned, deprived of their property, and deported for their activities. In 1817, William Davis Robinson, an American adventurer, noted the transformation of royalist attitudes toward women when he remarked, "The spirit of revenge and the cruelty of the immediate agents of Ferdinand VII appear to have taken the place of the former gallantry to the sex."[51]

The government's treatment of La Corregidora demonstrates the respect it developed for insurgent women as the warfare proceeded. Doña María Josefa Ortiz de Domínguez, wife of the corregidor of Querétaro, sent the famous message that sparked the call to arms in September 1810. Overhearing that the rebels' conspiracy had been discovered, she managed to alert them even though her husband had locked her in the house to prevent any such communication. After a brief imprisonment (which failed to daunt her resolution to fight for independence), she was released on her husband's recognizance. Miguel Domínguez, ordered by the viceroy to keep a close watch over his wife, promised to do everything in his power to control her. When the viceroy continued to receive reports of this "fearless" woman, whose "bold and audacious" acts made her a "true

2. An illustration for the poem "Call to the Women to Fight" (1812), exhorting Mexican women to join the struggle for independence. This propaganda piece, one of several that have survived, is evidence that the attempt to integrate women into various nation-building projects was well under way in the late colonial period.

Anne Boleyn," he had her imprisoned once more. An adviser urged him to arrest Miguel Domínguez also, on the grounds that husbands were accountable for their wives' behavior. By sparing doña Josefa's spouse, the viceroy tacitly admitted that she alone was responsible for her actions.[52]

Just as women's potential in the war effort became apparent to the colonial government, so was it recognized by the revolutionaries, who enlisted their aid through special propaganda efforts. Addressing women as a separate group with distinct concerns, an 1812 article entitled "To the Ladies of Mexico" appealed to women's pride. It urged them "to show those men who doubt it" that Mexican women had the spirit and valor to dedicate themselves to the liberation of their country. Women's maternal sentiments were also tapped in the reminder that their children, even if fathered by Spaniards, would be second-class citizens because they were born in the New World.[53] An insurgent "Call to the Women to Fight" encouraged women to seek revenge for the deaths of male relatives at the hands of the Spanish government. It exhorted American women to go to war "with cruel swords / to bring death to Callejas / and to see Señor Morelos." Although the call to arms may have been figurative, it was accompanied by an illustration of two women in martial hats crossing raised swords.[54]

The insurgents praised women's contributions to the cause both during and after the war. Their appreciation is exemplified in the treatment of doña Leona Vicario, the most famous heroine from Mexico City. Boldly defying her uncle and guardian, a staunch defender of the Crown, the wealthy orphan donated much of her fortune to the rebels, bought and smuggled arms to them, sent them information in secret code, and recruited soldiers for their army. In March 1813 doña Leona was imprisoned, and her property was subsequently confiscated. Escaping from prison, she joined the army of Gen. José María Morelos in Oaxaca and there married don Andrés Quintana Roo, her uncle's former law clerk. She rode with the rebel army, helped plan its strategy, administered its finances, oversaw the care of the sick and injured, and on January 3, 1817, bore her first child in a cave in Achipixtla. In recognition of her sacrifices, the government in arms declared her a national heroine and assigned her a monthly stipend (which it was unable to pay). After independence, the first Mexican Congress granted her an hacienda and three houses in Mexico City to reimburse her financial losses on behalf of the country, and the town of Saltillo temporarily changed its name to Leona Vicario in 1828. Upon her death in 1842, she was lavishly honored: President Antonio López de Santa Anna led her funeral procession, and the historian Carlos María de Bustamante wrote her obituary in the leading liberal newspaper, *El Siglo Diez y Nueve.*[55]

Collections of laudatory sketches of independence heroines began to appear soon after the Mexican victory. Fernández de Lizardi, who had previously admonished women to stay out of politics, published an almanac celebrating their feats. Ladies' magazines carried articles on the heroic acts of women in South America as well as Mexico. The fame of these women spread as far as Paris, where a book praising *Illustrious American Women* appeared in 1825. Arguing that women had made significant contributions to the independence movement, these publications show that in the early years of the republic women's roles were both recognized and chronicled.[56]

## Civic Participants

It is sometimes maintained that, beyond eliciting appreciation for past services, women's participation in the prolonged war effort had little impact on their status after independence. Elsa Chaney contends that in South America "the gallant ladies of the revolutionary *tertulias* returned to the silence of their colonial sleep," withdrawing from public affairs for another century; and Evelyn Cherpak likewise concludes that in Gran Colombia the struggle for independence had no effect on women's subsequent position or roles.[57] Yet the story is not that simple, at least in Mexico. There, where attitudes toward women had been undergoing important changes in the late colonial period, the wars accelerated these developments. Although not directly involved in republican governments, Mexican women began to organize in new ways after independence. The respect they had gradually earned from royalists and revolutionaries did not vanish overnight; women's increased wartime visibility, coinciding with improvements in their education and attempts to incorporate them into the labor force, contributed to a heightened appreciation of their talents. In some cases, it may have increased women's self-esteem. Like most changes in *mentalités*, these are subtle developments, difficult to document definitively and easy to overlook.

3. Leona Vicario (1789–1842), the most famous of Mexico City's independence heroines. A wealthy orphan who contributed heavily to the cause, she gained particular prominence in the movement because of her class standing. But she was only one of many women who helped in that struggle, most of them anonymously.

Certainly, there is much truth to the view that women returned to traditional roles after independence. Disapproval of female political activities in "normal" times remained strong; the new republic did not allow women to vote or hold public office, and prescriptive literature reaffirmed their domestic roles. Even an article lauding the heroines of independence concluded that the good wife and mother was "infinitely more admirable than the heroine of a novel."[58] The liberal writer Guillermo Prieto, in attempting to describe the ideal wife, made it clear that a woman should leave public affairs to men: "She should know how to sew, cook, sweep, . . . find pleasure and utility in virtue, [and] be religious, but never neglect my dinner for a mass. . . . The day she discusses politics, I'll divorce her!"[59]

But when women like doña Leona Vicario "retired" to the circle of Family and Church in 1821, their lives were clearly marked by their prior participation in politics. Doña Leona's obituary praised her for dedicating herself to husband and children, distributing alms to the poor, and adorning with her own jewels the saintly image of the Virgin in the Rosary Chapel of Santo Domingo.[60] Yet she had also maintained contacts with friends in government, who allegedly sought her advice. On at least one occasion she became embroiled in a public controversy that reflected the degree of public recognition she commanded. Meeting with President Bustamante on February 2, 1831, she asked him to ensure her husband's life, which she believed to be endangered by his opposition to the government. The meeting fueled a campaign against the couple. The pro-government newspaper, *El Sol*, accused doña Leona of insulting the president and claimed that she was her husband's attorney—a charge intended to discredit her spouse. The minister of foreign relations, Lucas Alamán, attempted to belittle her wartime activities, arguing that, like other women, she had been motivated not by true patriotism, but by her love for Andrés Quintana Roo. Incensed by this allegation, doña Leona defended herself in several letters published in *El Federalista*, her husband's opposition paper. Her open letter to Alamán, aimed at weakening the Bustamante government, embodies new attitudes toward women:

Confess, Mr. Alamán, that love is not the only motive of women's actions. They are capable of all the human emotions; and the desire for the glory and liberty of their country is not foreign to them. On the contrary, they tend to work more vigorously for their goals, because as always, the sacrifices of women . . . are more disinterested than men's, women seeking no more reward than that they be accepted. . . . As for myself, let me state that my actions and ideas have always been my own. Absolutely no one has ever influenced them; I have followed my convictions with total independence, without acceding to the opinions of those whom I esteem. I am persuaded that all women are the same, excepting the very stupid, or those who owing to their education have acquired servile habits. Of both classes there are also many men.[61]

Alamán's view that women would allow their passions to override their politics was not universally shared by his contemporaries, and several distinguished Mexicans rushed to Vicario's defense. Indeed, her friend Carlos María de Bustamante insisted that it was she who had first converted her future husband to the independence cause.[62] We can only guess the extent to which these responses were conditioned by wartime experiences. Would Mexican men otherwise have upheld a woman's capacity for devotion to high ideals? Would Vicario have dared—or even been in a position—to challenge Alamán publicly before that struggle? Probably not. The controversy reflects an increasing respect for women as well as their own growing self-confidence.

This incident illustrates the major characteristics of women's political activity during the first four decades of Mexican independence: both unusual and occasional, it took a different form from men's. In the broadest sense of the term,[63] the lower-class women who joined the 1828 riots at the Parián market in Mexico City, the elite women who sought support for their husbands in power, and the ladies who voiced their opinions in salons were all engaging in politics. Mexican women evidently took an interest in public affairs, for Fanny Calderón noted that "politics [is] a subject on which almost all women are well-informed."[64] Some, like the countess of Regla, may have gone beyond a mere interest: it is said that, as a confidante of Mexico's first president, she came close to arranging a change of his cabinet officers.[65] But these activities, however influential, represented at best an indirect participation in public affairs.

In more conventional terms, women's principal political weapon was the petition, which took on a new form and significance after independence. Before that, it was not uncommon for women to petition government offices on behalf of themselves or aggrieved relatives; they might, for example, appeal for a soldier's release from duty or the reduction of a prisoner's sentence, alleging that he was needed to care for his old mother or support his wife and children. These were the actions of isolated individuals attempting to further strictly personal goals; even the Parián riots lacked a formal organization and clear-cut demands. But after independence women began to join together to petition as a body. Although they still did so only rarely and may have been organized by men, women did nonetheless lobby as a feminine pressure group for the first time, taking a highly visible stance on public issues. Possibly, this pattern of collective action would have developed anyway, but it probably benefited from the organizing skills women gained during the independence struggle and built on the new awareness of women's potential effectiveness.

The collective petitions, signed exclusively by women, presented their arguments in terms of the special needs of their sex. An 1829 petition, protesting the decree expelling Spaniards from Mexico, was signed by more than 50 Mexican women whose husbands were affected. Describing the sorry plight of abandoned wives and children, they begged that their husbands be exempted from the decree. To elicit further sympathy, each woman followed her signature with a list of her children: "Carlota Silva, with five daughters, the eldest of seven years," or "María del Carmen Cacho de Estanillo, with four children, and her sister . . . with four more." These women watched from the galleries as the Chamber of Deputies debated the measure, and they organized a delegation headed by doña Mariana Cervantes that met with President Vicente Guerrero to present the document personally.[66]

Petitions submitted to the Constitutional Convention of 1856 opposing the measure on freedom of religion illustrate contemporary disapproval of women's participation in politics. A formidable body of one thousand women from Mexico City and smaller groups from other areas of Mexico joined the petition drive, which was probably led by the Church in view of its wide national scope. Deeming it necessary to excuse their actions, the women from Mexico City explained that "we have not come to meddle in the difficult questions of politics, completely foreign to our sex."[67] But they clearly had. The petition from Guadalajara, also recognizing that the signatories were stepping beyond the appropriate bounds of feminine behavior, began: "It must seem strange to the Sovereign Congress of the Nation that the women of this capital should raise their voices to the august precinct of legislation. . . . It must seem strange that women, not enjoying the right of citizenship, should take part, and with such enthusiasm, in a public question. Strange in truth will it seem to your sovereignty that women, whose destiny in society is commonly thought to be reduced to the care and attentions of the domestic home, should now manifest their opinions."[68] They claimed to defend Catholicism only because religion and morality were "vital and grave" to the rearing of children.

Although both groups justified women's intrusion into men's affairs as an extension of traditional female roles, the petitions in effect represented a break with those roles. Relying on the image of motherhood to legitimate women's political activity, the petitioners played on the ideal separation of women from politics to increase their effectiveness. Although they protested that it was their concern with children that emboldened them to raise their "weak voices" at this time, the fact is that these women *did* raise their voices on this occasion. No longer simply working behind the scenes to influence historical events, women now took an active part in lobbying against a specific piece of legislation, and they did so as a separate interest group, claiming to represent all of their sex.[69]

The emergence of charity organizations in republican Mexico similarly represents a new trend toward collective civic activity. Despite many gaps in their histories, we know that at least three such organizations were founded in Mexico City during the 1830's and 1840's under government auspices. The first, the Junta de Señoras of the Casa de Cuna, or Foundling Home, was established in 1836 and headed by the former marchioness of Vivanco (the Mexican nobility had lost their titles in 1826). According to Fanny Calderón's description of the enterprise, "The men furnish the money; the women give their time and attention." The Señoras helped administer the Foundling Home, visiting it regularly and knowing every baby and nurse by name. Each member had a certain number of children under her care and was responsible for arranging their eventual adoption. Fanny's comment notwithstanding, the Junta de Señoras also held fundraising events and collected donations in the capital's principal churches during Holy Week and other religious holidays. The Junta was still active as late as 1846, when it was praised in a report by José María Lafragua, the minister of the interior.[70] A second charitable organization, which has left no surviving records but was also observed by Fanny Calderón in 1841, was devoted to teaching female prisoners of the Acordada jail to read and write. The group was apparently formed by three of the capital's leading ladies, following a suggestion made by the Lancasterian Company in an article on prison reform.[71] The third known female organization, the Junta de Beneficencia del Hospital del Divino Salvador, was assigned by the government to supervise the hospital for demented women. Like the Junta of the Casa de Cuna, this group had a formal structure, including an elected president and officers. Doña Petra Barredo de Trigueros, its president in 1844, published a detailed report on the conditions in the mental hospital in that year.[72]

Although women's charitable activities were not new in Mexico, their organization was. Traditionally, a lady had "a circle of needy individuals of her acquaintance, a clientele of unfortunate souls to whom she distributes alms and articles of necessity."[73] But she had done so on her own. In Europe and the United States, women were already joining philanthropic societies by the late eighteenth century, often as an outgrowth of the religious revival taking place in the Protestant world. In Mexico, however, where there was no equivalent evangelical movement to mobilize women, there is no record of lay women having organized formally, elected officers, filed reports, or supervised municipal institutions before the independence wars.

In other parts of Latin America, a direct link has been established between independence and the organization of women's beneficence societies. Cynthia J. Little found that one of the Argentine government's first acts was the creation of a female Sociedad de Beneficencia, charged with establishing an elementary school system for girls and supervising social welfare services. Evelyn Cherpak's study of Gran Colombia shows that the first female beneficence society there was likewise created by the government, in this case during the actual fighting, to enlist women in the war effort.[74] In Mexico the Patriotas Marianas, organized during exceptional wartime circumstances, may have set the precedent for formal associations of women.

As elsewhere in Latin America, the mobilization of women after independence corresponded above all to the State's need for extraordinary aid from its citizens. Soon after independence, Mexico City's municipal government found itself unable to administer the capital's charitable institutions properly due to a severe shortage of funds. By the 1830's the city's financial problems were serious indeed: civil servants and soldiers went without pay for six months in 1833, and during the next decade employees were often put on half pay or released.[75] As municipal institutions fell into disarray, the government called on private citizens for help. Its inability to meet the public payroll made the volunteer services of elite women especially attractive. Their supervision of agencies serving other women and children could be justified as an appropriate extension of their traditional charitable roles.

Even then, support for women's taking on this limited public responsibility was extremely tentative. Most philanthropic organizations founded during this period were male,[76] and the three documented female groups probably had few members. Their emergence cannot be compared with the proliferation of female organizations in the United States and Europe, where women, without waiting to be invited, organized groups to aid female prisoners and prostitutes, pursue abolition and temperance, and work for other social reforms. Mexican women organized at the behest of a financially strapped government that did not originally set out to recruit them. Indeed, as soon as it was able, the Mexican government took back some of the duties it had delegated to women. An 1864 report on beneficence institutions informed its readers that "not so long ago, a Junta of Señoras was in charge of the daily administration of the Foundling Home." By that date, the Ministry of Development had taken charge.[77] In fact, I have found no record of female societies active in Mexico by the late 1850's.

The decline of women's charity associations by the middle of the century can be partially explained by the government's increased role in providing social services; but another important factor was the establishment in Mexico of the Sisters of Charity of St. Vincent de Paul in 1843. This French nursing order quickly took charge of many of the capital's beneficence institutions, eliminating the need for the continued mobilization of lay women. The Sisters of Charity also provided a formal channel for those women who wished to devote their lives to serving the public. By the time the order was expelled from Mexico in 1874—the last of the religious orders to be closed during the Reforma—355 Mexican women had joined the original French group.[78] Although the Empress Carlota briefly revived women's philanthropic organizations during the Second Empire (1864–67), it was only after the Sisters' departure left a vacuum in the capital's social services that lay women began to found the numerous charity organizations so familiar to students of the late-nineteenth-century Porfirian regime.

Even if short-lived, the appearance of women's charitable societies in the first few decades after independence shows a recognition of women's civic capacity. To be sure, that capacity was tapped only because of the national emergency persisting until the Reforma: Mexico's disastrous economy, continued political instability, and repeated foreign invasions were not conducive to women's total "return to the home." Thus the government temporarily recruited elite women to help administer municipal institutions, special interest groups organized female petition drives, and educators trained women to fulfill domestic roles responsibly. Reformers repeatedly insisted that without the integration of women in the national effort there would be no solution to Mexico's problems.

## The Idea of Women's Social Utility

Attempts to mobilize women in the late colonial and early republican period recognized that they had something to offer, not only to their immediate families, but also to the larger society beyond their homes. True, women were not always permitted to participate in national affairs in the same way as men. Women's education was oriented toward gender; reformers appealed to them as a distinct group; their organizations and petitions were exclusively female also. But women's special role in socializing the young, managing households, or recruiting soldiers was valued by contemporaries, just as their potential as workers, teachers, lobbyists, and members of charity organizations was not ignored.

The notion of women's social utility gradually supplanted the older ideal of female seclusion. This shift is reflected in the decline of Mexican nunneries and retirement houses, pivotal feminine institutions of the colonial period, which had for centuries provided refuge for spinsters, widows, and abandoned wives. Nunneries had traditionally sheltered elite women who wished to devote their lives to religious contemplation, could provide a dowry, and were able to demonstrate their legitimacy and purity of blood. Retirement houses, less rigid in their entrance requirements and not asking a lifelong commitment, likewise permitted women to live apart from the world in a religious atmosphere.[79] Both institutions originally reflected the philosophy that women without families of their own were vulnerable and of little value to society. As these ideas waned in the eighteenth and early nineteenth centuries, so too did these institutions.

Josefina Muriel's study of the retirement houses (*recogimientos de mujeres*) shows that by 1800 they had lost their protective function. During the second half of the eighteenth century some had been converted to female prisons or schools, and others had closed entirely.[80] There were several reasons why women shunned a life of retirement. Their rising literacy and expanding job opportunities made it easier for them to survive safely on their own; so did the pension system established for the widows and orphans of government employees in the late eighteenth century.[81] Furthermore, as Mexicans began to acknowledge that unattached women could make positive contributions to social and national development, they increasingly approved of such women leading a less sheltered life.

Mexican nunneries declined less precipitously than recogimientos owing to the foundation of two new religious orders. The Company of Mary, a teaching order, was brought to Mexico

in 1753 by the wealthy heiress doña María Ignacia Azlor y Echevers of the family of the marquis of Aguayo. The Sisters of Charity, who not only staffed the city's hospitals, but ran schools for
artisans' daughters, had likewise come to Mexico at the behest
of a noblewoman, doña María Ana Gómez, the former countess
of la Cortina. Both orders were dedicated to social service, and
both allowed their members a measure of freedom: the nuns of
the Company of Mary were less rigidly shut off from the public
than the other Mexican orders, though they were still a cloistered community; the Sisters of Charity did not observe the
cloister, renewed their vows annually, and were free to leave the
order at any time.[82] That the Sisters of Charity were able to venture out in public shows how far the change in attitudes toward
women had come.

Even so, Mexico lagged well behind Europe in this regard. Although both orders had existed on the continent for centuries,
the establishment of Mexican chapters had to await the modification of Mexican values. The sequence of their arrival is significant, for the Sisters of Charity, embodying more modern
ideas about women's potential for serving their country, reached
Mexico nearly a century after the Company of Mary; they were
established in Europe in the reverse order. Moreover, it is far
from coincidental that the Sisters of Charity was the only religious order founded in nineteenth-century Mexico; the temporary vows taken by its members were compatible with liberal
views of individual freedom as the permanent vows of other orders were not.[83]

But as these service-oriented orders were establishing themselves, other nunneries suffered a serious decline. The population of cloistered nuns in Mexico City decreased nearly 40 percent from 1790 to 1850, when it stabilized at about 540 until the
exclaustration in 1863. A similar, though weaker, trend is evident for Mexico as a whole (Table 2). In part this contraction reflects the new ideas about women, in part the secularization of
society during this period. This is not to say that the Church lost
its central place in women's lives. Scattered evidence suggests
that women participated actively in the religious rites of Catholic
Mexico, many attending daily mass and the yearly cycle of feast
days; altars and statues of saints are prominent in household in-

TABLE 2
Professed Nuns in Cloistered Orders, 1790–1859

| Year | Mexico City | Mexico | Year | Mexico City | Mexico |
|------|-------------|--------|------|-------------|--------|
| 1790 | 888 |       | 1843 |     | 1,609 |
| 1826 |     | 1,931 | 1849 |     | 1,541 |
| 1828 | 755 | 1,983 | 1850 | 541 | 1,494 |
| 1830 |     | 1,911 | 1859 | 542 |       |
| 1832 |     | 1,847 |      |     |       |

SOURCES: Mexico City. 1790, Alexander von Humboldt, Political Essay on the Kingdom of New Spain, 2d ed. (London, 1814), 4: 292; 1828, Juan Bautista Arechederreta, Estado general de los conventos de religiosas. . . . (broadside, Archivo General de la Nación, Justicia Eclesiástica, vol. 50); 1850's, Jan Bazant, Alienation of Church Wealth in Mexico (Cambridge, Eng., 1971), p. 218. Mexico. Bazant, p. 39.
NOTE: The non-cloistered Sisters of Charity are excluded from these figures.

ventories; and priests loom large among the people women turned to with personal problems. By the nineteenth century, however, Mexican writers no longer proposed the convent as an alternative to marriage, and the few who mentioned it discouraged women from that option.[64]

The Sisters of Charity nonetheless flourished precisely in the period when Mexican nunneries registered the sharpest decline. This timing suggests that those Mexican women who chose the religious life increasingly preferred an order that would permit them to serve their communities without having to retire from the world. Despite the gradual erosion of the Church's status, the Sisters of Charity ("instructing the daughters of the poor artisan without recompense [and] serving the sick without rest in the hospitals"[85]) found a warm spot in Mexican hearts. The angelic Celeste in Payno's El fistol del diablo is an unforgettable image of saintliness, floating through the city in drab garb to console dying soldiers during the U.S. invasion of Mexico City. Indeed, so much were the Sisters appreciated, even by liberals like Payno, that they were allowed to remain in Mexico for a decade after the other religious orders were suppressed and their property nationalized.

## Conclusion

The emerging notion of women's social utility, which went hand in hand with a recognition of their competence, was a positive development for Mexican women. The proliferation of girls' schools, the lifting of restrictions on women's work, the establishment of service-oriented religious orders, the mobilization of women during the independence wars, and the formation of female charitable organizations both reflected and reinforced these ideas. Mexicans viewed the expansion of women's responsibilities as part of the "social progress" of the century.[86] Indeed, as early as 1808 María Francisca de Nava condemned as "an abuse" women's previous relegation "to serving only for the sewing cushion and stove"; plainly, in her opinion, this situation had already begun to change.[87] Scattered comments by writers of the next half-century suggest that some Mexicans saw a clear improvement in women's position during their lifetimes.

Articles on women's education in particular noted an advance in women's status. Although today we might deride the level of instruction as superficial, contemporaries viewed it in a favorable light. A journalist's "Advice to Señoritas" in 1850 declared that "since independence, our education and customs have changed noticeably." The author saw the cultured and active women of the day as a vast improvement over those of "the time when, thanks to our conquerors, a Mexican lady was considered supremely happy if she did nothing."[88] Likewise, in 1836 Mora remarked that "the progress of Mexican civilization is especially evident in the Fair Sex." Admittedly, Mexican women in the past, "because of their ignorance and frivolity of character," had been "in truth worth very little" and purely "an object of courtship." But no longer. Their charming accomplishments and knowledge of world affairs now made them valuable companions for men. Beyond that, said Mora, "now that they can provide other pleasures than amorous flirtation, their old age is not burdened with the tedium caused by the loss of one's only joys, and the desperation caused by the impossibility of finding new ones. Today, music, drawing, reading, and friendship, which survive the charms of youth and the loss of beauty, are an inexhaustible source of pleasure for our ladies of advanced age."[89] A contributor to the *Panorama de las Señoritas* argued along similar lines: since education strengthened women, making them less vulnerable to "seduction and the downturns of fortune," it allowed them to lead a happier life.[90]

The fact that women like Ana Josefa Caballero de Borda were in the forefront of the movement to reform female education suggests that women themselves viewed it as beneficial for their sex. Caballero de Borda proclaimed that women's schooling would lift them from "the subjection and scorn with which the Fair Sex is viewed."[91] A Spanish woman quoted in the *Gazeta de México* offered an even more radical interpretation of the impact of female schooling, declaring that the denial of instruction to her sex was the "cruelest tyranny" exercised by men, one that "treats [us] as if we were not rational and a part of society."[92] We may assume that those Mexicans who shared her opinion would consider women's increased access to education during the first half of the nineteenth century a reduction of that tyranny.

It is likewise significant that women brought the two new service-oriented religious orders to Mexico. Both dona Maria Ignacia Azlor y Echevers and doña María Ana Gómez de la Cortina spent their fortunes and years of their lives arranging to have those orders transferred to their homeland so that Mexican women would have the opportunity to serve their communities. So fervently did they believe in their projects that both—one a young single woman, the other an elderly widow—themselves professed in the orders they had established for their compatriots.

The expansion of women's options may not have been immediately obvious, nor did it affect all women in Mexico City. Most women's lives still revolved around "religious vows, family responsibilities, and the management of the home."[93] But the gradual recognition that women could contribute to their country's well-being, in both sex-specific and class-specific ways, led to attempts to prepare them to be more valuable members of society. As educational, legal, and ideological barriers to their mobilization began to erode, they opened the way for the improvement of women's status. Many women in the Mexican capital may not have acquired a "regular education" during this period, or entered the labor force, or participated in the independence movement, or joined a charity organization, or petitioned a president. But we can speculate that those who did so gained satisfaction and self-confidence. Their education and effectiveness in new roles fostered an increasing respect for women, and even their traditional maternal role took on a heightened prestige because of its civic importance. It was these changes that Mexicans had in mind when they wrote of the "social progress" of the century and the "advancement" of the Delicate Sex.

# TWO

# Legal Status

THE LAW provides an essential framework for understanding women's lives. Although the Mexican legal system distinguished people on the basis of many factors, such as minor and adult, noble and commoner, legitimate and illegitimate, and Spanish, Caste, and Indian, gender cut across every one of these legal categories. In fact, women's distinct juridical status is a strong argument for studying them as a separate group. Granted, the relationship between law and behavior is far from simple: societies may interpret their laws differently at different times, individuals who fail to take advantage of their legal rights may in practice forfeit them, and, conversely, where local custom permits, individuals may have more freedom than the laws prescribe. Still, if legal systems rarely describe women's lives precisely, they establish boundaries within which women were supposed to operate and reflect ideas about women's roles and relationships to men. Changes in law, illustrating shifting social norms, in turn contribute to the further shaping of women's experiences.

The legal status of Mexican women thus illuminates several issues raised by this study. It demonstrates whether women were viewed primarily as wives and mothers and whether their activities were ideally restricted to the domestic home. It establishes areas where women exercised authority, with their right to make decisions formally sanctioned by law, and suggests those where they might exercise informal power, controlling the behavior of others by drawing on institutional resources provided by law. As lawbooks set forth restrictions on women's rights, they also explained the reasons for those restrictions. Modifications in both the law and the rationale for women's subordination furnish one measure of the depth of contemporary changes.

Although most legislation affecting women in late colonial Mexico was centuries old, it was largely accepted in the nineteenth century. The few republican departures from colonial law are telling indicators of new attitudes toward women. After independence, Mexicans reviewed colonial laws in order to modernize and simplify the inherited legal system. Part of a larger questioning of colonial structures, the process of legal revision provided an opportunity to bring women's legal position into line with contemporary ideas. The emerging view of women's social utility and competence conflicted with some of the traditional curbs on women's rights. The simultaneous spread of liberalism, with its hallmark beliefs in freedom and equality, logically demanded a reduction of differences between individuals. Indeed, racial distinctions were abolished in 1822, noble titles in 1826, slavery in 1829, and corporations in 1856. Finally, the shift from monarchy to republic carried with it the potential for the democratization of Mexican society. This chapter analyzes the definition of women's legal status at the opening of the nineteenth century and then explores how it changed in response to these developments.

Studies of Latin American women often remark on their inferior legal status but fail to define the exact nature and extent of that inferiority. It has been said that Hispanic law considered females an *imbecilitus sexus* whose mental deficiency justified a denial of many legal rights. By some accounts, women were legally barred from public activities, and by most accounts, they were legally dependent on men. Some writers contend that women had the status of perpetual minors, totally subordinated to husbands if married, otherwise subject to the lifelong tutelage of male relatives. Other scholars concede that the lone widow had some control over her destiny.[1] This grim picture of patriarchy, where the man ruled his wife and children without restraints, has some basis in fact but is inaccurate in many important respects.

The pitfalls of previous legal studies provide useful guides for an analysis of women's legal status. One persisting source of error is the failure to distinguish between laws that applied to all women and those that applied only to wives. Hispanic law accorded considerably more rights to single and widowed women than to married women, if less than to men of the same marital status. The law further differentiated "decent" women, be they single virgins or "honest" wives and widows, from "loose" women, such as prostitutes, who lost much of their protection before the law. These distinctions will be examined in this chapter, with the general principles applying to all women presented first, and those applying only to married women presented separately.

Another source of error is the confusion of Spanish law with Roman law in discussions of such institutions as the tutelage of women, a natural lapse given most Hispanic legal historians' training in Roman law. Although Spanish law derived in part from Roman law, the two diverged in their treatment of women, and it is Spanish law, passed on to the New World possessions, that is relevant to Mexico. The position of Spanish women improved under the influence of Christianity during the Middle Ages; their status then deteriorated somewhat, but without returning to the principles of Roman law, which placed women under perpetual male guardianship because they were deemed incapable of managing their own affairs. Women's legal status was largely defined by the Siete Partidas (a law code compiled in the thirteenth century under King Alfonso the Wise) and the Leyes de Toro (promulgated in that Spanish town in 1505), augmented by subsequent royal decrees and canon law. *Derecho indiano*, an ad hoc body of law developed for Spain's American colonies, had little to say about contracts, marriage, inheritance, and other areas central to women's status. In these matters, Spanish private law supplemented the fragmentary *derecho indiano*. Since the corpus of Spanish law continued with few exceptions to be in force in Mexico until the promulgation of the 1870 Civil Code, this analysis of Mexican women's legal status is relevant to women in Spain and Spanish America throughout the colonial period.[2] However, I have attempted to present the legal system as it was understood by Mexicans in the first half of the nineteenth century, limiting my discussion to those laws reproduced or cited in contemporary handbooks and compilations to avoid conclusions based on ancient laws long forgotten or ignored.

The majority of inaccuracies in the historical literature stem from superficial readings of lawbooks or the desire to simplify complicated statutes, for as lawyers in independent Mexico lamented, the corpus of Hispanic law was unwieldy and ambiguous. New laws were supposed to invalidate older ones, but both remained on the books. In contrast to common law's emphasis on previous judicial decisions, the Hispanic legal system emphasized the interpretation of the laws themselves. Since each lawyer unearthed the laws pertinent to a specific circumstance and argued their validity as opposed to other laws or local custom, a large body of interpretative literature arose that must be consulted. The numerous handbooks published to assist notaries and lawyers in sorting out the legal system are extremely useful, but they must be studied carefully, for laws pertaining to women are not consolidated in one place. Moreover, it is necessary to examine the exceptions listed for many statutes, because it is often in the qualification of general principles that the nature and meaning of women's legal status are to be found.

## Colonial Legal Status

### Restriction and Protection

The legal inequality of Mexican women was a combination of restrictive and protective measures. Legal handbooks explained that on the one hand men were "capable of all types of functions and obligations unless one of them [was] excluded due to a particular circumstance, whereas women just because of their sex [were] all presumed incapable of many activities." On the other hand, women enjoyed the privilege of protection because they were deemed weaker in body, mind, and character. A frequently cited axiom of law held that males were "superior" in matters of strength and dignity owing to their greater "prudence and firmness," and females were "superior with respect to matters excused by the fragility of their sex."[3] Yet on balance it is clear that the two did not offset each other. The principle of women's inferiority, explicitly set forth in the Siete Partidas, was reiterated by the *Teatro de la legislación*, a standard late colonial reference work, which flatly stated, "The woman is not of as high a status or as good a condition as the man."[4]

Hispanic law contained provisions consolidating the male's supremacy from the moment of birth until death because of his superior corporal strength. For instance, if a woman gave birth to fraternal twins of both sexes, it was presumed that the stronger male was born first—a presumption with important implications for the few wealthy families with entailed estates that went to the firstborn, female or male. Likewise, it was assumed that when husband and wife perished together in a shipwreck or fire, she died first because she was "naturally weak," again with important patrimonial consequences.[5] Yet the distinctions based on a woman's physical debility were not central to her legal status.

Until adulthood was reached at the age of 25, men and women shared a similar juridical position, except that in several circumstances the law recognized the earlier maturity of girls. Minors of both sexes were under the father's or guardian's tutelage, needing his permission to enter into contracts or litigate in court. Failure to obtain his authorization invalidated such transactions. In principle, minors also needed permission to marry, but because the Church guaranteed freedom of marriage, their marriages were valid (if there was no impediment such as consanguinity or affinity) as long as the girl had reached the age of 12 and the boy 14.[6] At these ages children, classified as *infantes* until age seven and then as *pupiles*, became known as *púberes*. Having entered puberty, they were considered ready for marriage, were expected to be familiar with the law, and, if orphaned, could make a will and name an administrator for their property. The same two-year age gap applied for granting minors a dispensation to administer their own property: girls were eligible at 18, boys at 20.[7]

There has been some confusion whether minors were released from their fathers' guardianship on attaining their majority, with some authors maintaining that adult men and women were both independent, and others that adult women were subject to perpetual guardianship by male relatives.[8] Neither was the case. Unless specifically emancipated, neither single sons nor single daughters were independent during their father's lifetime. Such *hijos de familia* continued to be subject to the *patria potestas* (paternal authority) and needed the father's permission for their legal transactions. *Hijos de familia* could be emancipated by their father voluntarily or by court order, if he abused them. They were released from his authority automatically if he was incapacitated by illness, committed incest, or was banished from the realm. Marriage also released children from the *patria potestas;* in fact, the minor daughter who married remained emancipated even if she was widowed while still underage. (But emancipation did not give minors the rights of adults, since they continued to need a guardian until they reached the age of majority.)[9] Men and women emancipated in any of these ways—or by a father's death—were released from guardianship at the age of 25. They could freely choose their domicile, administer their property, enter into contracts and litigation, and as a concomitant of this responsibility for their behavior, be tried and imprisoned as criminals. Only if insane or retarded were they subject to continued guardianship.[10] Thus though single daughters, like single sons, remained subject to their fathers' authority, widows and emancipated single women had complete sovereignty over their legal acts.

Despite these similarities, the legal status of adult men and women diverged substantially. Men, whether subject to the father's authority or not, were legally able to engage in any noncriminal pursuit; women were excluded from a series of activities involving leadership or governance. Women could not hold public office or vote; could not be judges, lawyers, or priests; could not be guardians or adopt children as they pleased, since Hispanic law considered the governance of children to be a "public ministry" suitable only for men. And women could not generally act as an advocate for someone in court or as a witness for another's will. To reinforce these restrictions, women were forbidden to dress like men, thereby perhaps circumventing the limitations placed on the female sex.[11]

It is difficult to ignore the parallel between women and the other categories of people systematically banned from positions of authority: minors, slaves, the mentally retarded, the insane, invalids, and criminals. This list might suggest that women were considered incapable of governing others. But the parallel should not be taken too far, since different reasons were given for keeping each group from a given function. The following discussion from the Siete Partidas of who could not be a judge is representative:

There are certain personal disadvantages under which men labor, and on account of which they should not be appointed judges. For, according to the ordinances of the ancients, a man who is ignorant or imprudent should not be a judge, because he would not have sufficient intelligence to hear or decide suits justly, nor, also, one who is dumb [mute], because he would not be able to question the parties when it was necessary, or answer them, or render decisions orally; nor deaf because he could not hear what is discussed before him, nor should a blind man hold an office, since he cannot see persons, or recognize them, or show them honor. . . . Moreover, a person of bad reputation, or who has committed [criminal] acts . . . is ineligible, for . . . a man of this kind should [not] sit in judgement upon others. . . . Nor can a woman be a judge, for it would not be becoming for her to be present in a crowd of men deciding lawsuits. [Nor] a slave [for] although he may be intelligent, he will not have free will to act [and] might sometimes be compelled to decide cases according to the wishes of his lord, and not according to his knowledge, which would be contrary to the law.[12]

These justifications draw an important distinction between women and other persons ineligible for judicial positions: all except women are regarded as deficient in some way, either because of age, a physical handicap, a criminal record, ignorance, or bondage. In contrast, although a general principle of Hispanic law held that women were less judicious than men, in specific instances mental inferiority was not given as the rationale for excluding women from leadership activities. Indeed, the term *imbecilitus sexus* does not appear in Hispanic lawbooks.

Rather, restrictions on women's activities were justified in terms of propriety and tradition. The Siete Partidas barred women from judgeships simply because it would be unbecoming for them to decide lawsuits in a crowd of men. They barred women from receiving holy orders "for although Holy Mary, the Mother of Jesus Christ, was greater, and of holier rank than all the Apostles, He was unwilling to confer upon her the power of absolution, but gave it to them because they were men." Both propriety and tradition were cited in the Partida prohibiting

4. One of the public scribes stationed in the archways of the Zócalo who, for a small fee, wrote letters or drew up documents for the large illiterate population of Mexico City. The artist, an Italian traveler named Claudio Linati, has fittingly chosen to make the scribe's client a woman, for fewer women than men knew how to read and write. This did not prevent them from conducting business, filing court cases, or—according to Linati—sending love letters taken down by the *evangelista*, as the public letter-writer was known.

women from acting as advocates for others: "first, because it is neither proper nor honorable for a woman to assume masculine duties, mingling publicly with men in order to argue cases for others; second, because in ancient times the wise men forbade it."[13]

Exceptions made to some of these laws implicitly recognized women's capacity to perform certain "masculine duties." Women could serve as attorneys for elderly relatives who had no one else to represent them in court, and for any relative in such serious matters as trying to commute a death sentence. Women could be the guardians of their own children and grandchildren, and could adopt a child with government permission.[14] In extraordinary cases women were permitted to hold an inherited public office, as were a few widows who took over their husbands' posts in the early unsettled period of the Conquest.[15] The impropriety of women's "mingling publicly with men" was apparently not sufficient cause to keep them from fulfilling these important family responsibilities. Indeed, the system of inheritance directly involved women in the business world and courts in order to defend their family property.

Hispanic law even more clearly acknowledged woman's full mental capacity in granting adult women the right to conduct their own legal affairs. Women could participate in a wide range of public activities. They were allowed to buy, sell, rent, inherit, or bequeath property of all kinds. They could lend and borrow money, act as administrators of estates, and form business partnerships. They could initiate litigation, be their own advocates in court, and appear as witnesses (except in wills). After the royal decree of 1799 ended guild restrictions against women in New Spain, they could engage in "all labors and manufactures compatible with their strength and the decorum of their sex."[16] Widows and emancipated single adult women needed no one's permission for these acts; wives and unemancipated single women could perform them with the husband's or father's consent.[17]

Some legal historians have concluded that women could allege ignorance of the law to annul contracts by which they had been injured, but this protective provision applied only where a woman, as executor of an estate, paid bequests from an improperly drawn will.[18] The only class of persons who could excuse their actions on account of unfamiliarity with the law were girls under the age of 12 and boys under 14. The first Partida also extended this privilege to "peasants who cultivate the soil or dwell in uninhabited places, . . . shepherds who conduct their flocks through the mountains and the deserts, and . . . women who dwell in similar places."[19] Thus, a woman's legal transactions normally had the same validity as a man's.

Given the implicit recognition of women's competence, their limited legal rights are difficult to explain. The rationale offered by Hispanic lawbooks is inconsistent: the dual issues of propriety and tradition were only raised in relation to a few activities that caused women to mingle with men. Women were kept from presiding over a court, but not from litigating in it; from notarizing a transaction, but not from appearing before the notary with a contract; from supervising the marketplace, but not from selling there. Although banned from office-holding in State, Church, and community, women were neither confined to the domestic sphere nor defined exclusively as wives and mothers. It was only the governance of others, not public activities in general, that was inappropriate for them.

The other side of these restrictions is the protection granted women in consideration of their differences from men. Several protective provisions recognized women's weak economic position in society. Fathers who had the means to do so were required to endow their daughters (unless they married against their father's will), and guardians were required to endow their wards. Because the dowry belonged exclusively to the woman, it ensured her a measure of economic independence during marriage and widowhood. A man could also give his bride a gift, called the *arras*, which would similarly belong to her and protect her economic position in the event that he went bankrupt or died. Privileged by law, both the arras and the dowry were beyond the reach of the husband's creditors.[20]

These provisions reflect the general principle of Hispanic law that "a woman's capital should not be lost or diminished, but rather be conserved."[21] Thus, for example, although a married woman needed her husband's permission to enter into a contract, its validity was upheld *a posteriori* if she profited from it, even if she had failed to obtain his permission.[22] Likewise, women were barred from providing surety because of the possibility that they would lose money in this way. This dictate might have restricted women as much as it protected them, except that the law listed seven circumstances in which they could provide surety, and further gave them the right to "renounce" the privilege of not binding themselves if they wished to risk their property.[23]

The economic position of women was also safeguarded by inheritance laws that guaranteed legitimate daughters and widows (as well as sons and widowers) a share of their parents' or spouses' estate. Generally speaking, a person could dispose of only one-fifth of his or her property freely; the other four-fifths had to be divided among the legitimate heirs, with children of both sexes receiving equal shares from both parents. Widows normally received half the community property, but an impecunious widow could inherit a larger share if the probate judge determined that she was in greater need of it than the other heirs. If a man died intestate and without other heirs, his widow inherited the entire estate. Furthermore, any condition placed on a woman's inheritance that violated her legal rights, such as her right to remarry, was legally invalid, since the law favored the right to inherit over an individual's freedom to bequeath.[24]

Legal measures protecting motherhood and women's reputations recognized their sexual vulnerability. Women were defended from male deceit by the law on *esponsales* (spousals, or engagements), which stipulated that if a man promised to marry a woman, even if the promise was never put into writing, he could be forced to keep his word or pay her compensation.[25] An unmarried mother had the right to demand child support from the father of her children if neither had any impediment to marrying, as when both were single and unrelated.[26] A man who offended a woman's reputation by pursuing her in the streets, sending her jewels, or kissing her publicly against her will was required to make financial reparations. Penalties for rape or seduction were severe.[27] Indeed, male relatives of a raped woman were permitted to kill the rapist on the spot, a right that was justified as a variant of murder in self-defense, in this case defense of the family honor.[28] The law thus acknowledged the importance of maintaining a woman's sexual virtue, upon which her marital possibilities and her family's honor and social standing rested.

Not all women qualified for protection, however, and the distinctions made by Hispanic law in determining a woman's eligibility reveal that if women were not primarily defined as wives and mothers, they were perceived as sexual beings first and foremost.[29] Many protective provisions applied only to "decent" women: virgins, nuns, and "honest" wives and widows. Prostitutes lost the right to demand child support, and the seduction, rape, or offense of a "vile" woman carried no penalty unless it involved physical violence. An "honest" woman who dressed like a prostitute lost the right to sue a man who offended her because she was assumed to be inviting mistreatment.[30] Protection in these cases was based on a woman's sexual behavior rather than marital status. In order to qualify, a woman had to have a "good reputation," that is, to be virgin when single, monogamous when married, and chaste when widowed. In contrast, a man's sexual behavior carried no legal consequences unless he had a criminal record for some past offense of a sexual nature, such as rape or adultery.[31]

Women's definition as sexual beings is further suggested by the fact that they were held entirely responsible for their sexual behavior. Whereas in some types of cases the law granted women the privilege of receiving milder punishment for their crimes than men, they were considered strong enough to suffer the full consequences of their sexual acts. For instance, women could not be incarcerated for debts, except those derived from criminal activity.[32] Yet such crimes as abortion, concubinage, incest, and bigamy were as harshly punished in women as in men, with abortion carrying the death penalty if the fetus was born alive.[33]

Moreover, women alone were punished for certain types of sexual activities. Prostitution was illegal; frequenting a prostitute was not.[34] A woman's adultery, always illegal unless she was raped or deceived, might cause her to lose her dowry and share of the community property, or to be imprisoned if her husband chose to have her prosecuted. A husband was even allowed to kill his wife and her lover if he discovered them *in flagrante delicto*. In contrast, a man's adultery was punishable in only four cases: if he committed it with a married woman, with his children's wet nurse while she was in his house, or with a domestic servant while she was in her master's household, or if the affair was conducted so openly as to create a public scandal. The first could result in his banishment or death (if the woman's husband caught him *in flagrante*), the others in imprisonment or a fine. Otherwise, a man's adultery carried no penalty whatsoever. Indeed, Hispanic law denied wives the right to accuse their husbands of adultery in secular court, though such suits occurred regularly in nineteenth-century Mexico.[35] Similarly, a widow's "licentious" behavior was punishable, whereas a widower's was not. The widow who fornicated lost both the guardianship of her children and her share of any community property; the widower suffered no penalty because, according to the *Febrero mejicano*, the law considered "indecency less condemnable and offensive in a man than in a woman."[36] Thus the double standard was closely embraced by Hispanic law.

## Married Women

Married women, bound by the same discriminatory laws as all women, were subject to an additional set of restrictions. In return for the support, protection, and guidance her husband was legally required to provide, a wife owed him nearly total obedience. Compelled to reside with him, she became subject to his authority over every aspect of her life, relinquishing sovereignty over most of her legal transactions, property, and earnings, and even her domestic activities. Although Hispanic law did not use the term guardianship to describe the authority of a husband over his wife, she effectively entered into his tutelage. As one nineteenth-century law text put it, exaggerating her position, "A married woman is bound by her husband's wishes in everything."[37] There was no comparable loss of legal rights for men who entered the married state.

Concurrently, the Catholic Church provided a model of marriage, embodied in canon law, that was more egalitarian than the one expressed in civil law. Although the Church discriminated against women (notably by excluding them from the priesthood and by recognizing the husband as the head of the household), it gave wives more rights and demanded a greater subordination of husbands' freedom than the State. Defining marriage as a sacrament aimed at procreating and educating children and at providing companionship, aid, and a remedy for concupiscence, canon law granted husbands and wives equal rights and obligations toward those ends. They were supposed to aid each other and share the responsibility for their children; their reciprocal consent was necessary to "make use of their bodies so as to propagate the species"; both were required to be faithful.[38] Either spouse's failure to fulfill these duties provided grounds for a separation. Although the marriage bond could be dissolved only by death or annulment, the Church could authorize what was called an ecclesiastical divorce, in fact a separation of bed and board. Since the Church did not condone a double standard of sexual behavior, adultery by either spouse was cause for such a separation. The penalty for causing it also applied equally to husbands and wives: the guilty party lost his or her share of the community property and had to pay the court costs; the innocent one gained custody of the children.[39] According to the *Sala mexicano*, it was because "canon law . . . considered justice principally in terms of men's relationship with God and not with society [that] it defined equally the rights of both spouses, classifying the violation of fidelity for both as adultery without distinction."[40]

But these egalitarian principles were teachings more than legal prescriptions, because the Church had no power to enforce them: it could not punish adulterous husbands, or those who ignored their wives' wishes in rearing children, or those who forced their wives to have intercourse. The Church's ultimate weapon—excommunication—was rarely invoked, and certainly not for domestic misbehavior. Church courts became involved only when one spouse sought a separation. As long as husband and wife remained together, their relationship was regulated by civil law, which had exclusive jurisdiction over temporal matters.

Under civil law, husbands controlled most of their wives' legal transactions and belongings. As a wife's legal representative, the husband did not need her permission to act in her name.[41] But a married woman could not represent her husband. In fact, she needed his permission to perform most legal acts on her own behalf, specifically, to enter into contracts, to renounce an inheritance or accept an encumbered one, to initiate a suit in court, or to donate alms to the poor. The husband's authority was not absolute. His consent was not required for a woman to accept an unencumbered inheritance (which could only benefit her economically), to testify in court (her civic duty), or to make her own will (for finally, at death, he lost control of her property).[42] The law also curtailed his rights over her property and allowed her to file suit against him (without his permission) in order to separate, recover her property, punish him for mistreating her, or force him to provide for the family. Still, there were few areas in which married women could exercise their will.

A married woman could own property, but her husband controlled most of it. Under the community property system that obtained in Hispanic law, property acquired during a couple's married life (the *bienes gananciales*) was jointly owned. The community property consisted of salary earned by either spouse, property bought with any type of funds, and rents from real estate or profits from their separate funds; it was liable for the legitimate debts of either spouse. When a marriage was terminated by death, the community property was usually divided equally between the surviving spouse and the deceased's heirs, regardless of how much money each had brought to the marriage or who had worked to produce it. The community property was also divided following an ecclesiastical divorce, with the guilty spouse suffering a financial loss. If favorable to widows in most cases, this system was unfavorable to wives: during a husband's lifetime he alone administered the community property, including any salary the wife might earn, and he could dispose of it without her consent.[43]

A married woman retained the ownership of her dowry, but again it was her husband who controlled it. Moreover, he could dispose of its earnings as he liked, for this income was awarded him to "help him carry the burden of marriage": providing for his family financially.[44] But a husband could never alienate the principal (unless the wife lost the dowry by committing adultery), and a woman recovered it on her husband's death or in the event of an ecclesiastical divorce. If she died first, the dowry was either divided among her children or returned to her parents, since it was legally an advance inheritance deductible from their estates. If there was an arras it was treated like the dowry, for it was considered a husband's way of endowing his wife.[45]

The only property a married woman both owned and controlled consisted of the *bienes parafernales*: the belongings she brought to the marriage other than the dowry (usually clothes and jewels) and any property she subsequently acquired through inheritance or donation. The *bienes parafernales* constituted a wife's separate fund, but her rights over it were ambiguous. The *Teatro de la legislación* stated that unless she specifically ceded its administration to her spouse in writing, she could manage and dispose of it without his permission. Although Mexican lawbooks suggest that husbands customarily managed this fund for their wives, the law clearly established that a man could not dispose of his wife's *bienes parafernales*.[46]

Hispanic law limited the husband's control of his wife's property in order to protect her from abuses. The Leyes de Toro prohibited a husband from acquiring his wife's belongings, specifying that the dowry, arras, and *bienes parafernales* could not be held liable for his debts, and that the wife could not legally donate these to her spouse. Contracts violating these provisions could be annulled.[47] If a wife could prove in court that her husband had disposed of the community property with malicious intent, she recovered it (either by invalidating the contract in which it had been alienated, confiscating the husband's property, or placing a lien on his salary). However, she could not do so if unforeseen circumstances had caused the community property to dwindle or if her spouse, albeit incompetent, was well intentioned. The dowry was another matter. As the *Teatro de la legislación* saw it, the husband was the "mere administrator" of the dowry, the wife retaining the "absolute and direct dominion" of it.[48] If a wife could prove that her husband mismanaged the dowry, whatever his intent, she could have it removed from his control; she could also sue for the restitution of the dowry if her husband failed to provide for the family. She could then appoint an administrator for the dowry and community property or, if a judge approved, administer them herself.[49] Under normal circumstances, though, a wife ceded the control of her belongings to her spouse.

In addition to controlling a wife's property and legal transactions, a husband exercised exclusive authority over their children through the *patria potestas*. Granted to the father alone, it made him his children's guardian with control over their education, legal transactions, and property. The *patria potestas* also gave him privileges that went beyond mere guardianship, since he enjoyed the usufruct of his children's property and had the right to enforce his wishes through physical punishment and legal action. Only he could legitimate a child and only he was required to give consent for a child's marriage; legally mothers did not have to be consulted.[50] Because freedom of marriage was guaranteed by the Church, fathers could neither force children to marry against their will nor prevent their marriages, so long as no legal impediments existed between the bride and groom. But the Partidas gave fathers the right to disinherit daughters who married against their wishes, and the Royal Pragmatic on Marriage of 1776, attempting to prevent marriages between unequals, extended this right to minor sons as well.[51]

Hispanic lawbooks claimed that the *patria potestas* was awarded to the father in return for the support, education, and inheritance he was required to provide his legitimate children. However, a father did not lose these rights when he failed to provide, and the mother, though she shared almost all of these legal obligations, did not enjoy the father's rights.[52] Observing this difference, several nineteenth-century legal handbooks drew a distinction between the *patria potestas onerosa* of the mother and the *patria potestas útil* of the father.[53] Although strictly speaking they were incorrect in using the term *patria potestas* at all in connection with a mother, their point still holds: she had the burden without the privileges. Not even the single mother was given the *patria potestas* over her illegitimate children, though the father did not have it either. Nonetheless, mothers legally bore the full responsibility of supporting, rearing, and leaving inheritances to their children with only two exceptions: first, a woman who had legitimate children was not required to bequeath property to her illegitimate ones; and second, a nun was freed from the obligation to bestow an inheritance on any illegitimate offspring. In contrast, fathers were fully responsible only for their legitimate offspring. Although required to support and rear natural children (those born to an unmarried couple having no impediment to marry), fathers did not have to leave them inheritances. They had no legal obligations whatsoever to any other types of illegitimate children (e.g., those born of adultery or incest, and those born to prostitutes, nuns, or priests).[54]

Only one prerogative of the *patria potestas*, that of granting consent for a child's marriage, was transferred to the mother on her husband's death.[55] Still, the widow did not assume all the father's authority in this matter. A royal decree of 1803, clarifying the Royal Pragmatic of 1776, introduced a distinction between the mother and the father by releasing a widow's children from the consent requirement one year earlier than if the father had lived (at 22 for girls and 24 for boys for maternal consent, compared with 23 and 25 for paternal consent). If the mother was also dead, they had to obtain the permission of a grandparent, guardian, or judge, again gaining their emancipation earlier.[56] The fact that children were not subject to a mother's authority as long as to a father's implies that her authority was not as valid as his; the grandparents', guardian's, or judge's was even less so.

Fathers also had more rights than mothers in the realm of guardianship. Whereas fathers were automatically the guardians of their children, mothers were not. A widow became her children's guardian only if her husband had failed to name someone else in his will. And her guardianship was conditional: she lost it if she lived "sinfully" or remarried, for it was thought that she would favor the children of her new marriage. In contrast, a widower retained the guardianship of his children regardless of his sexual behavior or remarriage.[57] Thus, only the father was recognized as the natural "ruler" of the child.

The discrepancy between parents' rights over their children is particularly ironic because the Siete Partidas acknowledged the mother's disproportionate sacrifices, explaining that marriage was called matrimony and not patrimony, because the mother endured so much more hardship with children than the father. Indeed, the law established a mother's greater responsibility for children under the age of three, the *edad de lactancia*, or nursing age.[58] Yet Hispanic law did not award mothers commensurate predominance in childrearing, instead upholding man's supremacy in the "woman's sphere."

## *Justifications of Women's Inferiority*

Although Hispanic lawbooks offered several reasons for women's legal inferiority, these do not adequately account for the differences in the status of men and women. They fail to explain, for example, why the paterfamilias retained the *patria potestas* even when he did not fulfill his responsibilities, why married women and single daughters were unable to conduct their own legal affairs as other women could, and why women could engage in all public activities save those governing others.

Easiest to dispense with is the argument of physical weakness. A man's greater strength, cited by Hispanic law as the reason the male was necessarily born before his female twin and died after his female companion, might account for the protection that husbands were required to give wives. But it explains neither the husband's control of his wife's property, legal transactions, and children, nor the activities from which all women were excluded, since most of these did not require physical strength.

Sex-role differentiation based on women's reproductive function was a second factor in the rationale for their subordination. The law defined women largely as sexual beings in establishing their eligibility for some types of protection. It explained a man's right to control his wife's and daughter's sexual behavior on the grounds that, as bearers of children, they were the perpetuators of lineage. An inheritance system based on the principle of legitimacy made the control of the wife all the more important, for every child born to a married woman was presumed legitimate and inherited equally.[59] As the editor of the *Sala Mexicano* put it, "A woman's sexual favors belong exclusively to her husband, but not conversely," because an adulterous wife could introduce a false heir into the family and upset the order of succession. A husband's infidelity, having no such consequences, was "not as pernicious as hers to the civil and domestic order."[60] By these standards, women's sexual virtue played a crucial role in maintaining the inheritance and class structure. A woman's confinement during pregnancy, childbirth, and the infant's early months might also explain why the husband had to protect and provide for her during that time.[61] But, again, it does not explain a husband's authority over his wife's property, legal transactions, and children, or the restrictions placed on single and widowed women, apart from those regulating their sexual behavior.

The parallels between wives, minors, and slaves suggest two alternative explanations, since minors were placed under the paterfamilias's dominion because they were considered incapable of conducting their own affairs, and slaves because of their status as chattel. There were indeed many similarities in the relationship of these three groups to the paterfamilias.[62] Wives, minors, and slaves alike normally needed his permission to bind themselves legally. They owed him obedience, respect, and submission, and if they left his house he could go to court to force them to return. Moreover, he controlled the property they owned and enjoyed its usufruct. Although they had legal recourse when he abused them, they did not become independent even in the extreme cases where the courts removed them from his authority, but remained under the control of a substitute, be it a new master, judge, or guardian.[63]

Yet in some respects the wife's status was ambiguous compared with that of other subordinates. For example, the law made disobedience of the father or master, but not specifically of the husband, a punishable crime. Men were explicitly granted the right to punish a "child, servant, slave, or pupil with moderation, but [not] immoderately with stick, stone, or other hard substances."[64] In contrast, Hispanic law never stated that a man could physically discipline his wife. To be sure, legal commentaries suggest that the practice was condoned to some extent. For example, in defining the crime of wife beating, they distinguished it from moderate physical punishment, which carried no penalty.[65] A husband's right to chastise his misbehaving wife is also implied in the penalties prescribed for the man whose beatings caused his pregnant spouse to miscarry: according to one legal commentator this act would normally be classified as homicide, but if "the wife provoked him or deserved her punishment" his penalty would be reduced.[66] Still, the law did not explicitly grant husbands the right to discipline their wives, nor did it allow them to press charges against their wives for disobedience, as it did for other subordinates.

If in some respects a man's authority over his wife was ambiguous, in others it was clearly less than his authority over children and slaves. Indeed, the Partidas defined the word potestas only as the power of a master over a slave, a sovereign over his subjects, a bishop over his priests, and a father over his children. It did not use the term to describe the power of a husband over a wife.[67]

The most obvious demonstration of the difference between wives and minors was in the law's recognition of a married woman's capacity to conduct her own affairs. A number of provisions allowed a wife to limit or circumvent a husband's authority in ways that children could not. Wives had some privileged property that they could remove from their husband's control simply if he mismanaged it; children had no privileged property and could only take a father to court if he disposed of their belongings. Wives could administer their separate fund; children (except for sons who earned a salary in the military or public office) had no such fund. Wives could bequeath their property without permission; children under the father's potestas could not.[68] Wives could represent themselves in court; minors (and incapacitated adults) could not appear in court on their own behalf, but had to be represented by a guardian.[69] Finally, the law distinguished between women and children by returning a woman's full juridical capacity to her on her husband's death; minors (and incapacitated adults) were not released from guardianship if the guardian died—they were simply given a new one.

A married woman's ability to think for herself is implicit in the qualifications to the law requiring a husband's permission for his wife's contracts—none of which applied to minor children. A woman's contract signed without her husband's consent would be ratified *a posteriori* if he stated that he approved of it; it would be ratified automatically if she profited from the transaction, no matter what her husband thought. A husband could give his wife a blanket permission for legal activities she might want to carry out or a general permission for certain kinds, such as selling in the marketplace. She could also obtain the necessary authorization from a judge if a husband withheld it. Conversely, she could annul a transaction he coerced her into, a provision that suggests a wife was not forced to follow her husband's advice.[70] A wife was, in effect, allowed to contest her husband's de-

5. Women's right to employment was guaranteed by Mexican law, and they constituted about a third of the identified labor force in Mexico City. A married woman, however, needed her husband's permission to work, and her earnings were subject to his control as part of the couple's community property. Food vending was the choice of many wives, especially among the Indian population, since they could set the pace of their work and coordinate it with child care and other household duties.

cisions over her legal acts. In a sense, though wives ceded their authority over their property and legal transactions on marrying, the ultimate control remained theirs because they could challenge a husband's authority in court. In contrast, most legal commentators agreed that children could contest only the father's denial of permission for their marriage, his disposal of their property, his attempts to prostitute them, or his physical abuse.[71] Therefore, despite certain similarities between wives and persons placed under guardianship because of mental deficiency, the law did not consider married women to be like these.

The parallels between wives and slaves, controlled by virtue of ownership alone, suggest that wives might have been considered a husband's property. But on close examination, that comparison also breaks down. The Partidas defined servitude as the "vilest and most contemptible thing that can exist among men [because] the party who is subject to it not only loses the power of disposing of his property as he desires, but he has not even control of his own person, except under the orders of his master."[72] A woman did not lose control over her own person, legal acts, and property to the same degree. A husband may have administered most of a wife's property and enjoyed its usufruct, but a slave's earnings became the master's entirely, so that he acquired not only its profits but the principal itself. Wives could make wills and administer their separate funds; slaves could not. Wives could question husbands' decisions in court; slaves could only protest severe mistreatment or the prevention of their marriages. Women alone were granted a series of privileges to buttress their inferior position, such as the prohibition against being incarcerated for debts or the special protection given to their property. Women could also perform governmental functions in extraordinary circumstances; slaves could not. Wives were automatically freed when husbands died; slaves were resold as part of the estate, unless the master emancipated them in his will.[73]

It could be argued that Hispanic law considered wives to be chattels because it gave a man the right to kill his adulterous wife. As we have seen, the law did in fact empower a husband to be his own judge and executioner in this case, deeming him personally injured by an act that "infringed upon his rights and authority" and classifying such a homicide as murder in self-defense.[74] But this right was far from absolute. Such a killing could be justified only if it occurred in a moment of temporary insanity when, discovering his wife in the act, a man was assumed to be unable to contain his "just wrath." Moreover, he had to kill both wife and lover to be free of a murder charge, a stipulation designed to prevent a husband and wife (or husband and friend) from setting up the third party. A husband lost the right to kill his wife if he had previously pardoned her adultery, returning the dowry and community property that an adulterous wife lost. Finally, the law denied the husband his wife's dowry when he killed her, to eliminate avarice as a possible motive.[75] Thus the Roman patriarch's absolute right to kill his adulterous wife had been qualified by Hispanic law; indeed, Mexican commentators who saw the Roman woman's oppression as rooted in her status as male property considered this principle foreign to their own society.[76] Its only remnant, the husband's right to kill his adulterous wife, was greatly weakened and unparalleled elsewhere in Hispanic law.

In sum, though there is some truth to each of these explanations for women's inferior legal status, none is entirely satisfactory: neither those emphasizing physical or mental inferiority, nor those emphasizing the role-differentiation that relegated women to reproductive functions, nor those emphasizing women's status as male property. Another reason hinted at by late colonial lawbooks furnishes a clue to an explanation that more adequately accounts for the restrictions placed on women of every marital status. It was "improper" for women to govern others but not to engage in other public acts, "improper" for married women and single daughters to conduct independently the legal transactions for which they were considered competent, and "improper" for a man to lose his authority even when he did not fulfill his responsibilities, because the subordination of women was held to be essential to the functioning of the corporate system of social control.

The ideal Hispanic society was composed of corporations (such as the nobility, clergy, military, guilds, and Indians) with particular functions and privileges, or *fueros*. In this system, individuals were not equal before the law, competing openly with each other as in a pluralist system; they were hierarchically arranged, knowing their places and living in harmony. The corporatist view of society was neatly expressed in an 1806 opinion of the Council of the Indies: "It is undeniable that the existence of various hierarchies and classes is of the greatest importance to the existence and stability of a monarchical state, since a graduated system of dependence and subordination sustains and insures the obedience and respect of the last vassal to the authority of the sovereign."[77]

The nuclear family played a crucial role in preserving the system, for it was the basic social unit on which the entire structure rested. Not only was it a metaphor for the corporate state, which like one big family was ruled by the king as a benevolent father rules his children; the man was the State's representative in the family, governing his wife and children as he, in turn, was governed by the king. Because conflict within the vertically segmented groups was unacceptable to this order, effective control from the top down required the inequality of husbands and wives.[78]

Late colonial decrees limiting freedom of marriage explicitly portrayed the hierarchy of husbands over wives and children, like the hierarchy of the social classes, as a source of social harmony. The Royal Pragmatic on Marriage of 1776, citing the threat posed to the "good order of the State" by the rising incidence of unequal marriages, required minors to obtain paternal consent to marry so as to "conserve the rightful authority of the father." Seven years later the Crown enjoined a mother from opposing her husband's decision by giving money on her own to a child disinherited for marrying against the father's wishes. Condemning the "lack of subordination of wives to husbands," this edict admonished wives to "recognize the authority of their consorts as heads of the family" so as to "maintain the order and tranquillity of families, upon which the State's in large part depends."[79] Thus the State required the obedience of wives as a guarantee of social cohesion.

This rationale for women's subordination, though not stated outright in earlier Hispanic lawbooks, was implicit in the language they used to describe the relationship between the sexes. Using metaphors of government, the Siete Partidas established the principle that "husbands should govern their wives," and that "the husband is, as it were, the lord and head of his wife." Later commentaries similarly represented the paterfamilias as the "ruler" of the entire household, with all its members, including slaves and servants, his "subjects." Limitations placed on his dominion were expressed in the language of governance as well, the *Teatro de la legislación* explaining that only among "savage" peoples did each family form an isolated "nation," with the paterfamilias an "absolute monarch" at its head; in a "civilized society" he was subordinate to the State. The *Sala mexicano* added that in modern times his authority was more that of "a legislator or judge" than that of a sovereign.[80]

According to this model, society was governed at the most elementary level through the male heads of nuclear families. Women ideally lived out their lives in male-headed households as daughters and wives (or entered religious orders and were placed under an alternative system of control). Wives and unemancipated daughters needed their husbands' or fathers' permission for most legal transactions because the head of the family was responsible for all of its activities. The paterfamilias enforced his wife's and daughter's sexual virtue because the honor and social standing of the family depended on it. He controlled their domestic activities in order to maintain harmony within the family home.

Single women and widows, outside this system of control, exercised full juridical capacity and could head their own households. But they were not accorded a well-defined place in this model. Female household heads did not exercise the full rights of *patria potestas*, and they were denied representation in the larger society through office-holding or voting.[81] Although those women whose nuclear families had been broken by the death of father or husband had far more rights than those whose nuclear families were still intact, they were nevertheless subject to overall male control through the male-dominated Church and State, since lines of authority passed from the sovereign down through men. The rights of all women were therefore restricted to those that did not conflict with patriarchal social control.

Yet Hispanic society was not a classic patriarchy, for all women were not directly controlled by men. Patriarchy had declined since Roman times and even further since the thirteenth century, when the Siete Partidas were compiled. In ancient Rome women of all marital statuses were subject to the authority of men in their extended family; and the Partidas had originally conferred the *patria potestas* on the grandfather as well as the father. But by this time Hispanic women were subject only to fathers and husbands. Even within the nuclear family the paterfamilias's power had decreased. A man no longer had the right, given him in the Partidas, to kill his adulterous daughter. The father's right to sell children in cases of extreme poverty, again accepted by the Partidas, had been revoked. Unlike the Roman patriarch, he could not force a child to marry, and he had no authority over married children. Finally, a husband's dominion over his wife was reduced, for he did not have an absolute power of life or death over her.[82] Although the State, concerned with the erosion of parental authority, attempted to reinforce the paterfamilias's control in the Royal Pragmatic on Marriage of 1776, his authority over wife and daughter was clearly circumscribed by the late colonial period.

## Authority and Power

If a woman's legal status was not as grim as some have portrayed it, neither was it as rosy as implied by those who argued that the protection given the Delicate Sex compensated for the restrictions of their activities. Under Hispanic law, protection was characterized by tentativeness, restriction by finality. Women engaging in improper sexual activity were denied protection from sexual crimes, and women wishing to make their contracts binding under all circumstances could renounce the provisions safeguarding their property. Indeed, it was customary for a woman's contracts to begin by waiving a series of protective provisions and stating that she had not been coerced into the transaction by her husband,[83] so that women regularly forfeited their right to protection. In contrast, restrictions could rarely be overcome.

Far from compensating, in fact, protection often reinforced the restrictions on women. For example, because the sexual protection afforded women could so easily be lost, it was a mechanism for enforcing their proper behavior. Likewise, the inheritance system that gave some women a power base in marriage and protection in widowhood or spinsterhood was a mixed blessing: since women automatically inherited from both parents, daughters might be subjected to strict supervision before their marriage by parents anxious to control the match; wives might be subjected to strict control after marriage by husbands attempting to prevent false heirs from inheriting their property.[84]

Moreover, provisions protecting women's property led to some misunderstanding about the validity of their contracts in general. Mexican legal commentators referred to the confusion arising from the numerous ways in which women's contracts could be invalidated (if a woman had provided surety for another, if she had donated her dowry to her husband, if she had acted under pressure from him, and so on). Just in case, notaries drawing up women's contracts renounced a standard list of laws, whether they applied or not. Fernández de Lizardi satirized this practice in his portrayal of the ignorant notary Chanfaina, who renounced a married woman's privileges in an emancipated single woman's contract.[85] But even well-educated men were confused. For example, the introduction to the *Febrero mejicano* stated as a general rule of law that women had the privilege of breaking contracts that injured them. The author later corrected his oversimplified statement in his detailed discussion of contract law, but advised readers to err on the safe side and avoid dealing with married women altogether.[86] To some extent, then, the protection of women's property made all their transactions suspect.

To be sure, provisions protecting married women's property might give them power in marriage. Because a wife could remove the dowry and *bienes parafernales* from her husband's control, his ability to use and profit from these ultimately depended on her acquiescence. The community property also gave her some leverage, because a husband was accountable to a wife if he misused it, though less accountable than with the other types of property he held for her. Furthermore, because an ecclesiastical divorce allowed a wife to obtain her share of this property during her husband's lifetime, the community property system predisposed a husband to oppose a separation, and made the threat of filing such a suit a way to alter his behavior. Thus property ownership gave women a potential source of influence and a cushion against a husband's power.

· Much of the institutional protection given women was passive, though, especially that available to wives and daughters, the only women subject to direct male authority. Because family matters were private, the courts would not actively step in on a woman's behalf when men abused their authority. A woman or her relatives had to take the initiative in demanding her rights: suing for child support, taking a deceitful lover to court for breach of promise, charging a husband or father with cruelty, filing for the restitution of the dowry or the removal of the community property from a husband's management, soliciting a judge's permission for legal transactions the paterfamilias prohibited. As records in the Judicial Archives show, some women did file suit on all these grounds, but even then they depended on a judge to rule in their favor. Moreover, such women were probably unusual. Thus many women, if they did not waive or lose their right to protection, never enjoyed it because they failed to go to court to enforce it. So it can hardly be said that on balance women's right to protection overcame their restrictions and put them on a par with men.

In keeping with the logic of patriarchal corporatism, Hispanic law granted women little authority over others in either the public or private sphere. Women may in practice have influenced other people, of course, but only men were formally given the right to command as community leaders, fathers, and husbands; the law did not sanction women's imposing their will except, perhaps, by bequeathing their property and, in specific cases, exercising limited authority over orphaned children or slaves. Women could make some decisions affecting their own lives, but their degree of personal autonomy depended on their rela tionship to men. Thus, though women were neither powerless nor totally without authority, and though they were permitted to engage in a wide range of activities, the law clearly subordinated them to men.

## Contemporary Views of Women's Legal Status

The inferior legal position of women was easy to justify as long as women tended to stay at home, were poorly educated, and were not considered valuable members of society. It was acceptable also as long as relations of dominance and subordination characterized all aspects of social life. When the legal system began to conflict more and more with nineteenth-century realities, however, some Mexicans proposed reducing the inequalities between the sexes. But their willingness to weaken patriarchy was tempered by their view of corporate social control.

It is not easy to trace discussions about women's legal status. Few changes in private law were enacted after independence because of the frequent turnover of governments, the preoccupation with establishing viable political structures, and the many pressing economic problems. The subject did not elicit widespread comment in the capital's journals or pamphlet literature either. Nonetheless, the legal handbooks published in Mexico City, in their discussions of centuries-old prescriptions about women, reveal much about the current views of women's legal status. Likewise, the short-lived civil codes enacted for the states of Oaxaca and Zacatecas in 1827–29 (and revoked when Mexico returned to the centralist system in 1835) introduced changes their authors considered appropriate. Justo Sierra's draft of a national civil code, written from 1857 to 1859, is also useful because, though never promulgated, it served as the basis for the 1870 Civil Code that finally replaced the corpus of Hispanic private law in force until that date.[87]

The controversy over women's legal status was limited to a handful of issues, for Mexicans generally approved of the legal definition of women's place. Typical of the discussions surrounding legislative reforms was an anonymous speech published in 1841, entitled *Discourse on the Law with Some Observations on Reforms That Should Be Made in Our Legislation*. Devoting only one short paragraph to women, it concluded, "The woman, according to our customs, holds an honorable and even prominent place in the family. The part of our legislation concerning her should remain intact for a long time." Even a pamphlet with such a promising title as *Without Equality Before the Law There Can Be No Liberty* did not mention women, being directed against Spaniards in independent Mexico.[88]

Commentators repeatedly observed that the legal status of

Mexican women was far better than that of women in many other places and times. For example, Fernández de Lizardi wrote in 1818 that women were "oppressed" over "more than half the globe": subject to "enclosure and domestic slavery" among Orientals and polygamy among Arabs, and "insulted" by the practice of lifelong tutelage among ancient Romans. In the 1850's the liberal politician Ignacio Ramírez contrasted the "emancipation" of contemporary women with their position as slaves in Asia and "movable goods" in Athens and Rome. The author of the *Nuevo Febrero* likewise decried the situation of women in the Orient, where "even today husbands have the right, not only of direction, but of true empire," and in ancient Rome, where "the wife became like a daughter to the family." Nowadays, he wrote, "there can be no advantage to a similar abjection of the Fair Sex."[89]

By the international standards of the time, Mexicans were justified in concluding that their laws concerning women were eminently reasonable. On the whole, women's rights were no more severely curtailed under Hispanic law than under contemporary U.S., English, or French law. In some respects, Mexican women had more legal protection than their foreign counterparts. For example, in England and the United States property was usually transmitted through the male line, bypassing daughters. By common law, husbands acquired all of their wives' belongings; since married women did not own property, they could neither enter into contracts nor make wills. After 1833 British women did not even retain their dowries if separated or widowed. According to Blackstone's formulation of the common law, "Under the law husband and wife are one, and that one is the husband." In contrast, a Mexican wife maintained an independent juridical personality: she could own property, bequeath it without permission, retain custody of children in most separations, and, symbolically, keep her maiden surnames and pass these on to her offspring. The favorable comparison between colonial Hispanic law and other legal systems partially explains why women's legal status was not questioned more profoundly in independent Mexico.[90]

Praising the protection of the "weak and needy" in their ancient law codes, Mexican lawmakers retained these provisions with only minor changes. Although legal commentators urged two changes in what Ramírez called the "privileges and prerogatives" conferred on women by colonial law,[91] neither represented a significant reduction of that protection. Most nineteenth-century legal commentators believed that only written spousals should be binding, a view incorporated into the Oaxaca and Sierra codes. Still, most jurists agreed with the *Nuevo Febrero* that "the law can never do too much to protect young girls."[92] The new codes, reflecting the decline of the dowry by the nineteenth century, also dropped the requirement that parents endow their daughters if they had the means to do so.[93] By expanding individual liberty, this proposal freed parents to use their property as they wished during their lifetimes. Yet because daughters continued to inherit automatically from both parents, and because the dowry had always been subtracted from their final inheritance, daughters sooner or later received the equivalent of the portion they were guaranteed at marriage under colonial law, merely losing the use of it during their parents' lifetimes. In fact, since a wife might have more control over an inheritance considered *bienes parafernales* than over a dowry, the shift away from endowing daughters may have given wives more control over property.[94] Thus this change, which at first glance appears to represent a loss of protection, may not necessarily have been so. Furthermore, the abolition in 1823 of entail, by which a few wealthy families had circumvented the rule of equal partition among heirs, strengthened that principle favoring women.

As with the laws protecting women, Mexicans generally accepted the laws curtailing their activities. After all, once their exclusion from artisan trades was rectified in 1799, women were legally able to engage in all public activities except those involving administration and governance. When, in 1824, the first Mexican Constitution granted citizenship—including voting rights—to all Mexicans regardless of literacy and wealth, women were excluded from suffrage. This restriction seemed so natural that it was not even specified in the constitution. Since the same practice was followed in subsequent constitutions, Genaro García, an ardent advocate of women's suffrage, was able to argue in

1891 that Mexican women were technically permitted to vote. But, of course, they could not do so.[95] In the 1850's, after learning of the Seneca Falls declaration in which U.S. feminists demanded suffrage, Mexican lawmakers explicitly rejected the call for the "emancipation" of women. Addressing the members of the 1856 Constitutional Convention, Ramírez in the same breath urged the strengthening of what he termed women's "social rights," or protection, and emphasized that he did not "mean to emancipate woman or give her political responsibilities." In another speech at the convention, he argued that women did not need a direct formal relationship with the State since they were adequately represented through the vote of their husbands or fathers.[96] In short, Mexican women did not share in the political democratization following independence because politics was considered inappropriate for the Fair Sex.

Although the legal definition of permissible female activities did not generate much controversy, that of their limited authority did. Mexicans wanted to expand women's authority within the family, and more particularly, over children. Mexican jurists regarded laws denying the widow guardianship and *patria potestas* over her children as especially unjust. It is difficult to document these views, since the law codes introducing reforms in this area did not express the reasoning of the lawmakers. Consequently, attitudes must sometimes be deduced from the changes made. Fortunately, these sources can be supplemented by the *Nuevo Febrero* of 1850–52, which included the anonymous author's "Philosophical Reflections" on each topic covered, possibly written by its publisher, Mariano Galván Rivera.

That handbook's extensive critique of the restrictions on a mother's authority responded to two major developments of the period. First, the growing belief in woman's competence, supplanting the older view of man's greater judiciousness, made it untenable to deny mothers authority over their children. Although numerous provisions of colonial law had implied that women were capable of engaging in all manner of legal acts, this view became increasingly explicit in arguments to change women's legal status. Second, the growing prestige of motherhood, now imbued with an important civic function, meant that mothers deserved recognition for their worthwhile contribution to society. It also entitled them to the power that would enable them to perform their duties more effectively.

In keeping with these new attitudes, the author of the *Nuevo Febrero* proposed that a widow automatically receive the guardianship and *patria potestas* of her children, retaining these even if she remarried. He also proposed that the *patria potestas* be shared between mother and father during the husband's lifetime, and that single mothers hold it over their natural children. Mothers could exercise this authority, he argued, because they were entirely capable of discerning their children's best interests. They deserved it because "the mother has an immense influence over the education and guidance of the children, perhaps more than their own father, since she is the one who deals with them most often, who knows them best, who forms their character during the tender age when they are so susceptible to perversion. . . . Thus how can we deprive mothers of the right to exercise this superiority and influence, which is so natural and useful?" Basing his appeal on his debt to his own mother, he wrote: "It would doubtless be a great ingratitude on the part of us men to deny our mothers recognition of the great efforts, inconveniences, and sacrifices we have caused them." Finally, he assured his readers that because a widow's great love for her children would prevent her from abusing her authority if she remarried, no matter how much she loved the children by her new husband, she should retain the guardianship and *patria potestas* over her children throughout her lifetime.[97]

Mexican lawmakers agreed with the *Nuevo Febrero* on the desirability of increasing a widow's rights over her children, but they were not unanimous about how far to go. The Zacatecas Civil Code automatically granted widows who did not remarry the guardianship of their children but denied them the *patria potestas*; the Oaxaca Civil Code granted widows both rights but removed the *patria potestas* from those who remarried; and Sierra's draft code granted widows guardianship and *patria potestas* and allowed them to keep both if they remarried. Still, in none of the three codes were the widow's rights exactly like the father's. The Oaxaca and Sierra codes gave the father the right to name in his will one or more advisers whom the mother was required to consult for the acts he specified. (But according to Sierra, she did not have to follow their advice if she did not consider it to be in her children's best interests, and would only lose the *patria potestas* if she behaved "maliciously.") The Sierra code placed a second limitation on the mother's *patria potestas*, specifying that she lost it if she had an illegitimate child, proof of a debauched life. The Oaxaca and Sierra codes also further qualified the rights of the widow who remarried, permitting her to administer her children's property only if a Family Council composed of local authorities and surviving relatives approved.[98] Nevertheless, these codes came closer to recognizing the natural rights of mothers over their children than did colonial law. Indeed the Sierra code, following the *Nuevo Febrero*, conferred the *patria potestas* on single mothers as well as widows.[99]

A weaker trend toward expanding women's authority over children can be seen in the Oaxaca code's provision that women over the age of 50 could adopt children and serve as guardians of minors other than their own children and grandchildren. These activities, previously defined as "public ministries," had been forbidden to women. As childrearing increasingly became a female domain, however, some lawmakers were willing to give women (or at least older women, who commanded respect in this society) rights over unrelated children. Yet these views were so tentative that the Zacatecas Civil Code, though it allowed women to adopt children, did not empower them to be guardians of any except their own descendants; the Sierra code did not grant women either right.[100] For most Mexican jurists it was motherhood, more than womanhood, that justified giving women authority over children.

Sierra considered the expansion of a widow's authority over her children such a significant improvement over colonial law that he singled it out for comment in the preface to his draft code. "I have substituted the mother in the absence of the father in all of the latter's rights relative to the *patria potestas*," he explained. "I believe nothing to be more just, more worthy of a reasonable society. It is high time that the rights of maternity be recognized as they should be, since the law can prevent abuses that might result from the weakness of the sex."[101] The law might step in if a widow's sexual behavior made her an unfit mother, if she lacked enough education or experience to administer her children's property, or if after remarrying she favored the children by her new spouse. As a general rule, however, widows would take on all the deceased father's rights over their children.

Most Mexicans were not so ready to grant mothers increased authority during their husbands' lifetimes, even though the civil codes took a few halting steps in that direction. The Oaxaca code required minor children to obtain both the mother's and the father's consent to marry, but specified that if they disagreed, only the father's consent was necessary. The Zacatecas code, incorporating the same provision, added that a mother's consent was necessary for the emancipation of legitimate children. In a measure linking the *patria potestas* to the fulfillment of parental duties, the Zacatecas code gave this authority to the mother if the father neglected his responsibilities. The Sierra code similarly awarded the *patria potestas* to a separated mother during the father's lifetime if he had provided grounds for an ecclesiastical divorce; the Oaxaca code conferred it on a mother during her husband's absence.[102] Furthermore, the legal commentators who described the responsibility of mothers over children as *patria potestas onerosa* stretched the law to its limit, since Hispanic law did not confer any sort of potestas on the mother. Although Mexicans were thus beginning to contemplate the possibility that mothers could exercise authority, the *patria potestas* still normally belonged exclusively to the father, as it had under colonial law.

Even the *Nuevo Febrero*, alone among legal commentaries in suggesting that wives share the *patria potestas* with their husbands, carefully limited that recommendation. It advocated the wife's participation in decision-making on the grounds that "a family's affairs will best be managed when they are based on the mutual consent of the spouses since, in truth, a woman can sometimes enlighten or give useful advice. Because of this, and also because of the esteem that husband and wife owe each other, it would be advantageous to introduce legislation requiring a husband to ask his wife's counsel in matters of import to the family, such as the alienation of real estate, the marriage of children, loans of money, and the assignment of dowries." But if the author of the *Nuevo Febrero* thus recognized women's competence, he would not grant the wife authority equal to that of her spouse. On the contrary, he stipulated that though men should consult their wives, "when the opinions of the couple conflict, it is the husband's that should prevail."[103]

The author of the *Nuevo Febrero* was careful to point out that he did not propose increasing women's rights in general; it was only a mother's rights over her children that should be expanded. Thus he insisted that the mother's *patria potestas* was not "a public charge that would be appropriate and exclusive to men; it is but a domestic authority based on the incapacity of the child." In his "Reflections" on the dowry and community property, he reiterated his approbation of traditional sex roles, commending a husband's management of these funds so that the wife could "limit herself to the interior of the family." He further advised wives to leave the administration of the *bienes parafernales* to their husbands, though they were not required to by law, in order to remove themselves from public affairs altogether.[104] Indeed, the notion that husbands should handle all family business was so widespread in nineteenth-century Mexico that the *Sala mexicano* incorrectly stated that the law made the husband the administrator of his wife's separate fund.[105]

The civil codes likewise retained the husband's authority over his wife's legal transactions, stating in almost identical language that "a husband owes his wife protection; a wife owes her husband obedience."[106] Although they did introduce a few modifications of colonial law in outlining areas where a wife needed her husband's permission, these were more changes of detail than substance, following the wording of the Code Napoléon in some cases and bringing Mexican law more into line with current interpretations of Hispanic law in others. On the one hand, the civil codes required a married woman to seek her husband's permission to accept an unencumbered inheritance as well as an encumbered one, whereas colonial law had not. On the other hand, she was relieved from the requirement of seeking his authorization to defend herself in a criminal suit. The Oaxaca code also allowed a married shopkeeper or market vendor to enter into legal contracts related to her business without a husband's permission. In effect, this provision simply spelled out current practice, for most legal handbooks assumed a husband's tacit approval had been granted if his wife engaged in a public trade; hence his permission was not required for her individual business transactions.[107]

Although legal commentators thus accepted the subordination of wives prescribed by colonial law, most regarded one aspect of a husband's power, his right to kill his adulterous wife, as too extreme. Fernández de Lizardi noted in his *Periquillo Sarniento* that the traditional punishment of adulterous wives had been "softened by the enlightenment of the times." The editor of the *Sala Mexicano* pronounced the husband's right "barbaric" and against the "morals of Jesus Christ," explaining that "private vengeances should be understood as abolished in the actual state of society . . . and reassumed by the government." In his handbook on criminal law, Rafael Roa Bárcena likewise termed a husband's right to kill his wife "barbaric," since she was "not his property." He assured his readers that in nineteenth-century Mexico this was an unheard of crime, but admitted that such a homicide would not be punished. Fernández de Lizardi observed that in most cases it would be punished, but less severely than murder of other kinds.[108]

This "softening" did not mean that Mexicans sided with the Church in their attitudes toward adultery. Most legal commentators stood somewhere in between the opposite poles represented by civil and canon law. They believed that traditional civil law punished adulterous wives too harshly, and that a husband's infidelity deserved at least some penalty, but less than the wife's. Consequently they approved of wives' suing adulterous husbands in secular court, a practice not formally sanctioned by Hispanic law.[109] The civil codes also took a middle position, adopting canon law's dictum that husbands and wives owed each other fidelity, while limiting the cases in which the husband's adultery provided grounds for separation.[110] The double standard was thus alive and well in nineteenth-century Mexico; more than anything else the questioning of the husband's power of life and death over his wife—the aspect that most conflicted with her basic civil rights—reflects the continuing decline of patriarchy as the State expanded its role in deciding justice and enforcing law.

A few Mexican jurists also contemplated reducing a husband's authority over his wife's property by introducing the possibility of marriage under the separation-of-property system established in the widely admired Napoleonic Code.[111] That system permitted a wife who renounced her right to the community property to retain and administer the property she brought to marriage as well as any she acquired or earned thereafter. The proposal was not as radical as it might seem, since it was not meant to replace the community-property system altogether; rather it was envisioned as a device to be used by a few wealthy women as an alternative to the more usual community-property arrangement.[112]

Surviving documents on the ensuing debate are scant and one-sided, yet they represent the side that won out during the first four decades after independence. Opposing any change in the marital regime, the author of the *Nuevo Febrero* challenged an argument some used in favor of the separation-of-property system: that it would correct the injustice of a wife's receiving half of the goods acquired during married life when she had earned none of it. On the contrary, he argued, the wife deserved her share because she contributed just as much to the family as the husband, if in a different way. In a passage recognizing the importance of a housewife's unremunerated labor, he wrote: "She dedicates her activity to other matters of great utility to the family, such as the care and upbringing of the children and the interior government of the household." Besides, he observed, it would be convenient for a wife to have a stake in the conjugal fund because this would encourage her to be thriftier in handling the household expenses. In short, he saw the community property as an assurance of the unity of interests of husband and wife. Another jurist simply referred to the controversy by stating that the community property was a "happy invention," protecting the married woman. Reflecting the dominant opinion, the Oaxaca and Sierra codes retained the community-property system intact; the Zacatecas code alone introduced the option of the other system.[113] Although the separation of property might benefit the working wife by allowing her to administer her earnings freely, the legal literature did not remark on its implications for women of that class. Apparently keeping their own wives and daughters in mind, most Mexican jurists were not ready to increase women's personal autonomy if it meant significantly decreasing their protection.

The idea of limiting a husband's authority, though it was discussed during this period, was therefore very tentative; limiting the father's authority was accepted to a far greater degree. Thus during the federalist interlude of the 1820's and 1830's several states lowered both the age of majority and the age at which minors no longer needed parental consent to marry. In an even more radical departure from colonial law, they removed single adults from the *patria potestas* during their fathers' lifetimes.

Here the details varied, but the direction of change is clear: individual freedom was augmented at the expense of patriarchal authority. For example, in 1826 the Constituent Congress of the state of Mexico, maintaining colonial gender distinctions based on women's earlier maturity, decreed that sons would be free from the *patria potestas* at the age of 25 and daughters at 23. The Zacatecas code set the age of majority and emancipation at 23 for sons, but maintained daughters under the father's potestas. Yet daughters could marry without parental consent at the age of 18 and sons at 20. The Oaxaca code set the age of majority and emancipation for both sons and daughters at 21, but required them to obtain parental consent for marriage until they reached 25 and 23. Three decades later, Sierra set the age of majority and emancipation at 21. However, he put limits on the autonomy of a daughter, who needed her parents' consent to move out of the family home if she was under 25, except when a widowed parent remarried, introducing a stepparent into the household. The partial subjection of daughters to continued parental authority until the age of 25, though it introduced a distinction between single men and women, still gave women more freedom than colonial law, which had subjected orphans to guardianship until that age and unmarried adult daughters to the father's potestas until his death. The expansion of children's autonomy can also be seen in a modification of the *patria potestas* in the Oaxaca and Zacatecas codes: both deprived parents of the usufruct of their minor child's independently earned income.[114]

## Conclusion

What do these changes tell us about nineteenth-century Mexico? Above all, that it was a time of shifting attitudes toward women. Although only two modifications of women's legal status applied to Mexico City before the promulgation of the 1870 Civil Code (those lowering the age of majority and freeing single adults from the *patria potestas*),[115] Mexicans were contemplating several measures to lessen sexual inequality. They wanted to grant widows, and to a lesser extent single mothers, the automatic guardianship and *patria potestas* over their children; they proposed allowing women to adopt children and be guardians of minors other than their own descendants; they considered increasing wives' authority to make decisions affecting their children; they rejected a husband's right to kill his adulterous wife; they discussed the possibility of reducing a husband's rights over his wife's property; and, finally, they removed adult daughters from the *patria potestas* and lowered the age at which they could control their legal acts.

Small as each of these proposed changes appears in isolation, together they suggest a trend toward increasing women's freedom and authority. These reforms would not only narrow the distinctions between men and women, but would also expand personal freedom for both, reflecting a heightened respect for women and a growing belief in individual liberty and equality. Even if we consider only the most universally accepted reforms— the restriction of the paterfamilias's authority over his children and the expansion of the widowed mother's over hers—these constituted a significant departure from colonial law.

Yet this trend, though discernible, was weak and discriminated among women of different marital statuses. Widows, already able to govern themselves with complete liberty under colonial law, were given the authority to govern their children. Single adult women, some of whom were already independent if emancipated, were in all cases released from the father's potestas. But wives, along with daughters the most restricted of any women under colonial law, retained approximately the same status. Some legal commentators tentatively proposed enlarging the wife's authority within the domestic sphere, but they did not go so far as to challenge the husband's control over the household.

The exclusion of married women from these legal changes might at first appear paradoxical. The recognition of women's competence, used to justify changes in the status of single and widowed women, could also have applied to wives. So too the growing prestige of motherhood could logically have led to an extension of married as well as widowed mothers' authority over their children. Furthermore, the abolition of slavery, the removal of Indians from the guardianship by which colonial rulers sought to protect them, and the release of adult children from the *patria potestas* made the wife's subjection to her husband's authority all the more anomalous. In the past, when single adult sons, slaves, and Indians were restricted, the curtailment of a wife's autonomy at least had a counterpart among men; it now made her the stark exception among adults. Thus, although married women's legal status remained largely unchanged, it deteriorated relative to advances made both by other women and by men.

These developments made it difficult for lawmakers to explain the continued subordination of wives. No longer content with the unqualified statements of women's inferiority of character and intellect that appeared in colonial lawbooks, they sought new ways to justify women's legal status. A comparison of the 1831 and 1845 editions of Sala's *Ilustración del derecho* illustrates this shift succinctly. When the editor of the 1845 version came to the passage explaining legal differences between men and women, he dropped the traditional statement that "men usually exceed women in prudence and firmness" and instead presented the differences as the result of custom.[116] The growing respect for women was thus undermining the older rationale for their subjection.

For the first time some legal commentators explicitly recognized a woman's "full capacity to govern herself." The author of the *Nuevo Febrero*, for instance, refuted allegations of women's mental weakness in a "Reflection" on the transactions of emancipated single women. Yet in praising women's business acumen, he was enough embarrassed that he felt the need to couch his praise in a satirical tone: "A woman," he wrote, "always perceives her interests perfectly clearly . . . when it comes to conserving her property. To say that she would more easily lend herself to a risky venture . . . is to grossly misunderstand feminine nature. After all, who is not familiar with her shrewdness in business affairs? Who has not observed how stingy she is in all her contracts? Who has not noticed how small her inclination to endanger herself in performing a favor for another?" So certain was he that women would take perfectly good care of themselves that he proposed striking the protective provision forbidding women to provide surety.[117]

Because of this evident appreciation of women's ability to manage their affairs independently, the *Nuevo Febrero*'s attempts to justify a wife's inferior position were clumsy and confused. In one "Philosophical Reflection" the author argued that "the man, be it due to his nature or education, has more knowledge and experience than the woman. Therefore, the [couple's] affairs will best be managed in his hands." Obviously uncomfortable with this statement, however, he immediately added: "This is not to say that all men are superior to all women in strength and instruction. In truth, contrary cases occur, but since these are uncommon, the law does well to adapt itself to the general facts."[118] This passage suggests that the differences between the sexes were socialized rather than inherent, with man's prudence due to his experience and education, not his innate character or intellect. Even more striking, it entertains the notion that the assignment of superiority to the husband might be arbitrary and even inappropriate in some cases.

The same "Reflection" resorted to an explanatory model that minimized the inherent contradiction between a married woman's full capacity for sovereignty and her subordination. Drawing heavily from the corporate ideal, it made explicit the issue of social control that had only been implicit in colonial lawbooks:

Because a married couple form a society composed not only of husband and wife, but also of children and servants, that is, of an entire family, it is essential that it be headed by a leader with the authority to direct it in necessary cases. This superiority is correctly vested in the husband. For when a diversity of opinion arises between husband and wife, as occurs despite their unity of interests and affection for each other, then what can be done? Resort to force? That is improper and inadmissible in the legal order. Such conflict can be avoided by designating a superior expressly for these instances. But to whom should this prerogative be given, to the husband or the wife? I have no reservation in conceding it to the former. Why? The reason is obvious: man, owing to his physical and intellectual faculties, is more fit than the woman to exercise it. In effect, the male is superior in force and courage, and is thus more suited to command his family's respect and defend it. Would not a society ruled by the wife be liable to the continual mutiny of the subjects against the established authority? . . .

The same reasons by which I have justified granting the husband the supervision and government of domestic affairs explain why wives should also be denied the faculty of conducting legal affairs on their own. If this were to take place, would it not risk the possibility that husband and wife would each undo what the other had done?[119]

Despite the nod to traditional justifications of the subordination of wives, this passage based it above all on the need for social cohesion. Only after first establishing to his satisfaction that someone had to rule the household did the author assign the inferior position to the wife. Although he threw in her physical weakness, timidity, and intellectual inferiority for good measure, it was basically because he believed effective government resulted from a hierarchical chain of command, rather than from consensus or negotiation among equals, that the author of the *Nuevo Febrero* justified a husband's authority over his wife. This is why he warned in another passage that "excessive freedom or prospects given to women might alter with more frequency domestic tranquillity and pleasures," and why he vigorously defended the "respect and authority" due the husband.[120]

It was this concept of social order that kept Mexicans from expanding the rights of married women. The new authority granted widows and spinsters did not conflict strongly with the paterfamilias's rule of the household since widows, and in many cases, spinsters, were outside this structure of control. In fact, the conferral of the *patria potestas* on widows, and in the Sierra code on single mothers also, strengthened the rights of female household heads. Consequently, the control of individuals through nuclear households was thoroughly upheld. Although patriarchal authority was reduced in families where adult children remained at home and fathers were still alive, contemporaries viewed this situation as exceptional, and justified it as part of a necessary defense of individual rights. However, the line was clearly drawn at wives: increasing their personal autonomy was perceived as a threat to the stability of the basic social unit. Egalitarian principles did not affect married women because their freedom was incompatible with the corporate vision of social harmony. This deeply rooted world view strongly limited the extent of possible legal reform and suggests that democratic and egalitarian views did not run very deep.

Nonetheless, the direction of the proposed legal changes is consistent. Contemporaries believed they would improve women's status by expanding their authority and freedom, while retaining the traditional protection of the Weak Sex that already made Hispanic law more favorable to women than the Anglo-American common law.[121] In fact, in some respects legal commentators of the period went beyond what would be accepted later. Although most reforms proposed in the early republic were incorporated into subsequent civil codes, during the heady post-independence decades when Mexicans experimented with new directions, when women were still desperately needed in the process of nation-building and had so recently shown that they could contribute to those efforts, some Mexicans were willing to consider ideas (like the remarried widow's retention of the guardianship of children and the wife's sharing of the *patria potestas*) that were to be rejected in the 1870 code.[122]

It is easy to overlook the egalitarian trend in legal reform because it was so tentative and manifested itself so sparingly. Certainly, there was tremendous continuity in ideas about women's legal status. Most of the old laws discriminating against women were not questioned: colonial provisions excluding women from politics, protecting and punishing them according to a double standard, and subjecting married women to their husbands' control were fully accepted in independent Mexico. But if much of the colonial legal heritage concerning women persisted, it was not swallowed whole. The mobilization and education of women and the spread of liberal ideas were beginning to have an impact, if a subtle one, on the legal status of Mexican women.

# THREE

# Demographic Patterns

IN EXPANDING the rights of single and widowed women, nine-teenth-century legal reformers recognized that many women did not fit into the structure of corporate control through nuclear families. Indeed, one of the striking aspects of demographic patterns in Mexico City is the extent to which women's experiences differed from prescribed roles. An exploration of census data allows us to get away from the ideas of reformers and lawmakers, and from their privileged circles, to learn how women of all classes actually behaved. Although statistics only provide an image of women in the aggregate, the demographic facts—the age at which women married, the proportion who did so at all, the number of children they bore, the life expectancy of their husbands and offspring, their chances of migrating or heading a household over a lifetime—shaped women's daily activities, responsibilities, and power. And because colonial censuses counted people of all classes, this source allows us to see, better than any other, whether women of different social backgrounds shared the basic features of personal life or were divided according to an accident of birth.

This chapter is based primarily on a sample from the manuscript census of 1811, by far the best one available for the capital during the late colonial and early republican period. Contemporary statisticians praised it as a model count, contrasting it to unreliable censuses taken in provincial towns and rural areas.[1] Although, like all censuses, it has numerous biases, it contains rich data on the city's inhabitants, listing the name, sex, age, race, marital status, place of origin, occupation, type of dwelling, and household composition for most of the individuals recorded.

Since the entire census was not available when I conducted my research, I have analyzed information on 3,356 people who lived in two contrasting areas of the capital (see Appendix A). One neighborhood was in the center, within the *traza* to which the Spanish population had been confined, and the Indian excluded, immediately after the Conquest; the other was on the city's eastern periphery. Although the rigid residential segregation of the early colonial period had broken down by this time, the densely inhabited city center remained the most elegant and Hispanic, with the surrounding areas becoming increasingly shabby, and occupied by an ever larger proportion of poor and colored people, the farther they lay from the *zócalo*, or main plaza. In the central sample area over two-thirds of the population was listed as being of Spanish descent; in the periphery almost three-quarters were Indians or Castes. In the center lived a noble family, a high court judge, many merchants and their clerks, and ranking military officers, along with the numerous artisans and servants who catered to these groups. In the periphery servants were a rarity among the manual laborers, textile workers, and small shopkeepers who serviced the community. In the center, where the majority of residents lived in apartments and modest houses, a fortunate 15 percent occupied *casas grandes*, the palatial residences of the wealthy. In the periphery there were no *casas grandes*, most people renting rooms in tenements, or *vecindades*, a type of building totally absent from the wealthier neighborhood. In addition, nearly all the foreign immigrants, most of them Spaniards, chose to settle in the center. The census takers, apparently equally loathe to venture into the periphery, collected the most complete information for the more affluent, Hispanic section.

Although the statistics obtained from this sample may not apply precisely to the entire city, there are several reasons to believe that they provide a good approximation of urban demographic patterns. First, the racial and sexual structures of the sample correspond to those given for Mexico City as a whole in the published summary totals of the 1811 census and other counts.[2] Second, the two neighborhoods sampled represent two major types of areas in the capital; moreover, though it is reasonable to assume that demographic patterns varied by class or ethnic group, it is unlikely that they were distinct in different areas of the city, except as a reflection of their different social compositions. The following analysis therefore treats both areas together, considering social groups separately after overall patterns have been established.

My attempts to discern long-term demographic changes by using earlier and later censuses were only partially successful. Since the manuscript schedules of the 1790 census—the only late-eighteenth-century count—have been lost for Mexico City, comparisons must be based on the general information in the published summary statistics, subject to the errors and limitations of aggregation. Although manuscript schedules survive for the 1848 municipal census, the best post-independence count, it too is of limited utility because of its uneven quality. Since the goal of the census, taken while U.S. forces occupied the city, was to compile a real estate list for tax-collecting purposes, the census takers faithfully recorded the rent of each occupied dwelling.[3] Many also recorded the name, sex, age, marital status, place of origin, and occupation for each person in their districts. Some, however, listed only household heads, omitting spouses and children altogether; others listed everybody but gave the occupation of household heads only; and still others were so careless as to make it impossible to determine when one household ended and another began. When I located the same two sections of the city as analyzed for 1811, I found that some of the information for the peripheral area was so deficient that it had to be discarded. Owing both to the poorer quality of the data and the smaller number of cases used, the 1848 census sample is therefore less reliable than the 1811 sample. Furthermore, since racial distinctions were dropped from official documents in 1822, that variable cannot be applied to the later data.

A sample of wills spanning the first half of the nineteenth century provides a check on the census data and allows some examination of demographic trends over time. I selected 600 wills from the years 1802–3, 1825–27, and 1853–55 (see Appendix B). Since these consistently give the testator's name, place of origin, marital status, times married, number of children, and use of a dowry, they can be used to study marriage patterns, fertility, and child mortality. In one respect, wills are superior to censuses as a source, because they list both legitimate and illegitimate children, including those who died. In other respects, wills are less useful. For one thing, though they distinguish between minors and adults, they only occasionally record ages, which are essential to the study of completed family size and the proportions of people never marrying. For another, because wills were made by people with some property, they generally describe the upper classes rather than the population as a whole.

There is no entirely satisfactory way of establishing the class background of people in the censuses. Many contemporary observers believed that the social structure of Mexico City followed its division into Spanish, Caste, and Indian groups, which were also the three racial categories allowed for in the printed schedules of the 1811 census.[4] But this triracial scheme was vastly oversimplified. Mexico had never had a rigid caste system, and by the opening of the nineteenth century its social structure was more fluid than in earlier years. Furthermore, Mexicans often distinguished people on the basis of economic rather than racial indicators. For example, Fernández de Lizardi and Mora used occupation, Bishop Abad y Queipo used acquisitive power, and the liberal social critic Mariano Otero used property ownership.[5] But all four used racial categories as well, and noted that race and class were usually interrelated, if not identical.

Although the relationship between race and class has elicited a heated scholarly debate in recent years, it is clear that the two were correlated, especially at the top and bottom of the social scale.[6] The upper class was almost entirely Spanish, including both Mexican- and European-born whites, and the lowest class was predominantly Indian. The 1811 census sample shows, for example, that the most prestigious occupations were held exclusively by people listed as Spanish. Likewise, 95 percent of the 145 household heads listed as having at least one domestic servant—whose residents presumably were the most affluent in the city—were of Spanish descent, as were all 27 of those with three or more servants (Table D.2). But the Spanish population, which represented nearly half the city's inhabitants, was larger than the upper and middle classes, which together represented approximately one-fourth. And the Castes were not a distinct

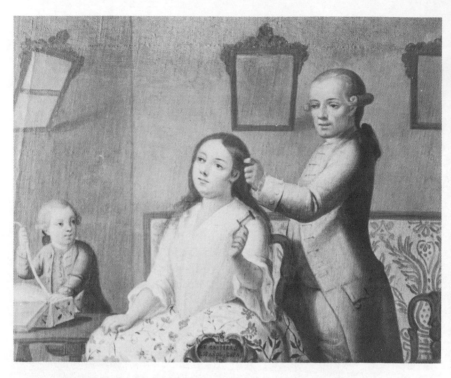

6. Three paintings from a series of sixteen depicting families of various ethnic backgrounds in the dress and occupations typical of their station. In this set of paintings, one of several versions of the series, the artist has not only associated each ethnic group with a particular social rank, but endowed it with certain moral characteristics. The first family is shown in a loving domestic scene to suggest the leisure and prosperity of the Spanish population. In the second, the family is shown working side by side, selling fruits in the market, with the daughter helping her Indian mother while the dark-skinned father, so impoverished that he is clothed only in a blanket, adjusts the awning to protect them from the sun. The third and most racially mixed family is the most degenerate in the artist's eyes, a point he conveys by showing the mulatto woman physically abusing her mate.

middle group, both because the middle classes were ethnically heterogenous, and because, of all the groups, the Castes were the most blurred by intermarriage. It is true that no group was an entirely separate entity since some intermarriage occurred between them, but recent studies of other areas of Mexico suggest that the majority of Indian and Spanish marriages were endogamous. When intermarriage occurred it tended to involve individuals in contiguous groups, so it was rare for an Indian to marry a Spaniard or vice versa, though either might marry a Caste.[7] The Caste group presents a further difficulty for analyzing demographic patterns, since it is so poorly represented in the sample (constituting only 17 percent of the population), that once the group is divided into two sexes, three marital statuses, and five-year age brackets, there are too few cases in each cell to allow for meaningful comparisons with other groups.

An individual's occupation or the number of servants in the household might give a more accurate indication of socioeconomic class than does race, but neither variable can be satisfactorily applied to the census data. Since such terms as *comerciante* could encompass anyone from wealthy merchants to ragged street peddlers, occupation does not always indicate class. Furthermore, many people cannot be classified at all using this variable because 14 percent of the men and 73 percent of the women aged 15 and over did not list an occupation. The number of servants in a household is also problematic. In some cases it cannot be clearly determined: households listing no live-in servants might have hired them by the day, and some servants (especially in households listing only one) might have been relatives or friends who worked as domestics in other homes. Moreover, the upper class selected by this criterion is too small to furnish reliable statistics for computations where it must be broken down by multiple variables.

The demographic patterns of different social groups have therefore been established by breaking the data down by race, although categories based on the numbers of servants have also been analyzed as a cross check on the racial variable whenever possible. Race at least has the advantage that it is given for nearly everyone in the census sample. It also allows comparison with other studies of the late colonial period that, following the original documents, use a triracial classification. Finally, since racial designations were largely self-declared by 1811, and there is evidence that people changed them as they rose in status, the census categories probably already reflected people's socioeconomic status to some extent, making race a more useful indicator of class than true ethnicity would be. Given the problems with the information on Castes, this chapter focuses primarily on Indian and Spanish patterns, though the Caste data are presented where pertinent. It should be remembered, however, that contrasts between the Indian and Spanish groups provide only rough approximations of the average behavior of those at the top and bottom of the social scale. They do nonetheless show the behavior of two ethnic groups that were acutely conscious of being different from each other throughout the nineteenth century.[8]

## Sexual Structure and Migration

The sexual structure of cities, heavily influenced by migration, helps determine people's chances of marrying, remarrying, and having children. It also defines the character of cities as frontier posts or settled communities, as poles attracting migrants or areas expelling them. Mexico City, like other settled urban centers of Latin America and Europe, was a city where women predominated.[9] Indeed, women have consistently outnumbered men in population counts ever since the eighteenth century, constituting 57 percent of the capital's inhabitants in 1790, 56 percent in 1811, 55 percent in 1842, and 59 percent in 1848.[10]

Still, these statistics must be treated as approximations, since men often tried to avoid a count that was made for the purposes of military recruitment or tribute. As the priest José Antonio Alzate wrote, with a flair for exaggeration, at the mere mention of a census "wives described themselves as widows, mothers neglected to list their sons, sisters left off their brothers, and some families simply disappeared."[11] Although the authorities took steps to solve this problem, some men undoubtedly escaped enumeration—certain Indians in 1790, attempting to avoid tribute payment, but primarily (since tribute was abolished in 1810 and even in 1790 many urban Indians were exempt)[12] men aged 16 to 36 attempting to avoid the military draft. The 1811 count, taken by security police in the midst of the independence war, was especially likely to have been perceived as a prelude to the levy.

But if the sexual imbalance was less pronounced than the censuses indicate, there is much evidence that it existed. Even in wartime many categories of draft-age men, such as married men and widowers with children, and those who held important posts, were exempt (at least in theory) from military service.[13] Furthermore, the censuses recorded fewer men than women in the age groups above 40, where men were no longer liable for military duty.[14] Although war deaths may account for some of the imbalance in 1811 and 1848, it also existed in years of peace and when military service was limited to certain racial groups. The 1790 census, for example, recorded a surplus of women in every racial category at a time when Indians and many Castes were ineligible for recruitment. The 1842 municipal census, which recorded the smallest sexual imbalance, may be the most accurate of the counts: taken in peacetime to determine male eligibility for voting, it was the least apt to encounter male evasion. Yet it also found an excess of women over men. Finally, the age structure of Mexico City's population cannot be explained by male evasion alone. Assuming that the gap in the young male population in the population pyramids reflects some undercounting, the dramatic excess of young women, out of line with any normal population distribution, shows that other factors were at work (Fig. 1; see also Fig. 2, below).

Many of the contemporaries who recognized the disproportion of the sexes linked it to patterns of migration. As Humboldt explained, "Country women come into the cities to serve in houses . . . and a great number of men leave them to travel through the country as muleteers, or to fix their abode in places with considerable mines." By his figures, Mexico City in 1790 had a male/female ratio of 79:100, compared with 105:100 for the country as a whole. The statistician Fernando Navarro y Noriega similarly noted that the sex ratio in Mexican cities was the reverse of that in rural areas, where men predominated.[15] It would therefore appear, though studies of out-migration from rural communities have yet to be conducted, that the rural crisis uprooted women as well as men. Whereas men could find work

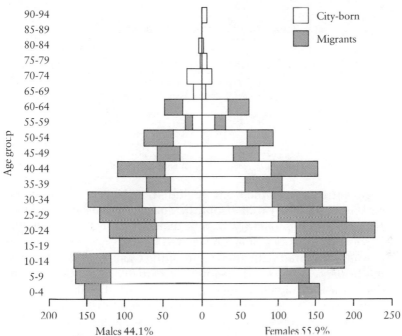

Fig. 1. Population by age and place of origin, 1811. Based on 1,422 males and 1,800 females whose age and place of origin are known. Excludes place of origin for those 65 and over.

on haciendas and mines, those locales provided few opportunities for women, who consequently turned to—or stayed in—the cities instead.

The available data suggest that the rate of female migration to the capital was very high. Women constituted 56 percent of the Mexicans arriving in the capital in 1811 or, since the few foreigners who ventured to Mexico City were almost all male, 54 percent of all migrants when foreigners are included (Table 3). Although the proportion of female migrants may actually have been smaller because of the undercounting of migrant men, it was still substantial when only women are considered: some 38 percent of all the females, adult and children, in Mexico City in 1811 had been born elsewhere, and the figure rises to 43 percent when those under age 15, more likely than their parents to have

TABLE 3
*Sexual Structure of Migrants by Race, 1811*

| Race | Females | | Males | |
|------|---------|---------|-------|---------|
| | Number | Percent | Number | Percent |
| Spanish | 291 | 51.5% | 273 | 48.4% |
| Caste | 112 | 51.4 | 106 | 48.6 |
| Indian | 274 | 58.3 | 196 | 41.7 |
| ALL RACES | 677 | 54.1% | 575 | 45.9% |

NOTE: All data for 1811 and 1848 in the tables in this chapter are from my Mexico City census samples. The groups studied across these tables may vary in size because the "unknowns" have been omitted. Percentages do not necessarily total 100 because of rounding.

been born in the capital, are excluded.[16] Most of these women had moved to the capital from the country's densely populated center,[17] and the majority were Indians or Castes. Thus only 38 percent of the city's Spanish women age 15 and over were migrants, compared with 45 percent of the Caste and 48 percent of the Indian women. Still, despite the heavy female in-migration, the female surplus was less marked among the migrants than among the city-born group, where women represented 57 percent of the total population. This difference suggests the importance of male out-migration as well as female in-migration in explaining the sex ratio of Mexico City.

As contemporaries noted, women migrants did not simply accompany their relatives to the Mexican capital. Poor women in particular often migrated on their own in search of employment in the capital's industries and service sector. Migrants of Spanish descent were thus relatively evenly divided between females and males compared with the Indian group. In 1785 Hipólito Villarroel, the chief prosecutor of the Acordada Tribunal, observed that women sometimes served as the advance guard for other migrants. By his account, rural girls left their villages to find work as servants or nursemaids in comfortable homes in the capital; once they had a roof over their heads, they were joined by "real or presumed" kin who moved into the servant quarters and forced the poor girls to support them by stealing from their employers. Villarroel complained that hiring migrant girls was therefore dangerous and contributed to the depopulation of rural areas, thereby causing the Crown to lose considerable tribute the villagers would have paid.[18]

Although the census does not indicate the ages at which female migrants arrived, the age distribution in Figure 1 confirms Villarroel's portrait of young girls leading the migration to Mexico City. Girls and boys were equally represented among migrants under 15, as might be expected if parents moved to Mexico City along with all their children. The percentage of women then increased dramatically, reaching a peak in the 20–24 group, where they constituted 64 percent of the migrants. Thereafter the figure declined, until by the age of 40 women represented approximately half the migrants, and the proportions remained relatively balanced beyond that age.[19]

A caveat on the census is in order here. The information on ages is not always accurate because people tended to declare or be assigned ages that were multiples of ten (and to a lesser extent of five), particularly after the age of 30. This trend is clearly visible in the population pyramids, where there are many more people in each round-decade age bracket past 30 than there are in the succeeding ones. Yet these figures are reliable enough for our purposes, since the heaping of ages should not affect the rough age distribution or the proportions of migrants (or, for later discussions, of men and women of various marital statuses) within each age group.

The influx of young female migrants explains the marked excess of women aged 15 to 29 in the population pyramid for 1811. For it was precisely in this age group that female migration was heaviest and, as will be seen in Chapter Four, this was also the group from which the majority of domestic servants were drawn. The reduced number of older female migrants suggests that some women may have returned to their birthplaces after working a few years in the capital, as they still do today. It may also indicate that the huge influx of women was a relatively recent phenomenon in 1811, with previous generations of men and women migrating in more even numbers. Although the cityward movement of young women seeking work as domestic servants was probably centuries old,[20] female migration may well have accelerated in the late colonial period as more and more rural villagers sought their fortunes in the thriving capital. Unfortunately, conclusions about the changing pace of migration from 1790 to 1811 must remain speculative because the sum-

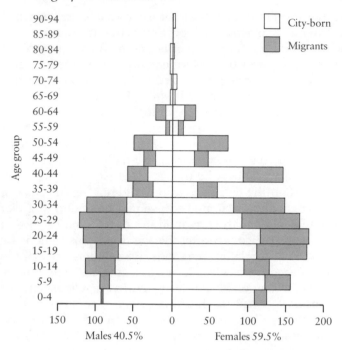

Fig.2. Population by age and place of origin, 1848. Based on 996 males and 1,462 females whose age and place of origin are known. Excludes place of origin for those 65 and over.

mary statistics for 1790 do not include information on place of origin.[21] Furthermore, people seeking refuge from the war-torn countryside may partially account for the large numbers of migrants—especially women—in 1811, since men might have sent their families to the capital for safety.[22] The wartime situation would not, however, explain the peculiar age distribution of female migrants.

That migration to the city in 1811 was no temporary aberration is clear from the fact that it remained both substantial and heavily female for decades. A comparison of the 1811 and 1848 census samples suggests that the total rate of migration to Mexico City remained constant, at the same time becoming more markedly female. Although some 37 percent of the city's female residents were migrants in 1848, as in 1811, the female share of all

Mexican migrants increased from 56 percent to 62 percent. Also as in 1811, the majority of female migrants were young, though now peaking somewhat earlier, at 15–19 years (Fig. 2). The proportions of women did not taper off among migrants over 30, however, since women continued to outnumber men. The persistence of female migrants may indicate that the influx of young women had been continuous for several decades or that older women had less of a tendency to return to their native villages. Too much should not be made of the differences between the two counts, given the smaller size and poorer quality of the 1848 sample, but it is clear, at least, that the female migration to Mexico City did not let up from 1811 to 1848.[23]

This predominance of women among migrants—and consequently among city residents—continues to characterize Mexican cities today, suggesting that solutions to Mexico's rapid urbanization will not be found until the reasons for rural women's migration are understood.[24] Furthermore, the widespread image of passive, sheltered country women is at odds with the extensive female migration that has taken place for at least two centuries.

## Marital Patterns

The traditional wisdom about women does not hold up any better for marriage patterns than it does for migration. The image of Latin American women who had few alternatives to early matrimony and motherhood would lead us to predict that most women in the Mexican capital married, and did so young. This prediction is not borne out by the 1811 census sample, which lists only 44 percent of the adult women (25 or older) as married and fully 22 percent as single. The high proportion single, moreover, is evident in the age group 45 to 54, a group that can be used to measure those in a population who never married:[25] 16 percent of the women were still single at that age (see Fig. 3).

These findings, if accurate, raise questions about the prevalence of marriage in early-nineteenth-century Mexico, for they represent a low marriage rate in terms of both traditional notions and contemporary Mexican standards. When the sample proportions are applied to Mexico City as a whole, they suggest that somewhere on the order of 52,500 women were unmarried,

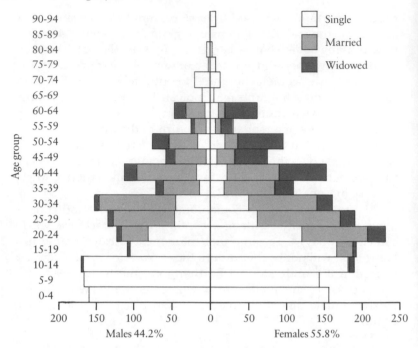

Fig.3. Population by age and marital status, 1811. Based on 1,444 males and 1,823 females whose age and marital status are known. Excludes marital status for those 65 and over.

either single or widowed, accounting for almost one-third of the adult population in 1811. To be sure, widows had originally opted for marriage, but they nonetheless failed to conform to the role of dependent wife within a male-headed nuclear family. And some 14,500 women over 45 had never fulfilled that role.

An assessment of these figures must begin by examining the meaning of the marital-status categories used in the 1811 census. Although consensual unions were widespread in Mexico City, particularly among the lower classes,[26] the census has only three designations of marital status: single, married, and widowed. The manuscript schedules indicate that census takers did not use the legal definitions of these categories, but consistently listed men and women who lived together as married, and women living with children but without husbands as widows.

(People who had obtained an ecclesiastical divorce, and were thus legally separated, were still considered married and would have been listed as such.) Only 3.5 percent of the mothers in my sample were recorded as single, a suspiciously low figure given the prevalence of consensual marriage and illegitimacy. Consequently, the term married appears to include those living together in consensual unions, and the term widowed to include single mothers. The broad definition of these categories may be considered an advantage rather than a drawback for this study: had the terms retained their narrow legal meanings, all single mothers and women living in informal unions would have been listed as single, creating a misleading picture for the study of sex roles. As it is, since the terms married and widowed encompass individuals who never married legally, the term single more nearly represents those who lived in a single state.

It is still possible that some women who listed themselves as single had previously been in consensual unions that ended through separation or the partner's death. The ones who had children, however, as many did, would have been recorded as widows. Although unmarried mothers might have hidden their babies from the census takers and declared themselves single, they were more likely to have declared themselves widowed because of the convenience and prestige of this marital status, as older women who had lost their consensual husbands of many years were wont to do.[27] Indeed, there is evidence that some single mothers were included in the category of widow, for despite a relatively small age gap between spouses, widows began to appear in the census sample from the age of 12, whereas widowers appear only after the age of 22.[28] Thus again it seems likely that most women listed as single were, for our purposes, truly "single," never having entered consensual unions or married.

To be sure, the undercounting of men might skew the female marriage patterns recorded in the census. In young age groups the proportion of married women was perhaps too low and that of widows too high, for some widows might have been wives hiding their husbands from the census takers (although most married men were theoretically exempt from the draft). But the incidence of lifelong spinsterhood, which defines the female marriage rate, would hardly have been affected, because that

TABLE 4

*Marital Status of Adult Will-Makers (25 Years and Over), 1802–1855*

| Category | 1802–3 | | 1825–27 | | 1853–55 | | Total | |
|---|---|---|---|---|---|---|---|---|
| | Number | Percent | Number | Percent | Number | Percent | Number | Percent |
| **Females** | | | | | | | | |
| Single | 24 | 27.3% | 22 | 24.7% | 32 | 33.0% | 78 | 28.5% |
| Married | 33 | 37.5 | 23 | 25.8 | 25 | 25.8 | 81 | 29.6 |
| Widowed | 31 | 35.2 | 43 | 48.3 | 35 | 36.0 | 109 | 39.8 |
| Divorced[a] | 0 | — | 1 | 1.1 | 5 | 5.2 | 6 | 2.2 |
| TOTAL | 88 | 100.0% | 89 | 99.9% | 97 | 100.0% | 274 | 100.1% |
| **Males** | | | | | | | | |
| Single | 32 | 37.2% | 27 | 28.7% | 24 | 27.0% | 83 | 30.8% |
| Married | 41 | 47.7 | 48 | 51.1 | 40 | 44.9 | 129 | 47.9 |
| Widowed | 12 | 13.9 | 18 | 19.1 | 23 | 25.8 | 53 | 19.7 |
| Divorced[a] | 1 | 1.2 | 1 | 1.1 | 2 | 2.2 | 4 | 1.5 |
| TOTAL | 86 | 100.0% | 94 | 100.0% | 89 | 99.9% | 269 | 99.9% |

SOURCE: Wills sample, Appendix B.
NOTE: Nuns and priests are excluded.
[a]Church-authorized separation.

calculation is based on an older age group where neither men nor their wives had reason to fear military recruitment. Furthermore, the proportions never married based on the female population alone are relatively reliable, for women were more completely counted than men and had little to gain from declaring themselves single if they were in fact married or widowed.

Nor can the high proportions single be dismissed as the result of unusual circumstances that would artificially inflate the numbers. They cannot be attributed to the presence of convents in the sample areas, since these areas did not include any nuns. Neither can they be attributed to the heavy migration of young single villagers to the capital. Because a young woman's move to the city probably delayed her marriage, slightly more migrant than native women were single from the ages of 15 to 24 (69 percent versus 67 percent; Table D.3). That age group was not, however, included in the calculation of single adults or never married. Among those 25 or over, migrant women in fact had a higher marriage rate than the city-born (23 percent versus 21 percent), and only 13 percent remained unmarried in the 45–54 group, against 18 percent of the city-born. Thus, the presence of migrants actually diluted the prevalence of spinsterhood among urban women.

The substantial number of single adults in Mexico City is corroborated by the sample of wills, a source not subject to male evasion or female deception about marital status. Wills do have limitations as a source for marriage patterns. For example, nuns and priests are disproportionately represented, nuns because they were required to renounce their worldly goods on entering a convent, and priests because they did not have automatic heirs. Once both groups are excluded from the testamentary data, though, we still find a high percentage single, indeed, far more than in the general population (Table 4).[29]

These marriage patterns cannot be directly compared with those revealed by the 1811 census because wills rarely give the exact ages of the testators. We can assume that the will-making group was older than the adult population in the census sample, since in the nineteenth century people customarily made wills only when they were so sick that death seemed imminent.[30] Indeed, 42 percent of the testators had grown children, putting

TABLE 5

*Marital Status of the Adult Population (25 Years and Over), 1790–1848*

| | 1790 | | 1811 | | 1848 | |
|---|---|---|---|---|---|---|
| Category | Number | Percent | Number | Percent | Number | Percent |
| **Females** | | | | | | |
| Single | 4,948 | 18.0% | 204 | 22.5% | 117 | 17.5% |
| Married | 12,941 | 47.2 | 399 | 43.9 | 276 | 41.3 |
| Widowed | 9,557 | 34.8 | 303 | 33.4 | 276 | 41.3 |
| TOTAL | 27,446 | 100.0% | 906 | 99.8% | 669 | 100.1% |
| **Males** | | | | | | |
| Single | 4,163 | 19.9% | 161 | 22.5% | 99 | 20.7% |
| Married | 14,318 | 68.5 | 451 | 63.0 | 335 | 70.1 |
| Widowed | 2,408 | 11.5 | 104 | 14.5 | 44 | 9.2 |
| TOTAL | 20,889 | 99.9% | 716 | 100.0% | 478 | 100.0% |

SOURCE: 1790 figures from Alexander von Humboldt, *Political Essay on the Kingdom of New Spain*, 2d ed. (London, 1814), 4: 292 (Table 3).

most of them in their forties at least, and many others were probably elderly. The mature age of testators might explain the presence of slightly more widows and widowers than in the population as a whole (compare Tables 4 and 5), but it hardly explains why there is a higher incidence of lifelong bachelors and spinsters. Indeed, if the will-makers were an older group, one would expect to find proportionately fewer single people than in the general adult population. Reasons for this discrepancy will be discussed later, when we examine class distinctions in marriage patterns. For now, the point of interest is that the low marriage rate is confirmed by a source not susceptible to the biases of the census data. We can therefore conclude that, despite the emphasis on marriage in didactic literature, there were socially viable alternatives to matrimony in the Mexican capital.

Although spinsters were too numerous to overlook in discussions of Mexican sex roles, the census sample suggests that five out of six women eventually entered legal or informal marriages, for if 16 percent of all women remained single at the age of 45–54, 84 percent did not. But only rarely did women spend most of their lives in a married state. To begin with, they did not marry as young as has often been assumed. In 1811 the average age at first marriage, calculated from proportions single using the method developed by J. H. Hajnal, was 22.7 years.[31] There were few instances, in fact, of marriages in the 14–17 age group (12 of 159 girls, including 3 identified as widows), and none among younger girls.

Because most women married relatively late, they may have had a fair degree of latitude in choosing a spouse, at least in comparison with societies where early marriages prevailed; indeed, contemporary Mexicans strongly disapproved of parents' forcing their daughters to marry, and the Church opposed it.[32] Moreover, the typical married couple were close in age, since the average man first married when he was 24.2 years old, only a year and a half older than the average woman. Thus, husband-wife relationships may well have been more egalitarian than where the man was much older than his wife.[33]

The average woman not only married late; she did not stay married very long. In a society with a high mortality rate, it was unusual for a couple to remain together into old age. The typical woman lost her legal or informal husband around the age of 40, after a union of some 20 years (see Fig. 3), and some 70 percent of all surviving wives aged 45–54 had lost their mates. Historians have not yet studied Mexican life expectancies for the time, so we do not know whether women tended to live longer than men.[34] Scattered literary evidence suggests that well-to-do women often lived to be 60, though such a life span was undoubtedly rare for the poor. An elite woman might consequently spend one-third of her life single, one-third married, and one-third widowed. Or, put another way, she was likely to be a widow for half her adult life. Among the poor, too, where men probably died relatively young, it is likely that women spent much of their adult lives on their own.

There is, therefore, some demographic basis for the legal historian José María Ots Capdequí's erroneous statement that in Hispanic societies "only the state of widowhood permits women to enjoy full civil rights."[35] The average woman, wed while still a minor, did pass directly from her father's to her husband's power, experiencing legal independence for the first time as a widow. To be sure, some women may never have experienced it because they died before their spouses, and others may have gained it at a relatively young age because they lost their fathers before they wed. And the many women who remained single were probably emancipated by their father's death long before reaching middle age. Nonetheless, widowhood marked an important transition to autonomy for most married women.

In fact, the prevalence of widowhood was the principal difference between the marriage patterns of women and men. For if men waited longer, on average, to marry or enter co-residential consensual unions, they did so at a similar rate as women, with 17 percent remaining single in the age group 45–54.[36] But the ratio of married to widowed adults sharply distinguished the sexes (Table 5). The proportions are somewhat deceiving: since there were fewer men than women in the census sample, a much greater percentage of the men were married, even though in absolute terms there was approximately the same number of husbands and wives.[37] In contrast, the widows vastly outnumbered the widowers—by something on the order of three to one.

In large part, the preponderance of widows was due to the fact that men were more apt to remarry if their spouses died, as can be deduced from the numbers of married men and women within each age bracket in Figure 3. The excess of married men over married women in older age groups, despite the small age gap at first marriage, suggests that widowers often wed promptly, many taking brides considerably younger than themselves the second time around. The surplus of women in the population undoubtedly made remarriage relatively easy for men. But this numerical advantage alone is not a sufficient explanation for their higher rate of remarriage, since many men remained single despite the large pool of eligible women. Instead of increasing the male marriage rate, the unbalanced sex ratio merely shortened the time men spent in a widowed state; quite likely, the greater propensity of widowers to remarry arose largely in their need for wives to care for their homes and children. In contrast, widows did not have the same opportunities for remarriage. There was no social dictum against widows remarrying, for one-tenth of the women who made wills had been married two or even three times.[38] Yet it is my impression that, unless they had some property, widows could not easily compete with younger, childless women for a match. The result was that most men, though they married somewhat later than their female counterparts, actually spent a larger part of their lives in a married state.

As far as can be determined, an excess of widows over widowers, and high proportions single, characterized Mexico City in 1790 as well as 1848. In fact, the proportions single are probably underestimated in the 1790 figures, since the marital statistics given for the city as a whole exclude male and female religious entirely. The inclusion of 923 nuns and novices and 1,409 male religious (monks, novices, lay brothers, and secular priests) would add 2.3 percent to the single women age 16 and over, and 4.6 percent to the men. By 1850, however, the impact of religious celibacy was negligible, with the city's 541 nuns representing less than 1 percent of the women age 16 and over.[39] Thus the marriage rate remained low despite the decline in religious vocations—and the concurrent rise in the prestige of motherhood and marriage.

A comparison of the three censuses does suggest that the marriage age was lower, especially for women, in both 1790 and 1848. Although marriage ages cannot be computed for 1790 because the data are overaggregated, the proportions married in the broad age categories provided by the published summary statistics permit some deductions (Table 6). There were proportionately fewer single adults in 1790 than in 1811, but this discrepancy apparently does not reflect a greater incidence of marriage in 1790, since the proportions never marrying (based purely on those 40 or older for lack of a finer breakdown in the published data) were very close. Rather, it reflects an earlier marriage age, for in 1790 most of those who were going to marry at all had done so by the age of 25, resulting in fewer single and more married adults than in 1811. The excess of single men over single women aged 16–25, which evened out by the next age group, also suggests a considerably younger marriage age for women than men in 1790. Although there were relatively more single men and women under 40 in 1811, beyond that age they had wed at a similar rate as in 1790. Without the manuscript census schedules for 1790, however, we cannot be certain that census takers defined marital-status categories in the same way as in 1811, so that too much emphasis should not be placed on differences between the two counts.

TABLE 6
*Proportions Single by Age Group, 1790–1848*

| Category | Age 16–24 | | Age 25–39 | | Age 40 and over | |
|---|---|---|---|---|---|---|
| | Females | Males | Females | Males | Females | Males |
| 1790 (n = 69,201)[a] | | | | | | |
| Total number | 12,440 | 8,397 | 17,121 | 12,409 | 10,325 | 8,480 |
| Number single | 5,608 | 4,819 | 3,237 | 2,508 | 1,711 | 1,655 |
| Percent single | 45.1% | 57.4% | 18.9% | 20.2% | 16.6% | 19.5% |
| 1811 (n = 2,210) | | | | | | |
| Total number | 383 | 205 | 462 | 358 | 444 | 358 |
| Number single | 247 | 161 | 129 | 104 | 75 | 57 |
| Percent single | 64.5% | 78.5% | 27.9% | 29.1% | 16.9% | 15.9% |
| 1848 (n = 1,681) | | | | | | |
| Total number | 331 | 203 | 376 | 287 | 293 | 191 |
| Number single | 167 | 126 | 81 | 83 | 36 | 16 |
| Percent single | 50.5% | 62.1% | 21.5% | 28.9% | 12.3% | 8.4% |

SOURCE: Same as Table 5.
[a]Figures exclude clergy and nuns.

With the 1848 census we stand on firmer ground, since we know that the marital-status categories were directly comparable with those of 1811, and we can precisely compute mean ages at first marriage. The average male in the 1848 census sample wed one year younger than in 1811, at 23.1 years, and the average female nearly three years earlier, at 19.9. Still, as in 1811, marriages of men under 18 or women under 16 were exceedingly rare (2 of 94 men aged 14–17, 4 of 48 women aged 14–15), and none were listed as married below the age of 14.

The later census sample, though less reliable than the 1790 and 1811 sources, suggests also that more men married, and remarried, in 1848 than previously. The incidence of lifelong bachelorhood fell from some 16–20 percent of the men age 40 and over in the earlier counts to 8 percent in 1848 (and from 17 percent of those aged 45–54 in 1811 to 9 percent in 1848). The incidence of widowerhood also fell—from some 12–15 percent of adult men to 9 percent. There were no comparable changes in female marriage rates. The proportion of never-married women only dropped from 16 percent (in 1811) to 13 percent, a variation that hardly merits attention, given the statistical flaws of the censuses. But the proportion of widows rose dramatically, from some 33–35 percent of adult women (in 1790 and 1811) to 41 percent in 1848.

It is difficult to know how to interpret these changes, especially because the evidence for them is rather slim. They are based on too few censuses for us to know whether we are looking at temporary ripples or more meaningful waves in marital practices. Some of the variations may reflect deficiencies in the censuses and the samples rather than any real alteration in behavior. And we do not yet know enough about the population of the country as a whole during this period to relate these changes to larger demographic trends. Although the differences in marriage ages between 1790 and 1811 need to be substantiated by future research and quantified with some precision,[40] we may speculate that the rise in widowhood in 1848 reflects male deaths in the preceding decades of war and civil strife. The increased marriage rate among men in 1848, higher than both 1790 and 1811, combined with a three years' drop in women's average marriage age, might also reflect an attempt to recover from the population losses. Since most of those lost were men, the survivors may have felt a heightened pressure to marry and remarry. Women could not hope to wed at a comparable rate given the male/female ratio of 72:100 in 1848, the sharpest imbalance registered in any census of the time, but they could marry younger, for every decrease in a bride's age increased her opportunities to bear children over a lifetime.

To the extent that these differences represent significant demographic trends, they probably affected men's experiences more than women's, for though marriage became more prevalent for men, the female marriage rate was strikingly consistent. Even if women married at different ages between 1790 and 1848, and were most likely to be widows in 1848, in all three counts, fewer than half of all adult women were married or living in coresidential consensual unions; at least one-third were widows (or perhaps abandoned wives, single mothers, or mistresses of men who lived elsewhere); and about one-sixth had remained single all their lives.

## Motherhood

Despite the large numbers of women who spent their entire lives in the single state, the majority at some point married or entered consensual unions, becoming widows as they aged. The number of children they bore tells us a great deal about their daily routines and helps illuminate the differences between the experiences of widows and spinsters, for the relationships between mothers and children often endured longer than those between husband and wife. Moreover, the likelihood that women would have children illuminates the process of urbanization, for only a high rate of fertility could sustain the capital's native-born population when so many women remained celibate.

Fertility cannot be derived from the censuses for several reasons. For one thing, they do not provide information on completed families, but merely record those children living at home at the time of the enumeration, excluding any siblings who had left the parental home as well as those who had died. For another, the census taker did not always specify family relations, so it is often unclear whether the children listed after a woman were her own.[41] Finally, the population pyramids suggest that, as with most contemporary censuses throughout the world, children were undercounted, especially girls (compare, for example, the proportions of city-born children under 10 in Fig. 1). Although this deficiency does not affect the analysis of adult marriage patterns and sexual structure, it biases any examination of motherhood, for mothers with unlisted infants would be overlooked.

The following analysis of fertility is therefore based on the sample of wills, which list all children ever born to a woman. The number of women studied in this case was larger than the 300 female testators themselves, because the male testators provided information on current and previous spouses. However, only 141 women could be used for the study of completed families, a calculation based on those who had reached the age of 45, and were thus presumably past their childbearing years. Since few wills recorded the testator's age, this group was largely identified by deducing the woman's approximate age from the date of first marriage or the age of the oldest child, information that was not always available.

Although testators occasionally made bequests to illegitimate children, the wills are not a reliable indicator of bastardy in Mexico City. Only four spinsters and three married women admitted to having had children out of wedlock, figures that cannot be applied to the society as a whole because the will-making group generally represents the elites, whose women were closely guarded to prevent sexual encounters outside of marriage. There is considerable evidence that illegitimacy was widespread among the urban lower classes. In a study of birth registers in five Mexico City parishes for 1830 to 1842, Frederick Shaw found that from 18 percent to 33 percent of births were recorded as illegitimate—a range that must be on the low side, given the tendency to conceal illicit affairs whenever possible.[42] The problem of unwanted children, and of "infanticides that mothers perpetrate to hide their frailty," was perceived as serious enough to warrant the establishment of the Foundling Home in 1767. And Fanny Calderón observed in 1841 that "the number of children in the hospital is proof that much vice and poverty do exist." Although elite women did not apparently live in consensual unions, illegitimacy was not unknown in that class. In 1806 the Poor House added a section for "Concealed Childbirths" that took only women of Spanish descent. Allowed to enter discreetly by a back door at any time of the day or night, its clients were cared for in absolute secrecy, their presence not revealed to anyone, not even their husbands, so that the women could preserve their "good reputations" and not have to "resort to abortions."[43] This evidence suggests, first, that the women who wrote wills were not likely to have borne illegitimate children, and second, that the few who had done so had probably given them up for adoption (and omitted them from their wills). The following analysis therefore is basically limited to the marital fertility pattern among the privileged.[44]

Apart from the matter of illegitimacy, however, these patterns were probably not too different from those of the capital's population as a whole. The women who made wills had fewer children than has often been assumed, in part because of the relatively late age at which they married, and in part because of a high rate of mortality that left many widowed before the end of their childbearing years and reduced the number of children who survived. Neither of these factors was peculiar to the upper classes. Indeed, the will-makers, if anything, may have had more children than the women of the lower classes, since the mortality rate was highest among the poor, who lived in insalubrious housing subject to seasonal flooding and could not afford to keep warm or eat an adequate diet,[45] and since malnutrition and ill health decrease a woman's chances of conceiving. Furthermore, the median age of the population in the census sample—24 years for both men and women—suggests that this was not a fast-growing population. (Although the undercounting of infants might artificially raise this number, it was probably compensated for by the presence of many young migrants.)

Humboldt's study of Mexican vital statistics tends to substantiate a relatively low rate of fertility in the capital. The Prussian scientist, though used to the high mortality rate in European cities, was nevertheless struck by the "very great mortality and . . . very small number of births in the capital." He attributed the high death rate to the "conflux of patients" who died after traveling to seek medical help from the city's doctors or hospitals, and the low birth rate to "the convents, the celibacy of the secular clergy, the progress of luxury, the militia, and the indigence of the . . . Indians."[46] What he missed, however, was the impact of migration and marriage patterns. The heavy immigration meant that some one-third of those who died in the capital had not been born there. Moreover, with so many women who remained single, and so many others who married late and were widowed early, it is easy to understand why the city reproduced itself mainly through migration instead of natural growth.

Although the 141 women over 45 had borne five children on the average by the time they reached that age, well over a third (36 percent) of the children had died before their mothers wrote their wills, leaving only three surviving children in the completed family (Figs. 4, 5). The child mortality rate is similar when the sample size is expanded to include the 417 mothers of all ages: 34 percent of their children had likewise died by the time the parents made their wills, a percentage that remained fairly constant throughout the first half of the nineteenth century. Sixty, or 5 percent, of the children died after turning 16; 32, or 3 percent, died between the ages of 3 and 16. If we assume that the rest, including those whose age of death was not specified or was only vaguely designated as "during infancy," perished soon after birth, we can calculate an infant mortality rate somewhere on the order of 27 percent.

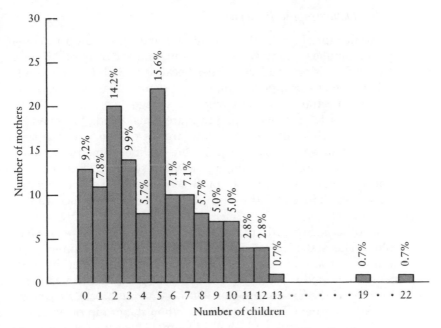

Fig.4. Completed family size: children ever born, 1802–1855. Based on 141 women aged 45 and over in wills sample. Mean, 5.02 children; median, 5; mode, 5.

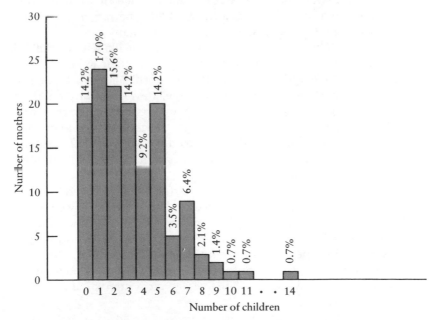

Fig.5. Completed family size: surviving children, 1802–1855. Based on 141 women aged 45 and over in wills sample. Mean, 3.2 children; median, 3; mode, 1.

Adult mortality also limited the number of children in completed families. Many women reaching the age of 45 had in fact stopped bearing children earlier because their husbands died; other families stopped expanding because the mother died. When only the 19 women whose marriages we know to have lasted intact for at least 20 years are considered, the average number of children ever born rises from 5.02 to 6.8 (and of surviving children from 3.2 to 4.6). One prolific woman who married young had 22 children, 14 of whom survived. But she was hardly typical: only one-fifth of these women had seven or more surviving children, and one-third had one or none (see Tables D.4 and D.5).

Another factor curbing the size of Mexican families was infertility. The statistics on completed families underestimate the number of infertile couples, since most of the women over 45 were identified from the ages of surviving children. Even so, 9 percent of the 141 married or widowed women past childbearing age had never borne children. When the group of potential mothers is expanded to include women known to have been married five years or more, the proportion childless rises to 12 percent. It was not unusual for women to declare in their wills, as did doña Salvadora Lavanes, that "during our marriage we had no children whatsoever despite the many years we were married." The widower don Francisco Varela likewise explained that he and his wife had no offspring during their 48-year union, and the widowed doña Ana Parado, fertile herself, since she bore a daughter in her first marriage, never had any children by her second husband, though they were together 26 years. Furthermore, many couples had far fewer children than they wanted. For example, the only baby doña María de la Torre bore was stillborn, and don Francisco Orozco had only one son after nine years of matrimony.[47]

On this evidence alone, it is clear that Gilberto Freyre's image of Latin American women reduced to "mere shreds" by constant childbearing does not apply to most women of Mexico City in the first half of the nineteenth century. This conclusion is substantiated in the 29 cases where child spacing can be calculated from the wills, for three-fourths of these children were separated by over two years. The average birth interval of 2.9 years may indicate that Mexican mothers breast-fed their infants when-ever they could, thereby depressing their fertility.[48] It is even possible—though the evidence on this point is slim—that a few elite couples, like their European counterparts, attempted to limit their families after they had at least three surviving chil-dren, since in the 19 families with four or more children where ages are given for all offspring, the average interval between the last two children was considerably longer than the interval between earlier births (3.7 versus 2.4 years). However, most women almost certainly did not practice contraception or abor-tion within marriage.[49]

It should be apparent by now that the average number of chil-dren is a misleading indicator of the prevalence of motherhood because the variation between individuals was so wide, even within the same social class. Fertility rates were relatively high—but only for those couples who were fertile and whose union lasted over a woman's childbearing years. Although the average wife who reached age 45 bore five children, three of whom sur-vived, nearly half had two or fewer, and the mode was one. Thus, for every Corregidora with a dozen children there were several like Leona Vicario with two or doña Salvadora Lavanes with none. Moreover, child mortality, like fertility, varied widely between individual families. For instance, don Pedro García Monasterio's wife bore a child every other year for 16 years, all eight of whom survived. But doña Antonia Grané, who had 14 children, lost ten of them in infancy and one in adolescence.[50] The celebrated "Güera" Rodríguez, a lady renowned for her beauty and wit, had but seven children despite her three hus-bands and tender marriage age of 17; only two survived her when she died at the age of 72.[51]

The censuses can add some dimensions to this portrait of motherhood by describing the situation of women with children still living at home. Although approximately two-thirds of adult women bore children at some point in their lives, well under half the adult women in both 1811 and 1848 had children at home at the time of the census enumeration (Table 7). Further, on aver-age, they had only 2.4, relatively few offspring to care for at one time. Finally, over one-third of these mothers in 1811 were either widows (32 percent) or single (2.8 percent).[52] By 1848 the propor-

TABLE 7

*Marital Status of Adult Mothers (25 Years and Over) with Children Living at Home, 1811 and 1848*

| Marital status | Total number of adult females | Mothers | | |
|---|---|---|---|---|
| | | Number | Percent of mothers | Percent of adult females |
| | | 1811 | | |
| Single | 204 | 11 | 2.8% | 5.4% |
| Married | 399 | 258 | 65.1 | 64.7 |
| Widowed | 303 | 127 | 32.1 | 41.9 |
| TOTAL | 906 | 396 | 100.0% | 43.7% |
| | | 1848 | | |
| Single | 117 | 3 | 1.0% | 2.6% |
| Married | 276 | 166 | 55.7 | 60.1 |
| Widowed | 276 | 129 | 43.3 | 46.7 |
| TOTAL | 669 | 298 | 100.0% | 44.5% |

tion of adult mothers who were widows had risen to 43 percent, probably reflecting the impact of the republican wars. Thus many children were brought up in single-parent families for at least part of their childhood, and many mothers were entirely in charge of their children's socialization.

Life could be rich and rewarding for widows with children, but it could also be exceedingly lonely. The "love and regard between parents and children" that so impressed foreign travelers led Fanny Calderón to remark, "I have seen no country where families are so knit together as in Mexico, where affections are so concentrated, or where such devoted respect and obedience are shown by the married sons and daughters to their parents."[53] Yet few older women were lucky enough to live surrounded by their children and, given the late marriage age and short life expectancy, even fewer knew their grandchildren. Less than half the widows in the census samples had children living at home with them, and in the will-making group, a widow over the age of 45 most commonly had only one surviving child. Even then, that child might not be around to comfort her in her old age, especially considering the poor communications of the time. As the widowed doña Juana Romero lamented in her will, she had not heard from her sole surviving son in many years, not knowing his whereabouts or indeed whether he was still alive. Another widow, doña Manuela Soria, outlived three children and two husbands to die without any close relatives and, like the elderly doña Josefa Barreda y Balladares who never had children and survived her husband and all her relatives, bequeathed her entire estate to charity.[54] The daily lives of widows like these might not have been too different from those of their single counterparts.

The variety of women's experiences, however, suggests the difficulty of generalizing about the meaning of widowhood or spinsterhood in Mexico City. Although five-sixths of Mexico City women married, and four-fifths of those had children, a substantial number never experienced marriage or motherhood, and about one-third of the adult women lived without the company of a husband or offspring at any given time. Thus, the "typical" female experience was not as typical in the first half of the nineteenth century as it is today, when the vagaries of death and infertility are more under control, when family size among the fertile is usually limited through contraception, and when marriage is more commonplace.

### Household Headship

There are many indications that women who were not wives were able to live self-sufficient and fulfilling lives. We have seen that by the opening of the nineteenth century, retirement houses, originally established to shelter unmarried women, had been transformed into schools or prisons, suggesting that it was no longer considered necessary for spinsters and widows to live in seclusion from the world. We have also seen that Mexican law gave these women contractual and property rights denied to their married sisters. Many widows and orphaned daughters from wealthy families could support themselves on inheritances and government pensions. And, as is documented in Chapter Four, numerous employment opportunities existed for lower-class women in the Mexican capital, though they were poorly paid. But this is not to say that all spinsters and widows were consequently independent.

We can begin to assess their independence by seeing how many of these women lived on their own. Women constituted one-third of the 655 household heads for whom gender is known in the 1811 census sample. Although the number of young female household heads may be somewhat exaggerated by the undercounting of male heads, it is likely to be accurate in the older age groups to which the majority of these women belonged. Table 8 shows that nearly two-thirds of the female household heads were widows, and they presided over 21 percent of the households in the sample.[55] After married men, widows and widowers headed households in the largest numbers relative to their size in the population, with some 44–46 percent of those 18 and over heading their own residences. These patterns reflect the ideal that married couples establish separate residential units; nearly half continued to keep their homes after the death of a spouse. In contrast, only one of 8 single women (and about one of 7 single men) was a household head.

There was apparently a long-standing tradition in Mexico City of women heading their own households, and it persisted over the first half of the nineteenth century. Asunción Lavrin found that one-third of the rental properties of the Regina Celi convent were let to women in 1756—an interesting comparison because her source was not susceptible to the undercounting of men that might bias the census results.[56] In 1848, as in 1811, approximately one-fifth of all women age 18 and over, primarily widows, headed their own residences. Perhaps because of wartime dislocations, however, women now headed a somewhat greater share of the total households (36 percent, against 33 percent), and proportionately more of them were widows. But again too much should not be made of differences between the two counts because of the carelessness with which census takers distinguished households in 1848. Rather, the 1848 census sample can be used to confirm the patterns revealed both by the convent records and the earlier count.

These documents suggest that for many women, widowhood conferred a degree of freedom—or at least the prestige of being mistress of a household and the responsibility of managing it—that they were much less likely to experience if they remained single. Likewise it was only as a widow that the typical woman

7. Many older widows had to work to support themselves, like this apartment-house manager, whose faded flowered skirt recalls more affluent days. The *casera* usually received a free room in a tenement building in return for collecting rents, locking the gate after dark, and monitoring the behavior of the tenants. The author of the article accompanying this illustration ridiculed the casera as a tight-fisted busybody; the artist has unsympathetically portrayed her as on the point of serving an eviction notice on some unfortunate tenant.

TABLE 8
*Household Heads Age 18 and Over by Marital Status, 1811 and 1848*
(As a percent of the population 18 and over of the
same gender and marital status)

| Category | Total number in marital group | Number of household heads | Percent of marital group | Percent of household heads |
|---|---|---|---|---|
| | 1811 | | | |
| Females | | | | |
| Single | 370 | 45 | 12.2% | 21.1% |
| Married | 498 | 30 | 6.0 | 14.1 |
| Widowed | 312 | 138 | 44.2 | 64.8 |
| ALL MARITAL STATUSES | 1,180 | 213 | 18.1% | 100.0% |
| Males | | | | |
| Single | 261 | 40 | 15.3% | 9.1% |
| Married | 492 | 353 | 71.7 | 80.6 |
| Widowed | 98 | 45 | 45.9 | 10.3 |
| ALL MARITAL STATUSES | 851 | 438 | 51.5% | 100.0% |
| | 1848 | | | |
| Females | | | | |
| Single | 242 | 37 | 15.3% | 19.1% |
| Married | 410 | 24 | 5.8 | 12.4 |
| Widowed | 288 | 133 | 46.2 | 68.6 |
| ALL MARITAL STATUSES | 940 | 194 | 20.6% | 100.1% |
| Males | | | | |
| Single | 181 | 37 | 20.4% | 10.5% |
| Married | 412 | 281 | 68.2 | 80.1 |
| Widowed | 44 | 33 | 75.0 | 9.4 |
| ALL MARITAL STATUSES | 637 | 351 | 55.1% | 100.0% |

NOTE: 1811 figures exclude 2 male household heads under 18; 1848 figures exclude 6 male and 2 female household heads under 18.

came to control, in practice as well as on paper, her own legal transactions and the major decisions affecting her life, such as how to handle her money or where to live. For it was more often widows than spinsters who were free from patriarchal supervision of their domestic activities.

The 1811 census sample shows that for both sexes the probability of heading a household depended not only on marital status, but also on age, since two-thirds of male and female household heads were 40 or over. Take single women, for example:

only 15 percent of those aged 25–29 headed their own house-holds, compared with 33 percent of those 50 or older. Widows' chances of heading their own residences grew even more dra-matically, from 15 percent among those 25–29 to 51 percent by the age of 40; about half of all widows continued to head house-holds in older age groups as well. This pattern suggests that for a substantial number of single and widowed women, old age brought increased autonomy.

The positive aspects of the situation of widowed and single women should not be overemphasized, however. For every Mexican observer who associated spinsterhood and widowhood with liberty, there was another who could muster only pity for lonely old women, or who despised them as "the surplus part of the human lineage."[57] For every learned, well-traveled, and so-cially active unmarried woman like the two Fagoaga sisters, for every self-supporting businesswoman like Cecilia in *Bandidos de Río Frío*, and for every strong-willed and enterprising widow like the countess of Regla, there were dozens of pathetic widows struggling to make ends meet or destitute orphans vulnerable to scheming men—both staples of contemporary novels.[58] For every single and widowed woman who took advantage of her legal sovereignty, there were many others, like doña María Josefa de Campo, who did not. Abysmally ignorant of the law, doña María declared in her will that when her husband died she had returned to her father's home and reentered his *patria potestas*.[59]

In fact, more than half of all the widows and the vast majority of adult single women in the 1811 census sample did not head their own households. Although the census data bank does not allow the study of household composition, scattered evidence suggests that if some of these women lived with others their own age (sometimes their sisters or work companions), most lived within their parents' or relatives' homes, where they were pro-tected and controlled. Furthermore, some of the women who headed their own households may have lived far from indepen-dent lives. A widow living with a married son or daughter, as often happened, may have been acknowledged as the head of the household out of respect, but the adult son or son-in-law presumably provided for, controlled, and represented the family in the outside world. Likewise, single and widowed women who might in reality be mistresses of men living elsewhere with their legal wives would be listed as household heads if they lived alone, though they too would be dependent on men. Still, because most female heads of household were older women, they were less likely to be mistresses than simply women whose families had died, leaving them with no one to depend on.

Whether or not they lived on their own, spinsters and widows often fulfilled traditional female roles within the extended family. The widowed *abuelita* and aging *tía* who cared for the children, clothed religious images, and frequented mass,[60] carried out clearly institutionalized functions. Indeed, it is likely that spinster aunts and widowed mothers—who appear to have lived with their relatives more often than bachelor uncles and widowed fathers—did so as much because they could help with child care as because of their vulnerability. It is therefore difficult to describe many of these women as "independent" in today's sense, no matter where they resided.

## Differences Among Social Groups

It has been argued for Mexico City that "very few women, especially in the higher classes, had the option of being single and independent, since the traditional roles of women in society were enforced more firmly among the upper classes," and that, conversely, lower-class women tended to have greater freedom from traditional roles because of their participation in the work force.[61] But the 1811 census sample suggests that the relationship was the opposite of what has generally been assumed, at least in the sense that women of the higher classes were less likely to be wives and mothers, and more likely to head their own households, than women of the lower classes.

These contrasts are evident when the population is broken down into racial categories that in turn shed light on socioeconomic status. As Table 9 shows, Spanish and Indian marriage patterns differed primarily in terms of the proportions single. Although Spanish men married more than two years later than the average (Table 10), the mean age at first marriage was similar for all women; widowhood also formed a common bond among them, for the majority of all women age 45–54 were listed as widows in both groups. But the Spanish population was dis-

## TABLE 9
*Marital Status of the Adult Population (25 Years and Over) and of the
Population Age 45–54 by Race, 1811*

|  | Single | | Married | | Widowed | | |
|---|---|---|---|---|---|---|---|
| Category | No. | Pct. | No. | Pct. | No. | Pct. | Total |
| **Females 25 and over** | | | | | | | |
| Spanish | 131 | 28.0% | 183 | 39.2% | 153 | 32.8% | 467 |
| Caste | 24 | 17.1 | 61 | 43.6 | 55 | 39.3 | 140 |
| Indian | 48 | 16.3 | 153 | 52.0 | 93 | 31.6 | 294 |
| ALL ADULT FEMALES | 203 | 22.5% | 397 | 44.1% | 301 | 33.4% | 901 |
| **Males 25 and over** | | | | | | | |
| Spanish | 106 | 26.9% | 225 | 57.1% | 63 | 16.0% | 394 |
| Caste | 22 | 21.1 | 68 | 65.4 | 14 | 13.5 | 104 |
| Indian | 32 | 15.0 | 155 | 72.8 | 26 | 12.2 | 213 |
| ALL ADULT MALES | 160 | 22.5% | 448 | 63.0% | 103 | 14.5% | 711 |
| **Females 45–54** | | | | | | | |
| Spanish | 20 | 21.7% | 17 | 18.5% | 55 | 59.8% | 92 |
| Caste | 2 | 8.0 | 5 | 20.0 | 18 | 72.0 | 25 |
| Indian | 5 | 10.0 | 18 | 36.0 | 27 | 54.0 | 50 |
| ALL FEMALES 45–54 | 27 | 16.2% | 40 | 23.9% | 100 | 59.9% | 167 |
| **Males 45–54** | | | | | | | |
| Spanish | 17 | 20.0% | 48 | 56.5% | 20 | 23.5% | 85 |
| Caste | 4 | 18.2 | 13 | 59.1 | 5 | 22.7 | 22 |
| Indian | 2 | 8.0 | 16 | 64.0 | 7 | 28.0 | 25 |
| ALL MALES 45–54 | 23 | 17.4% | 77 | 58.3% | 32 | 24.2% | 132 |

## TABLE 10
*Mean Age at First Marriage by Race, 1811*
(Based on population ages 10–54)

|  | Females | | Males | |
|---|---|---|---|---|
| Race | Mean age | Number | Mean age | Number |
| Spanish | 22.7 | 699 | 26.4 | 506 |
| Caste | 23.7 | 231 | 22.5 | 175 |
| Indian | 22.5 | 462 | 24.0 | 315 |
| ALL RACES | 22.7 | 1,392 | 24.2 | 996 |

**TABLE 11**

Proportions Single in the Adult Population (25 Years and Over) and in the Population Age 45 and Over by Number of Live-in Domestic Servants, 1811 and 1848

| Category | 0 servant | | | 1 servant | | | 2 or more servants | | |
|---|---|---|---|---|---|---|---|---|---|
| | Number of people in age group | Number single | Percent single | Number of people in age group | Number single | Percent single | Number of people in age group | Number single | Percent single |
| **1811** | | | | | | | | | |
| Age 25 and over | | | | | | | | | |
| Females | 610 | 95 | 15.6% | 109 | 38 | 34.9% | 89 | 32 | 36.0% |
| Males | 519 | 86 | 16.6 | 86 | 23 | 26.7 | 85 | 38 | 44.7 |
| Age 45 and over | | | | | | | | | |
| Females | 192 | 21 | 10.9 | 43 | 15 | 34.9 | 28 | 10 | 35.7 |
| Males | 174 | 23 | 13.2 | 36 | 7 | 19.4 | 31 | 9 | 29.0 |
| **1848** | | | | | | | | | |
| Age 25 and over | | | | | | | | | |
| Females | 510 | 74 | 14.5% | 41 | 9 | 21.9% | 34 | 9 | 26.5% |
| Males | 377 | 61 | 16.2 | 34 | 14 | 41.2 | 37 | 12 | 32.4 |
| Age 45 and over | | | | | | | | | |
| Females | 231 | 19 | 8.2 | 4 | 0 | 0.0 | 7 | 2 | 28.6 |
| Males | 171 | 5 | 2.9 | 11 | 3 | 27.3 | 12 | 4 | 33.3 |

NOTE: The numbers exclude the domestic servants themselves.

tinguished by the disproportionately large numbers of single adults, both men and women. The low Spanish marriage rate is evident not only among adults as a whole, for nearly twice as many Spanish as Indian men and women were single, but also among those who reportedly never married, for there were more than twice as many Spaniards as Indians who were still single at the age of 45–54.[62]

A similar pattern is visible when the population is divided according to the number of servants in their households. Again, the proportions single are highest in the upper-class group (those with two or more servants) and lowest in the lower-class group (those without any servants). And again, as we see in Table 11, these differences hold both for the entire adult population and for those 45 and older—though the upper-class never-married group, even if expanded beyond age 54, includes too few people to inspire great confidence. Even if the marriage rate in the lower class is somewhat inflated by the omission of domestic servants themselves from that group, the rate for the upper class is still low when compared to the population as a whole. In fact, the discrepancies between social groups identified by domestic servants are more dramatic than those between racial groups, with "Spanish" marriage patterns being far more pronounced among those with two or more servants than among the Spanish population as a whole. In this light, the many single people making wills are not so unusual, for they represented the elites more than the capital's population at large.

Educated Mexicans of the time recognized the low incidence of marriage among the upper classes. For example, in an article entitled "On the Necessity of Marriage," the author decried "the multitude of virgins," the resistance of the well-to-do to matrimony, and "the abandonment with which today this precious union is seen." And another writer wondered why it was that "among distinguished persons or those of some means there are so few marriages, not only in terms of absolute numbers, but also in comparison to the numbers of marriages among the poor and plebeian, even though they have the wherewithal to support the burdens of that sacred tie?"[63] Several writers even felt that marriage was becoming increasingly rare among the well-to-do. This opinion, already voiced by the anonymous author of

"On Luxury in Women" in 1810, was echoed by the liberal writer and politician Manuel Payno in his 1843 article "Feminine Celibacy," where he argued that "spinsterhood . . . is making rapid, surprising, and devastating progress."[64]

It is difficult to document the claim of a declining elite marriage rate. The evidence on this point is contradictory and probably reflects changing characteristics of the sources more than changing marriage patterns. Although the proportion of single women rose slightly in the will-making group (over the period 1802–55; Table 4), it decreased in the two-or-more-servants group (between 1811 and 1848; Table 11). In contrast, the proportions single decreased both among men making wills and among the adult men with two or more servants in the censuses, but increased slightly among men over 45. Some of the fluctuations in the census samples in the over-45 age group may be due to the small number of older people living in households with two or more servants. The increase in proportions married among upper-class adults in the census samples, a larger and therefore more reliable category, could reflect the younger marriage age in 1848 rather than a higher marriage rate. (Unfortunately, the mean age at first marriage cannot be calculated for the upper-class, either on the basis of race, which is not given in the 1848 count, or on the basis of number of servants, which provides too few cases in each age group for that complex computation.) The falling marriage rate among female will-makers could conceivably be caused by a changing age mix, with the addition of more young testators to throw off comparisons. The rising marriage rate among male will-makers almost certainly reflects a reduction in the number of peninsular Spaniards in that group, for Spanish immigrants were well known for bachelorhood.[65] Indeed, when only Mexican-born testators are considered, the proportions of single men were stable over the first half of the nineteenth century, averaging 24 percent. It is most likely, then, that the elites married at about the same rate during this period.

The evidence on changing marriage patterns is more solid for the people living in servantless households, because they constituted the majority in the census samples. By this measure the lower-class trends were, in fact, the reverse of what elite observers imagined, since the proportions never marrying decreased from 11 percent for women in 1811 to 8 percent in 1848 and, even more notably, from 13 percent to 3 percent for men. In addition, lower-class women married earlier in 1848 than in 1811, at 20 years, as did the sample population as a whole.

What alarmed elite observers, however, was the behavior in their own class, and the thing that worried them most was spinsterhood. It was not only that these men disliked the spectacle of women "free and without masters," in Fernández de Lizardi's phrase. At a time when population growth was considered a key to national development, female celibacy posed a serious threat to the "honest multiplication of the species."[66] (Bachelors, who were able to keep mistresses below them in social rank, were not so much of a problem except to the degree that they might have married women of their own class.) Thus enlightened leaders, both before and after independence, forbade prostitution and took steps to prevent abortion and the exposure of children because they "diminished the population."[67] But it was the "honest multiplication" of whites, or *gente decente*, that concerned them above all. For example, when the legal commentator Anastasio de la Pascua explained that women should not provide surety because they might thus lose their dowries, "a situation causing harm to the State . . . for it is convenient that women have dowries so that they marry and the population increase,"[68] he had propertied women in mind. In the wake of the Hidalgo revolt of 1810 and the Caste Wars of the 1840's, which highlighted the continuing division of Mexicans into conquered and conquering races, it became urgent to erase these divisions and shore up the "civilized" element.[69]

These concerns explain the harsh tone with which didactic writers, addressing themselves to educated audiences, insisted that women "were born but to be wives and mothers." Spinsters were denounced as "useless women—sterile monsters who commit a crime against the human race." Guillermo Prieto likened them to "a useless tree that never produced fruit or sheltered the traveler with its shade," and Manuel Payno termed female celibacy a "cancer of the very fabric of morality, gangrene of the population."[70]

Yet these moral strictures in many cases fell on deaf ears.

Fanny Calderón noted that little social isolation and stigma were attached to spinsterhood among her elite friends when she remarked (perhaps with some exaggeration) that "amongst the young girls here there is not that desire to enter upon the cares of matrimony which is to be observed in many other countries. The opprobrious epithet of 'old maid' is unknown. A girl is not the less admired because she has been ten or a dozen years in society; the most severe remark made on her is that she is 'hard to please.'"[71] Her comment that the derogatory term old maid was unknown is borne out in the literature of the period, where the term *solterona* does not appear. These remarks suggest that spinsterhood and bachelorhood were integral parts of early-nineteenth-century elite life.

This low marriage rate meant that elite women had more alternatives than their lower-class sisters to the traditional female roles of wife and mother. To the extent that the Spanish population represented the upper and middle classes, these women were also more likely to live without patriarchal supervision, for the likelihood of a woman's heading a household was greatest in the Spanish population that commanded the most resources. These sectoral variations will surprise some students of Latin America, since studies based primarily on societies with large Black populations have noted the incidence of matrifocal families in the lower classes.[72] Yet in Mexico City, perhaps because of a housing crunch that made it expensive to maintain a separate residence, only 13–15 percent of the Indian and Caste women age 18 and over headed their own households in 1811, compared with almost a quarter of the Spanish women. Similarly, only a third of the Caste and Indian widows were household heads, compared with more than half for the Spanish group (Table 12).

These differences were, in fact, more marked among women than men, for approximately half the men headed their own households regardless of ethnic group. Similarly, a woman's chances of having her own family and being sexually active depended more on her social background than did a man's, since many elite bachelors were not truly celibate, whereas most women listed as "single" were. Marriage patterns, in short, sug-

TABLE 12

*Household Heads Age 18 and Over by Race and Marital Status, 1811*

(As a percent of those 18 and over of the same
gender, race, and marital status)

| Category | Females | | | Males | | |
|---|---|---|---|---|---|---|
| | Total no. in marital group | No. of household heads | Pct. of marital group | Total no. in marital group | No. of household heads | Pct. of marital group |
| **Spanish** | | | | | | |
| Single | 211 | 35 | 16.6% | 155 | 28 | 18.1% |
| Married | 229 | 13 | 5.7 | 227 | 181 | 79.7 |
| Widowed | 155 | 85 | 54.8 | 58 | 33 | 56.9 |
| ALL MARITAL STATUSES | 595 | 133 | 22.3% | 440 | 242 | 55.0% |
| **Caste** | | | | | | |
| Single | 56 | 4 | 7.1% | 31 | 4 | 12.9% |
| Married | 76 | 5 | 6.6 | 73 | 52 | 71.2 |
| Widowed | 53 | 18 | 34.0 | 14 | 6 | 42.9 |
| ALL MARITAL STATUSES | 185 | 27 | 14.6% | 118 | 62 | 52.5% |
| **Indian** | | | | | | |
| Single | 101 | 6 | 5.9% | 73 | 8 | 11.0% |
| Married | 184 | 11 | 6.0 | 171 | 118 | 69.0 |
| Widowed | 101 | 34 | 33.7 | 25 | 5 | 20.0 |
| ALL MARITAL STATUSES | 386 | 51 | 13.2% | 269 | 131 | 48.7% |

gest that in the highly stratified society of the Mexican capital many of women's basic experiences were sharply distinguished by class.

## Explanations of Differences Among Social Groups

Well-to-do women presumably did not have the alternative of entering consensual unions because of the importance of maintaining their respectability. Why, though, did so many shun matrimony? Certainly, some did so out of conscious choice, since a few wealthy heiresses are known to have refused several offers of marriage.[73] We have other statements to that effect, from Manuel Payno, who assured his readers that he had overheard a young maiden exclaim that "women's happiness consists in remaining single," and from Guillermo Prieto, who observed that many elite women associated marriage with victimization and loss of liberty,[74] but I tend to read these as expressions of male fears rather than of women's opinions. In the absence of documents revealing why individual women decided to marry or not, any explanation of their motives must remain speculative. I would guess, however, that despite the satisfactions available outside of marriage, most women desired it, both because they wished to emulate their mothers and because only marriage brought opportunities for having licit sexual relations, bearing legitimate children, and, typically, becoming mistress of a household.

The popularity of religious careers might have discouraged marriage in the upper classes, but the evidence is that this was not an important factor. Despite the fears of the Mexico City cabildo in 1792 that "the disproportionate number of men taking up the celibate lives of ecclesiastics . . . would eventually result in the depopulation of the Kingdom," Navarro y Noriega was closer to the truth when he noted that, in contrast to Spain, ecclesiastical celibacy had little adverse impact on Mexican population growth.[75] For just as entrance into religious orders hardly affected the proportions single among the total population of Mexico City, it was not a significant alternative to marriage among the smaller Spanish group. Moreover, it had even less impact on women's marriage patterns than on men's. For example, in 1790, only 4.2 percent of the capital's Spanish women age 16 and over were members of religious orders, compared with 6.6 percent of Spanish men; and as time went along, fewer and fewer Spanish women opted for the religious life: some 2.5 percent in 1828 and 1.3 percent in 1850.[76] Actually, the percentage choosing to profess was even lower, since women from provincial towns also entered Mexico City convents, thereby expanding the potentially eligible population. It was not therefore the case, as some have suggested, that elite women had to choose between marriage and a nunnery.

To be sure, the Church may have encouraged spinsterhood to some extent by extolling celibacy as one path to perfection, but the idealization of celibacy had declined notably since the sixteenth century, when Fray Luis de León, Fray Martín de Córdoba, and Luis Vives clearly considered matrimony inferior to celibacy. Although Prieto commented on the "deeply rooted idea" held by elite women "that a woman upon marriage . . . renounced the perfect state of virginity that would lead her to Heaven,"[77] he himself disapproved of that attitude, and his contemporaries ignored it, attributing the low marriage rate to a variety of other factors, or simply lamenting it.

In a society where social status depended on the transmission of property, property became an important factor in restricting marriage. The inheritance system, by forcing parents to divide their belongings among all their children, tended to discourage matrimony in difficult economic times. As David Brading has observed, "If thrift and business talent could together create a fortune, death and a fertile wife could destroy it."[78] Bachelorhood (and spinsterhood), which limited the number of heirs, prevented the dissolution of property and maintained an extended family's future status. So did late marriage, since the size of families bore an inverse relationship to a woman's age at marriage. Indeed, late marriage was the safer of the two options because it did not threaten to terminate the family line. Unions of cousins, or of uncles and nieces (not uncommon among privileged groups), had a similar effect by keeping wealth within a family while guaranteeing its continuity; but even this strategy did not prevent the partition of estates. At one time families may have encouraged children to enter religious orders, since they would presumably have no offspring, thereby freeing family funds for their siblings.[79] But as the appeal of religious life diminished, such a response became increasingly rare. The scarcity of resources during the first half of the nineteenth century may have led the well-to-do to curb fertility instead through late marriage or bachelorhood. This development could explain why, though the marriage rate increased in the population as a whole after 1811 (in particular, among men), it remained low in the upper classes.

Although the desire to avoid the dispersal of property discouraged marriage, its very dispersal encouraged spinsterhood. The viability of spinsterhood for Spanish women was due in part to their access to wealth, assured by the inheritance system and, for some, by pensions paid to the dependents of government employees. This income enabled many well-to-do women to maintain their own residences; others were accepted into the large households that the Mexican elites maintained as a sign of their prosperity, status, and largesse. If wealth provided options making marriage less compelling, though, it did not necessarily make it less desirable. But some elite heiresses, who could afford to be highly selective in choosing a mate, may unintentionally have postponed marriage so much that the opportunity passed.

The relatively late marriage age of Spanish men compared with that of Indians and Castes is similarly related to their greater earning potential, coupled with the requirement that they support a family in suitable style. At the very least, well-to-do Mexicans expected the groom to provide his wife with a separate household "where she could live with the liberty and mastery to which she [was] entitled."[80] The author of "On Luxury in Women" believed that the "love of luxury directly destroys the population," since the expense required to sustain an elegant household put off prudent men.[81] Ambitious young men thus deferred marriage until they could attract a wife of high social standing. Since it was difficult, given the economic uncertainties of the time, to count on a well-educated and talented young man's improving his position through a successful career, men became eligible suitors only after they had established themselves in a profession or received an inheritance. (Indeed, a characteristic stage in an upwardly mobile youth's career required celibacy, because bachelors were preferred for such positions as clerks in commercial houses and junior military officers.[82]) Some men never arrived at the desired level, though, and by the time many others did, they had become confirmed bachelors.[83]

Such comfortable options were not available to the lower classes. Barely able to subsist on their meager earnings and lacking inheritances, pensions, or wealthy relatives to rely on, the women had little choice but to depend on a man for financial support, and given the precarious economic situation of their menfolk, they could not reasonably insist that a mate bring property or an established position to the union. The lower classes may also have viewed children as insurance against sickness and old age. And because poor families could not hope to leave property to their children, there was little fear of dividing fortunes among many heirs. Thus the high proportions marrying or entering consensual unions among the Caste and Indian population, and the relatively low marriage age of the men, might reflect the poverty of those groups.

It has often been maintained that dowries were a necessary prerequisite for matrimony among the upper and middle classes. Might this have accounted for the great number of Spanish women who remained single? If the wills sample is any indication, it did not, for most women in that group wed without dowries (Table 13). Indeed, it was not uncommon to find a will plainly stating that the bride brought nothing to the marriage, though she might be marrying a man of considerable means.[84] Furthermore, not only was the institution decreasing rapidly in Mexico City, where the dowry rate fell from 23 percent in 1802–3 (representing women who wed in the late eighteenth century) to only 13 percent in 1853–55, but this was merely the tail end of a broader trend: dowered marriages had been the rule in Guadalajara and Puebla in the seventeeth century, and were still the preferred custom in the eighteenth, but were the exception by the nineteenth century. This trend is also evident in a parallel development: in the earlier colonial period a favorite form of charity—and one that must have responded to a social need—had been the provision of dowries for orphaned and poor girls; by the nineteenth century most of these donated dowries were requested by (and assigned to) young women who wished to enter convents, rather than by girls planning marriage.[85]

The waning of the dowry may demonstrate an increasing regard for women's economic potential or at least a perception that they were less vulnerable because of the introduction of pensions ensuring the future security of many elite survivors. Or it may reflect a reluctance to give a husband control over his wife's property. Or it may simply show a growing unwillingness of parents to risk damaging the family's financial position by dividing their estates before death. In any case, the lack of a dowry was clearly not a critical obstacle to marriage for most women in Mexico City.

Despite the decline of the dowry, a family's wealth did not cease to influence marriage patterns. Dowries were still *de rigueur* among the nobility and highest circles of society during

TABLE 13
Dowered Marriages in Guadalajara, Puebla, and Mexico City, 1625–1855

| | Guadalajara | | Puebla | | Mexico City | |
| Period | Total marriages | Percent dowered | Total marriages | Percent dowered | Total marriages | Percent dowered |
| --- | --- | --- | --- | --- | --- | --- |
| 1625–75 | 108 | 75.0% | 63 | 82.5% | | |
| 1726–90 | 87 | 51.7 | 53 | 62.3 | | |
| 1802–55 | | | | | 455 | 17.0% |
| 1802–3 | | | | | 142 | 23.2% |
| 1827–29 | | | | | 161 | 16.1 |
| 1853–55 | | | | | 152 | 13.1 |

SOURCES: *Guadalajara and Puebla*. Asunción Lavrin and Edith Couturier, "Dowries and Wills: A View of Women's Socioeconomic Role in Colonial Guadalajara and Puebla, 1640–1790," *Hispanic American Historical Review*, 59, 2, (May 1979): 294. *Mexico City*. Wills sample, Appendix B.

the late colonial period; indeed, a royal decree of 1789 required the brides of ranking military officers to pay substantial sums (3,000 pesos) as a way of assuring that the marriages would reflect well on the Crown.[86] Other elite men undoubtedly demanded property—if not in dowry then as a prospective inheritance—from their brides. Moreover, the end of the dowry may have contributed to the late marriage age in 1811, assuming that some couples now waited for a woman's inheritance to help them set up a new household. For the same reason, the end of the dowry may have kept the marriage age high among elites when it dropped for the rest of the population in the middle of the nineteenth century. (This hypothesis, however, depends on the marriage age having been lower in the early colonial period, a fact that remains to be established.)

If the problem of raising a dowry does not entirely account for the high proportions of single women among the Spanish population, the difficulties of making appropriate matches—a process in which the dowry sometimes played a part—does. Because well-to-do Mexicans viewed marriage as a way to maintain or improve their family's status, they were highly selective in choosing a mate. Some families needed dowries or the prospect of an inheritance to attract suitable husbands for their daughters; family prestige and connections might suffice for others; the beauty or talent of a daughter might achieve the desired result for a few. The importance of a family's wealth and social prestige in facilitating marriage is underlined by the relatively high marriage rate among the Mexican nobility, for all but 10 percent of peeresses married from 1790 to 1826[87]—half the never-married rate for the Spanish female population as a whole. Conversely, according to the author of "On the Necessity of Marriage," numerous "well-educated and virtuous virgins" of the middle classes were shunned merely for lack of possessions, despite their talent for "making husbands happy" through "prudence, thrift, and willing subordination to marital authority."[88]

Regardless of what an individual or family had to offer, the problem of finding an appropriate partner was compounded by a limited marriage market. To begin with, universal marriage was an impossibility for women because of their numerical predominance in the population. And the sexual imbalance obtained in all ethnic groups, so that for every Spanish woman to wed, many would have had to marry outside of their ethnic group. There is evidence that some Spanish women did so, but for those at the pinnacle of a society that valued racial purity, this step was unacceptable. The sexual imbalance does not, of course, explain the large numbers of Spanish men who remained single, since sex ratios favored their marriage within their social group. Neither does it entirely account for the high proportion of Spanish spinsters, since in both 1790 and 1811 the excess of women was slightly more pronounced in the Indian population (Table D.6), which married or entered consensual unions at the highest rate.

Sex ratios were thus only one factor limiting the marriage market; the restricted geographic and social mobility of the period also narrowed the upper classes' chances of finding a socially and personally attractive mate among the relatively static circle of family friends. As Fanny Calderón noted in another of her incisive (and probably exaggerated) remarks, "Young people have so few opportunities of being together that Mexican marriages must be made in heaven, for I see no opportunity of bringing them about upon earth!"[89] Many men and women may have simply preferred to remain unmarried if they could not find a suitable spouse.

The crucial point is that, whether responding to economic, social, or demographic circumstances, a person's choice was conditioned by the cultural importance attached to maintaining status. It was only because social rank was related to family background, racial purity, property ownership, and an appropriate standard of living that these factors became significant. These values may in fact have been particularly Spanish, and therefore not shared by the lower classes of Indian descent, who were less concerned with appearances and defined suitable mates and living arrangements more broadly.[90]

Spanish notions of marriage as a means of sustaining the hierarchical class system are embodied in a series of royal decrees aimed at preventing marriages among "unequals." In the late colonial period the Crown increasingly restricted the freedom of marriage sanctioned by the Catholic Church. Members of the militia, nobility, and government bureaucracy needed official permission to marry after 1728; minors needed parental consent after 1776; those wishing to contract interracial marriages needed a dispensation from civil authorities after 1805.[91] It is my impression that these licenses were not often denied, so this legislation prevented few marriages. But it may have delayed some unions,[92] and it reinforced the already existing pressure to be highly selective in choosing a mate. Although the restrictive legislation was abolished with independence, that pressure remained strong among the highly status-conscious elites of Spanish descent, especially as the economic situation became more precarious.

Further evidence that cultural factors were at work in distinguishing the marital behavior of Spanish and Indian groups comes from a cross-cultural comparison of marriage patterns. J. H. Hajnal's study of global patterns reveals that from the sixteenth to the early twentieth century, Western Europe was characterized by late marriages and large numbers of adults who never married, in contrast to Africa, Asia, and Eastern Europe, where marriage was nearly universal and, especially in the case of women, people married young.[93] The 16–17 percent who never married in Mexico City in 1811 was well within the Western European range of 10–29 percent. Mexico City residents generally followed Europeans in terms of mean marriage ages too, although they married somewhat younger on average. The mean age at first marriage for women in Mexico City in 1811,

22.7, was within the Western European range of 22.2–30.0 years, if at the low end of the scale; the mean age for men, 24.2, was at the bottom of the range of 24.3–31.3 years. In 1848 (and probably in 1790 also) Mexico City residents married slightly earlier on average than Western Europeans, but their behavior continued to be more like the Europeans' than like that of people in other parts of the world, especially because of the low marriage rate for women.[94]

Aggregate statistics are misleading, however, in a society where marital behavior varied in different social groups. When the residents of Mexico City are divided by race, the Spanish population followed essentially Western European marriage patterns, the Indians were closer to Asian and African patterns (which in the following discussion should be read as applying to Eastern Europe as well), and the Castes were generally in between. It may be, then, that this society born of conquest had not, after three centuries of colonization, produced a new and homogeneous set of values about the basic institution of marriage.

This hypothesis rests in part on the fact that sectoral variations were more marked in Mexico than in Western Europe, where people of all social groups shared the same ethnic background. Although few European studies have examined class differences, it appears that marital customs were often similar among people of different classes. In cases where they varied, the fluctuations were within the European range, and even then the relationship between lower and upper classes was not necessarily the same as that between Indian and Spanish. Although the elites of Europe often had the lowest marriage rates, as in Mexico City, the lower-class women there often married the latest.[95] Furthermore, given the minuscule proportions remaining unmarried in Africa and Asia, it does not appear that upper classes with different cultural values behaved like those of European descent.

Differing rural marriage patterns in Mexico also suggest separate Spanish and Indian traditions. Again, the evidence is rather slim because of the dearth of research on the subject. Claude Morin and Cecilia A. Rabell both found that Mexican villagers married at earlier average ages (18 for women, 20–21 for men) and higher rates (all but 5 percent of the men and 7 percent of the women in Rabell's study, nearly universally in Morin's) than city dwellers.[96] The few available demographic studies of Latin America likewise suggest that rural patterns were close to those of Africa and Asia, whereas those of Hispanicized cities, like Mexico City's, were largely European.[97] Such marked contrasts between rural and urban areas were not characteristic of racially homogeneous Western Europe. Although European city dwellers sometimes married later and less often than the rural population, the variations were relatively small; moreover, in some areas country women actually married later than in cities.[98] Thus rural-urban differences alone do not appear to account for the magnitude of the discrepancy between Indian and Spanish patterns any more than class differences do.

We might speculate that the marriage patterns in Mexican villages were a modification of traditional Indian customs that had once conformed to the Asia-African model documented by Hajnal.[99] If, as in contemporary Mexican villages, unmarried villagers were not regarded as adult members of the community (so that young people, as well as widows and widowers, had to marry and remarry in order to enjoy community standing),[100] then cultural values were clearly operating. Following this line of reasoning, we could argue that in Mexican cities, despite the extent of acculturation to Hispanic ways, different patterns continued to characterize Spanish and Indian groups. Indeed, the few studies of other areas of the country, whether based on censuses, parish registers, or criminal records, have consistently shown that in cities as well as in towns Indians married in higher proportions and at lower ages than people of Spanish descent.[101]

Of course, the higher marriage rate in Mexican rural areas in part reflects the emigration of single people to cities, haciendas, and mines. It might be related to more balanced sex ratios in villages, although we have seen that Mexico City's marriage rate was much lower than the sexual imbalance alone would dictate. In addition, rural patterns might have been affected by the dependence of the rural economy on the husband-wife unit, which was undermined by the cash economy of the cities. And inheritance patterns could explain why the age of marriage was lower in Mexican villages than in European ones, for Indians who worked communal *ejidos* did not have to wait, as European peasants did, to inherit their own plot of land.

In Mexico City, where race and class were roughly correlated (especially in the censuses, whose racial designations may have already reflected people's social rank), it is difficult to know whether sectoral differences reflect distinct Spanish and Indian traditions, or whether they stem from socioeconomic factors related to the different locations of these groups on the social scale. It is likewise difficult to know whether Mexico City's characteristically "urban" marriage patterns stem from its high proportion of Spanish residents or from its diversified class structure, because Latin American cities were both more Hispanic and more heavily populated by members of the upper and middle classes than villages.[102]

In the final analysis, since cultural values and economic systems are inseparable, it may be fruitless to try to determine what differentiated Mexican rural and urban patterns, or distinguished African and Asian patterns from those of Western Europe. The point is that the society of Mexico City was, in terms of its economic system, its class structure, and its cultural values, very much a part of the Western world, and the society of the Indian villages was not. The variations in marriage patterns among the capital's ethnic groups thus reflect the process of Mexican social formation through conquest and colonization that resulted in a hierarchical class structure generally correlated with race.

## Conclusion

In terms of their basic demographic experiences, women in Mexico City appear to have differed considerably from most Mexican women, the vast majority of whom lived in rural areas.[103] If the capital's largely European marriage patterns cannot be said to represent Mexico, however, they were fairly typical of other Latin American cities that were the seat of Iberian settlement in the New World. The "enlightened Parisians who inhabited the city center," as Payno derisively dubbed the elites of Mexico

City,[104] consequently were more European in terms of some intimate life experiences than the Indian masses from whom they constantly strove to distinguish themselves.

In many ways social background fragmented Mexico City women more than gender united them. Contemporaries may have thought in terms of gender, educated children for different gender roles, and organized women along gender lines; laws may have differentiated between the sexes; and women of all social groups may have suffered male domination. But the likelihood of a woman's marrying or entering a consensual union, having children, migrating, and heading a household depended on her social rank, as did her standard of living and the respect she commanded from others. Indeed, in these areas sectoral cleavages divided women more than men, for women's chances of being sexually active, of heading a household—and of working—depended much more on their social background. In some senses, women at the top of Mexico City society had greater possibilities for diversified roles than did those at the bottom, because Spanish women had more freedom to stay unmarried and live on their own. In the twentieth century, as marital customs altered for all Mexicans, these sectoral variations may have been largely eliminated.[105] But they were still very much in evidence during the first half of the nineteenth century.

Exhibiting the slow pace of many social phenomena, demographic patterns changed little during the late colonial and early republican period despite the increasing prestige of marriage and motherhood and the decline of the celibate ideal. (Since these trends date at least from the eighteenth century, however, their impact should be measured over a much longer span.) From 1790 to 1848 elite behavior stayed about the same: difficult economic times, combined with the sexual imbalance and limited marriage market, encouraged members of the upper classes to restrict the formation of new families so as to preserve their social position over generations. In the lower classes marriage ages apparently dropped, especially for women, and the marriage rate increased, especially for men, whose rate of remarriage also rose. These new lower-class patterns may reflect the population's attempt to recover from decades of warfare and civil strife; they may also signal the beginning of the trend toward high marriage rates and low marriage ages that, combined with advances in public health, currently help give Mexico one of the fastest growth rates in the world. As we have seen, however, the demographic patterns of contemporary underdeveloped countries were not those of Mexico City for most of the first half of the nineteenth century.

FOUR

# Employment

THE MOST EASILY refutable aspect of the stereotype of the traditional Latin American woman is her isolation from economic activities. Even a cursory glance at contemporary travelers' accounts, novels, and newspapers shows that women were actively involved in production, commerce, and service trades. But recent studies, valuable as they are in documenting women's participation in the labor force and in a variety of business enterprises,[1] have not told us what proportion of women worked, what the sexual division of labor was, or what the conditions of women's employment were. Nor have they told us with any precision how class, migration, marriage, and age affected women's work. Yet these factors determined women's chances of employment in important ways.

Women's experiences in the labor market were also affected by contemporary changes in urban life. During the late colonial period Mexico City's rapid growth and nascent industrialization had the potential to transform women's work. So too did reformers' attempts to mobilize women for national development, to incorporate them in the labor force, and to prepare them to enter new fields, which culminated in the landmark decree of 1799 abolishing legal barriers to women's work. This chapter examines the extent to which these developments expanded and diversified women's job opportunities by the eve of independence and then explores the impact of republican instability and recession on their employment. For if the loss of men through war and military duty could have opened new jobs for women, economic stagnation and male unemployment worked in the opposite direction.

Some scholars argue that it is artificial to distinguish between working and non-working women because women's housework contributes to a family's well-being in essential ways. For instance, a housewife's judicious management of her husband's earnings and her provision of services that would otherwise have to be bought affect a family's standard of living; and the seemingly frivolous maintenance of a network of friends and relatives might prove useful to the family's prospects for employment and loans.[2] But this chapter reserves the term workers for those who produced goods or services for the market. This was the way nineteenth-century Mexicans defined work, for they clearly differentiated housework from activities that earned cash. Since some of these activities took place at home, the real distinction is not whether women worked inside or outside the home. Rather, the women workers examined here are those who conceived of themselves as having an occupation, or *destino*. The business activities of elite women, though not employment in this sense, will also be considered briefly.

Although this definition of the worker ignores the important economic roles of unemployed women, it includes most women who would today be counted as part of the economically active population. By the late eighteenth century, domestic manufacturing for family use was of little importance in Mexico City. Most basic consumer goods—whether bread or tortillas, soap or candles, cloth or clothes—were purchased rather than made at home. In the lower classes even meals were often taken at inexpensive sidewalk stands because crowded tenements lacked cooking facilities. To be sure, some outlying homes had small garden plots, but most city dwellers depended on fresh produce brought in from surrounding farms. And though artisans and shopkeepers usually worked out of their homes, perhaps assisted by their wives and daughters, many commercial establishments were separate from the owners' residences, and certain branches of artisanal production had already shifted to a factory-like setting, notably cigar manufacture in the huge government-owned Tobacco Factory, some textile weaving in the infamous *obrajes*, and bread making in *panaderías* that sometimes more closely resembled prisons than workshops. Consequently, the distinction between employment and housework in Mexico

City was more complete than in rural areas still dependent on household production by all members of the family.

A rich variety of sources document women's economic activity in Mexico City, but most do so impressionistically. The 1811 census sample, which permits the examination of work patterns for the entire population, is the principal source used in this chapter. Unfortunately, it is a less satisfactory source for employment than for demographic patterns. For one thing, censuses only list occupations if people declared them—and given the stigma attached to women's working and the illegal nature of some employment, there may be entire categories of women excluded from this analysis. Prostitutes and *cuberas* or *tepacheras*, who dispensed drinks from illegal taverns, are certainly excluded.[3] So, probably, are women who took in sewing and laundry now and then to supplement the family income. Women who helped out in their husbands' and fathers' shops may also be excluded; although artisans' wives and daughters occasionally listed an occupation related to the family business (for instance, edgers were often married to cobblers), most of them probably did not.[4] Still, the census is far more complete than any other source I have been able to locate; the rich data for those women who did declare an occupation are unparalleled in other sources; and the statistics based on it can be compared with the other studies based on censuses.

A second drawback derives from the use of a sample, rather than from the census itself. Because certain types of businesses were sometimes concentrated in specific streets or neighborhoods, the sample probably overlooks the variety of women's work. Still, there are several reasons to feel confident about the validity of the sample. Jorge González Angulo's study of artisans, the only work based on the entire 1811 census so far, located 1,018 seamstresses and 637 spinners who, by my estimates, represented roughly similar proportions of the work force as seamstresses and spinners in the sample.[5] Many of the conclusions about women's work are supported by other types of documents as well. And if the statistics in this chapter must be treated as approximations, they are nonetheless better than those we have had in the past.

Conclusions about nineteenth-century trends in particular

must remain tentative because the published summary totals of the 1790 census do not provide information on women's work and the 1848 census has spotty employment data, especially in the peripheral area of the sample. (One of the two census takers in the periphery excluded all women's occupations, reflecting the view that either women did not work or their work was unimportant. The other enumerated only employed adults, perhaps exclusively recording household heads. Omitting most young workers and the unemployed, his list cannot be used for studying the proportions of working women or their demographic characteristics, though it does illustrate the variety of adult women's occupations.) Therefore, for some calculations only the central sections of the 1811 and 1848 census samples can be directly compared (see Appendix A). Since this was an affluent neighborhood where most employed women were domestic servants, this area alone is far from representative of the city as a whole. The 1753 census of Mexico City, analyzed by Irene Vázquez Valle and Patricia Seed, does permit some discussion of long-term changes in women's work, though it provides less detail on working women than the 1811 count.

## The Division of Labor by Sex and Class

Women were far from marginal participants in the economy of Mexico City, for they constituted almost one-third of the labor force in the 1811 census sample (Table 14). This translates to some 20,500 women city-wide, or more than one-fourth of the urban female population. (Since so many of the female workers were young, the proportion of employed women was virtually the same whether based on the adult population or those age 15 and over: 28 percent vs. 27 percent.) Because of the deficiencies of the census, this figure undoubtedly underestimates the number of working women in Mexico City. Moreover, it omits the numerous Indian women from nearby villages who, entering the capital daily to sell fruits, vegetables, flowers, poultry, and fish, gave the city markets a distinctly female cast. Still, the level of female employment in the census sample was high even by twentieth-century standards.

Most identified female workers were lower class, for it was a sign of status for Mexican women not to work. Sewing for one's

TABLE 14

Employment of Females Age 18 and Over, 1753, 1811, and 1848

| Year | Total work force | Females | | | |
|---|---|---|---|---|---|
| | | Total number | Number employed | Percent employed | Percent of total work force |
| 1753 | 9,785 | 11,432 | 3,119 | 27.3% | 31.9% |
| 1811 | | | | | |
| Total sample | 1,057 | 1,221 | 327 | 26.8 | 30.9 |
| Central area only | 555 | 758 | 177 | 23.4 | 31.9 |
| 1848 | | | | | |
| Total sample | 876 | — | 321 | — | 36.6 |
| Central area only | 513 | 538 | 214 | 39.8 | 41.7 |

SOURCE: 1753. Irene Vázquez Valle, "Los habitantes de la ciudad de México vistos a través del censo del año de 1753" (M.A. thesis, El Colegio de México, 1975), pp. 397–98.

NOTE: All data for 1811 and 1848 in the tables in this chapter are from my Mexico City census samples unless otherwise noted. The groups studied across these tables may vary in size because the "unknowns" have been omitted. Percentages do not necessarily total 100 because of rounding.

own family was admirable, but to *coser lo ajeno*, or "sew for a stranger," was degrading, as doña María del Carmen Andrade lamented in her alimony suit, complaining bitterly of the "misfortune" of being obliged to work.[6] As Table 15 shows, employment clearly distinguished women of different social groups, though it was nearly universal for men. Among Spanish women age 15 and over only 13 percent listed an occupation, compared with 36 percent of the Caste and 46 percent of the Indian women. Thus Caste women were three times and Indian women nearly four times more likely to work than Spanish women. Because of these marked sectoral differences, it is in some ways misleading to argue that approximately one of every four women in Mexico City worked; the proportion was closer to out of two in the Indian group.

The majority of these women were domestic servants (listed as *sirvientes* and *criadas*), who represented 54 percent of the identified female workers in the 1811 census sample; if cooks and laundresses are included in this category as well, they represented 57 percent of the female work force. Domestic service was in fact the single largest occupational category in the entire urban economy, employing one of every four workers in Mexico City. The next largest group of female workers, 20 percent, were

TABLE 15

*Employment of the Population Age 15 and Over by Race and Marital Status, 1811*

| | Females | | | Males | | |
|---|---|---|---|---|---|---|
| Category | Total number | Number employed | Percent employed | Total number | Number employed | Percent employed |
| **Spanish** | | | | | | |
| Single | 266 | 36 | 13.5% | 203 | 140 | 69.0% |
| Married | 234 | 15 | 6.4 | 232 | 193 | 83.2 |
| Widowed | 163 | 32 | 19.6 | 65 | 41 | 63.0 |
| ALL MARITAL STATUSES | 663 | 83 | 12.5% | 500 | 374 | 74.8% |
| **Caste** | | | | | | |
| Single | 81 | 37 | 45.7% | 51 | 43 | 84.3% |
| Married | 81 | 19 | 23.5 | 78 | 69 | 88.5 |
| Widowed | 60 | 23 | 38.3 | 15 | 10 | 66.7 |
| ALL MARITAL STATUSES | 222 | 79 | 35.6% | 144 | 122 | 84.7% |
| **Indian** | | | | | | |
| Single | 142 | 94 | 66.2% | 92 | 70 | 84.8% |
| Married | 192 | 57 | 29.7 | 176 | 161 | 91.5 |
| Widowed | 104 | 49 | 47.1 | 27 | 22 | 81.5 |
| ALL MARITAL STATUSES | 438 | 200 | 45.7% | 295 | 261 | 88.5% |
| **All races** | | | | | | |
| Single | 489 | 167 | 34.2% | 346 | 261 | 75.4% |
| Married | 507 | 91 | 17.9 | 486 | 423 | 87.0 |
| Widowed | 327 | 104 | 31.8 | 107 | 73 | 68.2 |
| ALL MARITAL STATUSES | 1,323 | 362 | 27.4% | 939 | 757 | 80.6% |

involved in some aspect of the retail food industry. Preparing finished food products at home or buying fresh produce in bulk, they sold these goods from their homes, street corner stands, and market stalls. The pages of travelers' accounts and novels and the *costumbrista* paintings of the day depict these colorful vendors, the *tortilleras, atoleras, chieras, fruteras, tamaleras, trajineras, seberas, placeras, torteras,* "crying their wares and merchandise at the top of their voices."[7] All together, then, about three-quarters of the female workers in the 1811 census sample performed the same kinds of functions as housewives did for their families: keeping house, caring for children, and providing meals.

The others engaged in a variety of trades. They were *comer-*

8. Domestic service, the greatest source of employment for women in the nineteenth century, was considered humiliating work and was usually abandoned as soon as possible. Live-in household servants were likely to be young, single, and Indian; they were also likely to be newcomers to the capital.

*ciantes* who ran small neighborhood stores and *corredoras* who peddled jewelry, stockings, and combs from door to door. They were waitresses in *fondas*, *pulquerías*, and *mesones*. They worked in the Tobacco Factory, in small textile workshops, and in the city prisons and welfare institutions. Within their homes they sewed, took in laundry, salted hides, washed and spun cotton, embroidered, and made lace or ribbons and sometimes even shoes. They supplemented the established medical profession as midwives and curers, the *parteras* and *herbolarias* so much of the population preferred to the pharmacist and doctor. And as a perusal of nineteenth-century novels reminds us, they also worked as *caseras*, managing apartment buildings in exchange for free rent, and always informed of the neighbors' latest goings-on.

Although late colonial reformers attempted to increase women's employment, it appears that women in 1811 did not work in greater proportions than before. Vázquez Valle's analysis of the 1753 census, based on the population 18 years and over, shows that women were just under one-third of the identified labor force in 1753, as they were in 1811. Their rate of employment was virtually identical in both years, for some 27 percent of those 18 and over listed an occupation.[8] Despite the omission of many Indians from the earlier count, the female work force in 1753 was also similar in racial composition to the work force in 1811, with Indian women being nearly four times as likely to work as those of Spanish descent.[9] Since the 1753 enumeration omitted some areas on the city's periphery, the two censuses are not entirely comparable. But they suggest that the level of women's employment had remained roughly stable over half a century.

One thing had apparently changed, however. Women's work was more diversified by 1811. In 1753, fully 88 percent of all identified female workers fell into just two occupational categories: domestic servants (77 percent) and seamstresses (11 percent).[10] In contrast, though domestic service was still the most important occupation for women in 1811, only 54 percent of them were now so employed; and seamstresses now constituted just 3 percent of the female labor force. At the same time, the proportion of women in other trades more than tripled, from 12 percent to 43 percent. Thus women's job opportunities had expanded along the lines that reformers desired.

In some cases this meant entering trades formerly restricted to male guild members. According to the 1811 census sample, women constituted 30 percent of the apprentices, 13 percent of the weavers, and 6 percent of the cobblers. An odd woman here and there was listed as a candlemaker, dollmaker, or mattress maker, trades also regulated by artisan guilds. In 1805 one woman in Orizaba (Veracruz) became a master in the wax workers' guild—an event heralded by much fanfare in the capital's press. She was one of the very few women in the historical record who actually joined a guild; most female artisans worked entirely outside the guild structure.[11]

The entry of women into traditionally male fields may be partly attributed to the 1799 decree, though to some extent the decree

## TABLE 16
### Sexual Division of Labor, Selected Occupations, 1811 and 1848

| | 1811 | | | 1848 | | |
|---|---|---|---|---|---|---|
| | Total in occupational group (males and females) | Females | | Total in occupational group (males and females) | Females | |
| Occupation | | Number | Percent of total | | Number | Percent of total |
| Service | | | | | | |
| Laundress (lavandera) | 5 | 5 | 100.0% | 27 | 27 | 100.0% |
| Servant (sirviente)[a] | 298 | 218 | 73.2 | 164 | 122 | 74.4 |
| Cook (cocinera) | 15 | 9 | 60.0 | 12 | 12 | 100.0 |
| Porter (portero) | 4 | 0 | 0.0 | 18 | 10 | 55.6 |
| Food production and sale | | | | | | |
| Miller (molendera) | 35 | 35 | 100.0% | 67 | 67 | 100.0% |
| Tortilla maker (tortillera) | 17 | 17 | 100.0 | 3 | 3 | 100.0 |
| Torta vendor (tortera) | 13 | 13 | 100.0 | 0 | 0 | — |
| Atole vendor (atolera) | 4 | 4 | 100.0 | 2 | 2 | 100.0 |
| Fruit vendor (frutera) | 4 | 3 | 75.0 | 11 | 7 | 63.6 |
| Sweets vendor (dulcera) | 6 | 2 | 33.3 | 8 | 3 | 37.5 |
| Baker (panadero) | 6 | 0 | 0.0 | 41 | 1 | 2.4 |
| Crafts | | | | | | |
| Seamstress (costurera) | 11 | 11 | 100.0% | 56 | 56 | 100.0% |
| Spinner (hilandera) | 37 | 30 | 81.1 | 3 | 1 | 33.3 |
| Apprentice (aprendiz) | 23 | 7 | 30.4 | 8 | 0 | 0.0 |
| Weaver (tejedor) | 32 | 4 | 12.5 | 24 | 0 | 0.0 |
| Cobbler (zapatero) | 51 | 3 | 5.9 | 50 | 0 | 0.0 |
| Tailor (sastre) | 40 | 0 | 0.0 | 24 | 0 | 0.0 |
| Miscellaneous | | | | | | |
| Tobacconist (estanquera)[b] | 7 | 5 | 71.4% | 8 | 7 | 87.5% |
| Apartment manager (casera) | 17 | 10 | 58.8 | 3 | 2 | 66.7 |
| TOTAL WORK FORCE | 1,255 | 406 | 32.4% | 1,107 | 402 | 36.3% |

NOTE: The Spanish names of the occupations vary according to gender, in most cases ending with "a" for women and "o" for men. [a]Includes criadas, domésticas, recamareras, and amas de llaves. [b]Includes the variant estanquillera.

itself reflected the weakening of the guilds. During the eighteenth century it was not uncommon for widows and daughters of deceased artisans to take over their shops. The guilds countenanced this practice for one year after a member's death (so that his widow or daughter could use up his materials) or for a longer period, if his son was preparing to join the guild.[12] Otherwise, they lodged complaints against women engaged in craft manufactures, as they had against doña Josefa de Celis, the shoe embroiderer who initiated the process leading to the landmark ruling. The *Artesanos y Gremios* records in the Municipal Archive show that guild officials pressured these women to marry or hire accredited craftsmen to be in charge of their shops. Some female "interlopers," complaining that they could not afford to hire guild members, continued to operate workshops on their own.[13] Thus by the late eighteenth century, female artisans were already challenging the guilds, but the women were subject to harassment and ineligible for formal apprenticeships until the royal decree removed legal barriers to their training, employment, and freedom to market their wares.

Still, the degree of diversification of women's work should not be overemphasized. Although by 1811 women were beginning to benefit from the end of legal discrimination, they were still concentrated in the trades long defined as appropriate for their sex. And they continued to be barred from the clergy, the military, and the government bureaucracy—the three careers with the most opportunity for upward mobility. Even in the newly opened crafts the sexual division of labor bore the imprint of the guild system. Twelve years after the decree, only 5 percent of all working women were engaged in a trade formerly regulated by the guilds. As shown in Table 16, for example, all of the chocolate millers and tortilla makers listed in the 1811 census sample were female, but bakers (a guild occupation) were exclusively male. Similarly, because the primary stage of processing raw materials had not been regulated, women continued to prepare materials for use by male guild members, salting hides for the leather workers and spinning thread for the weavers.[14] (Although there had been a silk-spinners' guild, spinning was considered women's work to such an extent that this was the only Mexican guild to organize women; but by 1811 it existed in name only, owing to the decline of silk production in the face of Philippine imports.[15]) Women were also active in the cigar industry (never regulated by a guild), both as cigar makers in the Tobacco Factory and as *estanquilleras*, the tobacconists who sold cigars and snuff in government-licensed shops.

In some cases the reason why certain occupations employed women and others did not defies logic, since women did not predominate in all the trades that had been outside the purview of the guilds. Although women were rarely manual laborers, the sexual division of labor was not always related to the physical difficulty of the tasks. As one English visitor remarked with amazement, brawny fellows "with mustachios" might be found making flowers in a millinery shop, attesting to the legacy of the milliners' guild, while next door "a number of poor girls [were] on their knees on the floor, engaged in the laborious occupation of grinding chocolate."[16] Whereas atole, tortilla, and torta vendors were always female, fruit and sweets vendors might be male. Men and women were evenly divided among those who sewed, but men were called tailors and organized themselves in guilds, and women were called seamstresses and did not. Only women did laundry work, but many men worked as domestic servants and cooks. Both sexes worked as apartment managers, though caseras were so often women that they were portrayed as feminine "types"—along with chambermaids, refreshment vendors, midwives, seamstresses, and tobacconists —in a mid-nineteenth-century book depicting popular figures of the period.[17]

This division of labor persisted in 1848 with two important differences: the decline in domestic servants continued and the increase in female artisans did not. The proportion of working women listed as maids decreased from 54 percent to 30 percent; if laundresses, cooks, and porters are included in that category, the proportion dropped somewhat less, from 57 percent to 43 percent.[18] Women in commerce, food preparation, and various service trades offset this decline. For example, seamstresses increased from 3 percent to 14 percent of the women listing an occupation. Meanwhile, female artisans working in guild-regulated trades declined from 5 percent to a mere 1 percent of the identified female labor force. Women had in fact disappeared altogether from the two categories of weavers and apprentices.[19]

It is, of course, possible that the decline in female artisans represents a change in the nature of the sample neighborhoods, for as production and sale became separated, artisans moved out of the increasingly commercialized city center.[20] But it is unlikely that this process, already under way by 1811, proceeded quickly enough in the next four decades to explain all the decline between 1811 and 1848. Indeed, it appears to have been more precipitous in the peripheral neighborhood—to which artisans would presumably be moving—than in the center, for in the peripheral section of the sample female artisans decreased from 9 percent to 3 percent of all identified working women (in the center they held steady at 1 percent). And the decline in servants is also evident in the central section alone, where they decreased from 87 percent to 30 percent of the working women (or 91 percent to 43 percent, if laundresses, cooks, and porters are included).[21]

What the evidence so far available suggests is that if women had begun to move into formerly male crafts in 1811, they had backed off by 1848, being even more concentrated in traditionally female areas than four decades earlier. This interpretation seems all the more plausible because women's entry into artisan trades elicited no comment from republican writers, as it had in the late colonial period. It therefore appears that the expansion of women into new trades had not progressed very far before it was halted, and even reversed, by the recession and high male unemployment that plagued the Mexican republic.

These same economic difficulties may have caused more women to seek work in 1848 than before. Women rose from 32 percent of the labor force age 18 and over in 1811 to 37 percent in 1848. In the central neighborhood alone they increased from 35 percent of all workers to 42 percent.[22] There was an even more dramatic expansion of employed women as a share of all women. In the center, the only neighborhood in which such a calculation can be made for 1848, 40 percent of women aged 18 and over listed an occupation in that year, compared with 23 percent in 1811. These conclusions, based on only two areas of the city, need to be substantiated by further research. It is nonetheless reasonable to expect that if fewer women worked as domestic servants because the financially strapped middle classes could not afford to hire them, then more women would be forced by the same economic pinch to earn a livelihood, especially because there were more widows who had to support themselves in 1848 than in 1811. Still, these differences were but subtle shadings of the general picture in which a high level of female employment had been a constant feature for at least a century.

It is clear that many women of the lower classes had not been secluded even at a time when society considered it best for women to be separated from public life, and when nunneries and retirement houses vigorously embodied that goal. But what about the middle-class women, to whom the declining ideal of seclusion mainly applied? There is some evidence that during the nineteenth century these women began to move into the labor force in increasing numbers. The proportion of middle-class working women was so small, however, that the trend was not registered in the census samples and is therefore difficult to quantify.

A few women of the middle classes had traditionally been shopkeepers, an occupation more prestigious than manual labor and usually performed out of *accesorias* attached to their homes. Women continued to operate shops during the nineteenth century, but there is no evidence that they did so more than before. An 1854 guide to Mexico City, the *Guía de forasteros de la ciudad de Mégico*, which lists the most highly regarded commercial establishments, suggests that few women were engaged in commerce at that date. Women owned only 121, or 7 percent, of the 1,734 businesses listed. To be sure, the guide is far from comprehensive. Women were probably more prevalent in the poorer establishments that did not make the list. And they were apparently prominent as owners of illegal taverns, another category obviously excluded, for Michael Scardaville's research shows that women, mostly Spanish, ran approximately half of the 850 such establishments from their homes.[23] In addition, the guide would not have listed women who managed restaurants and other businesses, receiving a fixed salary from the owner,[24] or those who worked in their husbands' shops, in which they presumably had a stake as part of the community property, or those who owned businesses in partnerships listed under "Hermanos" or "Cía." Despite these omissions, however, there is no doubt that women were a distinct minority of shopkeepers in the city's most highly capitalized businesses.

9. Shopkeeping was one of the few careers open to middle-class women. The shopkeeper here, a tobacconist (*estanquillera*), is perhaps fortunate enough to have a government-licensed shop, for such an *estanco* might turn a tidy profit, allowing her to retreat into the respectability of her home while a subordinate ran the business. The right to an estanco was eagerly sought by the widows and daughters of deceased government employees; it was often preferred to a government pension that might be paid only irregularly.

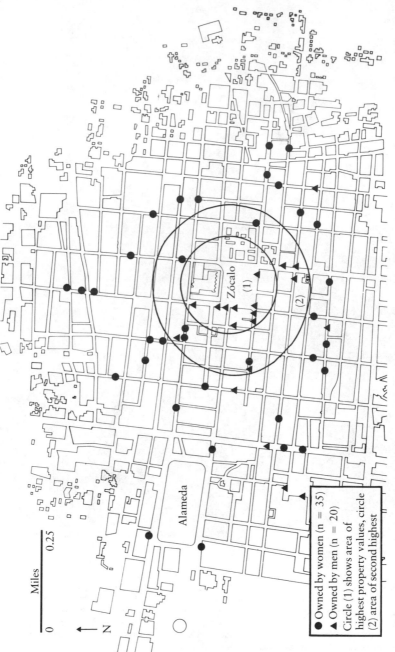

Fig. 6. Location of Mexico City *sederías*, 1854. Sources: *Guía de forasteros. . .; (Mexico City, 1854), pp. 292–94; property values based on María Dolores Morales, "Estructura urbana y distribución de la propiedad en la cd. de México en 1813," *Historia Mexicana*, 25, 3 (Jan.–Mar. 1976): 394 (Fig. 5), and in consultation with the author. The *sederías* are accurately positioned by the block in most cases but not within the blocks. Three male-owned shops could not be located.

The guide tells us little about the nature of these enterprises. We do not even know whether all of them were retail stores; some may have been workshops, or *fábricas*, as they were called at the time. Nor do we know whether the women listed as owners were middle class; some may have been extremely wealthy women who owned but did not manage their businesses, and some may have been artisans who might not have been considered *gente decente* by their contemporaries. We do know that the largest share of female businesses listed was in the clothing industry, where women owned 18 percent of the shops, including 22 of 24 *cajones de modistas* (dressmakers' shops), 35 of 58 *sederías* (cloth, or perhaps exclusively silk, shops), and 6 of 55 *rebocerías* (shawl shops). They also owned 6 of 46 bathhouses, 6 of 56 candle factories, 8 of 105 pawn shops, and 2 of 48 shoe stores. Despite their importance in feeding the city, women owned surprisingly few food-processing operations: 6 of 14 noodle factories, but only one of 39 bread bakeries, one of 55 pastry shops, one of 11 chocolate factories, and 2 of 30 *tocinerías* (where pork was processed and sold). Women also owned few restaurants: only one of 15 *fondas*, and none of the cafes and *mesones* listed.

On the whole, female businesses appear to have been less prosperous than men's, and run by women of the lower-middle class. When the *sederías* are located on the map of Mexico City, for example, a clear pattern emerges of men owning the majority of the elegant, centrally located shops, with women predominating in the more modest, peripherally located establishments (Fig. 6). A few successful dressmakers did open shops in prestigious commercial areas catering to a wealthy clientele. One was the Frenchwoman doña Eugenia Segault, who separated from her tailor husband don Pedro Ouvrard in 1829 and set up her own shop on the Calle de Plateros.[25] In fact, judging by the last names listed in the guide, all but two of the female owners of dressmakers' shops in 1854 were likewise foreign, most of them French. This impression is reinforced by Fanny Calderón's comments on the French *modistes* who outfitted her friends, in her opinion "persuading them into all sorts of follies."[26] Apparently, at least after foreigners began arriving in Mexico after independence, Mexican women failed to join the ranks of the highly regarded modistes because of the prejudice in favor of Europeans and their fashions. In any case, if running a dressmaking shop might have represented upward mobility for a poor seamstress, it was not considered a desirable step for women of the middle classes.

Other sources provide scattered evidence of additional enterprises operated by women. Doña María Dolores Zepeda, "wife of Don Pedro Gómez," for example, advertised her special medical potion, available at her home, in the *Gazeta de México*. At least three women, apparently widows, owned publishing houses or printing shops in the first half of the nineteenth century and, according to Secretary to the U. S. Legation Brantz Mayer, a former marchioness ran the Hotel Vergara in the 1840's. (However, taking in boarders was uncommon in upper- or middle-class households, though clerks and apprentices might live in an employer's home.) The rarity of such activities is suggested by the fact that none of the hotels or printing shops listed in the 1854 guide were female-owned.[27]

Still, middle-class women in straitened circumstances sometimes had no choice but to work. Such was the case for three of the wives who were in the midst of divorce proceedings. One had a maid sell embroidery and sweetmeats that she herself made. The others opened *fábricas de rebozos* in their homes, probably because the primitive looms required so little capital outlay.[28] One of the shops wove silk consigned by a merchant capitalist; of the other we know only that it wove and embroidered "cloth, shawls, and other pieces of this sort." We do know that all three women worked with the greatest reluctance. The first refused to deal with the public directly, and the other two only supervised production, which they considered beneath them, hiring female operatives to do the actual weaving. The stigma of working was so great in this class that doña Plácida Herrera, owner of one of the textile shops, attempted to dispel the suspicion of the working woman's virtue by insisting that she "lived in the utmost retirement, without going out day or night."[29]

A few "respectable" jobs opened for middle-class women when welfare institutions were founded by enlightened officials in the second half of the eighteenth century. The Foundling Home, the Poor House, and municipal hospitals all employed women to supervise the female sections and teach the female inmatcs. Although there were only a handful of these positions, petitions to the city government suggest that they were in much demand.[30] These jobs displayed a characteristic that would mark the other new middle-class occupation as well: they employed women to provide services exclusively for a female clientele rather than for the population at large.

The most important career that increasingly opened to middle-class Mexican women was teaching, the "recourse of the unfortunate woman . . . forced to support herself with honor."[31] In the eighteenth century the amigas who taught young children were decidedly *déclassées*, though they earned enough to place them in the lower middle class.[32] Portrayed by contemporaries as ignorant old babysitters, some of the amigas were Indians and Castes, to the chagrin of the municipal authorities who issued licenses for schools and insisted that school mistresses be of "pure blood." The teaching profession began to be upgraded with the establishment of the Company of Mary in 1753; young ladies who wished to be teachers thereafter took religious vows. Then, with the expansion of primary education for girls, the demand for secular teachers grew. Because public education improved slowly, and because women did not teach boys at that level, there were probably no more than 150 female teachers in Mexico City at the middle of the nineteenth century. Although they were strikingly few in comparison with Europe and the United States (in New England, for example, it is estimated that one-fifth of all white married women had taught school in their youth), they represent a sevenfold increase from 1753, when the municipal census listed only 21 female teachers, and twice the number registered in 1802.[33] For the women involved, the rising quality of female schooling brought respect and prestige, especially when it involved the instruction of older girls.

As with the successful dressmakers, many of the women who ran the most fashionable schools were foreign, especially from the 1840's on. To be sure, the majority of the 55 female primary school teachers in the 1854 guide to Mexico City had Spanish surnames, and a few Mexican teachers achieved some renown, as did doña Guadalupe Silva, whose school was visited by President Guadalupe Victoria in 1826.[34] Most advertisements for girls' schools in the city's newspapers, as well as many applications to the city government for teaching licenses, however, were placed by women with such non-Hispanic surnames as Gregoria Pleimbert, Dolores Chivilini, Cecilia Poulet—or Isaura de San-Vital who, "having just returned from New York," had the "honor of announcing to the capital's mothers" her Casa Francesa for girls.[35] The prevalence of foreign women in teaching, as in dressmaking, reflects the unwillingness of Mexican middle- and upper-class women to take on wage work even though their services might be in demand.

But this does not mean that all such women were necessarily "house prisoners" isolated from the business world.[36] Since nuns monopolized some jobs in welfare institutions and teaching, a few elite women who wished to devote themselves to a career took religious vows; many others were involved in the investment and management of their inheritances. Prominent among city landlords, women held one-fourth of all privately owned buildings in the capital in 1813; indeed, two of them, doña Hipólita Giral and the marchioness del Apartado, were among the 41 largest property holders in that year.[37] Women were thus involved in buying, selling, renting, attempting to collect rent on, or evicting delinquent tenants from houses and apartment buildings throughout the city. Women who lived in Mexico City also owned rural estates along with profitable businesses like slaughterhouses and bakeries.[38] They might take an active role in administering these enterprises; the countess of Regla even scolded the supervisor of her hacienda for trying to tell her what to do, assuring him that she would always do as she saw fit.[39] It bears repeating, however, that they left the daily management of these enterprises to subordinates.

Such business endeavors were probably most prevalent among the capital's wealthiest women. Linked to the inheritance system that divided property evenly among daughters and sons, activities of this sort were acceptable extensions of family responsibilities. Consequently, doña María Josefa Adalid did not consider it beneath her to advertise in an 1852 city directory that "very fine bottled pulque" from her country estate could be purchased at her home, a mansion situated on the capital's elegant Calle de Cadena.[40] Moreover, since these enterprises did not require the owner's full-time attention, they did not conflict with domestic roles.

TABLE 17
*Notarial Transactions, 1803–1853*

| Year | Females | | | Males | | |
|---|---|---|---|---|---|---|
| | Number of trans- actions | Percent wills | Percent powers of attorney | Number of trans- actions | Percent wills | Percent powers of attorney |
| 1803 | 78 | 28.2% | 41.0% | 289 | 11.4% | 56.0% |
| 1827 | 112 | 9.8 | 43.8 | 287 | 5.6 | 52.6 |
| 1853 | 111 | 4.5 | 38.0 | 276 | 3.6 | 37.7 |
| TOTAL 1803–53 | 301 | 12.6% | 41.2% | 852 | 6.9% | 48.9% |

SOURCE: Transactions sample, Appendix B.
NOTE: Only transactions signed by women alone have been considered "female," not those transacted for women by their attorneys. Excludes 47 transactions signed by couples or representing convent business.

Because well-to-do women did not conceive of themselves as having an occupation, their business activities were not recorded in municipal censuses. But a random sample of 1,200 notarial transactions for the years 1803, 1827, and 1853 (Appendix B) reveals that women signed every type of notarized business instrument; although elite women were not the only ones represented in those records, they were in the majority. All told, women signed just over a quarter of these documents. Like men, they most frequently sought the services of a notary either to make a will or to grant a power of attorney (Table 17). But almost half the female transactions involved other sorts of activities: executing an estate, buying or selling property, borrowing or lending money, accepting guardianship of children or grandchildren, and so forth.[41]

Perhaps because of the instability of republican life, which increased the incidence of widowhood and sent some wealthy men into temporary exile or prolonged residence in Spain, women were slightly more active after independence than before, signing 28 percent of the notarial instruments in 1827 and 1853 as compared with 21 percent in 1803. Elite women also took advantage of new republican business opportunities for, as in most recessions, those with capital could profit from others' difficulties. Thus women were among those who bought Church property and speculated in urban real estate, and, though most lent money at 5 or 6 percent interest, women could also be found among the *agiotistas* who lent money to the government at usurious rates.[42]

In fact, as new opportunities arose, wills decreased from 28 percent to a mere 5 percent of the female transactions.

Women's business activities are also reflected in civil court records, where they were involved as either plaintiff or defendant in 345 of 1,150 cases examined for the first half of the nineteenth century.[43] Although women went to court to enforce a variety of personal rights—or were brought to court charged with everything from drunkenness to physical assault[44]—most of the civil court cases involved economic matters, with women suing or being sued to recover debts, widows and daughters challenging the division of an estate, and occasionally even orphaned minors charging the administrators of their estates with mishandling their inheritances.

None of these documents tells us much about what these business activities meant to elite women. On the one hand, it is possible to find competent and enterprising women like doña María Ana Gómez de la Cortina, whose husband trusted her with his power of attorney and whose biographer praised her business acumen; on the other, there were women who relied wholly on their husband's advice, allowing him to represent them in all financial dealings and having little idea of what they owned when they became widows.[45] Some property owners like the countess of Regla personally directed their affairs, and others were owners only in name, like doña Dolores Escandón, whose brother, about to leave for exile, gave her his businesses, still administered by his partner, merely as a way to protect them.[46] But interestingly enough, women appear not to have named others to represent them any more often than men, who in fact granted powers of attorney at a slightly higher rate. What is clear is that, even if some wealthy women preferred to relinquish control over their property, many were nevertheless involved in economic pursuits.

## A Demographic Portrait of Women Workers

The traditional literature gives the impression that the Mexican women who entered the labor force or business world were usually widows, and occasionally orphans—that in normal circumstances families lived on the earnings of their male head.

The implication is that women's work was exceptional or merely supplemental. The census data, however, show that this was not the case for most working women. Not only was the loss of a spouse far from exceptional, but the likelihood of a woman's working depended as much on her place of birth and age as on her marital status, and it depended most of all on her class. In the absence of documents telling us how women felt about their work, an examination of these factors not only tells us who the working women were, but also suggests why they may have worked.

Some members of all social classes appear to have accepted the ideal of the man as the sole breadwinner and the woman as the homemaker. In ecclesiastical divorce records we find evidence of the strains that sometimes arose over the wife's employment. Many men were flatly opposed to their wives' working. The tailor don Pedro Ouvrard, for one, complained of his wife's dealing "with everyone under the sun in the guise of doing business in a public store." And don Pedro Padilla, resolving a long-standing bone of contention, agreed to hire "persons of confidence" to run his store so that his wife "would never have to attend to customers, and could always remain in the interior of the house, dedicating herself to the care of our children and the fulfillment of her other duties." At the same time, women like María Rita Gómez used their husbands' inability to support them as an argument that they were unfit spouses. María, whose humble status precluded the title of doña in her divorce papers, complained that she was forced "to labor ceaselessly" because of her husband's "absolute indifference to one of his principal duties, which is to provide for our subsistence and clothing."[47]

Yet work and marriage were not mutually exclusive for women, since one-fourth of all working women were listed as married. Marriage did, however, reduce the chances of a woman's working: when employed women of each marital status are compared with their share in the population age 15 and over, it is evident that married women were the least likely to work (Table 15). Single and widowed women were in fact nearly twice as likely to work as wives. These differences sharply distinguished the sexes, for most men of all marital statuses, like most men of all classes, were part of the labor force.

The correlation between marital status and employment was strongest among Spanish women. In that group, where men's earnings were normally sufficient to maintain a family, it was rare for a wife or daughter to work. Thus it was widows who predominated among Spanish working women, in contrast to the other two groups, where single women predominated. Indeed, Spanish widows were nearly four times more likely to work than wives, and one-and-a-half times more likely than single women. Other sources tend to confirm this picture. For example, Tanck Estrada found that though a few couples opened schools together (with the husband teaching boys and the wife teaching girls), most teachers were self-supporting spinsters and widows.[48] Similarly, the census of the Poor House in 1848 lists the four middle-class women who worked there (the Rectora de Niñas, the Rectora de Ancianas, the Maestra de Bordado, and the Maestra de Primeras Letras) as widows (and relatively young ones, from 28 to 41 years of age).[49] In the Spanish population, then, it appears that women entered the labor force only when obliged to by the loss of the male breadwinner. It is therefore likely that the 6 percent of Spanish wives who listed an occupation in the 1811 census sample were abandoned, separated, or married to disabled men. Their employment, like that of spinsters and widows alone in the world, could scarcely be called supplemental because these women were the sole support of themselves and their families; it was, however, exceptional.

The picture was not so simple among the Castes and Indians, where employment levels were more uniform for women of different marital statuses. Although in both groups the married women worked less than the single and widowed, even Caste and Indian wives were more likely to work than Spanish widows, the most widely employed of Spanish women. Among the Indians, for example, nearly one-third of all wives, one-half of all widows, and fully two-thirds of all single women listed an occupation, compared with only one-fifth of all Spanish widows. Social background thus differentiated women's chances of working far more than did marital status.

Although Caste and Indian wives may have shared the ideal of domesticity, they could not always afford the luxury of devoting themselves exclusively to family and home. In the 1840's, ac-

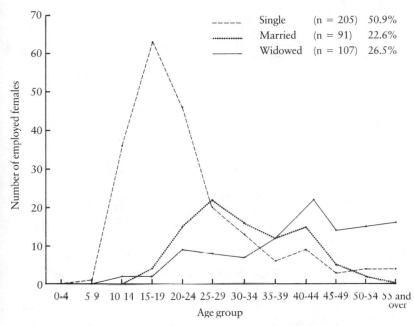

Fig.7. Female employment by age and marital status, 1811. Excludes five females whose age or marital status is unknown.

cording to Frederick Shaw's estimates, the adult male artisan or manual laborer rarely earned enough to provide for a family of four;[50] many families therefore could not subsist without the wife's earnings. So the work of these women cannot be characterized as merely supplemental to that of the male breadwinner, even though the women may have considered it secondary to their roles as wife and mother. In the lower classes, where there was no family wage, the very concept of the sole male breadwinner may not have applied.

There is some evidence that lower-class women preferred to stop working when they married. Figure 7 shows that the majority of female workers were young and single, and their numbers dipped dramatically at about 23 years—the mean age at marriage. Josefa Vitorero's petition to the Tobacco Factory in 1815 likewise suggests that many lower-class women saw work as a young woman's affair, to be left behind with matrimony

TABLE 18
*Employment of Mothers with Children Living at Home*
*by Race and Marital Status, 1811*

| Category | Total number of mothers | Employed mothers | | |
|---|---|---|---|---|
| | | Number | Percent of mothers | Percent of employed females |
| Race | | | | |
| Spanish | 236 | 18 | 7.6% | 19.8% |
| Caste | 84 | 23 | 27.4 | 26.4 |
| Indian | 164 | 55 | 33.5 | 23.1 |
| ALL RACES | 484 | 96 | 19.8% | 23.1% |
| Marital status | | | | |
| Single | 17 | 6 | 35.3% | 2.9% |
| Married | 333 | 52 | 15.6 | 56.6 |
| Widowed | 137 | 37 | 27.0 | 34.6 |
| ALL STATUSES | 487 | 95 | 19.6% | 23.5% |

whenever possible. Explaining that she had worked in the factory until her marriage, Josefa asked that her single daughter be employed there now, since her husband was sick and no longer able to earn a living.[51]

Those women who did not leave their jobs when they married often did when they had children. As shown in Table 18, mothers with children living at home at the time of the census enumeration entered the labor force less often than other women—and this pattern holds for women of every racial group. Still, nearly one of three Caste and Indian mothers declared an occupation. Here again, as in the case of married women, it was Spanish mothers who were most able to attain the domestic ideal, for only one of thirteen Spanish mothers claimed a trade.

If marriage and motherhood ended some women's employment, for others it simply shifted the types of jobs they took. Young, single women usually entered domestic service; indeed, three-fourths of all employed single women were maids in 1811. Their distribution by age and marital status (Table 19) suggests that they left their jobs when they married and had children, and their places were not filled by women in older age groups. Married women who continued to work instead chose jobs that allowed them to live in separate households with their families. Domestic service alone did not, since only rarely did a family

## TABLE 19
Female Live-in Domestic Servants and Other Female Workers by Age and Marital Status, 1811

| Category | Age 15–24 | | Age 25–34 | | Age 35–44 | | Age 45–54 | |
|---|---|---|---|---|---|---|---|---|
| | Number | Percent | Number | Percent | Number | Percent | Number | Percent |
| Servants[a] | | | | | | | | |
| Single | 80 | 87.9% | 19 | 54.3% | 13 | 37.1% | 5 | 26.3% |
| Married | 5 | 5.5 | 7 | 20.0 | 2 | 5.7 | 2 | 10.5 |
| Widowed | 6 | 6.6 | 9 | 25.7 | 20 | 57.1 | 12 | 63.2 |
| TOTAL | 91 | 100.0% | 35 | 100.0% | 35 | 99.9% | 19 | 100.0% |
| Other workers | | | | | | | | |
| Single | 29 | 60.4% | 14 | 27.5% | 2 | 4.9% | 2 | 8.3% |
| Married | 14 | 29.2 | 31 | 60.8 | 25 | 61.0 | 5 | 20.8 |
| Widowed | 5 | 10.4 | 6 | 11.8 | 14 | 34.2 | 17 | 70.8 |
| TOTAL | 48 | 100.0% | 51 | 100.1% | 41 | 100.1% | 24 | 99.9% |

[a]Includes sirvientes, criadas, domésticas, amas de llaves, and recamareras.

serve together in a master's house (only 2 percent of maids served with their husbands in 1811 and only 7 percent brought a child with them). Although some older widows returned to domestic service, perhaps because they found shelter in a master's household, married women avoided it whenever possible.

The profile of domestic servants therefore contrasts considerably with that of working women in other trades. In 1811 only 7 percent of female servants were married, compared with 41 percent of the others, and servants were much younger, with a median age of 22 compared with 30 for the others. In 1848 also, where reliable demographic data are available only for domestic servants, they were predominantly young, single women (Table 20). In both years approximately two-thirds of the female servants were under 30, and two-thirds were also single.

Because so many of the married working women were self-employed, they were able to combine household duties with work, supervising their offspring while they spun thread, cooked meals to sell, operated small stores out of their homes, or peddled their wares on the city streets. Those who worked in the Tobacco Factory could also bring their children along (673 children accompanied their mothers in 1794). Some of these children may have helped to increase their mother's output, which was paid by the piece, but nurses were provided to care for the youngest, and older children could attend school in the factory during the workday. Because of these facilities, a relatively high number of married women were apparently employed in cigar manufacturing as well as in casual home-based trades.[52] We cannot therefore conclude, as has been argued for Europe, that factory work in Mexico City introduced a new conflict between women's productive and reproductive roles;[53] that conflict had already existed in domestic service, and was in fact attenuated in the Tobacco Factory because of the State's paternalistic attitude toward its employees.

If marriage and motherhood did not preclude economic activities for many women of the lower classes, it often caused their employment to be temporary or irregular, coinciding with periods of their lives when they were not bearing children or caring for infants. These patterns are reflected in the age breakdown of

TABLE 20
*Female Live-in Domestic Servants by Place of Origin,*
*Marital Status, and Age, 1848*

| Category | Number | Percent | Category | Number | Percent |
|---|---|---|---|---|---|
| Place of origin | | | Age group | | |
| Migrant | 63 | 52.9% | 10–19 | 50 | 42.0% |
| City-born | 56 | 47.1 | 20–29 | 34 | 28.6 |
| | | | 30–39 | 16 | 13.4 |
| Marital status | | | 40–49 | 12 | 10.1 |
| Single | 85 | 70.8% | 50 and over | 7 | 5.9 |
| Married | 6 | 5.0 | TOTAL ALL | | |
| Widowed | 29 | 24.2 | CATEGORIES | 120 | 100.0% |

NOTE: Based on central section of the census sample only. "Servant" includes sirvientes, criadas, domésticas, recamareras, amas de llaves.

working women in 1811. Although the largest group of female workers was young and single, the increase in employed women from the ages of 35 to 44 suggests that some wives and especially widows returned to the labor force after their children had grown up, or at least after a daughter was old enough to mind her younger siblings. Few women were able to work after the age of 55, however, forcing many to rely on children or charity for support.

These trends in female employment over the life cycle again suggest that we should not think in terms of only one-fourth of urban women working; in the lower classes, where close to half the women worked at any one time, nearly all women were employed at some point in their lives, usually when they were young and single and, for some, intermittently thereafter. In the Caste and Indian groups, women's work was thus hardly exceptional.

The prevalence of young girls in the work force indicates that the majority of single workers were not lifelong spinsters obliged to support themselves for lack of a male breadwinner. On the contrary, as shown in Chapter Three, spinsterhood was most widespread in the Spanish population where women worked the least. In fact, only 26 percent of the women who remained unmarried in the 45–54 age group listed an occupation. An even smaller proportion of the single women who headed their own households claimed a trade (22 percent; Table D.8). Their level of employment was thus somewhat lower than that of the female population as a whole.

Insofar as two-thirds of all employed single women were under the age of 25, they were more likely to be daughters contributing their earnings to the parental household than orphans alone in the world. Indeed, a teacher in one of the Indian barrios of the city complained that parents regularly took their "frail daughters" out of school, preferring them to "earn a half *real* or one *real*" making tortillas or working in shops.[54] Although he insinuated that the parents' desire for greater income was frivolous, and that they would be better served by educating their children, the families' inability to subsist on a single wage gave them little alternative; a girl's wages were particularly crucial when, as often happened, the family was headed by a widowed or abandoned mother. Since lower-class families could not easily forgo their daughters' earnings, it is difficult to classify such employment as supplemental, as though these girls were working merely for pin money.

The age patterns of female employment show how childhood and old age differed for women of different social groups. The few Spanish working women in the 1811 census sample began working later and retired sooner than the Castes and Indians, since Spanish parents were better able to support their children, and Spanish adults had a better chance of accumulating savings, receiving pensions, or finding relatives able to help them in their old age. The youngest employed female, a nine-year-old servant girl, was Caste; five other girls entered the work force at 10; by 12 childhood was over for many more, for 20 percent of all 12-year-old girls listed an employment. Indian girls worked at the highest rate: 38 percent had already entered the labor force between the ages of 10 and 14, making them almost five times more likely to work than Spanish girls of that age. By age 15–24 the majority (55 percent) of Indian girls worked, compared with 40 percent of the Caste and 14 percent of the Spanish girls. Since employment for young girls usually meant leaving home to work as maids, Spanish women were able to remain with their families longer, probably moving out only to marry; the transition to adulthood began sooner for Indian girls. The disparities in women's experiences were even more marked when they reached old age: approximately one-third of the Indian women 55 and over still had to work to survive, compared with less than 5 percent of the elderly women of Spanish descent (Table D.7).

These sectoral age patterns distinguished women from men, for whom work was a constant throughout their adult lives, until they too began to retire as they approached 60, a respectable old age for the time. Because boys received more secondary schooling, they tended to enter the labor force later than girls. Although more men than women worked in every age group, the percentage of women who worked was highest from the ages of 15 to 19, the age group (not including those under 15) in which it was lowest for men. Working men were consequently older on average than working women: their median age was 30, compared with 26 for women. As in the other aspects of their working experiences, these differences were more pronounced for women of different ethnic groups than for men.

This portrait of working women suggests that employment was not a happy prospect for women of the lower classes; despite the satisfaction and sociability some may have found in their work, most appear to have been driven into the labor force out of pure need. Although the majority of working women (56 percent) were Indians, they were not, as a group, the most desperately poor; that status was reserved for rural villagers fleeing the crises in the Mexican countryside. Of all women, migrants were the most likely to be employed. As Table 21 shows clearly, they predominated among female workers of all racial groups, marital statuses, and ages in the 1811 census sample. The differences were greatest in the 15–24 age group (the group with the highest female participation in the labor force), where 42 percent of the migrants listed an occupation, compared with only 26 percent of the city-born—and where fully 65 percent of the Indian migrants did so, compared with only 48 percent of the city-born Indian women. The prevalence of migrants among working women suggests that the opportunity for jobs drew many provincial women to the capital in the first place. Their extreme need set them apart from women born in Mexico City, who reflected their families' greater prosperity by working less.

The vast majority of migrants, who were young and single,

TABLE 21
*Employment of Females Age 15 and Over by Place of Origin,*
*Race, Marital Status, and Age, 1811*

| Category | Migrants | | | City-born | | |
|---|---|---|---|---|---|---|
| | | Employed | | | Employed | |
| | Total | Number | Percent of total | Total | Number | Percent of total |
| Race | | | | | | |
| Spanish | 251 | 42 | 16.7% | 404 | 40 | 9.9% |
| Caste | 99 | 40 | 40.4 | 119 | 38 | 31.9 |
| Indian | 206 | 103 | 50.0 | 227 | 96 | 42.3 |
| Marital status | | | | | | |
| Single | 202 | 86 | 42.6% | 282 | 81 | 28.7% |
| Married | 228 | 45 | 19.7 | 276 | 44 | 15.9 |
| Widowed | 130 | 54 | 41.5 | 192 | 49 | 25.5 |
| Selected age groups | | | | | | |
| 15–24 | 175 | 74 | 42.3% | 244 | 64 | 26.2% |
| 35–44 | 109 | 37 | 33.9 | 147 | 37 | 25.2 |
| 55–64 | 42 | 6 | 14.3 | 49 | 6 | 12.2 |
| TOTAL ALL CATEGORIES | 561 | 185 | 33.0% | 753 | 176 | 23.4% |

entered domestic service, in the now-classic pattern of the twentieth century. In fact, 70 percent of the migrant working women in the 1811 census sample were maids, as compared with only 30 percent of the city-born. So Humboldt was not that far off the mark when he attributed the excess of women in Mexican cities to "country women [who] come into the cities to serve in houses."[55] The large numbers of single migrants seeking work in urban households, especially in the age group 15–24, explains why the greatest difference in economic participation between migrant and city-born women was in that age group and why the difference was least marked among married women. It also made the typical female worker in Mexico City a young, single Indian from one of the villages surrounding the capital, who worked as a maid and probably sent her earnings home to her family.

A demographic portrait of elite women who engaged in business enterprises is more difficult to come by, based as it must be on a sample of notarial records. Still, those records show that, as with poorer women, elite women of all marital statuses were active in the business world (Table 22). As with poorer women

TABLE 22
*Female Notarial Transactions by Marital Status, 1803–1853*

| Year | Single No. | Single Pct. | Married No. | Married Pct. | Widowed No. | Widowed Pct. | Divorced[a] No. | Divorced[a] Pct. |
|---|---|---|---|---|---|---|---|---|
| 1803 | 18 | 24.7% | 24 | 32.9% | 31 | 42.5% | 0 | 0.0% |
| 1827 | 22 | 25.9 | 21 | 24.7 | 41 | 48.2 | 1 | 1.2 |
| 1853 | 11 | 22.4 | 17 | 34.5 | 18 | 36.7 | 3 | 6.1 |
| TOTAL | 51 | 24.6% | 62 | 30.0% | 90 | 43.5% | 4 | 1.9% |

SOURCE: Transactions sample, Appendix B.
NOTE: Excludes 94 transactions where marital status was not declared.
[a]Separated by an ecclesiastical divorce.

also, well-to-do wives participated relatively less than their proportions in the population (30 percent vs. 39 percent of the adult Spanish women). But marriage affected these women's chances of signing a notarial instrument less than it did the lower-class woman's chances of being employed. This evidence suggests that many elite wives, unlike their lower-class counterparts, saw no conflict between familial responsibilities and business ventures. Their participation in such endeavors was not often a substitute for absent or incapacitated husbands: a wife who appeared before the notary almost always did so with her husband's permission even though he was in town. Marriage did not seem to handicap these women: they went about their business duly appending their husbands' authorizations to the records, along with a declaration that they "had not been compelled, forced, or intimidated by their spouses," but were acting out of their "free and spontaneous will."[56]

What distinguished elite businesswomen is the high proportion of widows among them, which far exceeded their share of the population (44 percent of those signing notarial instruments vs. 33 percent of the adult Spanish women). As we have seen, widows were also the most active of the few Spanish women in the labor force. The fact that historical generalizations are often based on the elites, in combination with the widely held assumption that the number of single women in Mexico City was insignificant, may have led to the stereotype that it was primarily widows who engaged in economic and legal activities; this was in fact a highly class-specific phenomenon.

The prominence of elite widows in the business world reinforces what we already suspected from the frequency with which they headed their own households: old age brought many well-to-do women independence, along with new financial responsibilities. They had by then inherited from parents and husbands, and even middle-class women might be collecting a pension if their spouses had been in the military, government service, or managerial positions in the Tobacco Factory.[57] Furthermore, since the dowry was in decline, most widowed mothers of the propertied classes now kept their estates to themselves rather than endowing their daughters. Many elite widows thus experienced increased respect, freedom, and power.

Widowhood and old age had a very different meaning for lower-class women, who suffered more economic hardship and had less security with advancing years. Unable to accumulate property and usually eligible for pensions only if their husbands had died in military service, they either continued working, although their infirmities made it harder for them to earn a living, or became dependent on children, relatives, or charity. The divergence of women's experiences from adolescence to old age is one reason why, despite the importance of gender, women of different classes had little in common with each other.

## The Conditions of Women's Work

"A woman's means are very limited when she seeks them by honorable paths," lamented doña María Vargas in her divorce suit.[58] Providing another rare glimpse of working women's thoughts, 25 Tobacco Factory employees gave us this description of women's work in a petition opposing the mechanization of cigar production, which they feared would cost them their jobs:

In our society it is undeniable that employment is scarce even for men; it is no less true that women are reduced to a still more wretched situation. The economy is based on the assumption that families subsist on the earnings of their male head, and when he is lacking, when a mother has to support and educate her children, or when daughters or sisters are forced to provide for their own subsistence, it is fair to say that given the present organization of industry, no recourse is open to them [other than employment in the Tobacco Factory] save domestic service, repugnant because of its humiliation. In the manual arts that women perform they can barely eke out a living due to the scarcity of work and the even more miserable wages with which it is rewarded.[59]

These statements, written in 1836 and 1846, respectively, could easily apply to women throughout the late colonial and early republican period. For if women's job opportunities had begun to expand in 1798, when the viceroy had remarked that women "lack branches of industry for their subsistence and that of their families,"[60] they constricted again after independence. On the whole, women were plagued by unemployment or underemployment; they were confined to a few trades and, within those, work was not only scarce but poorly compensated.

Beyond that, the pace and organization of women's work varied so much from trade to trade that it is difficult to generalize about their working conditions. Some women worked out of their homes as shopkeepers, food producers, seamstresses, and artisans. They might entirely control their work, buying raw materials, processing them, and selling the finished goods directly to the public. Or they might, like many in the textile industry, do piecework for merchant capitalists or prepare materials for male artisans and never deal with the public; because they worked at home they suffered the least dishonor. Other women sold goods on the city streets, also setting the pace of their work, but more stigmatized because they risked their virtue by venturing out. Still others were wage laborers in restaurants, small workshops, or factories, which were usually unmechanized until the 1830's, but boasted a complex division of labor. Many more lived with their employers, relinquishing control over their work and personal life in exchange for shelter and sustenance. A few women were proprietors but not wage earners, a distinction that was increasingly to be found in food production, textile manufacture, and retailing, though the processes of specialization and proletarianization that had accompanied the growth of Mexico City's primitive industries in the late eighteenth century slowed down as the economy stagnated.

Over half the women who worked were domestic servants, an occupation that, as the Tobacco Factory workers indicated, Mexicans considered repugnant and humiliating.[61] To be sure, there was a hierarchy of servants, with *amas de llaves* (housekeepers) above cooks, who were in turn above chambermaids, *galopinas* (kitchenmaids), children's nurses, and laundresses. Some maids fared better than others, either by working for the very rich or by staying all their lives with the same employer. Foreigners often remarked that Mexican servants were treated like family members, and contemporaries occasionally used the term "family" to include servants as well as children, perhaps indicating that servants were treated well.[62] But the evidence suggests that this was not always the case. For most women, domestic service was repugnant because they were daily reminded of their social inferiority. Servants legally owed their masters "submission, obedience, and respect," which might apparently include consenting to sexual advances, a fact some wives held against husbands in divorce cases.[63] Even when the servant's relationship with the employer was a good one, the job, far from granting her independence, caused her to live under strict surveillance, at the master's beck and call from early morning to late at night. Finally, it usually entailed a separation from her family, for as we have seen, only a few couples served together in an employer's household.

These conditions caused a high turnover among domestic servants. Fanny Calderón's unsuccessful attempt to train a 12-year-old servant illustrates why girls rarely persisted in this employ. Fanny, who promised the child's mother to teach her to read, sew, and dress hair, and to see that she went to church regularly, could not understand why the girl soon quit her job. Although Fanny concluded that the incident showed the "universal indolence and indifference to earning money" of the Mexican poor, her journal reveals that the child was terribly homesick. When her family visited, "they would have dinner, light their cigars, and together with little Josefita, sit and howl and bemoan themselves, roaring, crying, and lamenting her sad fate in being obliged to go out to service," which, according to Fanny, they considered more degrading than begging for a living.[64]

Another explanation that Fanny, as an employer, could not admit, was the paltriness of servants' wages. Since these were negotiated with each family, they varied. *Amas de llaves* might earn a decent salary, but few households in Mexico City could afford one. Most of the families that hired domestic servants had only one maid who did all the chores, often working for little more than room and board. In many cases servant girls were probably unable to send wages home to their parents, but merely relieved them of the burden of having one more mouth to feed.

There is no evidence that these girls saved any money, as their European counterparts did. In fact, domestic service appears to have been a more debased occupation in Mexico than Europe, where, it is said, women preferred it to factory work.[65]

Given the large pool of needy women, there were always some who had to hire themselves out as maids. Most often these were Indians, or migrants (or likely both), who often arrived in Mexico City without a roof over their heads, marketable skills, or family connections. Domestic service, then as now, played an important role in acculturating provincial women into the urban lower class.[66] It was particularly appropriate for young girls who did not have the option of living on their own and who would benefit, in theory at least, from the protection of a master's household. However, since domestic service was the most plentiful employment available to women, it drew women of every age, race, and place of birth.

Other trades gave women personal liberty and allowed them to live with their families, but they were hardly lucrative. "Sewing and other handiwork appropriate to women," such as spinning, embroidering, knitting, flower making, and the like, were the fallback of abandoned wives, widows, and orphans.[67] Even *gente decente*, like the kindly spinsters who took in the orphaned Guillermo Prieto, sometimes took up sewing to make ends meet.[68] The relatively high social standing of these workers is suggested by the fact that they were the most Spanish, the least likely to have migrated, and the oldest of any group of working women in the 1811 census sample. For example, as shown in Table 23, more than two-fifths of the seamstresses, spinners, and other female apparel workers were Spanish, and almost three-quarters were born in Mexico City. Their median age of 36 reflects the large share of widows in the group, higher than in any other. Thus women in the apparel industry were often those who would normally have depended on a man to support them. But even within this group, a distinction must be drawn, for the spinners appear, on average, to have been of lower rank than the seamstresses and women in other branches of the industry: only 30 percent of the spinners were Spanish, compared with 63 percent of the others; and 43 percent were married, compared with only 21 percent of the others.[69]

TABLE 23

*Female Employment in Domestic Service, Apparels, and the Food Industry by Race, Marital Status, and Place of Origin, 1811*

| Category | Domestic service | | Apparels | | Food industry | |
|---|---|---|---|---|---|---|
| | Number | Percent | Number | Percent | Number | Percent |
| Race | | | | | | |
| Spanish | 52 | 23.9% | 21 | 42.9% | 3 | 3.8% |
| Caste | 47 | 21.6 | 14 | 28.6 | 11 | 13.9 |
| Indian | 119 | 54.6 | 14 | 28.6 | 65 | 82.3 |
| Marital status | | | | | | |
| Single | 149 | 68.7% | 14 | 28.6% | 17 | 21.8% |
| Married | 16 | 7.4 | 17 | 34.7 | 43 | 55.1 |
| Widowed | 52 | 24.0 | 18 | 36.7 | 18 | 23.1 |
| Place of origin | | | | | | |
| Migrant | 130 | 61.3% | 13 | 27.1% | 32 | 40.5% |
| City-born | 82 | 38.7 | 35 | 72.9 | 47 | 59.5 |
| TOTAL ALL CATEGORIES | 218 | 100.0% | 49 | 100.0% | 79 | 100.0% |

NOTE: Servants include sirvientes, criadas, domésticas, amas de llaves, and recamareras. Apparels includes costureras, hilanderas, tejedoras, and devanadoras. Food workers include tortilleras, atoleras, dulceras, fruteras, torteras, vendedoras plaza, molenderas, and molenderas de chocolate.

Sewing and other handiwork were so badly paid, according to Fernández de Lizardi, "that even the most industrious [women] cannot support themselves with the needle, and if one manages to do so, it is at the cost of her health and she is always on the verge of misery." For Prieto's benefactresses too, it was a constant struggle to make ends meet, despite the long hours they spent hunched over their work. Fernández de Lizardi attributed the poor earnings of women's handiwork to the huge pool of seamstresses—200 for each shirt, he claimed—which lowered the price of their products "in the extreme."[70] The position of spinners was similar. A business that took so little to set up created an excessive supply of spinners, lowering the profits they might have made. Furthermore, they were at the mercy of whatever prices the merchants and weavers might set, since most spinners were forced to sell their thread quickly in order to purchase the raw materials for the next day's work.[71] Women's testimony in court cases and petitions supports this view of the low pay involved in "women's work," as do official reports on employment and education. Nineteenth-century observers agreed with Manuela Gaitán de Vergés that sewing "barely allows us to maintain ourselves miserably."[72]

Contemporaries believed that the situation of these women worsened in the first half of the nineteenth century as mass-produced goods from abroad invaded the Mexican market. Because these observers used the term sewing rather loosely to include textile work and handicrafts as well as dressmaking and mending, they did not distinguish the plight of seamstresses from that of spinners and weavers. It is the last two, not the first, who would have been affected. During the 1790's the cotton industry flourished in Mexico City, creating jobs for women in small workshops and in their homes.[73] But overproduction sent textile manufactures into decline at the turn of the century, and they were dealt a staggering blow as experiments with free trade, especially after independence, opened Mexican ports to yarn, thread, ribbon, and woven cloth. Although the government, responding to the protests of Mexican industrialists and artisans alike, periodically attempted to protect domestic production, contraband imports could not be halted.[74] Many women, struggling before, were now unable to make do, like María Dolores Rondero, who petitioned for a dowry to enter a convent in 1853, explaining that though she worked whenever sewing was made available to her, she could never save "because a woman's work is so miserable and precarious owing to the introduction of foreign goods."[75]

It is not clear whether the recovery of the textile industry in the 1840's benefited women in Mexico City because much research remains to be done on the new cotton mills. Although in some parts of Mexico women were a substantial part of the mill labor forces,[76] there is no evidence that this was the case in the capital. Most of these mills were apparently in the provinces or villages surrounding the capital, rather than in the city itself, and the mechanized mills established by French investors in Mexico City employed mostly French and English workers.[77] Indeed, the new mills probably displaced many women in Mexico City from cottage industries, a trend suggested by the disproportionate decline in the number of spinners between 1811 and 1848 (Table 16). Thus when, in 1845, Manuel Payno praised the *hilanderas* "in their curious national garb" as talented and "constantly laboring" women, who "twenty years ago" did all the work of spinning thread, it may largely have been an exercise in nostalgia.[78] Those women who continued to manufacture thread and cloth at home for lack of an alternative must have suffered from the dramatic drop in prices that accompanied the mechanization of the textile industry.[79]

The women employed in the food industry, one-fifth of the working women in the 1811 census sample, probably experienced fewer changes in their working conditions than those in the textile industry. Unfortunately, we know very little about them beyond picturesque descriptions of what they wore and the cries they used in hawking their goods. The census data suggest that they were of a lower social standing than artisans and seamstresses, since they were the most Indian of all working women. Nearly half (35 of 79) were *molenderas;* 16 were specifically listed as chocolate millers, the others simply as millers, perhaps again of chocolate or of corn for tortillas. All worked as hired hands in workshops, usually owned by men. The rest of the food workers were self-employed, selling fresh produce, or tortillas, atole, tamales, soups, sweets, and the like that they prepared themselves. Working out of their homes and on the streets, they could, like seamstresses and spinners, combine their work with household chores and childcare. Food vendors consequently tended to be somewhat older and have more family responsibilities than molenderas; their median age was 30 (compared with 28 for molenderas), and only 13 percent were single (compared with 31 percent for molenderas). But approximately half of both groups were married, the highest proportion of any group of working women.

Because so many food vendors and producers were Indian and so many were married, they appear to have been a particularly impoverished group of women whose husbands could not support them. Payno's prosperous fruit vendor Cecilia in *Bandidos de Río Frío,* who bought herself pretty clothes and eventually married a lawyer, was thus a figment of the author's imagination, forgivable since an ocean and half a century separated him from the driving poverty of which he wrote. Unlike Cecilia, women in the food industry lived a precarious existence, working sporadically without formal contracts, catering to a mostly poor clientele, and having no security in the event of sickness or old age.

We know far more about the women who worked in the Tobacco Factory. As a government enterprise, it kept extensive records, which were eventually transferred to the National Archive; as the first modern factory in Mexico, it drew the attention of travelers and Mexicans alike. After the Real Fábrica de Puros y Cigarros was established as a royal monopoly in 1769, the independent cigar shops were outlawed. The owners and employees of these small shops—at least a third of them women[80]— now had to work in the State-owned factory that put thousands of workers together under one roof. Entering the factory in the morning, they brought their lunches and spent the day, as the traveler William Robertson found them in 1849, at "work in suites of long rooms, ranged from one end to the other, with ample space and air, and a forewoman to look over each."[81] Although the factory was not mechanized, the organization of labor was clearly industrial, with all workers on a standard work schedule and production organized into a division of tasks. The labor relations were also industrial. Nearly all the women worked at the lowest level, paid by the piece. Only the guards and supervisors, about 2 percent of the female work force in 1795, received salaries. All the higher level managers were men.[82]

The transformation of cigar making from artisanal production to the factory system caused a deterioration of working conditions for those women who had previously made cigars at home. It created a conflict between their domestic duties and their employment, and for Spanish women in particular, who because of their social status could not risk the loss of their reputations by working outside their homes, even less to work alongside the *infima plebe* at the factory, it either forced them out of the cigar industry, pushed them into illegal production—or, according to one government official, sacrificed them to "prostitution and shame."[83] On the other hand, new jobs were created for Caste and Indian women, at least for a while, particularly as production was increasingly divided into simplified tasks so that more unskilled workers could be hired. There may thus have been some substance to critics' charges that soon after it opened the factory caused an acceleration of migration to the capital and a shortage of domestic servants.[84] For if factory work was less desirable than home-centered production, it was better than domestic service—and probably no worse than employment in the independent cigar shops.

Authorities took special care to protect the factory women's reputation, but the view of factory work as dishonorable persisted. From the start, men and women worked in separate rooms and entered by separate doors, and women worked under female supervisors exclusively. In 1792 the director further ordered women to enter half an hour later to avoid meeting male factory workers on the streets (women thus worked 11 hours a day, compared with 11.5 for men). Government officials repeatedly tried to convince the public that the factory protected poor women from the "dangers" and "risks" to which they were frequently exposed in making a living. Still, the factory continued to be criticized for bringing together workers of both sexes, leading to "perverse and dangerous conversations."[85] These attitudes were still widespread in 1837, when Estevan de Antuñano attempted to combat them in his pamphlet encouraging his fellow industrialists to employ more women in their textile mills.

Despite the stigma of working in the Tobacco Factory, its employees were the elite of manual laborers in terms of both wages and the opportunity for steady work. They were also the only lower-class female workers with some type of social security provided by their employer; all workers were eligible for pensions if disabled, and supervisors (*maestras, sobrestantes,* and *guardas*) retired at one-third of their salary after they had worked at least 20 years.[86] Robertson considered the "clean, neat, well-appointed set of factory girls" to "stand quite above the rest of the surrounding population." For all that they were "from the lowest class," it seemed to him that "their general morals [were] many grades higher." "After they have once joined or been admitted into the Fabrica as operatives," he added, "there is nothing that the women so much dread as losing caste, or being dismissed for bad conduct. They have all piece-work set them, and the most industrious and expert make excellent wages."[87]

The women themselves were less sanguine about their jobs, but they clearly considered themselves luckier than other working women of their class. In their petition to the government opposing the proposed mechanization of cigar production, they argued that they needed the work, not because it was lucrative, varied, safe for their health, or pleasant (indeed they intimated that it was none of the above), but merely because it allowed them to subsist. Nevertheless, they made clear their preference for work in the factory over "humiliating" domestic service or the "miserable" sewing trades. The long waiting lists for jobs in the Tobacco Factory further attest to their attractiveness.[88] Even government officials recognized the scarcity of comparable work when they decreed that weak or pregnant women should not be suspended from their jobs for infractions of work rules because they would have no "honest" alternatives if "thrown out into the street."[89] Thus, as is still the case today in Mexico with the *maquiladoras* (offshore assembly plants), the most modern work was highly desirable in comparison to other options open to lower-class women.

The Tobacco Factory continued to be a privileged place to work even though the conditions there worsened after it opened. In 1777 the piece-rate was reduced, and by 1792 the workday had lengthened from eight hours to eleven. The practice of allowing workers to take cigar paper home at night to prepare (which allowed them to get a head start on the next day's work with their family's help) was discontinued in 1794; though temporarily restored after workers (including 400 angry women) protested, the practice had been barred again by the time Robertson arrived. Payment in copper coins replaced silver in 1841, sparking another protest by the employees.[90]

Despite these expressions of dissatisfaction, reductions in the size of the factory's work force disposed workers to accept the employer's terms. Three years after it opened, the factory had 7,400 workers. By 1803 the figure had been halved, to 3,464. The work force had shrunk even more dramatically, to approximately 600, when Joel Poinsett visited in 1822, and it remained at that size when Robertson visited a quarter century later.[91] Although little is currently known about the Tobacco Factory after independence, it is possible that there were periodic increases in employment between 1822 and 1849, since the government at various times attempted to revive the monopoly. The overall trend, however, was clearly downward. To a large extent, this decline reflects shortages of imported paper in the 1790's, followed by the government's loss of control over the cigar industry after independence. But it also reflects the consensus among government officials that it was dangerous to gather so many of the *ínfima plebe* together in one place. The fear of social disturbances led officials to consider dividing the factory into several small units and establishing new factories in the provinces (plans that did not, apparently, materialize for Mexico City, though a new factory was established in the nearby Villa de Guadalupe). It also led them to favor women, thought to be more docile and careful, over men, a view embodied in the viceroy's order of 1797 that no new men be hired at the factory except to do the heavy work that women were incapable of performing.[92]

Although the preference for women increased their share of the factory's work force, their absolute numbers decreased as the work force itself shrank. In 1772, a year after the *patio de mujeres* (women's workroom) opened, 1,600 (or 30 percent) of the factory employees were women, roughly the proportion who had been displaced from the independent shops. By 1794, their numbers had nearly doubled, to 3,055 women, and their share had risen to 40 percent. But in 1798 the factory hired only 2,640 women, now representing 61 percent of the work force. Even as their proportions swelled to three-fourths or four-fifths, their numbers continued to decline—to 1,985 in 1803 and to approximately 450 by 1849.[93] Thus, after its initial flourish created new jobs for women, the Factory probably hired fewer than the independent shops had.

The reduction of positions in the Tobacco Factory narrowed the options available to women in the work force. Where the factory had employed somewhere on the order of one of every 10 female workers in Mexico City in 1803, it only employed one of 45 by 1849. Women unable to work there took whatever jobs they could find. Their alternatives were increasingly limited, however, since opportunities in spinning and artisan crafts declined at the same time. This may explain why there were five times as many seamstresses in the 1848 census sample as 35 years earlier, and why their earning power diminished. It may also explain why the proportion of women migrants in domestic service dropped from 61 percent in 1811 to 53 percent in 1848; as city-born women became more pressed for work, they may have squeezed migrants out of the available service jobs and into even more precarious trades. It is therefore likely that female unemployment and underemployment, already a problem when the colonial government decreed the end of legal barriers to women's work, grew after independence.

For many middle-class women, earning a living was no less of a problem. Positions in welfare institutions probably decreased after independence as these became impoverished. Shopkeepers, the majority of working women in this class, shared the economic hardships of their clients. So did the many middle-class women who relied on pensions for an income, for these too were hard hit when the government's revenues shrank. Petitions from widows in the files on *Tabaco* and *Montepíos y Pensiones* in the National Archive indicate that this problem was most acute in the 1830's and 1840's, when the government was often several years behind in its payments. Complaining that in any case the pensions were not nearly enough to live on, many widows requested that they instead be granted a tobacco shop (*estanquillo*) to manage or lease out for a profit, but there were long waiting lists for these as well, and such positions were increasingly hard to come by as the government's control of the cigar industry weakened.[94] So the economic position of many, indeed probably most, self-supporting middle-class women declined during the first half of the nineteenth century.

A few middle-class women nonetheless benefited from the heightened emphasis on female education. Not only did their job opportunities expand as the demand for girls' schools grew, but the occupation of schoolmistress gained prestige as more qualified teachers taught older students at a higher level than before. Teachers showed a growing professionalism and even a sense of mission as the century progressed. Already in 1813 one woman applying to the municipal government for a license to open a school proposed to call it an *escuela de niñas* rather than an *amiga*, indicating that she hoped to set new educational standards for girls, preparing them to succeed in the "grave ministry of motherhood" and "any other calling to which divine providence might destine them."[95] After independence teachers like doña Guadalupe Silva campaigned for modern teaching methods, denouncing the rote method that taught children to "read in a fashion causing nausea in the listener." [96] Others held out lofty goals for women's education. Doña Ana Josefa Caballero de Borda, seeking the municipal government's permission to establish a "Mexican Academy" for girls in a public building, expressed her desire, "moved by my love for the country in which I was born and the sex to which I belong," to elevate her compatriots by teaching them "principles of refined politics and healthy morals." [97] By the 1840's Mexico City journalists were ready to pronounce teaching a vocation, where it had once been condemned as the last refuge of those who could not get along in any other career. [98]

The prestige and professionalism of teachers did not for the most part rub off on other women's work. Midwives may have been one exception, since they became increasingly professionalized after 1822, when the government set up an obstetrical school to train them and began to license its graduates. [99] But though this allowed women like María Montaños to advertise as *parteras recibidas*, the government's intervention in this traditional female occupation does not seem to have raised its status in any way. [100] The theater may also have been an exception, for this glamorous and well-paid profession expanded with the opening of two new theaters in Mexico City in 1843 and 1856. Actresses, singers, and dancers could earn several thousand pesos in a season, an excellent salary for the time. Although contemporaries did not consider acting a respectable profession, actresses were the only women—besides historical figures—to be written about in ladies' magazines, their pictures accompanying articles that praised their lives and accomplishments. Many leading entertainers were foreign, however, another instance where new positions did not benefit Mexican women much. [101]

Even though working men were often badly paid, the available evidence suggests that they fared better than women. An industrial census of 1849, listing the weekly earnings of servants, laborers, and artisans, shows that the average woman earned less than one peso, compared with nearly three for the average man. In addition, the salary range for women was narrower: the highest-paid woman (a laundress) earned only three pesos, the same as the average man; the highest-paid man (a glovemaker) earned nine. [102]

10. A midwife (*partera*), usually a mature widow, is shown here with the tools of her trade, including the birthing chair that she took to each delivery. In keeping with a popular superstitious practice, she has invoked good fortune by turning the picture of the saint upside down and lighting a candle to him. Midwifery was one of the few careers that earned women respect and prestige, particularly after the government professionalized it by training and licensing the practitioners.

The gap between male and female earnings in part reflects the fact that most working women were unskilled or possessed skills that were in abundant supply, such as sewing, cleaning, and cooking. Although reformers realized that any betterment in women's situation would have to begin with an improvement in their education, vocational programs in this period did not progress beyond teaching girls such barely profitable skills as needlework, lacemaking, and the like.[103] Even the increased emphasis on literacy did not help beyond providing new opportunities for schoolmistresses; the sorts of work available to most women simply did not require it. Thus women were largely relegated to low-paying jobs in fields with little opportunity for advancement.

Furthermore, women were paid less for equivalent work than men because their work was considered temporary and supplementary to the work of the male breadwinners—a reason the Tobacco Factory workers understood full well when they noted in their petition that the "miserable wages" of women's work were caused by an "economy based on the assumption that families subsist on the earnings of their male head." According to the industrial census, female servants in 1849 earned from one to six pesos a month, against the male servants' one-and-a-half to eight. The Calderón de la Barcas' best-paid maid, a housekeeper, earned 12 to 15 pesos a month in 1840, compared with 40 pesos for a coachman, the best-paid manservant.[104] Even in the Tobacco Factory, managed by enlightened administrators, maestras in 1803 earned 350 to 450 pesos a year, and maestros earned 600. In addition, most of the female cigar makers, paid by the piece, earned less in a day than the men because they started work half an hour later.[105] Women who worked at home may have had similar problems, producing less than men because they had to interrupt their work to attend to children and household duties.

In these circumstances, it is no surprise to find that the feminization of poverty that U.S. journalists so suddenly discovered in the 1970's is far from a new phenomenon. The pitiful plight of widows and orphans was a constant theme in nineteenth-century novels and newspaper articles, with reformers urging the creation of "honest" jobs so that women without fathers or husbands would not have to turn to vice to survive.[106] The government also recognized women's vulnerability: the widows and daughters of deceased employees were entitled to pensions as long as they remained unmarried, whereas sons were cut off at the age of 25; moreover, men were released from military duty (in theory, at least) if they were the "sole source of support" of widowed mothers or orphaned sisters.[107] For every doña Manuela de Roa, who was able to say in her will that she had acquired everything she owned—a house, its furnishings, and a rental property—through "my personal industry and work, . . . for [my husband] left me nothing,"[108] there were dozens of other widows, likewise left penniless, who were hounded by creditors and forced to sell their belongings, search garbage heaps for food, or beg for a living. Faced with a shortage of jobs and an even greater shortage of well-compensated ones, often prevented from working (or working enough hours) by family responsibilities, women made up the bulk of the poor and destitute of Mexico City. And yet they continued to migrate to the capital for lack of anywhere else to turn.

## Conclusion

There is considerable debate in the field of women's studies on the question of whether working improves women's position in society by increasing their independence, status, and power. For Mexico City in the first half of the nineteenth century the answer is a clear negative. Employment may have permitted some women and their families to survive, but it did not normally make them prosperous and emancipated, nor was it an avenue for upward mobility. On the contrary, the pressure would have been downward, since the working woman was widely stigmatized. If a few middle-class women, already of respectable status, did not lose prestige by opening a store or school, they did not gain it either. Lower-class women, forced to take work that contemporaries considered degrading, and that called their honor into question, hardly raised their status through their labor. The ill-repute of women's work, reinforced by limited job opportunities and the absence of economic incentives, made domesticity and patriarchal protection attractive.

It is difficult to know what the opportunity for work—however poorly compensated and disagreeable—meant to individual women, since their opinions have rarely been recorded in Mexican historical documents. In addition, no single generalization could adequately encompass the variety of their experiences. It is nonetheless doubtful that Mexican women entered the job market in search of personal fulfillment or freedom; most clearly did so to contribute to their own and their family's survival. Indeed the majority of working women, who served as maids, saw their liberty sharply curtailed by the requirement that they live with their employers; the young servant girls who migrated to the capital and continued to send their wages home certainly did not gain autonomy. On the whole, the most "independent" of the working women in terms of their legal rights and relationship to men, widows and spinsters, did not live as comfortably as dependent women. Their inability to equal a man's income usually meant that they suffered a decline in their standard of living when they lost the male breadwinner. To be sure, a few of them prospered, and widows, spinsters, and abandoned wives were at least able to subsist because of their employment. The question of choice is crucial, however, to evaluating the meaning of women's work. In most cases women did not choose to be independent, nor did they choose to work.

Even though so many women worked and did not marry, employment was not a desirable alternative to marriage. In fact, the most employed group was also the most married. Indian women's high rate of employment did not generally allow them to live more independently than elite women, since Indians were the most likely to marry or enter consensual unions and the least likely to head their own households. Spanish women, who married least often, rarely entered the labor force; it was their inherited fortunes and pensions, not acquired wealth, that permitted some unattached women to live in comfort. Marriage was a much better economic alternative than a career: it was more likely to provide security and it might occasionally mean a step up the social ladder, something that women could not achieve on their own.[109] There is consequently no evidence that employment weakened the institution of marriage.

For those married women who worked it is almost impossible to ascertain how employment affected their relationships with their husbands. One man credited his wife with having increased their assets through her "efforts, work, and constant care," for he admitted that his soldier's salary barely covered their needs,[110] but whether her financial contributions gave her increased freedom or power we do not know. What is certain is that as a wife she could not legally control her earnings, since these became part of the community property managed by the husband. The employment of the wife was a sufficient source of tension to bring a few couples before the ecclesiastical divorce court. And finally, because married women of all social groups were underrepresented in the labor force, we can reasonably assume that most did not consider employment beneficial, under the prevailing circumstances, either to their own or to their family's well-being.

The female labor force mirrored the class divisions in Mexican society. Central to the conception of elite status was the fact that women did not work; since servants were easily available even housework was demeaning, although supervising it was not.[111] Upper-class women might own inherited businessses and real estate, and they might be personally involved in overseeing their investments, but they ordinarily left the day-to-day management to hired subordinates. A few middle-class women worked as shopkeepers, teachers, employees of beneficence institutions, and managers of wealthier women's enterprises. But it was primarily lower-class women who entered the job market. Because of their poverty, many of them were unable to attain the ideal of domesticity, even if they shared it.

As the market for women's labor changed, it reinforced the social structure. During the late colonial period the expansion of Mexico City's economy increased and diversified lower-class women's job opportunities, but these favorable trends were undone, or at least arrested, by the recession that followed. While the capital's economy was growing, reformers felt that women could contribute to further prosperity: thus the attempts to incorporate women into the labor force by removing legal, educational, and ideological barriers to their work. After independence, when the stagnant erconomy did not require a larger labor force, reformers no longer raised the issue of women's work. Women retreated from the artisanal trades they had be-

gun to enter and, even in traditional female crafts like cigar making and spinning, they lost ground in the face of factory production and mechanization.

At the same time, the employment picture improved for some
middle-class women. They were the only ones with "respectable" alternatives in the labor market, and the only ones whose
job opportunities grew and gained prestige during the first half
of the nineteenth century, especially with the elevation of the
teaching profession. Although middle-class women began to enter the work force in substantial numbers only at the end of the
century, when normal schools were founded and the universities opened their doors to women, a glimmer of this trend was
already visible. Thus the pattern that has characterized women's
work in the twentieth century was established much earlier: as
Helen Safa has observed, the principal beneficiaries of the expansion of women's employment in Latin America are the well-
educated, middle-class women, who step into prestigious and
lucrative jobs, thereby blocking the possibilities of upward mobility for lower-class workers, both female and male.[112] In early
republican Mexico, where middle-class women were reluctant to
enter the labor force, it was often foreign women who took advantage of these opportunities with the same effect. Although
their work might open new horizons for those women who
moved into these jobs, it did nothing to lessen the stigmatiza-
tion or to ameliorate the conditions of lower-class women's work.
Modernization did not therefore have a uniform impact on wom-
en's work in the late colonial and early republican periods.

Coming closer to our own time, it appears that in Mexico, as
Louise Tilly and Joan Scott argue for Europe, women's work over
the last two centuries "has not altered in amount, nor even in
intensity, only in character."[113] The composition of the work force
has changed as lower-class women's work opportunities stagnated and middle-class women benefited from the expansion of
public education, the liberal professions, and the white-collar
sector. Yet the level of female employment has neither increased
nor declined substantially, since roughly one-third of the labor
force is female, and one-fourth of all Mexico City women are
part of the labor force, as they were in the eighteenth and nineteenth centuries. With the exception of cigar making, which has

long since left the capital, women continue to dominate the same trades as before, playing crucial roles in domestic service, food processing and distribution, and the apparel industries. In fact, the high proportion of domestic servants in the urban economy persists, despite their declining proportions in more developed countries. The migration of provincial women to work in the capital is another pattern of long duration. Indeed, women's high rate of migration and participation in the urban economy, which distinguishes contemporary Latin America from Arab Africa and Asia,[114] have characterized Mexico for at least two centuries. Finally, the changing job market has not altered women's roles, for most working women, now as then, are young single girls who leave their jobs when they marry and, if necessary, enter the work force only sporadically thereafter.[115] Thus even patterns of female employment suggest that marriage and motherhood are the goal of most Mexico City women, despite the opportunities for them in the labor market.

# FIVE

# Marital Relations and Divorce

MARRIAGE is a key institution for understanding the experiences of the women of Mexico City, for most of them entered legal or informal unions at some point in their lives. Lawbooks show that married women were the most restricted of any women and the only ones whose legal status did not improve over the first half of the nineteenth century. Ecclesiastical divorce records give us another perspective on marriage, not so much by showing the behavior of individual couples, since the cases are too few and unusual from which to generalize, as by illustrating husbands' and wives' definitions of women's place, the causes of conjugal conflict, and the response of Church and State to marital difficulties. Because divorce was above all a female recourse, with wives filing most of the suits in the first half of the nineteenth century, these cases show to what extent married women might wield power or protect themselves by turning to the courts. They also demonstrate how the mobilization of women, the growing respect for the Fair Sex, and the rise of individualism affected marital relations. Perhaps the best measure of the strength of these changes is how they affected the most private of institutions, one that society gave men the right to rule, and that placed women in an unequivocal position of dependence.

Ecclesiastical divorce records are an extraordinarily rich source for the study of domestic life. Full of intimate details of family life, they are one of the few historical documents that express attitudes of women as well as men, poor as well as rich, litigants and witnesses as well as lawyers and judges. Although some of the records are fragmentary, many contain the written testimony of the entire judicial proceedings; a few are hundreds of pages long. A case began with a petition in which one spouse filed for divorce, presenting charges against the other. Then followed the defendant's reply and countercharges. Depositions continued from both spouses and, if the case was brought to trial, family members, servants, employers, friends, and neighbors testified on the character of the spouses and on specific incidents. The records closed with the final arguments of both parties, the detailed opinion of the *promotor fiscal* (an attorney appointed by the court to assist in the examination of evidence and to serve as official accuser), the verdict of the Vicar General, and the reactions of plaintiff and defendant to the decree.

Even the fullest of these records have their drawbacks. For one thing, the couples who came before the divorce court were far from typical, being both exceptionally unhappy and exceptionally daring.[1] Furthermore, only a fraction of the suits processed by the court in the period 1800–1857 have been preserved in Mexican archives. Although the total cannot be established with certainty, two notebooks kept by the court scribe indicate that, on average, 15 suits were filed in Mexico City each year from 1754 to 1818, about nine-tenths of which have since been lost.[2] The 81 surviving cases manifest no obvious biases, but because they are few and unevenly distributed chronologically (see Appendix C), any conclusions based upon them—especially about trends over time—are tentative at best.

Another drawback is that the depositions put before the court had been filtered through the couple's lawyers.[3] Still, apart from the conventional formulas used in the opening and closing phrases, the language and arguments used by petitioners exhibit considerable diversity, and the testimony of witnesses was usually transcribed verbatim. The accusations were, of course, intended to appeal to the court, and so were framed to conform to canon law. Although in many cases the charges seem true, in others they seem to mask the real motives for conjugal discord that emerge incidentally from long written disputes between husband and wife. Fortunately, the litigants' attempts to impress the ecclesiastical judge, with each spouse striving to appear exemplary, is an asset in the sense that arguments in this vein presumably expressed the society's norms of acceptable marital behavior. By the same token, in the often-protracted proceedings, the Church's views of marriage and sex roles were also expressed. Not least, the conditions under which divorce was sought and obtained show the boundaries of what wives were willing to tolerate and the effectiveness of that recourse in enforcing a woman's rights.

## The "Sad Recourse" of Divorce

*Divortium quo ad thorum et mutuam cohabitationem*—or simply divorce, as it was referred to at the time—was at best a difficult and limited recourse. The Church-authorized separation of bed and board did not sever the marriage bond, for Catholic doctrine held that "those whom God united under the bond of marriage cannot and should not be parted" except by death or annulment, which declared a marriage invalid in the first place.[4] A divorced person was not free to remarry as long as the other spouse lived. Expected to "maintain entirely Christian conduct, continent and abstinent" during their separation, couples were urged to prepare for an eventual reunion in the hope "that the passage of time would erase the impressions presently influencing the emotions of the consorts and that, reflecting in a Christian manner on the ties that bind them and on the well-being of their children, they would return to common life."[5] Although it was not the solution to every couple's problems, ecclesiastical divorce was the only form of legal separation available at the time, since annulments were almost impossible to obtain and rarely sought;[6] civil separation was introduced only in 1870, and absolute divorce only in 1917.

Because the permanence of the marital union was considered crucial to the well-being of society, the Church granted divorces only in the gravest circumstances, to "avoid greater misfortunes" and "save the spouses from . . . eternal damnation."[7] Canon law recognized several circumstances in which a divorce might be warranted: if one spouse was cruel to or physically abused or threatened to murder the other; if one spouse had an incurable contagious disease, such as leprosy; if one spouse attempted to compel the other to perpetrate criminal acts, especially if a husband involved his wife in prostitution; if one spouse's "spiritual fornication" (e.g., heresy or paganism) might weaken the other's faith. Divorces were also granted when one spouse violated the marital vows by committing adultery or, in the case of the husband, abandoning his wife and failing to provide for her over a period of years. Adultery alone could justify a perpetual divorce because it broke a couple's promises absolutely; all other grounds gave rise to a temporary divorce, which might be decreed for a fixed number of years or for an indefinite period of time.[8]

Canon law required that the charges be substantiated by unimpeachable evidence. A spouse's confession of guilt, even under oath, was not acceptable, since this would have made it relatively simple for couples mutually bent on a separation to obtain it. All charges had to be proved by eyewitnesses, except adultery, which could be proved by presumption. (It was considered to have occurred, for example, if a married woman was found in the company of a man whom the husband had three times forbidden to see his wife.)[9] Neither was it sufficient to prove that the offenses were real; the plaintiff had to convince the judge both that the danger posed by continued cohabitation was extremely serious and that the delinquent spouse was incapable of reform. Implacable hatred, habitual drunkenness, and insanity were accepted as demonstrations of incorrigibility.[10] In the case of adultery or abandonment, which did not pose a danger to either spouse, the impossibility of reconciliation had to be shown.

Men or women seeking a divorce not only needed a strong case against their consorts, but had to be innocent of wrongdoing themselves, for divorces were decreed "in favor" of one spouse or the other. This distinction had important legal implications, since the guilty party suffered severe financial and personal losses. A guilty husband lost the custody of his children, was denied the use of his wife's dowry and share of the community property, was required to provide support for his family (*ulimentos*) during the separation, and had to pay the expenses of the trial (*litis expensas*). A guilty wife lost the custody of children over three years of age, was denied rights to her husband's future earnings, and had to pay the court costs; if she had committed adultery she lost her dowry and share of the community property as well.[11] Divorce was not granted if both spouses were at fault; and if both were guilty of an offense such as adultery, they even lost the right to accuse each other. Ecclesiastical divorce was not, therefore, an option when both spouses behaved badly, and it was certainly not an option when both behaved respectably.

That incompatibility by itself could not be grounds for a divorce under canon law was clearly explained to the litigants in an 1833 divorce suit. Responding to her husband's charges of cruelty and adultery, doña María Dolores Izedo said that she was willing to separate, but wanted to avoid "a lawsuit that would certainly cause substantial expenditures . . . and inconvenience." After considering her arguments, the *promotor fiscal* admonished the couple: "Once a marriage has been contracted, it is not only the individual spouses who have a vested interest in it, but also the public, which benefits from the education of children and from peace and union between husband and wife. Thus it is not sufficient for them to desire or even mutually consent to a separation. In order for it to be granted, they must prove that there is just cause for it."[12] Canon law permitted a couple to separate by mutual consent only if one of them wished to enter a religious order, an act the Church regarded as serving a higher cause than society.[13] Consequently, ecclesiastical divorce was useful primarily for those seeking protection from a dangerous spouse or separation from a delinquent partner. It was never intended as a remedy for marital conflict.

It is not surprising, then, that divorce was overwhelmingly a female recourse, with wives filing 88 percent of the 77 suits where the initiator is known. In practice, unless a woman committed adultery, it was difficult for a husband to have a strong case for divorce in his favor. Women also had more to gain from divorce, since they were more restricted by marriage than men. Although divorce did not liberate either spouse from the marital bond, it released a wife from the duty of cohabitation and restored her juridical capacity.[14] If she was the "innocent" party, she could live with her children, recover her dowry and half the community property, and continue to be supported by her husband— without having to reside with him or be subject to his authority. Men, because of their superior legal and social position, were less in need of divorce than women and normally benefited less. As doña María Josefa Mijares observed in 1816, a husband could live virtually independent of his wife, "devoted to his vices, . . .

and at the same time have [her] tied down at home to prepare his meals, care for his clothes, and tend to his other needs."[15] Moreover, apart from the financial losses the divorced man suffered (unless his wife was convicted of adultery), his honor was sullied simply by being involved in such litigation.[16]

It was only the strong-willed woman who dared file for divorce, though, since ecclesiastical officials—and sometimes her own lawyer—pressured her to return to her husband. Like a marriage counselor, the *provisor* (ecclesiastical judge) made every attempt to reconcile the couple, exhorting them from the bench and in private meetings to remember the "honorable aims of matrimony," their "pious duties" toward their children, and social conventions. In some cases he prescribed that the man attend mass and confession regularly or enter spiritual exercises in the hope that this "would cause him to change his way of life and subsequently treat [his wife] well."[17] In a few cases in which the woman seemed to be in physical danger, the provisor required the husband to post a bond as surety that he would not injure his wife during their reunion.[18] In general the provisor tried to preserve marriages at all costs, subordinating the happiness of individual spouses to the institution of matrimony.

Attempts to reconcile the couple were not only practiced throughout the case at the judge's discretion, but also institutionalized in the formal judicial procedure. Before the divorce petition could be acted on, the couple was required to submit to a *juicio de conciliación* (trial of conciliation), a face-to-face meeting of husband and wife, along with their attorneys. After independence this trial was usually presided over by a justice of the peace, rather than a provisor, but the purpose remained unchanged.[19] A standard component of Mexican judicial procedure designed to encourage an out-of-court settlement, the juicio in divorce actions was particularly aimed at persuading plaintiffs to drop their suits altogether. If they persevered, they were often given a few days to reflect on their decision, after which a second juicio was held. Only if these efforts failed to produce a reconciliation (as attested to by a written certificate inserted in the court record) was the divorce petition accepted by the ecclesiastical court.[20]

Besides having to face these pressures, a woman who persisted in seeking a divorce had to be willing to suffer consider-able inconveniences. Immediately after initiating the suit she was taken from her home and placed in a *depósito*, literally "de-posited" in the trust of a respected member of the community for the duration of the trial.[21] Although the depósito had to be acceptable to her (as well as her husband, who was required to pay her expenses there), many women found the disruption of their daily lives and the restriction of their freedom intolerable. For the depósito, representing a familiar combination, con-trolled women at the same time that it protected them.

Ecclesiastical authorities originally envisioned the depósito as a "negative sanction" to discourage separations without just cause. In 1585, the Third Mexican Provincial Council, whose dic-tates were still in force in nineteenth-century Mexico, had or-dered that divorce trials be conducted without delay, with the woman "immediately placed in an honorable house" to prevent the "diabolic deceit" of "some who file divorce actions but pur-sue them halfheartedly, or abandon them altogether, in order to devote themselves freely to vice."[22] The council evidently regarded the depósito above all as a method of defending the stability of marriage, but the practice had a number of impor-tant functions quite apart from the initial sixteenth-century justification.

In theory, the depósito protected the interests of both hus-band and wife. Since husbands were expressly forbidden from entering it under penalty of criminal prosecution, it gave women freedom to litigate without coercion or mistreatment.[23] Indeed this institution, unique to the Hispanic world, was a blessing for some women, making divorce possible for many who would not have dared file suit without the shelter and sustenance it pro-vided. At the same time, the depósito upheld the husband's honor by guaranteeing the wife's fidelity during the proceed-ings. The *depositario* who took the woman in pledged to "watch over her conduct," and the woman, expected to live in "modest retirement," had to ask permission to leave the house or receive visitors. Because her reputation was thus guarded, the depósito also helped ensure that a woman's property would be returned, since the adulterous wife lost her dowry and share of the com-munity property.

Yet no similar precautions were taken to ensure the husband's fidelity, though canon law held it equally desirable. This distinction in part reflects the traditional view that women lacked the moral strength to care for themselves; it also reflects the double standard that regarded a wife's adultery as a greater threat to the well-being of marriage and society than a husband's. But this was not the reason ecclesiastical officials gave to explain why only the wife's chastity was institutionally imposed: they argued instead that the depósito was a service rendered the husband in return for the money he paid to support his wife.[24] In practice, however, the majority of Mexican husbands did not pay their wives' expenses during the proceedings, giving rise to litigation in secular courts, which handled the temporal aspects of divorce, and imposing a financial burden on the person who agreed to act as depositario;[25] all wives who filed for divorce were nonetheless subjected to the depósito. Although a few women suffering from extreme want were eventually released from the depósito in order to earn a living, they remained under the supervision of the court, which instructed them to live in the company of "an honorable matron who would be responsible for [their] conduct" and to register their residence with the court.[26]

It was because the depósito was largely a substitute for the husband's control over his wife that there was no equivalent mechanism to supervise the male. The depósito was thus far more than a simple precaution against the wife's infidelity or a guarantee of her physical safety and freedom to deliberate. Temporarily free of her husband's direct authority, she now fell under the authority of the provisor, through whom the husband's wishes were mediated.[27] Not only was the depósito contingent on the husband's approval; he also retained the right to ask the provisor to prevent his wife from seeing particular people he mistrusted, from suspected lovers to concerned kinfolk. In effect, a woman could be held virtually incommunicado at her husband's request. Doña Rosalia Ramírez, for example, was by order of the provisor forbidden from "seeing or communicating, in person or through a third party, with any of her brothers and sisters, other relatives, or any person who might entice her to live separately from her husband, and shall only be allowed to

communicate with her procurator and attorney in order to prepare her case." Similar though less extreme rulings were made
throughout the first half of the nineteenth century at the request
of husbands who argued that "whether the divorce is declared
or not, the husband retains the authority vested in his station
[*estado*]."²⁸

In practice, the rigidity of the depósito varied considerably
from case to case. The depositario was often chosen by the litigants from among their friends and relatives. Most women took
their children with them (especially infants under three), arranging for the father to see them if he so requested;²⁹ those of
comfortable means took a maid as well. Approximately half the
women were placed with relatives, although sometimes only
after complaining and being transferred from the original depó-
sito.³⁰ A woman was placed with a stranger only when the couple
could not agree or could not find a *casa de confianza* (trusted
house) willing to accept her. It was primarily the poorer litigants, whose friends could not easily accommodate additional
members in their households, or women with numerous children who were placed with strangers. In these instances the
court appointed the depositario, often a respected widow or, if
no one else could be found, a notary, constable, or other official
involved in the case.

Some women lived quite happily in their depósitos; some husbands neither raised objections nor placed restrictions on their
wives; some depositarios found no cause for complaint. But in
the majority of cases, the depósito was the source of problems
for at least one of these parties, becoming the subject of lengthy
petitions and accounting for the bulk of the procedural motions
and rulings in the divorce records. The typical woman changed
her depósito at least once during the divorce proceedings, and
two did so as many as five times.

Husbands repeatedly charged that their wives enjoyed excessive liberty in the depósito. These allegations were most frequent when the woman was living with her relatives, especially
her parents. For example, the soldier don Isidoro Medina asked
that his wife be transferred to a stricter house, claiming, "I have
found her many times in the street, which should not be allowed in the *depósito*, since its object is to keep her safe and

withdrawn until the conclusion of this business." Likewise, don Pedro Ouvrard, a French tailor residing in Mexico, described his wife's depósito with her mother as "a total farce . . . to the extent that my wife has been seen in public promenades and in dangerous *tertulias* [salons]. She cannot deny that she was [recently] at the Theater, . . . dancing with all who asked her in an arrogant display of contempt for my rights and a mockery of the *depósito* amounting to an insult to this court."[31] Several husbands requested that their wives be placed in a convent, where their modest behavior would be ensured, but the use of convents for this purpose had been expressly forbidden by Archbishop Núñez de Haro at the end of the eighteenth century.[32]

Even more frequent than husbands' charges about the laxity of the depósito were wives' complaints about its onerousness. Several labeled it an instrument of "affliction," "pain," or "bitterness" that "oppressed" them, and many argued that its restrictions were unwarranted. Doña Teresa Carrero reasoned that "the *depósito* . . . is but a precautionary measure taken to guard the reputation of the married woman and guarantee to the utmost the fidelity required in marriage; it is not, nor should it be, a punishment, or a measure dictated solely for the pleasure of mortifying and disturbing a poor woman." Doña María Ignacia ("La Güera") Rodríguez, a well-known figure among the capital's high society, complained that in preventing her from communicating with everyone except her attorney and procurator, the court was treating her "like a defendant before the Inquisition" (a prescient statement, since she would indeed be brought before it a decade later, under suspicion of donating funds to the independence cause). And the humble Paula Pasarán declared the depósito "a prison without sentence," to which she was subjected while her husband, the criminal, "wandered freely in the streets."[33]

In condemning the depósito, these women reflected a view increasingly held by their contemporaries, as evidenced by the changes made in the new civil codes. The Zacatecas code of 1828 left it to the spouses to decide if the wife's depósito was necessary, and Sierra, in his draft code of 1859, abolished it except when a wife was accused of wrongdoing or requested it for her own protection.[34] The view that married women should be un-

der direct patriarchal control—if not the husband's, then the ecclesiastical judge's as his surrogate—was therefore being undermined by the idea that innocent women who sought divorce
might have the option of living independently during the proceedings and should not be penalized for seeking relief from an
abusive spouse.

Although some jurists were thus ready to acknowledge the injustice of the depósito, many husbands continued to argue that
married women needed to be kept under this kind of tight control. As late as 1855 don Simón Imhoff, a Swiss resident of Mexico, echoing the words of the Third Mexican Provincial Council,
maintained that the depósito should not be too pleasant since it
was intended "to prevent the deceit of astute women who use
divorce suits only to seek liberty." Others went even further.
Don Pedro Ouvrard was sure that once a woman tasted true
freedom, she would never want to return to her husband again.
"How can we expect that a woman who has enjoyed and enjoys
the benefits of a free existence would ever allow herself to be reduced to conjugal subjection?," he asked. "How could this operate in favor of marriage?" [35]

These attitudes found some support in the procedures followed after a divorce was granted. A wife, even if innocent, continued—at least in theory—to be under the ecclesiastical court's
supervision, whereas a husband, even if guilty, remained free.
Divorce decrees admonished the woman to live in a *casa honesta*
(honorable house) in order "to avoid an offense to God," and
required her to notify the court of her residence so that the ecclesiastical judge could "watch over her conduct and take the necessary steps in the event that [her behavior] should be inappropriate to her condition and the fidelity she owed her husband." [36]

A woman seeking a divorce had to be especially determined
to put up with the hardships of the depósito because the ecclesiastical court was exceedingly slow, a complete suit usually taking two to three years. [37] The time spent in carrying out judicial
formalities was in part responsible for the delay. For instance,
whenever a petition was received, the opposing party was informed and given ample time to respond before any action was
taken. Both spouses had the opportunity to appeal procedural
rulings before they were enforced (unless a woman's life was in

danger, in which case the court immediately sent her to a depósito without awaiting her husband's approval). And, of course, recalcitrant spouses could manipulate these procedures to prolong the litigation. Common delaying tactics included requests for extensions in the time allotted for a response, a husband's objections to his wife's depósito, which had to be resolved before the case could proceed, and appeals of procedural rulings and final sentences.

Another reason the litigation was usually so drawn out was that the court did not actively pursue divorce cases. One of the spouses had to initiate each stage in the process, complaining, for example, when the other failed to present evidence within the given time period, and requesting that the delinquent party be censured. In most instances the court merely responded to these actions without conducting its own investigation or attempting to impose the law of the Church.[38] Since the direction and speed of the process rested largely with the litigants themselves, most cases lay idle for weeks or even months at a stretch. (The court's passivity was also the key—for those bold enough to take advantage of it—to obtaining greater flexibility during the litigation. The few women who dared simply to leave a depósito they disliked and move into another were allowed to remain there, provided their husbands did not object. But few dared.[39])

Thus divorces were not to be sought lightly. The prolonged period of the suit could be highly unpleasant for a woman who was placed in the house of a stranger, or was not provided for by her husband, or, as occasionally happened, was separated from her children. Additional lawsuits usually had to be filed in secular courts both during and after the trial to seek child custody, living expenses, payment of court costs, and recovery of the dowry and community property. If one spouse wanted the other punished for a criminal offense such as physical abuse or adultery, it entailed yet another lawsuit in a criminal court. Furthermore, divorce carried considerable social stigma in nineteenth-century Mexico. Although there is some evidence of its increasing acceptance by midcentury, divorce was usually sought only when a marriage was intolerable. Many litigants had originally resisted taking the step "for the sake of appearances," to "protect the honor of my husband and family," and "so as not to cause scandal for my unfortunate children." And many women must have been discouraged from taking the step at all because of their economic dependency and poor job prospects; whether upper class or lower class, most women would suffer a decline in their standard of living if they left their husbands. Finally, though, some women reluctantly resolved, as did doña Concepción Morales, "to seek the security of my life in the sad recourse of divorce." [40]

## Women and the Courts

Divorce was usually the last resort. A woman had several other options when her husband stepped out of line, and these tended to be more effective and easier if she merely wanted to pressure him into improving his behavior. Most of the women bringing divorce actions had previously turned to priests, employers, or judges, hoping, as doña Josefa Salazar put it, "that this person of respect would be able to curb the excesses of my consort." Indeed, she claimed there was not a judge who had not been acquainted with her situation.[41] Wives could also file criminal complaints in the secular courts when admonishment failed to produce reform. Doña Ignacia de León, who charged her husband with cruelty in a secular court, frankly admitted that her goal was "to aspire to [his] correction," for she did not want a separation.[42] In at least nine of the 81 divorce cases, the wife had filed criminal charges before turning to the ecclesiastical court—and the proportion may have been higher, since a couple's history is not always complete in the divorce records. These actions sometimes had the desired effect, at least temporarily, for several husbands had promised to mend their ways. Moreover, a woman who accused her husband of abuse or adultery in a secular court could obtain his imprisonment or fine while continuing to live in the family home and carry out most of her normal activities. To be sure, the threat of a divorce action might also keep a wayward spouse in line, but the effect could often be achieved by simply initiating a *juicio de conciliación*, as had 10 wives who eventually filed for divorce. Examples of these types of litigation abound in Mexican archives.[43] It was usually only after such measures failed that aggrieved wives resorted to divorce, one having tolerated her "degrading" situation in a state of "virtual slavery" for 42 years.[44]

Although divorce suits were expensive, they were surprisingly accessible for those who resolved to take the step. Normally, the lawyers who represented the two parties, the notaries who recorded each transaction, the constable who accompanied the woman to the depósito, and even the *promotor fiscal* who consulted in the case charged for their services, and every petition was written on stamped paper for which there was a separate charge. A complete suit cost a minimum of 150 pesos in 1854 (and much more if the depositions were lengthy or numerous),[45] a prohibitive price for the manual laborer who earned approximately 100 pesos a year, let alone the spinner who earned only about 35. It could be just as much beyond the reach of the woman of some social standing who did not receive payments from her husband while in the depósito and did not yet have access to her own property. But after 1808, when judicial fees were abolished for indigents,[46] the ecclesiastical court appointed attorneys to represent needy litigants free of charge, ordered the court notaries and other officials to provide their services without fee, and accepted petitions on unstamped paper. By the 1830's it was generously granting assistance to those requesting *ayuda por pobre*. As one judge explained, "as a general rule" the court helped "all those who solicit [assistance] without requiring proof of need, persuaded by previous experience that even people of some comfort allege their insolvency, and even believe in it. If these parties were allowed to present evidence to substantiate their need, they would provide plenty of it, only adding to the work load of the court, without yielding any fruit."[47]

The Church succeeded in making its court available to people from all classes of Mexico City society: the majority of the litigants in divorce suits were neither wealthy nor well educated, especially after the option of financial assistance became widely known. Indeed, approximately one-third of the women who initiated divorce actions had to sign their names with a cross. Although the records do not contain detailed socioeconomic information on all the litigants, sufficient information is available in 73 cases to categorize them according to such criteria as occupation, salary, number of servants, type of dwelling and furnish-

## TABLE 24
### Class Background of Couples Seeking Ecclesiastical Divorce by Period, 1800–1857

| Couple's class[a] | 1800–1819 | | 1820–39 | | 1840–57 | | Total 1800–1859 | |
|---|---|---|---|---|---|---|---|---|
| | Number of couples | Percent | Number of couples | Percent | Number of couples | Percent | Number of couples | Percent |
| Upper | 8 | 44.4% | 6 | 23.1% | 5 | 17.2% | 19 | 26.0% |
| Middle | 3 | 16.6 | 4 | 15.4 | 8 | 27.6 | 15 | 20.5 |
| Lower-middle | 6 | 33.3 | 9 | 34.6 | 10 | 34.5 | 25 | 34.2 |
| Lower | 1 | 5.6 | 7 | 26.9 | 6 | 20.7 | 14 | 19.2 |
| Unknown | 1 | — | 3 | — | 4 | — | 8 | — |
| TOTAL | 19 | 99.9% | 29 | 100.0% | 33 | 100.0% | 81 | 99.9% |

NOTE: The tables in this chapter are based on the ecclesiastical divorce records, Appendix C. Percentages do not necessarily total 100 because of rounding.
[a]Wives and husbands are assumed to be of the same class.

ings, or value of the wife's dowry. The resulting class breakdown, admittedly very rough, indicates the range of people
involved.[48]

The cases fall into four categories covering a wide spectrum of
urban society (Table 24).[49] About a fifth of the couples were of
the lowest urban class. The husbands either worked in unskilled
jobs, such as bricklaying, or did not work at all (even if trained in
a skill) and were described as vagrants. Almost all the wives
worked as food vendors or servants. Earning less than 150 pesos
a year, these litigants were rarely accorded the honorific don or
doña in the court records. Slightly more than a third of the
couples belonged to what could be called the lower-middle class.
All these husbands worked (perhaps as artisans or trumpeters
in the Army), earned up to 800 pesos annually, and kept a servant; the wives sometimes took in sewing or assisted at their
husbands' shops. Another fifth of the couples were comfortably
middle class. The husbands were shopkeepers, lower-level bureaucrats, or military officers who earned up to 2,000 pesos a
year; most of the wives, unlike those in the two previous groups,
knew how to write and had not worked before filing for a divorce. The remaining fourth of the couples were of high status
and considerable wealth, living grandly in *casas grandes* and assisted by many servants. During the colonial period five of these
couples (7 percent of the total) were members of the Mexican nobility: one held the title of the counts of San Pedro de Alamo; the
others were untitled members of the gentry.

Although divorce was not the exclusive resort of the well-to-
do, they were disproportionately represented in these cases.
When compared to their share of the population of Mexico
City,[50] the 4 percent of the capital's dwellers who might be considered upper class (having 3 or more servants) provided fully
26 percent of the litigants. The same phenomenon is visible to a
lesser extent among the middle sectors (with 1–2 servants), who
constituted 18 percent of the population but furnished 55 percent of the litigants. In contrast, the lowest class (having no servants) constituted 78 percent of the city's population but only 19
percent of the litigants.

The high cost of the process could account for the low rate of
divorce among the lower classes before the court instituted as-

sistance for the needy—and until its availability became widely known. But even after independence, the middle and upper classes were overrepresented, though to a lesser degree. The poor may still have been deterred by the cost of divorce, which at the very least deprived the wife of her earning capacity during the trial unless she could manage to have the depósito lifted. Although women of all classes, including illiterates, dared to file divorce suits, those with a certain degree of education were more likely to have learned about the recourse. Perhaps some social standing or connections also helped people feel comfortable about using the court system. Furthermore, since the lower classes were the most likely to live in consensual rather than legal marriages, they had the least need to resort to divorce.

On the whole, the people who sought divorce received fair treatment from ecclesiastical authorities, though many rules governing the process were inherently more onerous for the wife than the husband. The provisor showed considerable prudence in separating false evidence from true and in denying unreasonable requests from husband or wife.[51] The court safeguarded the rights of both spouses by scrupulously carrying out the many formal mechanisms designed to guarantee impartial justice, including the defendant's right to attend the swearing in of witnesses and to challenge them in person. To avoid arbitrary decisions, the provisor consulted with the *promotor fiscal* before issuing significant rulings and always before the final verdict. Finally, divorces do not seem to have been granted more readily to one or the other complainant, for only one of the 7 men initiating divorce actions obtained a ruling in his favor, against 10 of the 70 women.

An exception to the ecclesiastical court's impartiality was its clear prejudice in favor of the nobility. Under apparent pressure from aristocratic litigants, it resolved two cases in a manner that deviated from both its own established policies and the dictates of canon law.[52] Within six weeks of receiving the first petition from the countess of San Pedro de Alamo, her suit was resolved on the basis of what would normally have been considered invalid evidence. Accepting her husband's confession of prolonged and public adultery with two actresses, the court declared a perpetual divorce in which neither spouse was declared guilty. The *promotor fiscal* reasoned that this solution, preventing "scandal and defamation to the honorable person of the count," would be most likely to lead to the eventual reunion of the couple by avoiding "the lengthy procedure, odious incidents, vexation, and great discord caused in the hearts of litigants by suits of this nature."

The case of doña Francisca Pérez Gálvez, the daughter of a count, against her husband don Lorenzo García Noriega was more complicated, but resolved in an equally irregular manner. Don Lorenzo first charged his wife with adultery in a criminal court; she retaliated by filing for divorce in the ecclesiastical court on the grounds of his adultery and cruelty. Depositions and proofs presented over the next 28 months strongly suggest that both spouses were guilty of infidelity, making them ineligible for divorce under canon law. Nonetheless an "absolute divorce" was declared, in which, once again, neither spouse was pronounced guilty. The decree emphasized that the divorce did not "in any way denigrate the honorable conduct nor impugn the high regard in which [both spouses] were held." Furthermore, in both of these cases the noble wives were "deposited" in the convent of their choice, which they preferred to being placed in a *casa de honra*, despite Archbishop Núñez de Haro's prohibition of this procedure. These cases attest to the great weight of the nobility in colonial Mexico, at least among officials of the ecclesiastical court. As doña Francisca Pérez Gálvez herself put it, in lamenting her husband's refusal to pay the court costs, "[He] is accustomed to doing as he wishes inside and outside of the courts."

Most cases were not so readily resolved. As shown in Table 25, only 12 of the plaintiffs obtained a divorce, five of which were perpetual and seven temporary. Eleven couples reunited and dropped the case, usually within the first three months of the litigation, as though not firm in their determination to separate. But five of them resumed the suit later. One petition was settled by the death of the defendant and one was rejected by the court because it was filed by both spouses on the grounds of incompatibility. Of the remaining divorce suits, seven are frag-

**TABLE 25**

*Results of Divorce Actions by Class, 1800–1857*

| Couple's class | Divorce | | Reunion | | Abandoned | | Other[a] | | Total cases |
|---|---|---|---|---|---|---|---|---|---|
| | Number of cases | Percent | Number of cases | Percent | Number of cases | Percent | Number of cases | Percent | |
| Upper | 6 | 31.6% | 0 | 0.0% | 10 | 52.6% | 3 | 15.8% | 19 |
| Middle | 3 | 20.0 | 0 | 0.0 | 12 | 80.0 | 0 | 0.0 | 15 |
| Lower-middle | 2 | 8.0 | 4 | 16.0 | 18 | 72.0 | 1 | 4.0 | 25 |
| Lower | 1 | 7.1 | 1 | 7.1 | 10 | 71.4 | 2 | 14.3 | 14 |
| Unknown | 0 | — | 1 | — | 4 | — | 3 | — | 8 |
| TOTAL | 12 | 14.8% | 6 | 7.4% | 54 | 66.6% | 9 | 11.1% | 81 |

[a]One of these cases was settled by the death of the defendant; one was rejected by the court because it was filed on the grounds of incompatibility; and seven are fragments in which the outcome is unknown.

ments and 54, or two-thirds of the total, appear to have been abandoned by the litigants at some point in the proceedings (though a few records may be incomplete).[53]

Although less than a fourth of the petitions concluded in divorce or reunion, most couples probably obtained what they wanted of the litigation, for it appears that those who abandoned their suits remained informally separated. Subsequent information is rarely available on couples who dropped their divorce actions, but the records of several cases that were abandoned for a number of years and then resumed show that the woman left the depósito and the couple lived apart during that time.[54] There is no evidence that ecclesiastical judges either made use of their authority to "ask for the reunion and cohabitation" of the couple[55] or attempted to determine whether husband and wife continued to live apart. Instead, the court scribe, reviewing the documents many months later, often noted that "no person has appeared to pursue this case as of this date" and filed the records in the archive of the Archbishopric.[56]

Because the ecclesiastical court did not intervene in unauthorized separations, it is likely that most temporary divorces also resulted in permanent separations. In only one case do we know that a couple reunited after being granted a temporary divorce.[57] The case of Román Punzalán Zapata and his actress wife, Ana María Zendejas, appears to be more typical. Granted a three-year divorce in 1795, they were still living apart in 1809, when Punzalán had a change of heart and appeared before the ecclesiastical court to request that his wife be returned to him. Even though the three years had elapsed, the court did not issue a new ruling; Ana María refused to rejoin her husband, and the couple remained separated without further litigation.[58] In practice, then, both temporary and permanent divorces probably lasted as long as the couple wished.

Even if formal divorce decrees were rarely obtained, there was an important advantage to initiating the process. After the first petition was filed, the woman received a certificate stating that she had brought action for a divorce. The certificate not only allowed her to request child custody and alimentos in a secular court, but enabled her to make legal transactions without her husband's permission.[59] Because it gave a quasi-legal standing to the subsequent separation, some women may have initiated the suit merely to obtain this certificate. Indeed, approximately one-quarter of the suits (21) were dropped immediately after the first petition was filed and the certificate issued; another quarter (23) were dropped shortly thereafter.

For some litigants, the certificate of having filed for divorce was not sufficient. A formal divorce decree was required if there was community property or a dowry to recover. This fact explains the considerably higher degree of success among the upper and middle classes evident in Table 25 and, conversely, the higher rates of abandoned litigation in the other social groups. A decree was also required when a husband actively opposed a separation, the situation of the only lower-class woman who persevered until she obtained a divorce, and of the only other lower-class woman who pursued the litigation past the formal proofs to the final deposition.[60]

A plaintiff who persisted energetically in the litigation usually succeeded in obtaining the divorce decree. In fact, not a single one of the 17 cases that reached the formal proofs was denied, though 5 cases were abandoned at that point. The close correlation between persistence and success suggests that the ecclesiastical court might not have been as firm as canon law required, for it eventually helped the litigants who insisted strongly enough. But the success of those who persevered might also reflect a process of self-selection in which plaintiffs who realized they had weak claims abandoned their actions. Such was clearly the case in the scandalous suit of doña Dolores Medina against her husband don Domingo Pintado. Once he submitted her secret love letters to the court, demonstrating that she—not he—was guilty of wrongdoing, she quickly dropped the suit so as not to lose her share of the community property.[61]

The passivity of the ecclesiastical court meant that in practice there was another alternative for unhappily married couples: they simply separated without first filing for divorce. Indeed, one-fourth of the litigants referred to previous unauthorized separations in which neither ecclesiastical nor civil authorities had intervened. In eight cases, it was the husband's opposition to an informal separation that prompted the wife to take formal action in the first place; these women might never have instituted proceedings had their husbands not gone to court to have them ordered home.

There is widespread evidence, in both ecclesiastical and secular court records, of such informal separations, some of many years' duration. For example, José María Pabón, in his petition to be declared free to remarry, indicated that his wife, Dolores Durán, had left him after 10 years of marriage and had remained separated until her death 14 years later. One of the couples who petitioned for an annulment of their marriage had been separated 31 years, during which time both spouses had entered consensual unions with new partners. The records of civil and military courts also contain frequent petitions for support from women who had been abandoned by their husbands; if the husband's employer could not convince the wayward spouse to rejoin his wife, the woman was usually granted a monthly payment amounting to a third of his salary without first being required to pass through the divorce court.[62]

The option of simply leaving an unhappy marriage was primarily available to members of the lower classes. Although well-to-do women occasionally left their homes for a short time when a marriage was unbearable (as had 7 of the 19 upper-class wives), I have not found any cases of a long-term informal separation or desertion by an upper-class husband. In contrast, three of the lower-class husbands had abandoned their families, as had one each in the two middle groups. The lack of such an informal alternative to divorce may be one reason, in addition to those discussed earlier, why the upper classes were disproportionately represented among the litigants. Social constraints pressured middle- and particularly upper-class couples either to live together, maintaining outward appearances, or to formalize their separations—at least to the point of being able to say, as did doña María Josefa Candelaria Alvarez in 1809, that she was separated from her husband "for lawful reasons, which have been taken up in court," though her divorce petition was apparently never resolved.[63]

In short, though lower-class women were more likely to marry or enter consensual unions than other women, they also had greater freedom to leave unhappy relationships. In the upper classes, the preoccupation with honor and appearances made marriage more permanent and confining, though less frequent. Even for the elites, however, there was considerably less formal social control in nineteenth-century Mexico City than the divorce laws suggest, a situation that women could use to their benefit.

## Marital Relations

The charges wives brought against husbands basically centered on cruelty and abuse, adultery, and failure to provide (see Table 26 in the next section). Of the 63 wives whose charges against their husbands are known, all but one accused them of cruelty, and 57 specifically complained of physical abuse as well, describing scenes of being beaten and kicked, dragged along stone floors, threatened with swords, bayonets, shovels, knives, or pistols, and of being forced to call the servants for help, run into the streets, or throw themselves from *azoteas* (rooftops) to escape. Most wives brought multiple charges: 26 alleged that their husbands did not provide for them financially and 25 that they committed adultery. Others accused their husbands of being drunkards (14), of gambling (6), of suffering from syphilis (6), of not being a good Catholic (6), of abandoning them (5), of locking them up in the house (3), of trying to force them into prostitution (2), of homosexuality (1), and of insanity (1). Twenty-eight women were able to substantiate their allegations, 10 of them obtaining a divorce.

Nearly a third of the accused husbands (21) failed to respond to the initial petition, with the result that our understanding of these marriages is one-sided and incomplete. Only one-quarter (16) filed counter-charges, 14 charging their wives with adultery and 4 with cruelty (2 charged both). The other 26 husbands had no complaints about their wives, 15 stating that, on the contrary, they wished to reunite. Don José Avila's response was representative of that of many husbands, especially in the lower classes. According to the scribe at his *juicio de conciliación*, Avila admitted that "it is true he has sometimes struck [his wife], and equally true that he is given to drink, for he does not drink holy water, and also that he has occasionally failed to provide her *alimentos*. . . . He added that he was willing to separate, if that was what she wished; . . . nonetheless he has always been content

with his wife's conduct."[64] Upper-class husbands, greatly concerned with protecting their honor—and keeping the community property—confessed to their faults less often and contested
their wives' petitions more frequently.[65] Indeed, 7 (or 54 percent)
of the 13 accused husbands of this class filed counter-charges
against their wives, compared with only 4 (33 percent) of the 12
middle-class husbands, 2 (9 percent) of those in the lower-middle
group, and 2 (15 percent) of those in the lower class. But even
so, nearly half of the accused upper-class husbands failed to file
counter-charges against their wives.

The causes cited by the seven husbands who initiated divorce
actions were principally adultery (5) and cruelty and abuse (5).
By abuse a man meant that his wife provoked quarrels, cursed,
or was stubborn and disobedient, not that she threatened his life
or physically abused him. To these were added such charges as
desertion (3), continual drunkenness and failure to fulfill household duties (2), refusing to have sexual relations (1), and pressing charges against him in a secular court (1)—though neither of
the last two was recognized as grounds for divorce. Only one of
the accused wives desired a reunion with her husband; five
wanted a divorce, and two of the five filed counter-charges of
cruelty, physical abuse, and failure to provide. One of the seven
husbands was granted a perpetual divorce in his favor after he
proved his adultery charge; the other six dropped their suits.

Discussions of these charges show what the litigants expected
of each other. Exemplary husbands and wives emerge from the
depositions as kind and pious, fulfilling their marital duties and
attending mass and confession regularly. The good husband
was "prudent," "honest," and "industrious," providing for his
wife and protecting her. He was an *hombre de su casa* (a "family
man"), who did not drink excessively, gamble, use obscene language, quarrel, or stay out late in the evenings.[66] The good wife
was even more home-oriented, with her roles as wife, mother,
and homemaker so intimately linked that the term *madre de familia* denoted all three. Devoting herself to the children and the
"domestic and economic government of the household," she
"cared for the housecleaning and her husband's clothes, and
saw to it that dinner was ready on time." Not "too gay or fes-
tive," she avoided familiarity with other men, "kept herself oc-

cupied with her household and family," and "left home only to attend to necessary matters."[67] These ideals were expressed by members of all social classes, including working women who, though they could not dedicate themselves entirely to the household, still tried to stress their modesty, decency, and fulfillment of household duties. More than one woman presented as proof of her husband's inadequacy that he could not fully support the family, forcing her to seek employment.[68]

The participants in the divorce cases were agreed that husbands and wives should treat each other with affection, living in peace and harmony. It was harmony based not on equality, though, but on the wife's acceptance of "the submission that a married woman owes her husband and the reverence with which she should treat him." A wife "came into a husband's power" upon marriage and was supposed to "obey him in everything reasonable."[69] It was not only the men who spoke of the wife's subordination; women also recognized the husband's "supremacy and authority" as legitimate. For every husband who complained of a wife who was "unruly," "unmanageable," "disobedient," "impertinent," and "disrespectful"—terms that do not describe the interaction of equals—there was a wife who emphasized her "docility," "submission," "forbearance," and attempts to accommodate her husband's wishes.[70] The Church underscored the inequality of husbands and wives when it admonished husbands, in the marriage ceremony of the time, "We do not give you a slave but rather a wife."[71]

A married woman's desire to be free from her husband's authority was considered entirely improper. One man explained that only the bad wife "doesn't tolerate dependence on her husband." Another charged his wife with wishing to obtain a divorce merely to "remain free from subjection to her husband." And a third thought his wife wanted to "live in liberty, as though having no husband," and "shake the yoke she so dislikes."[72] Women invariably defended themselves from these charges, for if the court became persuaded that the desire for freedom was the true motive of their actions, their suits would have been thrown out.

A surprising use of the term *fueros* (privileges) in connection with the husband's prerogatives in marriage appears in two of the divorce cases, one colonial and one republican. In 1816 the Spanish merchant don Ramón Martínez Calderón complained that his wife "never wished to observe the *fueros* and respect owed a husband, but wished to proceed with liberty in everything." Likewise, in 1846 the captain don Marcos Arellano charged that his wife, by arranging to be transferred to a depósito where she could live "with complete breadth and freedom," was "ridiculing the *fueros del marido*."[73] In a sense, then, the popular mentality classified husbands as a distinct corporation in society with its own fueros, which included the right to control their wives' behavior. The corporatist view of society, used by legal commentators to justify women's inferior legal position, was thus shared by these litigants in divorce cases.

Although Mexicans believed that wives should be subordinated to husbands, they disagreed on what that meant in practice. An undercurrent of male opinion regarded a wife as her husband's property, to treat as he liked. Whereas a husband's desertion was termed "abandonment," husbands often referred to their wives' desertion as an "escape" (*fuga*), as if she were a prisoner or a slave.[74] Several husbands viewed a wife's exercise of her legal rights as an insufferable affront to their authority, like don Antonio Esteves, who cited as proof of his wife's recalcitrance that she had filed suit against him in criminal court. Others agreed with Félix Morales who, by arguing that the divorce action was invalid because he supported his wife, implied that he could do whatever he pleased with her as long as he maintained her. "She's mine," he declared, and "not even the Pope has the right to take her away from me."[75] Such expressions of possessiveness were cruder and more widespread among the lower classes than the elites, but it is difficult to tell whether elite men felt differently or simply knew enough to keep these thoughts to themselves.

Most wives did not accept the extreme definition of a husband's powers. Even the submissive doña Josefa Escalona, who pledged in her reunion compact that she would obey her husband whenever possible and never leave the house without first asking his permission, wrote in provisos to protect her rights. These included freedom to see her relatives and go to Church, and regular access to spending money. Other wives rejected similar terms for reunions, especially when their husbands wished to prohibit them from seeing relatives and friends.[76] Doña Dolores Pérez, lamenting "the weakness [and] miserable condition of my sex," argued: "Neither nature nor law can deny me the recourse open even to slaves, that of changing their master and domicile when they have been as mistreated and detested as I have been."[77] And doña María de los Remedios Omaña clearly believed a husband's rights should be limited by the "laws of equity":

> In order for the conjugal partnership to be felicitous and stable, it should be regulated by the laws of equity. This balance should compensate for the inequality of strength and resources that nature establishes between the associates. Thus the husband, who is the stronger, does not acquire the right to be unfaithful or to oppress his wife, who is the weaker. Their duties and privileges are reciprocal on this point. . . . The supremacy and authority of the husband, as is true of all those that exist legitimately on this earth, are based on the advantages and protection that he should bestow upon the spouse who is subordinated to him.[78]

Differing interpretations of the legitimate bounds of the husband's authority caused severe strains in Mexican marriages. Conflicts over the proper extent of a wife's subordination emerge most dramatically from the discussions of wife abuse, but also appear in fights over property, adultery, and in-laws. For even when charges involved a husband's failure to fulfill his marital duties, most women sought divorce because they felt their husbands had abused their superior position. Their complaints suggest pervasive sources of marital tensions in Mexico City.

*Wife Abuse*

Physical abuse was the primary reason women gave for seeking divorce. Despite the many divorce actions dropped before reaching the final resolution, 26 women were able to prove their allegations convincingly. In 15 of the cases the charges were confirmed at the stage of formal proofs by the graphic testimony of eyewitnesses; in the others the husbands themselves confessed their guilt or the charges were substantiated by medical certificates attesting to contusions and broken bones.

Although some of the women may have invented or exaggerated their charges in order to get out of an unhappy marriage, the problem of wife abuse revealed in divorce records appears to be part of a wider behavioral pattern. It is attested to in the records of secular courts, where there was no similar advantage to filing a complaint on a trumped-up charge, since the wife's goal there was not to obtain a separation, but to change her husband's behavior by having him temporarily jailed or fined. Wife abuse also appears in a variety of contemporary published accounts. Not surprisingly, even the English traveler W. Bullock, in his short stay in the capital, noted enough drunken husbands beating their wives on the city streets to write of it, for as Fernández de Lizardi remarked, "Thousands of these iniquitous husbands . . . are to be seen daily among us. Judges, prisons, presidios, streets, and houses are witnesses to this truth." The legal scholar Anastasio de la Pascua similarly considered the "monstrous excesses [of] brutal husbands" against wives "an all too frequent crime, . . . especially among persons of poor education."[79]

Despite some observers' belief that wife abuse was a problem of the lower classes, the divorce records indicate that it existed at every level of Mexican society. Even the gentry had its share of chronic wife-beaters, like don José Villamil y Primo, married to "La Güera" Rodríguez. Several highly respected Mexican citizens chanced to find her "bathed in blood and with her visage black and blue" from her husband's blows. After suffering eight years in silence "to avoid worrying her parents and dishonoring her husband," she pressed criminal charges against him for attempted murder on July 4, 1802, when Captain Villamil shot at her with his pistol. The details of their marriage emerged only because her husband, after his release from house arrest in August, brought a divorce suit against her for adultery. This charge, which one of her confessors, the Vicar Francisco Manuel Arévalo, felt was "undoubtedly intended only to excuse the abominable fact that he had beaten her many times," appeared to be as false as her countercharges of cruelty and abuse were true.[80]

But domestic violence may have been less prevalent among the elites. Table 26 shows that women in the upper and middle classes charged their husbands with physical abuse less often than those of the lower classes—but the difference is too slight

TABLE 26

*Principal Charges Against Husbands by Class, 1800–1857*

| Wife's class | Cruelty alone | Cruelty and physical abuse | Adultery | Lack of financial support | Drunken- ness | Number of wives filing charges |
|---|---|---|---|---|---|---|
| Upper | | | | | | |
| No. of charges | 1 | 10 | 9 | 1 | 0 | 12 |
| Pct. of wives | 8.3% | 83.3% | 75.0% | 8.3% | 0.0% | |
| Middle | | | | | | |
| No. of charges | 3 | 7 | 1 | 1 | 2 | 10 |
| Pct. of wives | 30.0% | 70.0% | 10.0% | 10.0% | 20.0% | |
| Lower-middle | | | | | | |
| No. of charges | 0 | 24 | 8 | 12 | 5 | 24 |
| Pct. of wives | 0.0% | 100.0% | 33.3% | 50.0% | 20.8% | |
| Lower | | | | | | |
| No. of charges | 1 | 12 | 5 | 11 | 7 | 13 |
| Pct. of wives | 7.7% | 92.3% | 38.5% | 84.6% | 53.8% | |
| Unknown | | | | | | |
| No. of charges | 0 | 4 | 2 | 1 | 0 | 4 |
| Pct. of wives | 0.0% | 100.0% | 50.0% | 25.0% | 0.0% | |
| All classes | | | | | | |
| No. of charges | 5 | 57 | 25 | 26 | 14 | 63 |
| Pct. of wives | 7.9% | 90.5% | 39.7% | 41.3% | 22.2% | |

NOTE: Most wives brought more than one of these charges against their husbands.

to be conclusive. A few upper-class women defined cruelty and abuse more subtly,[81] making much the same distinction that Payno made in *Bandidos de Río Frío*, where the sophisticated count threatens his young wife by brandishing a dagger he keeps under the pillow, whereas the brawny carpenter Evaristo mercilessly beats his wife in full view of his apprentice. Certainly, the goriest descriptions of wife beating were provided by the lower-class litigants. But this may simply be because they used coarser language than the more educated groups and, awed by the court, were readier to confess their faults. It may also be that, because of the nature of the recourse, the few lower-class women who came before the divorce court were particularly desperate. The only certain conclusion is that wife abuse, to the extent that it existed, was better hidden among the elites who greatly valued their honor and considered it stained by the admission of such ungentlemanly behavior.

Studies of present-day wife abuse in the United States relate the phenomenon to three circumstances: a husband's drunkenness, a wife's economic dependence, and a wife's pregnancy when the husband does not want another child.[82] These factors were occasionally associated with the violent incidents in the Mexican divorce records, but the correlation was not a strong one. Drunkenness was linked to a husband's abuse in only one-fifth of the cases. Yet as a legally recognized demonstration of incorrigibility, it was likely to have been cited whenever it existed. The charge was more prevalent descending the social scale, supporting the contemporary opinion that excessive drinking was a problem primarily of the lower classes.[83] Even among these groups, however, the strongest link was between drunkenness and neglect or failure to provide. Five women mentioned that they were pregnant during a violent episode, but only doña Josefa Urrutia connected the pregnancy with the beatings, explaining that "each of my pregnancies has been a series of sufferings because my husband despairs to see his family increase when he lacks the means to support it."[84] Nor were the beatings clearly tied to economic dependency, since wives who contributed to the family income through work or dowry were victimized, as were those who did not. Thus the divorce records show no consistent pattern of circumstances giving rise to domestic violence.

Wife abuse was, as elsewhere, intimately linked to the ideology granting husbands the authority to control wives. The divorce records demonstrate that many nineteenth-century Mexicans believed a husband's authority included the right to administer corporal punishment as a means of guiding his wife's behavior. Husbands often admitted to hitting their wives, justifying their actions as attempts to "reduce her to her duties." As don Mariano García, a professor of medicine, explained, he had not beaten his wife, but only slapped or pushed her occasionally "to correct her pride and rebelliousness, an action that should be considered a moderate punishment, well within a husband's right to dispense."[85]

The humble merchant José Magdaleno Rosales similarly defended his right to punish his wife. After six years of marriage, Paula Pasarán requested a divorce on the grounds of his extreme cruelty, claiming that he caused her to live in constant terror. She alleged, among other things, that he hit her for the first time on their wedding day. Then,

when she was pregnant . . . with her first child he whipped her with a metal rod [causing her to miscarry]. . . . Soon afterward he struck her with a sword and with a shovel, and on that occasion would have killed her had not some passersby come to her defense. . . . Several days later he was going to throw her into the *acequia* [canal] that runs along their house, after having beaten her with the heel of a shoe, causing much blood to flow. [Another time] he threw some jars of boiling water at her. [Once] because she found him embracing another woman and reproached him, he struck her with a butcher's knife, and this time Rosales's own father defended her. Finally, . . . during their [recent] visit to her parents' house, there were days when he beat her with a stick in the morning, hit her with a club and slapped her at night, and [one day], being very drunk (as he is habitually), . . . he took her to a maguey field, hurled himself upon his victim, beat her, dragged her by the hair, struck her with a pole, and threatened to end her life; of the latter incident there are records in the Municipal Court of Texcoco.

Addressing each allegation individually in his defense, Rosales explained that on one occasion his wife's "haughtiness and disrespect" had "obliged him to lift his hand against her," and that on another her insults had likewise forced him "to reform her insolence." He assured the provisor that he had not touched his wife before the miscarriage, but concluded that "the other cases to which she refers in her . . . deposition [were] quarrels provoked by her . . . pride, and in all these instances I merely used a husband's authority to establish order in my house, for this has always been my duty." [86]

Although wives did not question their husbands' right to administer moderate physical punishment (at least not in the divorce records), they invariably defined acceptable bounds much more narrowly than the men did. The issue in women's depositions was not whether a husband had hit his wife; it was whether he had done so ruthlessly and whether she had given him motive for his acts. Still, the wives consistently censured what one called her husband's "cruel and constant correction." [87]

Women's resistance to this kind of treatment found vigorous support among Mexican writers throughout the first half of the nineteenth century. In 1806 the *Diario de México* saw fit to print a summary of a court case against a brutal husband, "so that the spectacle of the execution of justice may serve as an example for the readers and dissuade them from similar acts." In 1818 Fernández de Lizardi pronounced husbands who mistreated their wives "vile," "roguish," "infamous," "irreligious," "despotic," "tyrannous," and "barbarous," arguing that "the civilized man who knows the laws of humanity and honor never takes advantage of [a woman's] weakness to injure her." Echoing his words in a speech to the Constitutional Convention in 1856, Ignacio Ramírez found it "shameful in a civilized country" that "many unfortunate women are beaten by their husbands."[88]

Disapproval of wife abuse was apparently on the rise, for laws on domestic violence were tightened in 1845. In contrast to the 1828 decree that set up the Vagrants Tribunal, the 1845 vagrancy code included wife beaters—along with drunkards and gamblers—among those to be tried by that body. Still, its definition of antisocial behavior was limited to the husband who mistreated his wife "frequently without any motive, scandalizing the community with his conduct." Although the new law gave the State the power to arrest and punish violent husbands, wife abuse, as a private crime, was normally investigated only if a woman or her relatives filed a formal complaint.[89]

Furthermore, the distinction between wife beating and moderate physical force, applied as part of the legitimate exercise of the husband's authority, was highly subjective. Society disapproved of clear-cut wife abuse, but there was a gray area in which it was tolerated to some degree. Eyewitnesses occasionally disagreed about a husband's treatment of his wife, some finding it reasonable, others seeing it as unduly harsh. The lack of consensus is illustrated in doña María Antonia Reyna y Vega's suit against her second husband, don Ramón Martínez Calderón. She charged that her life was endangered by his irrational and brutal behavior; he replied that, if anything, his punishments had been "too mild," for they failed to correct her "insulting behavior" and "desire to dominate." One witness, a young clerk in Martínez Calderón's shop, testified that during their fights don Ramón had not hit his wife "excessively." But her brother-in-law don Celestino Porras testified that, though she was not the easiest woman to get along with, her husband had definitely "gone too far in trampling her."[90]

Even in cases of "undue" wife abuse, there was no agreement on how much a wife should endure. Many ecclesiastical officials and respected citizens drawn into the divorce suits believed that the importance of preserving a marriage outweighed all other considerations unless a woman's life was in imminent danger. For instance, two of the priests to whom "La Güera" Rodríguez turned for advice sympathized with her plight and exhorted her husband to moderate his behavior. But their recommendations to her were to confess regularly, pray that "the All Powerful would quiet the spirit of her consort," "be patient," and "endure the yoke of matrimony as best she could."[91]

These conflicting views of the problem made a battered wife's position ambiguous. Secular and ecclesiastical courts provided a recourse for her to use against an abusive husband, and social commentators supported her decision to bring him to justice. At the same time, the community pressured her to put up with mistreatment in deference to her husband's rightful authority and in order to preserve the marriage. In the end, it was up to the woman to decide how much she was willing to tolerate.

## Money and Property

Failure to provide was the second most frequent charge wives brought against husbands. In contrast to wifebeating, failure to provide was primarily a lower-class phenomenon—and not unexpectedly, given the high incidence of unemployment and marginal employment in the Mexican capital. The two middle- and upper-class litigants who raised this charge simply meant that their husbands were stingy. It was in the two lower groups that women complained of husbands who did not work or spent their earnings on drinking, gambling, and mistresses.

Conflicts over property were more widespread than the formal charges suggest. Middle- and upper-class,litigants frequently cited disputes over property as the underlying cause of their marital strife. Seven wives, three of them widows who had remarried, accused their husbands of mishandling the property entrusted to them or of disposing (or attempting to dispose) of the wife's dowry against her will. Doña Dolores Pérez, whose second husband gambled away her dowry and her children's inheritance from their father, complained that she was forced to work to support herself, making candies that her maid sold in the marketplace. The other cases, not associated with gambling, had less drastic effects. However, five of the wives contemplated going to court to remove their property from their husband's control. Only one had actually done so by the time of the divorce suit, lamenting that her husband's cruelty and beatings dated from the day he "ceased to be the administrator of my small wealth."[92]

The charge of failure to provide did not, as one might expect, merely involve a husband's nonfulfillment of his marital duties; on close examination it often masked a form of abuse of authority. Lower- and lower-middle class women whose husbands abandoned them usually went to work and had little reason to file for divorce. The majority of those who came before the divorce court (15 of 23) complained instead of husbands who expected to be supported by their wives and who beat them when they did not have any money to give them. In a few extreme cases husbands wandered about, seeking out their wives only to seize the money they had managed to earn on their own. One of these unfortunate wives was María Hilaria Hernández, who brought a divorce action against her husband, Félix Morales, in 1839. According to her depositions and the testimony of witnesses, when he used to work as a tailor he spent all his earnings on his mistress. Then, when she herself took a job as a servant, he broke into her employer's house, beat her, and stole all her clothes and savings. After that, when she opened an *atolería*, he presented himself regularly to quarrel and steal her earnings, forcing her to close the shop, and he was repeating this pattern in the house where she was presently serving, endangering her employment. María's divorce suit was therefore an attempt to protect her livelihood as well as her life.[93]

As with the charges of failure to provide, most of the disputes over property revolved around how much authority over her belongings a wife was willing to relinquish. In many cases a woman's desire to scrutinize the management of her property was regarded by her husband as an encroachment on his rights. For example, after don Mariano García lost a large sum of money, his wife, doña María Josefa Mijares, asked to be kept informed of his business dealings. He considered her request "scandalous" and "in no way consonant with the submission that a married woman owes her husband." Twice she threatened to go to court to remove her dowry and share of the community property from his dominion. Labeling these acts "despicable and abominable," her husband accused her of "trying to dominate him" in this way. Sympathy was on his side in this matter: the two gentlemen she approached to administer her property refused, "so as not to contribute to the ruin of a marriage."[94]

A woman's attempts to control her property during marriage therefore carried considerable social opprobrium, making her legal rights difficult to enforce. The enterprising doña Josefa Escalona managed to persuade her husband to renounce the administration of her property as a condition for their reunion, threatening him with a divorce action otherwise.[95] But she was the exception. A wife's recovery of her belongings was usually accepted only in the case of a separation. Consequently, in at least three cases the wife's resolve to seek a divorce stemmed primarily from this desire, and it may have impelled many more women who did not choose to reveal their true motives to the court. Again, even disputes over property demonstrate the extent to which divorce was a recourse for women seeking protection—of property or person—rather than a remedy for unhappy marriages.

## Adultery

Adultery was the source of strain in many marriages, but it was not the primary reason women sought divorce. Although it was the most solid ground for separation under canon law, only 25 of the 63 wives cited it in their divorce actions. Even then, 24 of them presented it as of secondary importance to the beatings or threats to property that compelled them to seek a separation.[96] Several women felt as doña María Josefa Mijares did. She explained that she could have borne the infidelities had "he hidden them from me, fulfilled his duties, [and] attempted to treat me with affection . . . even if it were feigned."[97] It thus appears that wives had internalized the double standard to the point where they did not consider their husband's infidelity a serious violation of the marriage vow.

Such a violation on the part of the wife, however, was taken seriously enough by the men. Fourteen of 23 husbands who brought charges or counter-charges against their wives exclusively alleged adultery, compared with only one of 65 wives, and men brought the charge in 71 percent of their suits or counter-charges, compared with 38 percent of the women's. It was not that wives committed adultery more often than men; the contrary was true. Rather, husbands were less willing to tolerate a wife's infidelity because, as the colonel don Manuel Camacho explained, it "robbed me of my honor." Several husbands considered a wife's affair so grave a transgression that they filed for divorce merely on suspicion of her misconduct. Their obsessive jealousy even led a few husbands to question the intentions of their wives' lawyers; don José Villamil y Primo suspected his attractive young wife of having an affair with almost every man who laid eyes on her. Many a husband maintained constant vigils against the possibility of a wife's affairs, and his suspicion was often the cause of the couple's quarrels and his violence. For example, don Mariano García, after he found his wife talking to a carpenter who was working in their house, "slapped her a few times to make her understand . . . that under no circumstance should she speak to a stranger with such familiarity . . . for [this behavior] was unbecoming to a married woman."[98] Indeed, whereas women in half the cases substantiated their allegations of their husbands' adultery with eyewitnesses or previous convictions in criminal court (notwithstanding the large number of actions that were dropped), the majority of the husbands' adultery charges appear to have been quite unfounded.

Still, if the double standard was widely accepted, it was not absolute. It was certainly not accepted by the ecclesiastical court, which followed the doctrines of canon law. In fact, for the *promotor fiscal*, the extremely cruel treatment María Navora Soberanis had received from her "perverted" and "barbarous" husband, the blacksmith Pedro Rivera (not only had he beaten her mercilessly with his tools, but he had crippled his own father when he intervened on his daughter-in-law's behalf), seemed weaker grounds for divorce than Rivera's scandalous affair with

Pioquinta Campos. Consequently, Rivera's adultery was given as the principal reason María was granted a perpetual divorce in her favor.[99] Neither was the double standard fully accepted by the secular authorities, who routinely prosecuted men for adultery even though Hispanic law expressly prohibited women from bringing their husbands to court on that charge.[100]

Although most women did not consider a husband's infidelity important enough in and of itself to seek a divorce, they did not meekly accept it either. Many had raised the issue in private, as had doña María Antonia Reyna y Vega, who "reminded [her husband] several times about the fidelity he owed me."[101] Two of the three wives who discovered that their husbands were having an affair with a maid immediately dismissed her, thus registering their disapproval, as did the numerous wives who accused their husbands of adultery in the secular courts. Many women singled out their husbands' affairs as the turning point in their marriages: half of the wives who included adultery charges in their divorce suits specifically stated that this was the major cause of the beatings they endured, for husbands often reacted violently to their wives' reproaches.

Another indication of the only partial acceptance of the double standard was that it (and stern legal penalties) did not keep women from having extramarital affairs. Four husbands were able to demonstrate that their wives had been unfaithful, presenting eyewitnesses and incriminating love letters as proof. Doña Francisca Pérez Gálvez, confessing to her husband's charge (substantiated by a carefully drawn diagram of a trysting place she rented under a servant's name and entered by ladder), attempted to place some of the blame on her spouse. Her explanation that since he "denied her the [marital] debt she was forced to seek elsewhere what she did not find in her marriage" suggests that some Mexican women considered sex both necessary and enjoyable.[102] The defense put up by doña María Josefa Arriaga, accused in criminal court of adultery with a cadet, seems to imply a fairly relaxed attitude toward a wife's affairs in at least some segments of society. Insisting that she "loved the cadet," she argued that "[this] was not unusual, both because ladies of more status than she had *cortejos* (lover-escorts) and because it was common in this city."[103] The very use of the word

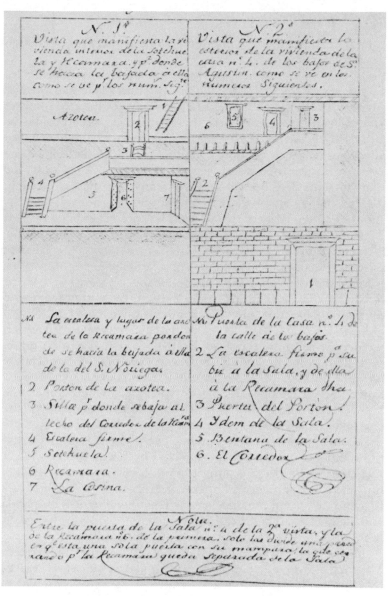

11. In an ecclesiastical divorce case prosecuted over the years 1818–22, don Lorenzo García Noriega submitted this diagram to the court, showing how his wife, the aristocratic doña Francisca Pérez Gálvez, had entered the adjoining house, rented as a trysting place, by mounting a ladder from the roof (*azotea*) of their home. Although both spouses were apparently guilty of infidelity and thus ineligible for divorce under canon law, their social background must have swayed the court, which granted them a rare "absolute divorce" and absolved both of any wrongdoing.

cortejo indicates that the phenomenon was widespread enough to warrant a specialized term.

Other sources likewise demonstrate that women in Mexico City were far freer in practice than the double standard would suggest. Firsthand observers like Joel Poinsett, the U.S. Minister to Mexico in 1822, commented that married ladies "are said to be faithful to the favored lover, and a liaison of that nature does not affect the lady's reputation." The German Carl Sartorius, who lived in Mexico for several years three decades later, observed that "intrigue does not enter every family; it is more frequent in the luxurious capital than in the country." Fanny Calderón, shocked by the laxity of morals and the "perfect indifference" to "liaisons" existing among her circle of friends, wrote her family: "As long as a woman attends Church regularly, is a patroness of charitable institutions, and gives no scandal by her outward behavior, she may do pretty much as she pleases. . . . I must, however, confess that this indulgence on the part of women of unimpeachable reputation is sometimes carried too far."[104]

Although these travelers may have exaggerated for effect, women in large metropolises like Mexico City were no doubt freer than in small towns with close community control. The reluctance of city people to interfere in the affairs of others is illustrated in doña Dolores Medina's divorce case, where a man who had gone out of his way to satisfy his curiosity about what she and a lieutenant colonel, don José María Salazar, were doing in the dining room one evening while everyone else was in the living room—and who was scandalized by his discovery—never told doña Dolores's husband of her infidelity until after she left him and filed for divorce. The reason he kept silent, he said, was to avoid discord in the marriage.[105] The unwillingness of friends and neighbors to become involved was thus partly rooted in their desire to maintain the stability of the marital union.

But the degree of social tolerance should not be exaggerated. Most wives accused of adultery in criminal as well as ecclesiastical court professed shame and remorse—as well they might to avoid losing their dowry and community property. For instance, doña Luisa Solórzano, whose husband was granted a perpetual divorce, confessed to having acted in "a moment of weakness" and begged her spouse to forgive her and take her back. Moreover, the divorce records indicate that women went to great lengths to try to keep their affairs secret, arranging clandestine meetings and sending love letters disguised in the margins of newspapers.[106]

Few unfaithful husbands, on the other hand, either expressed any regret for their actions or tried to hide their affairs from their wives. Don Ramón Martínez Calderón allegedly told his wife that "he would like to have her handcuffed and be able to love 10 or 25 women." Two men brought illegitimate children home to their wives, and three brought their mistresses. Félix Morales even forced his wife to wait on his mistress on one occasion; on another, he came home alone and, in the presence of a visitor, demanded that his wife feed him immediately, saying that "he was not going to his other woman because it was his wife's obligation to serve him, not the other's."[107] Indeed, the fact that a reproachful wife frequently got a beating for her pains indicates that husbands may have considered it their right to commit adultery, though they did not dare try to justify it before the ecclesiastical court.

It is tempting to argue that upper-class wives were less willing to accept the double standard than other wives, since they charged husbands with adultery at nearly twice the average rate, and the only wife who filed suit solely on the basis of a husband's infidelity was a countess, doña Dolores Valdivieso y Valdivieso. Even though it is possible that upper-class women, accustomed to their privileged social position, demanded more respect for themselves and would not countenance the scandal of a husband's affair, another explanation is plausible. Lower-class women, able simply to leave a relationship that soured, would not have bothered to file for divorce on that charge. (Not that they were more tolerant of a husband's affairs: lower-class women were far more likely than upper-class women to bring criminal charges against unfaithful husbands in secular court.) In contrast, some upper-class women, needing to formalize a separation, may have used that transgression to buttress their cases, though they still sought divorce primarily for protection.

Although the differences of opinion on the gravity of adultery did not necessarily follow class lines, they existed nonetheless, with attitudes ranging from the double standard to the Church's

TABLE 27
*Principal Charges Against Husbands by Period, 1800–1857*

| Period | Cruelty alone | Cruelty and physical abuse | Adultery | Lack of financial support | Drunkenness | Number of wives filing charges |
|---|---|---|---|---|---|---|
| 1800–1819 | | | | | | |
| No. of charges | 1 | 14 | 8 | 4 | 3 | 16 |
| Pct. of wives | 6.3% | 87.5% | 50.0% | 25.0% | 18.8% | |
| 1820–1839 | | | | | | |
| No. of charges | 2 | 21 | 10 | 12 | 4 | 23 |
| Pct. of wives | 8.7% | 91.3% | 43.5% | 52.2% | 17.4% | |
| 1840–1857 | | | | | | |
| No. of charges | 2 | 22 | 7 | 10 | 7 | 24 |
| Pct. of wives | 8.3% | 91.7% | 29.2% | 41.7% | 29.2% | |
| Total 1800–1857 | | | | | | |
| No. of charges | 5 | 57 | 25 | 26 | 14 | 63 |
| Pct. of wives | 7.9% | 90.5% | 39.7% | 41.3% | 22.2% | |

NOTE: Most wives brought more than one of these charges against their husbands.

egalitarian teachings. A dramatic drop in the incidence of adultery charges in divorce cases indicates that a more tolerant view of the husband's adultery was on the rise (Table 27). Since upper-class litigants charged adultery most frequently, it is not surprising that fewer adultery charges were made as divorce became accessible to a wider spectrum of people. This satisfactorily explains the slight decrease between 1800–1819 and 1820–39, but it does not explain the precipitous fall-off thereafter, when the class background of the litigants was approximately the same as in the previous 20 years. Since it is unlikely that men committed adultery less often as the century progressed, this trend suggests that women either tolerated their husbands' adultery more than before or selected their charges to appeal to current opinion, more sympathetic to the physically abused wife than the one whose husband had been unfaithful. In the second case, one might suppose that a wife whose case was weak on the grounds of mistreatment but strong on adultery would not have tried to file for divorce, as she might have earlier.

The apparent strengthening of the double standard may reflect the secularization of society and circumscription of the Church by liberal reforms. Indeed as the Church, defender of equal matrimonial duties for husbands and wives, continued to lose ground, the more discriminatory secular view of adultery came to govern divorce law. Although the 1859 Reform law establishing secular jurisdiction over divorce maintained the same grounds as canon law, the civil codes of the second half of the nineteenth century made a man's adultery grounds for divorce only in certain circumstances, whereas a woman's was in all cases.[108] The removal of divorce from clerical jurisdiction was not, therefore, favorable to wives because it reduced the grounds on which they could obtain separations. In practice, however, these legal changes merely reflected a weakening of canonical principles that was already in progress, despite the Church's continued insistence on the fidelity that husbands owed their wives.

### In-Laws and Family

After adultery and money problems, the interference of relatives was the most frequently cited source of marital conflict. This was primarily a male complaint: 21 husbands (43 percent of the 49 men petitioning for divorce, filing counter-charges, or merely responding to their wives' petitions) held in-laws responsible for the couple's strife. Only two wives complained of their in-laws, and children were hardly ever mentioned as a reason for domestic disputes. Although a few women accused their husbands of setting a bad example for the children, only María Navora Soberanis accused her husband of beating a child.[109]

It was the wife's parents, especially her mother, whom husbands blamed, though in four cases brothers- and sisters-in-law were reproached as well. Don Esteban Enciso claimed that his wife's mother "always fans the flames of our arguments" and José María Rosales insisted that his mother-in-law "seduced" his wife and gave her bad advice, "being the principal cause of the disturbances of our marriage." Several husbands suspected their in-laws of being "allies and perhaps accomplices" in the liaisons of their wives, and one brought a criminal suit against his mother-in-law for aiding and abetting his wife in what proved to be a nonexistent affair.[110] Four men threatened to kill their mothers-in-law, and many husbands attempted to prohibit their wives from seeing parents and relatives, both during the marriage and, more often, during the divorce proceedings.

Husbands sometimes felt that their authority was threatened by the competing claims of in-laws over their daughter and her property. If a married woman's parents were alive and living in Mexico City, she would usually see them daily. Several husbands charged that a wife would rather live with her parents (and in one case, sister) than with him.[111] Most wives turned to their parents for support and advice with marital problems; those who temporarily left their husbands usually returned to the family home, as did many women who were abandoned by their spouses or obtained a divorce.[112] Fathers occasionally accompanied daughters to file for divorce or bring criminal actions against husbands, and one mother quit her job in the provinces to be with her daughter in Mexico City during the difficult period of the divorce proceedings.[113]

The mother of "La Güera" Rodríguez believed that but for the proximity of relatives, don José Villamil y Primo would have abused her daughter still more than he had. When the couple left Mexico City to spend a season at his hacienda, the mother, "grieved by the separation from the daughter [and fearful] of any harm that her husband might do her . . . so far from her parents and relatives," asked the local parish priest to watch over her.[114] Thus both parents and husbands saw the wife's family as a balance to her husband's power.

It was perhaps for this reason that many husbands were bent on maintaining some distance from their wife's relatives. For instance, in their reunion compact, don Pedro Padilla and doña Josefa Escalona pledged—at his insistence—"to prevent the interference of our respective families in our domestic dissension." Padilla, for his part, promised "not to prohibit my wife from seeing . . . her family, taking her myself to her sister's house whenever she wishes and I am able, for I also desire to encourage and preserve the good harmony and intelligence that should prevail among relatives."[115]

It was rare for married couples to live with their parents, and for five couples this arrangement was the source of animosity. One woman complained that her husband had "not even provided [her] with a hut where she could live with the liberty and mastery to which she [was] entitled" as mistress of a household. Ecclesiastical officials agreed with another protesting spouse that "a married couple should [live] alone." Indeed, one reunion was explicitly made conditional on the couple's moving into their own home. In another case, the ecclesiastical judge presiding over a *juicio de conciliación* advised the man to build "a separate house where his wife could live apart from his parents."[116] Because all five cases date from the late 1840's and the 1850's it is possible that Mexicans increasingly believed that couples needed privacy and distance from their kin, perhaps to the detriment of some women who relied on relatives to mitigate a husband's abuses. But the divorce cases indicate that, as foreign travelers remarked, Mexican families were very close, perhaps more so than in the United States where by the nineteenth century the parents of divorcing couples were minimally involved in their children's problems and the couples rarely referred to in-laws in their depositions.[117]

## Changing Expectations

Although it cannot be proved statistically, the divorce records suggest subtle changes in attitudes toward marriage during the first half of the nineteenth century. The increasing respect for women led to a redefinition of the wife's place that put her on a more equal footing with the husband. The expansion of individualism, with its emphasis on the right to personal freedom and fulfillment, led to a growing acceptance of divorce and proposals for divorce reform. Both resulted in a liberalization of divorce procedures and a weakening of the principles of canon law that envisioned separation merely as a protective mechanism and subordinated the individual to the defense of matrimony.

These changes are barely visible in the formal charges made by the couples seeking divorce. Table 27 shows that, though cruelty was the primary charge wives brought against husbands over the entire period, women were slightly more likely to accuse husbands of abuse after independence than before. However, that shift probably reflects the increased proportion of lower-class women seeking divorce, rather than an increase either in wife abuse or in women's resistance to it. Because of broadening class participation also, lack of financial support and drunkenness were cited more frequently after independence. Only the dramatic decrease in the charges of adultery cannot easily be explained by the changing class mix alone. As already noted, this trend probably reflects a growing tolerance of men's adultery rather than a behavioral change. Accompanying the erosion of the more egalitarian religious view of society, the strengthening of the double standard can also be seen as part of the expansion of individual freedom; because of women's reproductive role and the importance of legitimacy in the inheritance system, this liberty was extended only to husbands and not to wives.

That the attitudes toward divorce changed is far easier to document. Beginning in the 1830's several litigants asked for a liberalization of that recourse, arguing that they should be granted a divorce because they no longer wanted to live with their spouses. Only the lieutenant colonel don José María Arrieta and his wife, doña Marciala Neira, were brazen enough to seek a divorce jointly on the grounds of mutual consent, in 1833. In 1836 doña María de los Remedios Omaña, charging her husband with adultery and cruelty (but not physical abuse), described matrimony as a "contract whose goal is the worldly happiness of the spouses and the fruits of their love," and urged that it be rescinded when it ceased to satisfy the needs of both partners, causing them only "anguish, pain, and affliction." In 1855 don Antonio Esteves, charging his wife with having filed an unsuccessful criminal suit against him, explained that by now they were so filled with hatred that "each had become insufferable to the other." In 1856 doña Severa Vázquez, stating only that she could no longer live with her husband (and that proof of his misdeeds would follow), asked the court to approve her divorce petition "considering how difficult it is for two wills, once divided, to live beneath the same roof without discord." These new attitudes were voiced predominantly by well-educated people who knew full well that incompatibility was not legally valid grounds for divorce, but they persisted.[118]

During the 1850's two women, both guilty of adultery themselves, filed for divorce (one on wildly invented charges) in an attempt to separate from spouses whom they despised but who were not abusive. Although they did not dare to confess their motives openly, as the other litigants had done, they too turned to ecclesiastical divorce primarily to end unhappy marriages rather than to protect themselves. Both women were frustrated by their husbands' opposition to a separation: doña Dolores Medina, fearful of losing her property, desisted in her action once her affair was discovered; so did doña Teodora Villar, after her husband filed criminal charges against her and obtained a warrant for her arrest.[119] Nevertheless, their efforts to leave their husbands after the love between them died, like the efforts of litigants seeking divorce on the basis of mutual incompatibility, manifest a growing belief that individuals should be free to find happiness through divorce.

During the colonial period two noblemen had similarly attempted to use divorce as a remedy for an unsatisfactory marriage, but both accused husbands were guilty of adultery. The difference after the 1830's was that a few litigants turned to the divorce court without having strong cases against their spouses. Not surprisingly, it was the well-to-do who sought divorce under these circumstances, since it was difficult for them to separate informally. But this trend should not be exaggerated, for the majority of women still sought divorce for protection above all, especially the lower-class women who initiated suits only in desperation. Because divorce was so difficult to obtain and continued to carry a social stigma, it was not a viable alternative for most hapless marriages.

Although very few people acted on the new views about divorce, there is some evidence that many subscribed to them. In 1834 Pascua, editor of the *Febrero mejicano*, reported that some spouses who desired a separation avoided the strict dispositions of canon law by asking a secular court to ratify a temporary separation based on a written compact. It is difficult to know how widespread this practice was, since I have located only one such compact.[120] But the very fact that Pascua deemed it necessary to warn his readers that such a divorce had no legal force suggests that some Mexicans no longer accepted the canonical strictures that allowed divorce only in extraordinary circumstances and when one spouse was at fault.

In 1850 the anonymous author of the *Nuevo Febrero* noted that divorce reform had been the subject of a heated debate in Mexico since revolutionary France adopted absolute divorce by mutual consent in 1792. According to his discussion, some Mexican jurists maintained that "whenever a couple is so incompatible in humor, customs, ideas, and inclinations that they come to hate each other . . . and quarrel constantly," it was advisable to separate them, because "the happiness of society results from the well-being of families, and this depends principally on the love between spouses." A few jurists apparently even argued that marriage, like a civil contract, should be dissolved when it ceased to satisfy both parties, so that they could remarry and find happiness.[121]

The author of the *Nuevo Febrero* affirmed that by midcentury no consensus had been reached on introducing absolute divorce or separation by mutual consent. He himself opposed any change in the divorce laws, fearing that if separations were easy to obtain the wife, the most vulnerable member of the couple, would be injured. In his view, the current difficulty in obtaining a divorce protected the aging wife; under the proposed reforms a husband, tiring of the wife who had lost the beauty of her youth, might pressure her into appearing to consent to a separation, thus leaving her abandoned in her old age.[122] Most of the authors of the Mexican civil codes agreed that indissoluble marriage favored women by providing security. Sierra in his 1859 draft code insisted that "the mutual consent of the spouses is not cause for a divorce, nor does it authorize a voluntary separation." Only the Zacatecas code of 1828 allowed separation based on "the mutual and free consent of the spouses," even then limiting it to marriages where the wife was younger than 45 years. When civil separation was established by the reform law of July 23, 1859, the prohibition against separation purely on the grounds of incompatibility was retained.[123]

The controversy over divorce reform suggests that Mexicans were increasingly ambivalent about how to reconcile social obligations with individual liberty. The Spanish term for separation on the grounds of mutual consent, *divorcio voluntario* ("voluntary divorce"), shows that it represented an expansion of the sphere of individual will. As Mexicans began to demand such an option, they rejected the Church's teachings on the primacy of the institution of matrimony over personal happiness.

The new emphasis on sentiment rather than duty as the basis of marriage is likewise revealed in a few of the divorce deposi-

12. The public exaltation of motherhood by mid-century is exemplified in this idealized print from a popular magazine of the period. Although the importance of love in marriage was increasingly emphasized by journalists and other writers as the century wore on, the woman as mother was adulated in a way that the woman as wife and companion never was. In this picture, curiously captioned "The Happy Couple" ("Los esposos felices"), the husband is conspicuous by his absence.

tions dating from the late 1830's onward. When, in 1836, doña María de los Remedios Omaña described the goal of matrimony as "the worldly happiness of the spouses"—and spoke of "the love so necessary" to that union—it is difficult to know whether the ideal she had in mind was one of harmony and affection or one of romantic love. But doña Carmen Rodríguez de Ayala clearly meant romantic love when, in 1852, she complained that her husband's adultery deprived her of his affection. Using language that did not appear in earlier divorce records, she charged him with having "said he didn't love me because he had given his heart to his lover."[124]

The ideal of marital relations based on love and mutual esteem contributed to a gradual reassessment of the power relations between the sexes. Reflecting the companionate ideal, the *Nuevo Febrero* stated: "The wife gives herself to her husband to complete her happiness and not for slavery; both are companions in their good or bad fortune, both are equal. . . . It is only to direct family business that the man is conceded some preeminence." Likewise, the anonymous author of an 1851 tract on educational reform believed that a wife should be her husband's "friend, helping him in his work [and] sharing in his fortune." In 1852 a Mexican journalist considered the "submissive" wife, "deprived even of her natural liberty and humiliated at her husband's feet like a servant rather than companion," a specter of the past. Similarly, Ignacio Ramírez, speaking to the Constitutional Convention of 1856, proclaimed that "the woman is equal to the man in marriage."[125]

Although Ramírez's proclamation was premature, the new talk of equality and the increasing respect for women did have a visible effect on some wives in divorce cases, intensifying their unwillingness to tolerate mistreatment. From the 1830's onward they were increasingly vocal in resisting their husbands' heavy-handed control, again using language that had not appeared in earlier divorce cases. Doña Dolores Pérez, arguing that "I do not have the vocation of a martyr . . . and see no reason why I should have to put up with [my husband's abuse]," pleaded that, in the name of justice, judges readily grant divorces "to the unluckily married and against the cruel oppressors of frail and helpless women." And doña María de los Santos Morales condemned her husband's "tyrannical" desire to "make her feel the iron yoke of [his] authority."[126]

As the century progressed, some women endured difficult situations for considerably less time before filing for divorce. This pattern is not reflected in the overall average: of the 47 cases in which the length of the marriage before filing is known, the typical couple had been married for nine years throughout the first half of the nineteenth century.[127] The majority of women still said they had endured bitter unhappiness for all but a short period after the wedding, and most tried other alternatives before seeking divorce. But increasingly, some women neither put up with years of suffering nor saw divorce as a last resort. Women married for five months or less appeared before the ecclesiastical tribunal for the first time in the 1830's (3 of 25 filed within six months of marriage in the 1830's, as did 6 of 33 in the next two decades). By the 1840's and 1850's, 12 of the 33 couples seeking divorce had been married two years or less, compared with only one of 19 from 1800 to 1819.[128]

The changing expectations women brought to marriage, whether of kind treatment, personal happiness, or love, are also suggested by their increased boldness in making use of "the sad recourse" when they needed it. Divorce, already a woman's recourse, became ever more so during the first half of the nineteenth century: in 1840–1857, women filed 96 percent of the 31 suits where the initiator is known, compared with 89 percent of 28 suits in 1820–1839, and only 83 percent of 18 suits in 1800–1819. Moreover, notarial records reveal an ascending incidence of divorce among Mexico City residents. In the sample of female transactions, divorced women rose from none in 1802 to 3 (6 percent) of those signing notarial instruments in 1853; in the sample of wills divorced women rose from none in 1802–3 to 6 (5 percent) of the female will-makers by 1853, and divorced men from one to 4.[129] Although their numbers were still miniscule, this pattern is further proof of the growing willingness to resort to divorce.

There is some evidence that the Church itself was beginning to accept a liberalization of divorce. In the 1830's divorce records became markedly shorter in length, as though the court were requiring less documentation. This trend culminated after 1854 in the granting of divorces on the basis of proof and on terms that were invalid according to canon law (though they had been used in the colonial period for a noble couple). Between 1854 and 1857 four couples obtained temporary divorces in less than four months, avoiding the lengthy judicial process by convincing the provisor in private discussions that there was just cause for a separation, without having to present formal demonstrations of their charges.[130] The divorces were granted for a fixed period of time (ranging from one to five years), and neither spouse was declared guilty. In three of these cases the couple signed a contract, approved by the provisor, which outlined the behavior they expected from each other during their separation. It appears that this simplified procedure was used only when the litigants persisted and had a strong case, for it did not appreciably affect the proportion of divorce petitions that were granted after 1850 (16 percent, compared with 14 percent for 1800–1849). It nonetheless streamlined the difficult divorce process for those who deserved help.

The new reliance on this procedure may reflect the view that abused women should find speedy protection through divorce— an attitude that suggests a growing sympathy for victimized wives. It may also reflect a response to the liberal criticism of clerical inefficiency, especially since the Church came under increasingly heavy fire from Reforma liberals after the Ayutla revolt of 1854. Or it may reflect the Church's acceptance of incompatibility as valid grounds for separation, an idea that goes hand in hand with a growing belief in the importance of happiness in marriage. Indeed, the two petitions submitted during the 1850's in which the plaintiff requested divorce because of incompatibility were not immediately thrown out of court as the earlier joint petition had been.[131] Although the divorce court gave no hint of its intentions, it was becoming more responsive to the individual's needs at the same time that individuals were more insistent in expressing them.

## Conclusion

These changes in ideas about marriage were subtle ones, by no means affecting all women involved in divorce suits. As doña Teresa Carrero put it in 1857, "The wife is still the weaker half of the couple despite all the proclamations about the equality of the spouses."[132] Litigants in divorce cases, contributors to popular literature, legal commentators, educators, and reformers continued to believe that husbands should govern wives. Because society sanctioned the moderate physical punishment of wives as a legitimate exercise of a husband's authority, some men ultimately used violence to maintain their superior position. Others dissipated their wives' wealth or attempted to control every detail of their daily activity. Although the degree of an individual woman's subjection to her spouse and the treatment she received depended on her personality and the man she married, the possibility for her oppression was inherent in the society's norms about marital relations, which gave him the power to rule and her the duty to obey.

But if in broad terms Mexicans believed that wives should be subordinated to husbands, they disagreed on the extent of that subordination. The couples who came before the divorce court argued about the circumstances under which the husband's domestic discipline was warranted, how much right he should have over a wife's earnings and property, whether he was entitled to commit adultery, and the degree to which he could control what she did and whom she saw. Most wives, even when they charged their husbands with failure to fulfill their marital duties, sought divorce because they saw themselves as "oppressed" and "tyrannized" by husbands who had abused their privileged position. Sexual inequality was therefore not without accompanying tensions, nor did it remain totally unchallenged.

Husbands and wives often tried to pit conflicting institutions and ideals against each other. Men relied on contemporary sexism, their wives' economic and legal dependence, and society's desire for the stability of marriage to back their more extreme definition of a husband's rights. Women appealed to the Church's egalitarian norms in demanding respect and fidelity; they manipulated their property, family relations, "persons of respect," and ecclesiastical and secular courts to provide external checks on their husbands' power. Although the wife who filed suit against her husband was rare, women's use of legal and extralegal recourses shows that there was a limit to how much subjection some wives would tolerate. It also shows that their desire to enforce those limits found support among some contemporary institutions and sectors of public opinion.

As the century progressed, public opinion slowly began to shift toward more egalitarian norms. Reflecting the trend toward modern conceptions of family life throughout the Western world, Mexicans began to speak of the ideal companionship of husbands and wives, citing love and happiness as the principal goals of matrimony. Wife-beaters increasingly came under community censure. Women were increasingly vocal in resisting attempts to be controlled. The patriarchal supervision of women during divorce proceedings was questioned, and their option of living independently at least considered. A few litigants called for divorce based on mutual consent, arguing that separations should be granted when marital expectations were unfulfilled, even if neither spouse had broken the marriage vows. As divorce gained in acceptance, some women began to seek it more readily when their marriages soured. The greater leniency of ecclesiastical officials in granting divorce by the 1850's suggests that they may have shared these sentiments. Thus even in this most private of institutions, Mexican society was far from static during the first half of the nineteenth century.

# Conclusion

NORTH AMERICAN scholars, concerned with explaining the weakness of feminist movements in Latin America, have suggested that women wield considerable power within the household where men supposedly rule. Evelyn Stevens argues that the characteristic Latin American *machismo*, the cult of virility, is counterbalanced by *marianismo*, the cult of female spiritual superiority.* In her view, women, by virtue of the belief in the sacredness of motherhood and their own moral preeminence, gain an emotional leverage that allows them to manipulate husbands and sons. For Stevens, this informal influence satisfactorily offsets women's lack of authority, making them "separate but equal" rather than inferior to men. Building on this perspective, Jane Jacquette goes farther, to argue that through marianismo women control events beyond the domestic sphere. Because extended families are so important in Latin America and because so many public decisions are made during gatherings of kin, women who dominate male relatives can exercise political and economic control without leaving the home. Both Jacquette and Stevens deny that role differentiation and its attendant machismo/marianismo myths are a source of oppression. Quite the opposite: they are the key to women's power.[1]

Stevens presents marianismo as a characteristically Latin American phenomenon, rooted in Iberian culture, but developed on New World soil during the colonial period. Yet marianismo bears a striking resemblance to the Victorian "cult of

*Note that *marianismo* as used by these scholars is distinct from *mariology*, the veneration of the Virgin Mary, or *hembrismo*, the passivity that is the opposite of the macho's aggressiveness.

true womanhood," which some historians credit with raising women's status in Europe and the United States. These scholars argue that with the separation of home and workplace in the nineteenth century, sex roles became highly differentiated, and the domestic sphere became a female and ultimately idealized domain. As the prestige of wife and mother grew, a romantic view of woman's moral perfection and spiritual strength took hold. Victorian women are said to have capitalized on these changes, stressing their differences from men in order to increase their power and autonomy within the family and, eventually, to justify excursions into public arenas requiring their purifying influence.[2]

The data for Mexico City strongly suggest that marianismo was not in fact a deep-seated Latin American cultural trait, but merely a variant of Victorianism introduced in the second half of the nineteenth century. To be sure, marianismo had much in common with traditional Hispanic views of women, since corporatism assigned each member of the State an equally important but different role to fill, and Catholicism insisted on the equality of Christian souls and the equal obligations of husband and wife. And certainly the view of the sacred mother was not new in a society with a strong Virgin cult, though there is no evidence that the idolization of Mary corresponded to a secular veneration of women.[3] These ideas may have made Latin Americans particularly receptive to marianismo, but corporatist and Catholic thought was clearly patriarchal, subordinating the wife to the husband and recognizing him as the moral and intellectual superior of the two.

During the late colonial and early republican years, Mexicans began to modify their conceptions of the inequality of the sexes. The older belief in female inferiority was increasingly tempered by a heightened respect for women. Reformers argued that women could make valuable contributions to national development, not only as enlightened mothers and frugal consumers, but also as productive workers, teachers, and supervisors of welfare institutions. Educators insisted that women and men had equal intellectual abilities and attributed women's deficiencies solely to a faulty education. Legal commentators questioned men's natural superiority and recognized women's full capacity to govern themselves. Popular writers and litigants in divorce cases began to speak of the equality of the sexes and the companionship of husbands and wives. Indeed, there is some evidence that by the middle of the century the acceptable degree of wives' subordination was reduced, with society censuring wife abuse more harshly and some women being less willing to tolerate mistreatment than earlier.

Few Mexicans believed, however, that women were spiritually superior to men.[4] Although some women may in practice have dominated their homes because of their purity, piety, and moral strength, that was not how society conceived of them as a group. As late as the 1850's, some writers still considered a virtuous woman less a reflection of her own inherent nature than a credit to the wise man who shaped her. Men were often regarded as better able to resist the temptations of adultery than women, whose moral convictions were weaker. Religion and charity were not yet feminized, although women began to be viewed as allies of the Church in the republican conflict with the State.[5] Women were referred to not only as the Fair and Delicate Sex, but as El Sexo Débil, El Sexo Flaco, the feeble part of the human race. Neither tracts on educational reform nor divorce depositions hint at women's spiritual perfection. Even though women were considered necessary to social reform, they were not deemed capable of redeeming wayward husbands or spearheading the moral renovation of society. On the contrary, poorly educated women were portrayed as the source of social ills.

Furthermore, husband and wife were not regarded as equals reigning in separate spheres. Although Mexicans acknowledged women's responsibility in managing the household, they were careful to distinguish the wife's "purely domestic and economic government" from the husband's overall dominance of the domestic sphere. It was only at the end of the nineteenth century, with the arrival of full-fledged Victorianism, that women would be seen as custodians of moral values, high priestesses ruling the home with delicate touch.[6]

Still, a few concepts associated with marianismo and Victorianism did begin to surface in Mexico in the 1840's and 1850's. The most widespread was the romantic exaltation of motherhood. To be sure, earlier commentators had recognized the value of women's maternal role, but the father was seen as having the primary responsibility in childrearing, as in Fernández de Lizardi's *Quijotita*, where the good colonel closely supervises his wife's efforts. By midcentury the socialization of children was assigned to "the exclusive care of the mother." Motherhood began to be hyperbolized as an "august function," a "saintly" and "sublime mission" that gave women a "sacred" position in society.[7]

A few Mexicans even stepped beyond this veneration of motherhood to praise women in general as being more virtuous than men. One of the first to do so was Lucas Alamán, who in the preface to his *History of Mexico* claimed that on the whole "the women in America were worth more than the men." Other writers lauded woman's beneficent influence on society, exercised through her "domestic empire." One journalist, terming it an "angelic influence, divine," asserted that "in the bottom of all hearts there is the need to obey woman, to love her, to venerate her."[8] But these voices were still few and far between, most often sounded in French and British articles reproduced in the capital's periodicals or in the writings of Mexicans who traveled abroad.

The clearest expression of the new ideas came in an anonymous treatise on women's education published in 1851 by an "American Lady" (that is, Latin American as opposed to European) who had lived abroad. Impressed by the relationship between the sexes in Europe, she called for "a revolution in the moral order," analogous to the political revolution caused by independence, to "change the state of Mexican womanhood." She contrasted the happiness of English women, considered "sacred objects," with the misery of Mexican women, who were either scorned or viewed as objects of passion, and consequently ignored or abused. To remedy this situation, she proposed educating women for a more responsible domestic role, for wives who were "worthy companions" to their husbands would deserve "respectful love" and "even reverence." Although she thought Mexican women needed considerable improvement before they could attain that position, she was one of the first to write of husband and wife ruling in separate spheres: "The laws of society that exclude us from the grand stage of public life give us sovereignty in the domestic and private sphere. . . . The family is our empire; we take care to satisfy its needs, direct its activities, maintain its peace, and preserve it as a sacred haven for proper behavior."[9]

Thus by the middle of the century Mexico was moving toward marianismo, with its elevation of women in the family. Along with the new emphasis on domesticity came a decline in the mobilization of women, as the earlier efforts to incorporate women in the labor force, enlist their help in political struggles, and recruit them to serve in welfare institutions were abandoned. Although these developments eventually might have led to more egalitarian sex roles, the rise of marianismo ended this possibility. By the 1850's, when Mexicans spoke of raising women's status it was only to give them a more prominent role in the family. There is no evidence that anyone in Mexico, woman or man, advocated female suffrage.[10] Educational reformers did not espouse equal education for men and women. Legal reformers carefully emphasized that they did not support the emancipation of women or the expansion of their authority except over children. The growing prestige of motherhood had come into conflict with women's civic roles.

This shift reflects an increasing dilemma posed by the earlier developments. The improvement of women's education—the most sustained and far-reaching of the changes affecting women —potentially challenged the social order, since well-educated women could conceivably compete with men. Other, more tentative trends—the abolition of the legal barriers to women's work, the movement of women into previously male trades, the expansion of single and widowed women's legal rights, the participation of women in the independence movement, and their presence in republican lobbying groups—were also beginning to lessen distinctions between the sexes. Women's subordination became increasingly hard to justify if they were the intellectual and spiritual equals of men. A few European articles reprinted in the capital's newspapers even entertained the notion that women could do anything men could do.[11] But most Mexicans were not ready to accept the full equality of women. The tension between women's competence and their subjection was resolved by assigning them a separate sphere to rule, a solution that avoided the radical step of granting them the same rights as men.

The desire to reconcile the changing status of women with traditional gender distinctions explains why liberal ideals were applied to women with such timidity during the first half of the nineteenth century. Equality as it applied to women was of a very special kind. It was neither equality in the public sphere nor equality in the family, for despite the increased prestige of motherhood, the wife's subordination to her husband persisted as a social ideal. "Equality," as Mexicans used the word, was instead a sense, as Nancy Cott puts it, that women were "different" rather than "inferior." [12] Individual freedom, another tenet of liberalism, was not directly extended to women either, since liberals feared what women might do with too much freedom. Indeed, Manuel Payno went so far as to denounce the "vigorous partisans" of spinsterhood who praised the word *soltera* (single) because it implied *soltura* (freedom). [13]

To combat women's alleged desire for independence, Payno and his fellow liberals engaged in a campaign to portray marriage as a source of bliss, the paramount institution for "the felicity of the human species, . . . increasing the pleasures of life." [14] They even agreed to uphold the Catholic Church as an institution that kept women in their place. The measure on freedom of religion was defeated in the Constitutional Convention of 1856 by men who argued, among other things, that religious toleration would "bring on rebellion" and cause "the domestic home [to] disintegrate into chaos." [15] By supporting the Church as a bulwark of social order, liberals implied that coercion might be needed to control the Fair Sex.

The rationale for making the home a female domain was therefore to preserve social control. Since it was a way of combating increased options for women through education, civic participation, and work, women who shunned domestic roles were portrayed in ever harsher terms. Fernández de Lizardi's admonishment, in 1818, that "erudite and manly women" were "more to be admired than copied" was bland compared with such indictments of the overeducated woman as this one, from 1842: "The learned woman is not exactly a woman, neither is she a man;

she is an intermediate being, doubly dispossessed." Or this one, made in 1851 by the American Lady: "No one can ignore that a woman educated in the principles and habits of a man offers a monstrous contradiction, upsets the social order, breaks its equilibrium, and becomes a mixed being, which without having the strength and predominance of the one sex, lacks the sweetness and modesty of the other."[16]

It is difficult to know how this literature affected its limited readership. Although the new prestige of women in the family may have been a positive development in the long run, encouraging egalitarian marital relations, in the short run it narrowed acceptable female roles—at least at the level of official ideology—and may have brought social norms closer to the stereotype of Latin American women. Certainly, the introduction of the derogatory term *solterona* (old maid) at the end of the century indicates an increased pressure for women to marry. The changing reactions of Mexican travelers to the United States reflect the same trend. Where the visitors of the 1830's and 1840's admired the freedom and social participation of women in the United States, later Mexican travelers condemned these developments on the grounds that they made women poor housewives and mothers.[17] Indeed, as the enthusiasm for mobilizing women faded, no more books praising the heroines of the independence wars were published in Mexico until the emergence of the feminist movement in the early twentieth century.[18]

Marianismo responded to several long-term changes evident in Mexico as well as throughout the Western world. The decline of patriarchy within families accompanied the rise of the State as the paterfamilias surrendered power to sovereign, judge, and school. The view of women as different instead of inferior accompanied their improved education and the separation of home from work. The growing prestige of motherhood accompanied the development of an increasingly isolated and child-centered nuclear family; it was also a product of the erosion of the Catholic ideal of celibacy in a secular world. And the insistence on domesticity accompanied changes in sex roles wherever they were believed to have gotten out of hand.[19]

The timing and strength of marianismo in Mexico also reflect peculiarly Mexican developments, for Mexicans did not blindly import European ideas. In the late eighteenth and early nineteenth centuries, the mobilization and education of women prepared the way for the recognition of women's competence; the program of defensive modernization enhanced the value of their maternal role. But full-fledged marianismo did not immediately follow, for the threat implicit in the changing status of women was distant in Mexico compared with other areas of the Western world. Because of the economic recession that followed independence, women's education did not improve as much as reformers wished, and women did not move far into male trades. Their participation in civic activities was very limited at a time when their counterparts in Europe and the United States were plunging into reform movements under the impact of evangelical religion. And the idealization of women was difficult when female education was still highly circumscribed and when it was women who socialized the "deficient" citizens believed to bear much of the blame for republican problems.

The same difficulties that delayed marianismo also made it attractive. When the burgeoning economy of the late colonial city had promised enough jobs so that women need not compete with men, and when the reformers' ambitious plans required that women take on new responsibilities, many men were confident that they could adjust to whatever changes in sex roles might result. After independence, as the plummeting economy and failure to establish a viable government dashed the earlier optimism, most men felt threatened by incipient changes in women's roles. Furthermore, the increasing link between population growth and national defense in a country with thinly settled borders provided another incentive to persuade women to fulfill domestic roles. Although the new respect for women and their new self-respect made it difficult to return them to the old inferior position, the same goal was accomplished by allowing women to rule the home, and restricting them to it.

As in so many other areas of Mexican life, then, the failure of independence may have been a lost opportunity, for the seeds of industrialization, democracy, and egalitarian gender roles planted in the late colonial period shriveled during the next half century. Despite the patriotic view propounded by liberals, the late colonial period was in some ways more dynamic for women

than the early republic; independence, far from bringing progress to "backward" Mexico, instead thwarted some possibilities
for a change in women's status. In fact, Catholic and corporatist
traditions were reinforced by marianismo, which transferred the
religious spirit surrounding the worship of Mary to secular motherhood and strengthened corporatism by emphasizing the differences between women and men. In this respect, Mexico may
have been more "colonial" in the second half of the nineteenth
century than in the first, when liberalism was ascendant.

In Europe and the United States women eventually pushed
the concept of their moral superiority to its logical conclusion,
using it to support demands for equal rights and public roles. In
contrast, Mexican women largely stayed with the cult of domesticity and accepted their differences from men. The first half of
the nineteenth century, the formative period for the women's
movement in the United States and Europe, provides clues to its
weakness in Mexico. Highly educated European and North
American women, active in reform movements that increased
their sense of worth and led them to lecture and travel about to
proselytize their causes, felt frustrated by the legal contraints
they faced. In Mexico the mobilization of women for the needs
of an enlightened State did not compare to the mobilization of
women by evangelical religion; the education of women was far
less advanced; and their legal inferiority was less glaring because of the considerable protection and property rights they
enjoyed under Hispanic law. Furthermore, since democracy was
but tenuously established in Mexico, women did not feel sin-
gularly deprived because they could not vote.

Meanwhile, the gulf between Mexican women of different
classes, already wider than in Europe and the United States,
deepened. During the late colonial period, lower-class women
had benefited from the new public schools and job opportunities in the capital, but after independence their economic situation deteriorated, and the much-needed vocational programs
failed to materialize when women were no longer needed in the
work force. Middle- and upper-class women, already the most
affected by late colonial value changes, since they alone had been
subject to seclusion, were the only ones favored by the limited
republican changes: their work expanded and gained prestige;

they participated publicly in charity and lobbying organizations; they had opportunities to achieve more than a rudimentary education. Taken together, these developments made women's traditional inferiority untenable and ushered in marianismo. It is unlikely, however, that lower-class women profited from the new attitudes and the legal changes they occasioned. The elevation of women in the family was of little or no benefit to those women who were forced to work to survive and who often had no home to rule while sharing living space in crowded vecindades. And the problems of unequal pay and inadequate education that plagued them in the workplace would not be solved by elite reformers who thought of women in terms of domestic roles. Even the expansion of widows' legal rights and the emancipation of adult daughters from the *patria potestas* probably affected only propertied women in practice. Certainly, the liberalization of divorce meant less to lower-class women who had the freedom to leave unhappy marriages than it did to elite women constrained by social convention. Thus republican trends, like so much else, discriminated among women on the basis of class.

In retrospect, the first half of the nineteenth century brought few changes to Mexican women. It was in no sense an era of emancipation: egalitarian impulses were highly selective; and the direction of change was inconsistent, for by the middle of the century the mobilization of women declined as marianismo rose. Sex roles and family patterns must have seemed reassuringly stable to people confronting the problems of self-rule, foreign invasions, the loss of half the national territory, Caste uprisings, governmental instability, and recession. Yet contemporary observers noted an improvement in women's position, led by educational advances and visible in the expansion of women's responsibilities, in legal changes, and in women's enhanced status within the family. Although we cannot simply dismiss their views, neither should we forget that elite writers had a myopic view of progress, based on the experiences of women of their own class. The divergence of women's experiences after independence provides the final clue to why, despite the significance of gender, female solidarity did not come to outweigh class identification in Mexico.

# Appendixes

# 1811 and 1848 Census Samples

This sample of the 1811 census of Mexico City ("Padrón formado con arreglo al nuevo reglamento de policía de agosto de este año, 1811," AGN *Padrones*, 53–77) includes Bloque 22 in the center and Bloques 1, 3, and 6 in the periphery, as shown in Figure A.1. These areas were chosen as part of an agreement with the Seminario de Historia Urbana of the Departamento de Investigaciones Históricas, Instituto Nacional de Antropología e Historia, of which I was a member in 1974–75. That research team aims to compile a data bank of the complete 1811 census, but had completed little more than the sample sections when I conducted my analysis. Although they kept all the information from the manuscript census except for names, their coding does not permit the study of relationships between people in a household. Fortunately for my purposes, women were identified as mothers or wives, and the presence or absence of domestic servants was noted for everyone in a household.

I took the sample of the 1848 census from the manuscript census schedules for the same two areas of the city analyzed in 1811. For the central area, I used Cuartel Menor 11, Manzanas 94, 98, 99 (AAA *Padrones*, 3408), which roughly corresponds to Bloque 22; for the peripheral area, I used Cuarteles Menores 26 and 27, Manzanas 208, 209, 215 (AAA *Padrones*, 3409), which roughly correspond to Bloques 1, 3, and 6. Because the information in the peripheral area in 1848 was much poorer than that in 1811, however, I had to discard some data.

Only one section of the 1848 peripheral area could be used for the demographic analysis in Chapter Three: Cuartel Menor 26, Manzanas 208–9 (or Periph 3). In the other peripheral areas the census takers only recorded demographic information for em-

Fig. A.1. Areas of census samples, 1811 and 1848. The bloque numbers are for 1811; the equivalent 1848 areas are explained in the accompanying text.

ployed people. In order to compare the 1848 and 1811 data, the information from Periph 3 has been weighted to maintain the same balance between the two neighborhoods as in 1811. When multiplied by two, the data from Periph 3 represent 41.8% of the sample in 1848, compared with 42.6% for the entire periphery in 1811. In addition, the peripheral area in 1811 contained the Hospital de San Lázaro, whose 121 patients have been excluded from household statistics for 1811. Since their demographic portrait was similar to that of the population as a whole, these patients did not alter the other analyses in Chapter Three.

The 1848 data on employment are more problematic. Only one peripheral section was valid for the occupational analysis in Chapter Four: Cuartel Menor 27, Manzana 215 (Periph 4). But even then, the peripheral data are not directly comparable to those of 1811 because the list of people is incomplete. The census taker in that area listed primarily employed people: only 8 of 79 women and 3 of 176 men did not list an occupation. Yet the census taker cannot have listed all employed people because almost no young workers are included. the youngest man was 16 and the youngest woman 22; the median age for men was 38, against 40 for women. It is possible that only household heads were enumerated, since women's share of the sample section (31%) is close to their share of household heads in other areas (35%). The marital status breakdown also shares some similarities with that of household heads: 4% of the women in Periph 4 were single, 20% married, and 75% widowed; 4% of the men were single, 85% married, and 11% widowed (compare with Table 8). However, the hypothesis that only household heads were listed is not entirely satisfactory because so few female household heads were employed (Table D.7). What is clear is that Periph 4 cannot be used either for a demographic portrait of working women or for a comparison with unemployed women. Such calculations are therefore based exclusively on the central section for 1848. The peripheral section does shed some light on the occupations and composition of the adult work force, though. For calculations using both sections, Periph 4 has been weighted by multiplying it by 1.5 in order to maintain the 1811 balance between the peripheral and central neighborhoods. Unless otherwise noted, the information on 1848 in Chapter Four is based on both sections of the sample.

## TABLE A.1
### Racial Structure, 1811

| Race[a] | Center Number of people | Center Percent | Periphery Number of people | Periphery Percent | Combined Number of people | Combined Percent |
|---|---|---|---|---|---|---|
| Spanish | 1,306 | 68.2% | 345 | 25.1% | 1,651 | 50.2% |
| Caste | 264 | 13.8 | 290 | 21.1 | 554 | 16.8 |
| Indian | 345 | 18.0 | 739 | 53.8 | 1,084 | 33.0 |
| Unknown | 11 | — | 56 | — | 67 | — |
| TOTAL | 1,926 | 100.0% | 1,430 | 100.1% | 3,356 | 100.0% |

NOTE: The 1848 census does not record race. In this table and those that follow, the un-knowns are not usually figured into the percentages, and percentage totals may not equal 100 because of rounding.

[a] Although these were the only racial categories printed on the census schedules, others were occasionally penciled in by the census taker. I have included a single Mulatto in the Caste category, 47 Indios Caciques in the Indian category, and two Europeos as well as 53 peninsular Spaniards in the Spanish category.

## TABLE A.2
### Sexual Structure, 1811 and 1848

| Gender | Center Number | Center Percent | Periphery Number | Periphery Percent | Combined Number | Combined Percent |
|---|---|---|---|---|---|---|
| | | | 1811 | | | |
| Females | 1,114 | 58.1% | 725 | 52.1% | 1,839 | 55.5% |
| Males | 808 | 42.0 | 666 | 47.9 | 1,474 | 44.1 |
| Unknown | 4 | — | 39 | — | 43 | — |
| TOTAL | 1,926 | 100.1% | 1,430 | 100.0% | 3,356 | 100.0% |
| | | | 1848 | | | |
| Females | 826 | 58.4% | 307 | 58.8% | 1,440 | 58.6% |
| Males | 588 | 41.6 | 215 | 41.2 | 1,018 | 41.4 |
| Unknown | 0 | — | 0 | — | 0 | — |
| TOTAL | 1,414 | 100.0% | 522 | 100.0% | 2,458 | 100.0% |

NOTE: The 1848 figures for the periphery are based on Periph 3, which has been weighted for the combined figures by multiplying by two.

### TABLE A.3
*Place of Origin, 1811 and 1848*

| Birthplace | Center Number of people | Center Percent | Periphery Number of people | Periphery Percent | Combined Number of people | Combined Percent |
|---|---|---|---|---|---|---|
| | | | 1811 | | | |
| Mexico City | 1,199 | 62.3% | 781 | 57.5% | 1,980 | 60.3% |
| Mexico | 666 | 34.6 | 575 | 42.3 | 1,241 | 37.9 |
| Foreign | 58 | 3.0 | 3 | 0.2 | 61 | 1.9 |
| Unknown | 3 | — | 71 | — | 74 | — |
| TOTAL | 1,926 | 100.0% | 1,430 | 100.0% | 3,356 | 100.1% |
| | | | 1848 | | | |
| Mexico City | 1,004 | 72.5% | 275 | 52.8% | 1,554 | 64.1% |
| Mexico | 356 | 25.7 | 245 | 47.0 | 846 | 34.9 |
| Foreign | 24 | 1.7 | 1 | 0.2 | 26 | 1.1 |
| Unknown | 30 | — | 1 | — | 32 | — |
| TOTAL | 1,414 | 99.9% | 522 | 100.0% | 2,458 | 100.1% |

NOTE: The 1848 figures for the periphery are based on Periph 3, which has been weighted for the combined figures by multiplying by two.

### TABLE A.4
*Households with Live-in Domestic Servants, 1811 and 1848*

| Number of servants | Center Number of households | Center Percent | Periphery Number of households | Periphery Percent | Combined Number of households | Combined Percent |
|---|---|---|---|---|---|---|
| | | | 1811 | | | |
| 0 | 260 | 65.8% | 257 | 96.2% | 517 | 78.1% |
| 1 | 73 | 18.5 | 9 | 3.4 | 82 | 12.4 |
| 2 | 35 | 8.9 | 1 | 0.4 | 36 | 5.4 |
| 3 or more | 27 | 6.8 | 0 | 0.0 | 27 | 4.1 |
| TOTAL | 395 | 100.0% | 267 | 100.0% | 662 | 100.0% |
| | | | 1848 | | | |
| 0 | 214 | 69.3% | 131 | 98.5% | 476 | 82.8% |
| 1 | 34 | 11.0 | 1 | 0.8 | 36 | 6.3 |
| 2 | 10 | 3.2 | 0 | 0.0 | 10 | 1.7 |
| 3 or more | 18 | 5.8 | 1 | 0.8 | 20 | 3.5 |
| Unknown[a] | 33 | 10.7 | 0 | 0.0 | 33 | 5.7 |
| TOTAL | 309 | 100.0% | 133 | 100.1% | 575 | 100.0% |

NOTE: The 1848 figures for the periphery are based on Periph 3, which has been weighted for the combined figures by multiplying by two.

[a]Unknown here represents those households with one servant where it is unclear whether the servant worked there or simply lived there. Adding these households to the one-servant households would bring the 1848 proportions more in line with those of 1811.

TABLE A.5
*Sexual Structure of the Labor Force, 1811 and 1848*

| Gender | Center Number of workers | Center Percent | Periphery Number of workers | Periphery Percent | Combined Number of workers | Combined Percent |
|---|---|---|---|---|---|---|
| | | | 1811 | | | |
| Females | 236 | 35.2% | 170 | 29.1% | 406 | 32.4% |
| Males | 434 | 64.8 | 415 | 70.9 | 848 | 67.6 |
| Unknown | 2 | — | 6 | — | 8 | — |
| TOTAL | 672 | 100.0% | 591 | 100.0% | 1,262 | 100.0% |
| | | | 1848 | | | |
| Females | 260 | 42.0% | 71 | 29.1% | 402 | 36.3% |
| Males | 359 | 58.0 | 173 | 70.9 | 705 | 63.7 |
| Unknown | 0 | — | 0 | — | 0 | — |
| TOTAL | 619 | 100.0% | 244 | 100.0% | 1,107 | 100.0% |

NOTE: The 1848 figures for the periphery are based on Periph 4, which has been weighted for the combined figures by multiplying by 1.5.

TABLE A.6
*Marital Status of the Adult Population (25 Years and Over), 1811 and 1848*

| Gender and marital status | Center Number | Center Percent | Periphery Number | Periphery Percent | Combined Number | Combined Percent |
|---|---|---|---|---|---|---|
| | | | 1811 | | | |
| Females | | | | | | |
| Single | 162 | 28.9% | 42 | 12.1% | 204 | 22.5% |
| Married | 203 | 36.3 | 196 | 56.6 | 399 | 44.0 |
| Widowed | 195 | 34.8 | 108 | 31.2 | 303 | 33.4 |
| Unknown | 1 | — | 2 | — | 3 | — |
| TOTAL | 561 | 100.0% | 348 | 99.9% | 909 | 99.9% |
| Males | | | | | | |
| Single | 112 | 27.9% | 49 | 15.6% | 161 | 22.5% |
| Married | 232 | 57.9 | 219 | 69.5 | 451 | 63.0 |
| Widowed | 57 | 14.2 | 47 | 14.9 | 104 | 14.5 |
| Unknown | 1 | — | 6 | — | 7 | — |
| TOTAL | 402 | 100.0% | 321 | 100.0% | 723 | 100.0% |
| | | | 1848 | | | |
| Females | | | | | | |
| Single | 97 | 24.7% | 10 | 7.2% | 117 | 17.5% |
| Married | 124 | 31.6 | 76 | 55.1 | 276 | 41.3 |
| Widowed | 172 | 43.8 | 52 | 37.7 | 276 | 41.3 |
| Unknown | 0 | — | 0 | — | 0 | — |
| TOTAL | 393 | 100.0% | 138 | 100.0% | 669 | 100.0% |
| Males | | | | | | |
| Single | 69 | 27.4% | 15 | 13.3% | 99 | 20.7% |
| Married | 163 | 64.7 | 86 | 76.1 | 335 | 70.1 |
| Widowed | 20 | 7.9 | 12 | 10.6 | 44 | 9.2 |
| Unknown | 1 | — | 0 | — | 1 | — |
| TOTAL | 253 | 100.0% | 113 | 100.0% | 479 | 100.0% |

NOTE: The 1848 figures for the periphery are based on Periph 3, which has been weighted for the combined figures by multiplying by two.

# Notarial Records Samples

## Wills Sample

This sample of wills, used for demographic analysis, consists of 300 women's wills and 300 men's wills, 100 each from 1802–3, 1827–29, and 1853–55. (The single years used in the Transactions Sample could not be used alone for this sample because they did not yield 100 female wills.) The dates selected were not notable for epidemics or other crises that could affect mortality or marriage.

The wills are taken from the following notaries who practiced in Mexico City: 1802–3, notaries number 32, 84, 92, 155, 158, 210, 359, 417, 424, 483, 519, 711, 713, 738, 749; 1827–29, notaries number 155, 158, 361, 417, 426, 427, 531, 711; 1853–55, notaries number 41, 169, 170, 242, 290, 362, 426, 464, 550, 611, 658, 721, 722, 725. In most cases, I used all the wills in the books listed. These documents are housed in the Archivo General de Notarías, Mexico City.

## Transactions Sample

This sample, used for an analysis of women's economic activity, consists of 1,200 transactions from 1803, 1827, and 1853. One hundred were selected randomly from the books of the following Mexico City notaries in the Archivo General de Notarías: for 1803, Francisco Calapiz (No. 155), *José Mariano Díaz (No. 210), *Félix Zamorano (No. 749), José Martínez y Zuleta (No. 424); for 1827, Francisco Calapiz (No. 155), Francisco Madariaga (No. 426), José Vicente Maciel (No. 427), Severiano Quesada (No. 549); for 1853, *Francisco Calapiz, son (No. 170), Ramón de la Cueva (No. 169), Francisco Villalón (No. 722), José Querejazu

(No. 550). Because the three starred notaries' books did not contain 100 transactions, the remaining number were taken from the other notaries listed for the same year.

Although most transactions recorded were for members of the elite, I attempted to choose notaries representative of different kinds of clientele. The first two notaries listed in each year were the most prestigious and were used by the wealthiest families of Mexico City; the last two had a more varied clientele. However, I did not find significant differences in women's level or type of participation on this basis.

# Ecclesiastical Divorce Cases

The analysis of ecclesiastical divorce is based on the following 81 cases heard at the Metropolitan Cathedral in Mexico City, nine of which involved residents of nearby towns like Coyoacán that are now part of the Federal District. Since these are all the cases I was able to locate in Mexican archives for 1800–1857, they are not strictly speaking a sample. But they probably represent only a fraction (perhaps one-tenth) of the divorces filed during those years. (In fact, some new cases have recently surfaced in the warehouse of the Archivo General de la Nación, though they are not yet available to the public.) Nineteen cases date (by year of filing) from the period 1800–1819, 29 from 1820–39, and 33 from 1840–57. The records are unevenly distributed, with none filed in 1810–15 or 1819–26. There is no reason to believe that the chronological distribution is significant; rather I attribute it to the vagaries of documentary preservation in Mexico. The fact that more than half of the cases are from six years (1816, 1833, 1836, 1854–56) reflects the original arrangement of documents in bundles by years, with some bundles faring better than others. Further evidence to support this conclusion is that two notebooks kept by the court scribe for 1754 to 1818 ("Cuaderno de Divorcio," 2 vols., in Filmoteca de la Sociedad Genealógica Mexicana, Mexico, D.F., Roll 1116) show little fluctuation in the number of divorces sought in any given year—about 15 a year.

I have used the honorifics don and doña only if they appeared in the original document. In five cases no plaintiff is shown, as indicated by the word "and" rather than the customary "vs." In one (C.32) the suit was pursued by mutual consent; in the others it is not clear which spouse initiated the action. And one case, filed in 1827 and reopened in 1837, has been used in the statistics for both years (C.20 and C.47). It resulted in a temporary divorce the first time and a permanent divorce the second.

In the list below the most frequently cited ramos of the National Archive (AGN) are abbreviated as follows: AGNBN, *Bienes Nacionales*; AGNJ, *Judicial*; AGNM, *Matrimonios*. A citation like AGNBN 854, 3, is to be read: AGN Bienes Nacionales, legato (or volume) 854, no. 3. Unnumbered files are indicated by "n.n." Selections from cases 3, 9, 18, 34, 45, 47, 48, and 63 are reproduced in Silvia M. Arrom, *La mujer mexicana ante el divorcio eclesiástico (1800–1857)*, (Mexico City, 1976).

1. Doña Apolonia Gutiérrez de Rosas vs. don Esteban Enciso, 1800–1809, AJ *Divorcio*, n.n.

2. Doña Gertrudis Guerrero vs. José María Andrade, 1801–9, AJ *Penal* 12, 1

3. Don José Villamil y Primo vs. doña María Ignacia Rodríguez, 1802, AGN *Criminal* 582, n.n.

4. Doña Plácida Herrera vs. José Carrillo, 1806–9, AGNBN 854, 3

5. Doña Ana Antonia Larios vs. don José Montesinos de Lara, 1806–7, AGNBN 854, 16–17

6. Don Joaquín Ovando and doña María de las Nieves Bienpico, 1808, AGNBN 1067, n.n.

7. Doña Antonia Rodríguez vs. don Juan de Dios Soni, 1809, AGNJ 32, n.n.

8. Doña Rosalia Ramírez vs. don Francisco Hernández, 1809–10, AGNJ 32, n.n.

9. Don Juan José Domínguez Sotomayor vs. doña Josefa Tovar de Zárate, 1809–11, AGNJ 32, n.n.

10. Doña Manuela Joaquina de Alcázar vs. don Manuel Ampucho, 1816, AGNM 68, 7

11. Doña Dolores Valdivieso y Valdivieso vs. don Francisco Xavier de Valdivieso y Vidal Lorca, 1816, AGNM 68, 8

12. Doña Joaquina Vinsoneo vs. don Santiago Saul Rolero, 1816, AGNM 68, 9

13. Doña María Josefa Rodríguez vs. don Antonio Azevo, 1816, AGNM 68, 10

14. Don Miguel Molina vs. doña María de la Luz Ibáñez, 1816, AGNM 68, 11

15. Doña Micaela Gutiérrez Coronado vs. don Pablo Villegas, 1816, AGNM 68, *13*
16. Doña Joaquina Avila Hernández vs. don Angel Caso, 1816, AGNM 68, *24*
17. Doña María Antonia Reyna y Vega vs. don Ramón Martínez Calderón, 1816–17, AGNJ 11, n.n.
18. Doña María Josefa Mijares vs. don Mariano García, 1816–17, AGNJ 11, n.n.
19 Doña Francisca Pérez Gálvez vs. don Lorenzo García Noriega, 1818–22, AGNBN 898, n.n.
20. Doña Eugenia Segault vs. don Pedro Ouvrard, 1827–29, AGNBN 470, *30*
21. Doña Francisca Soria vs. José María Sánchez, 1829, AGNBN 967, n.n.
22. Doña Josefa Urrutia vs. don Mariano José Giral, 1829, AGNBN 967, n.n.
23. Doña Gertrudis Raso vs. don Mariano Martínez, 1829–30, AGNBN 967, n.n.
24. Don José López Guazo and doña Angela Trujillo, 1831–32, AGNBN 1045, *49*
25. Doña Mariana Manzano vs. don José María Camacho, 1832, AGNBN 88, n.n.
26. Doña Severa Estrada vs. don Severo Yoldi, 1832, AGNBN 1045, *34*
27. Doña Francisca Pliego vs. don José Inojosa, 1832, AGNBN 1045, *35*
28. María de la Luz Escobar vs. Félix López, 1833, AGNBN 1047, *28*
29. Don Mariano Flores Alatorre vs. doña María Dolores Izedo, 1833, AGNBN 874, n.n.
30. Doña María Andrea Azcarraga vs. don José Castera, 1833, AGNBN 874, n.n.
31. Doña Luisa Ayala vs. don José María Coria, 1833, AGNBN 874, n.n.
32. Don José María Arrieta and doña Marciala Neira, 1833, AGNBN 874, n.n.
33. Doña Andrea Zavala vs. don Manuel Leiva, 1835–36, AGNBN 470, *16*
34. Doña Dolores Pérez vs. don Mariano Rodríguez, 1835–37, AGNBN 470, *39*; 1045, *50*

35. María García vs. Guillermo Alvarado, 1836, AGNBN 470, 4
36. Doña María de los Remedios Omaña vs. don Catalino Barroso, 1836, AGNBN 470, 8
37. Doña Susana Soriano vs. don José María Carrera, 1836, AGNBN 470, 10
38. Doña María Vargas vs. don Macedonio Contreras, 1836, AGNBN 470, 11
39. Doña María de las Nieves López vs. don José María López, 1836, AGNBN 470, 17
40. Doña María del Refugio Valois vs. don José María Martínez de la Pascua, 1836, AGNBN 470, 24
41. Isidoro Medina vs. Guadalupe Ramírez, 1836, AGNBN 470, 25
42. María Rita Gómez vs. Mariano Mercado, 1836, AGNBN 470, 26
43. Luisa Riofrío vs. Antonio González, 1836–37, AGNBN 470, 14
44. Doña Dolores Ortega vs. don Manuel Moreno, 1836–37, AGNBN 470, 23
45. María Navora Soberanis vs. Pedro Rivera, 1836–38, AGNBN 470, 40
46. Doña Rafaela Campusano vs. don José Antonio Castañeda, 1837, AJ *Tocas Civiles*, 1839–42, n.n.
47. Doña Eugenia Segault vs. don Pedro Ouvrard, 1837–40, AGNBN 470, 30
48. María Hilaria Hernández vs. Félix Morales, 1839–44, AGNBN 370, n.n.
49. Doña Marcelina Espíndola vs. don José María Martínez, 1842, AJ *Tocas Civiles*, 1842–44, n.n.
50. Don Marcos Arellano and doña Dolores Ochoa, 1846, AGNBN 509, 5
51. Doña Plutarca Parra vs. don Leonardo Arrieta, 1846, AGNBN 927, 41
52. Doña María de los Santos Morales vs. don José Rodríguez Noriega, 1848, AGNBN 513, n.n.; 528, 7
53. Doña Antonia del Mar vs. don Francisco Bustos, 1849, AGNBN 609, n.n.
54. María Serapia Terán vs. José María Pompa, 1849, AGNBN 609, n.n.
55. Josefa Salazar vs. José María Galván, 1849, AGNBN 609, 242

56. Don Teodoro Chávez vs. doña Luisa Solórzano, 1849, AGNBN 1047, *19*
57. Doña Teodora Villar vs. don Joaquín Velásquez, 1850–51, AGNBN 528, *34*
58. Doña Carmen Rodríguez de Ayala vs. don Pedro Desés, 1852, AGNBN 528, *20*
59. Navora Córdoba vs. Abundio Morales, 1853, AGNBN 513, *96*
60. Margarita Godines vs. Toribio Jiménez, 1853, AGNBN 513, *98*
61. Doña Ana Granados vs. don José Avila, 1853, AGNBN 513, *133*
62. Doña Soledad Jiménez vs. don Manuel Nápoles, 1854, AGNBN 513, *116*
63. Doña Dolores Medina vs. don Domingo Pintado, 1854–55, AGNBN 513, *120*
64. Doña Isabel Aguilera vs. don José Quijano, 1854, AGNBN 513, *131*
65. Doña Soledad Adelaida Arellano vs. don José G. del Canizo, 1854–55, AGNBN 513, *137*
66. Doña Josefa Leiva vs. don Manuel Iturria, 1854–56, AGNBN 76, *21*
67. Don Antonio Esteves vs. doña Antonia Lozano, 1855, AGNBN 513, *111*
68. Don Juan Luna and doña Ana Gávito, 1855, AGNBN 513, *147*
69. Doña Soledad Díaz vs. don Vicente Espinosa, 1855, AGNBN 513, *148*
70. Doña Isabel Rosel vs. don Simón Imhoff, 1855–56, AGNBN 513, *151*
71. Doña Concepción Morales vs. don Dolores Martínez, 1855–56, AGNBN 76, *6*
72. Paula Pasarán vs. José Magdaleno Rosales, 1855–56, AGNBN 76, *16*
73. Doña Mariana Pérez vs. don Higinio Núñez, 1856, AGNBN 75, *4*
74. Luisa López vs. Carmen Trejo, 1856, AGNBN 76, *11*
75. Doña Clara Segura vs. don Luis Tangassi, 1856, AGNBN 76, *15*
76. Doña Luganda Carrillo de Nava vs. don Clemente López, 1856, AGNBN 76, *42*
77. Doña Josefa García vs. don Juan Hajo, 1856, AGNBN 76, *43*

78. Agustina Vargas vs. Narciso Barrón, 1856, AGNBN 76, 45
79. Doña Severa Vázquez vs. don Santos Bastida, 1856, AGNBN
     76, 46
80. Soledad Palofox vs. Toribio Castillo, 1856, AGNBN 76, 47
81. Doña Teresa Carrero vs. don Gregorio Castañares, 1856–57,
     AGNBN 76, 39

APPENDIX D

# Statistical Tables

All data for 1811 and 1848 in the tables are from my Mexico City census samples (see Appendix A). The groups studied across the tables may vary in size because the "unknowns" have usually been omitted; and totals may not equal 100% because of rounding.

TABLE D.1
*Population of Mexico City and Mexico, 1742–1857*

| | Mexico City | | Mexico | |
|---|---|---|---|---|
| Year | Population | Average annual growth (percent) | Population | Average annual growth (percent) |
| 1742 | 98,000 ⎫ | | 3,336,000 ⎫ | |
| 1790 | 112,926 ⎪ | 0.8% | 4,483,529 ⎪ | 1.4% |
| 1793 | 130,602 ⎬ | | 5,200,000 ⎬ | |
| 1803 | 137,000 ⎭ | | 5,800,000 ⎭ | |
| 1810 | — | | 6,122,354 ⎫ | |
| 1811 | 168,846 ⎫ | 1.4% | — | 0.6% |
| 1813 | 140,000 ⎬ | | — ⎬ | |
| 1820 | 179,830 | | — ⎭ | |
| 1824 | 160,000 ⎫ | | 6,500,000 ⎫ | |
| 1838 | 205,430 ⎪ | | 7,004,140 ⎪ | |
| 1846 | 200,000 ⎬ | 0.3% | 7,000,000 ⎬ | 0.8% |
| 1856 | 185,000 ⎪ | | 7,859,564 ⎪ | |
| 1857 | 200,000 ⎭ | | 8,283,088 ⎭ | |

SOURCES: *1742.* Joseph Antonio Villaseñor y Sánchez, *Theatro americano, descripción general de los reynos, y provincias de la Nueva-España.* . . . (Mexico City, 1746): 1: 35. *1790–1857.* Keith Davies, "Tendencias demográficas urbanas durante el siglo XIX en México," *Historia Mexicana,* 83 (Jan.–Mar. 1972): 482–83, 501.
NOTE: 1790 and 1811 figures are drawn from censuses; the others are estimates. See Davies' discussion of these statistics on pp. 501–3.

TABLE D.2
Heads of Households with Live-in Domestic Servants by Race, 1811

| Servant group | Spanish | Caste | Indian | Unknown |
|---|---|---|---|---|
| 0 servants | | | | |
| Household heads (n = 517) | 239 | 83 | 181 | 14 |
| Percent by servant group | 46.2% | 16.0% | 35.0% | 2.7% |
| Percent by racial group | 63.6% | 93.3% | 98.9% | |
| 1–2 servants | | | | |
| Household heads (n = 118) | 110 | 6 | 2 | |
| Percent by servant group | 93.2% | 5.1% | 1.7% | |
| Percent by racial group | 29.3% | 6.7% | 1.1% | |
| 3 or more servants | | | | |
| Household heads (n = 27) | 27 | | | |
| Percent by servant group | 100.0% | | | |
| Percent by racial group | 7.2% | | | |
| TOTAL HOUSEHOLDS (n = 662) | 376 | 89 | 183 | 14 |

NOTE: One household listing 4 servants, headed by a Caste, has been placed in the no-servant category since it was a restaurant whose servants were not domestics, but employees of the business.

TABLE D.3
Female Proportions Single by Age and Place of Origin, 1811 and 1848

| Category | Age 15–24 | Age 25–34 | Age 35–44 | Age 45–54 | Age 55+ | All age groups |
|---|---|---|---|---|---|---|
| | | | 1811 | | | |
| Migrants | | | | | | |
| Total number | 175 | 157 | 110 | 68 | 50 | 560 |
| Number single | 120 | 48 | 18 | 9 | 7 | 202 |
| Percent single | 68.6% | 30.6% | 16.4% | 13.2% | 14.0% | 36.1% |
| City-born | | | | | | |
| Total number | 251 | 199 | 152 | 101 | 72 | 775 |
| Number single | 168 | 63 | 21 | 18 | 20 | 290 |
| Percent single | 66.9% | 31.7% | 13.8% | 17.8% | 27.8% | 37.4% |
| All females | | | | | | |
| Total number | 426 | 356 | 262 | 169 | 122 | 1,335 |
| Number single | 288 | 111 | 39 | 27 | 27 | 492 |
| Percent single | 67.6% | 31.2% | 14.9% | 16.0% | 22.1% | 36.8% |
| | | | 1848 | | | |
| Migrants | | | | | | |
| Total number | 130 | 143 | 80 | 58 | 28 | 439 |
| Number single | 69 | 27 | 8 | 6 | 4 | 114 |
| Percent single | 53.1% | 18.9% | 10.0% | 10.3% | 14.3% | 26.0% |
| City-born | | | | | | |
| Total number | 228 | 174 | 94 | 62 | 30 | 588 |
| Number single | 96 | 38 | 21 | 9 | 3 | 167 |
| Percent single | 42.1% | 21.8% | 22.3% | 14.5% | 10.0% | 28.4% |
| All females | | | | | | |
| Total number | 358 | 317 | 174 | 120 | 58 | 1,027 |
| Number single | 165 | 65 | 29 | 15 | 7 | 281 |
| Percent single | 46.1% | 20.5% | 16.7% | 12.5% | 12.1% | 27.4% |

## Number of Children Ever Born by Duration of Marriage, 1802–1855

| Years married | Number of children ever born | | | | | | | | | | | | | | | Number of mothers |
|---|---|---|---|---|---|---|---|---|---|---|---|---|---|---|---|---|
| | 0 | 1 | 2 | 3 | 4 | 5 | 6 | 7 | 8 | 9 | 10 | 11 | 12 | — | 22 | |
| 1–4 | 6 | 0 | 7 | | | | | | | | | | | | | 13 |
| 5–9 | 4 | 1 | 5 | 7 | 5 | 6 | 2 | | | | | | | | | 30 |
| 10–19 | 3 | 3 | 1 | 0 | 5 | 3 | 6 | 0 | 1 | 2 | 0 | 0 | 3 | | | 27 |
| 20 or more | 2 | 3 | 1 | 0 | 0 | 2 | 0 | 1 | 3 | 1 | 3 | 2 | 0 | | 1 | 19 |

SOURCE: Wills sample, Appendix B.

## Number of Surviving Children by Duration of Marriage, 1802–1855

| Years married | Number of surviving children | | | | | | | | | | | | | | | Number of mothers |
|---|---|---|---|---|---|---|---|---|---|---|---|---|---|---|---|---|
| | 0 | 1 | 2 | 3 | 4 | 5 | 6 | 7 | 8 | 9 | 10 | 11 | 12 | 13 | 14 | |
| 1–4 | 5 | 1 | 7 | | | | | | | | | | | | | 13 |
| 5–9 | 4 | 3 | 7 | 9 | 6 | 2 | 1 | | | | | | | | | 30 |
| 10–19 | 4 | 2 | 1 | 3 | 5 | 3 | 4 | 2 | 2 | 1 | | | | | | 27 |
| 20 or more | 4 | 2 | 0 | 1 | 1 | 4 | 3 | 1 | 1 | 0 | 0 | 1 | 0 | 0 | 1 | 19 |

SOURCE: Wills sample, Appendix B.

## Sexual Structure by Race, 1790 and 1811

| Race | Females | | Males | |
|---|---|---|---|---|
| | Number | Percent | Number | Percent |
| | 1790 | | | |
| Spanish | 29,250 | 55.5% | 23,456 | 44.5% |
| Caste | 15,661 | 59.2 | 10,790 | 40.8 |
| Indian | 14,371 | 56.1 | 11,232 | 43.9 |
| ALL RACES | 59,282 | 56.6% | 45,478 | 43.4% |
| | 1811 | | | |
| Spanish | 898 | 54.8% | 742 | 45.2% |
| Caste | 293 | 53.3 | 257 | 46.7 |
| Indian | 631 | 58.6 | 446 | 41.4 |
| ALL RACES | 1,822 | 55.8% | 1,445 | 44.2% |

SOURCE: 1790. Adapted from Alexander von Humboldt, *Political Essay on the Kingdom of New Spain* (London, 1814), 1: 293. 1811. 1811 census sample.
NOTE: These figures omit religious of both sexes.

## TABLE D.7
### Age Structure of the Labor Force by Race, 1811

| Age group | Females | | | | Males | | | |
|---|---|---|---|---|---|---|---|---|
| | Spanish | Caste | Indian | Total | Spanish | Caste | Indian | Total |
| **10–14** | | | | | | | | |
| Number in age group | 101 | 26 | 64 | 191 | 79 | 47 | 47 | 173 |
| Number employed | 8 | 6 | 24 | 38 | 25 | 24 | 14 | 63 |
| Percent employed | 7.9% | 23.1% | 37.5% | 19.9% | 31.6% | 51.1% | 29.8% | 36.4% |
| **15–19** | | | | | | | | |
| Number in age group | 80 | 38 | 74 | 192 | 56 | 17 | 35 | 108 |
| Number employed | 13 | 13 | 43 | 69 | 34 | 15 | 28 | 77 |
| Percent employed | 16.3% | 34.2% | 58.1% | 35.9% | 60.7% | 88.2% | 80.0% | 71.3% |
| **20–24** | | | | | | | | |
| Number in age group | 116 | 44 | 71 | 231 | 51 | 23 | 47 | 121 |
| Number employed | 14 | 20 | 37 | 71 | 38 | 20 | 42 | 100 |
| Percent employed | 12.1% | 45.5% | 52.1% | 30.7% | 74.5% | 87.0% | 89.4% | 82.6% |
| **25–29** | | | | | | | | |
| Number in age group | 93 | 29 | 71 | 193 | 65 | 24 | 47 | 137 |
| Number employed | 8 | 11 | 32 | 51 | 49 | 23 | 42 | 114 |
| Percent employed | 8.6% | 37.9% | 45.1% | 26.4% | 75.4% | 95.8% | 89.4% | 83.2% |
| **30–34** | | | | | | | | |
| Number in age group | 75 | 29 | 58 | 162 | 82 | 20 | 50 | 152 |
| Number employed | 6 | 10 | 19 | 35 | 67 | 16 | 46 | 129 |
| Percent employed | 8.0% | 34.5% | 32.8% | 21.6% | 81.7% | 80.0% | 92.0% | 84.9% |

| | | | | | | | | |
|---|---|---|---|---|---|---|---|---|
| **35–39** | | | | | | | | |
| Number in age group | 64 | 15 | 30 | 107 | 32 | 11 | 30 | 73 |
| Number employed | 9 | 5 | 16 | 30 | 25 | 11 | 28 | 64 |
| Percent employed | 14.1% | 33.3% | 53.3% | 28.0% | 78.1% | 100.0% | 93.3% | 87.7% |
| **40–44** | | | | | | | | |
| Number in age group | 78 | 25 | 48 | 152 | 60 | 12 | 40 | 112 |
| Number employed | 13 | 11 | 22 | 45 | 45 | 9 | 36 | 90 |
| Percent employed | 16.7% | 44.0% | 45.8% | 29.6% | 75.0% | 75.0% | 90.0% | 80.4% |
| **45–49** | | | | | | | | |
| Number in age group | 39 | 12 | 22 | 73 | 39 | 10 | 9 | 58 |
| Number employed | 9 | 4 | 8 | 22 | 35 | 8 | 7 | 50 |
| Percent employed | 23.1% | 33.3% | 36.4% | 30.1% | 89.7% | 80.0% | 77.9% | 86.2% |
| **50–54** | | | | | | | | |
| Number in age group | 53 | 13 | 28 | 95 | 47 | 12 | 16 | 75 |
| Number employed | 7 | 2 | 12 | 21 | 35 | 10 | 13 | 58 |
| Percent employed | 13.2% | 15.4% | 42.9% | 22.1% | 74.5% | 83.3% | 81.3% | 77.3% |
| **55 and over** | | | | | | | | |
| Number in age group | 65 | 17 | 40 | 122 | 73 | 16 | 23 | 111 |
| Number employed | 3 | 4 | 13 | 20 | 51 | 11 | 20 | 82 |
| Percent employed | 4.6% | 23.5% | 32.5% | 16.4% | 69.7% | 68.8% | 87.0% | 73.9% |

TABLE D.8
*Female Household Heads by Marital Status and Employment, 1811*

| Marital status | Total number | Number employed | Percent employed |
|---|---|---|---|
| Single | 45 | 10 | 22.2% |
| Married | 30 | 5 | 16.7 |
| Widowed | 138 | 29 | 21.0 |
| TOTAL | 213 | 44 | 20.7% |

TABLE D.9
*Marital Status of the Labor Force, 1811*

| Marital status | Females | | Males | |
|---|---|---|---|---|
| | Number | Percent | Number | Percent |
| Single | 205 | 50.7% | 332 | 39.5% |
| Married | 92 | 22.8 | 434 | 51.7 |
| Widowed | 107 | 26.5 | 74 | 8.8 |
| TOTAL | 404 | 100.0% | 840 | 100.0% |

# Notes

# Notes

Complete authors' names, titles, and publication data for works cited in short form in the Notes are given in the Bibliography, pp. 355–68. All archival materials except those from the Archivo de Notarías are cited by the name of the *ramo*; volume (or legato, or year); number, if any; and folio, if appropriate. Materials from the Archivo de Notarías are cited by notary number; year; volume, if any; and folio. Citations of Las Siete Partidas, based on Samuel Scott's translation, are abbreviated as P.7.33: 12, to be read as Partida 7, Title 33, Law 12. Citations from the *Novísima recopilación de las leyes de España* . . . (Madrid, 1805–29) are abbreviated as *Nov. rec.* 5 (6.3: 11), to be read as Volume 5, Book 6, Title 3, Law 11. The ecclesiastical divorce cases listed in Appendix C are cited by the parties' family names, along with a C-number.

Other abbreviations used in the Notes are as follows:

AAA   Archivo del ex-Ayuntamiento de la Ciudad de México, Mexico City
AGN   Archivo General de la Nación, Mexico City
AJ   Archivo Judicial del Tribunal Superior de Justicia del D.F., Mexico City
AM   *El Album Mexicano*
AN   Archivo General de Notarías, Mexico City
AP   Archivo General de los Juzgados Unitarios Penales D.F., Mexico City
DM   *El Diario de México*
HAHR   *Hispanic American Historical Review*
Oax. Code   Oaxaca Civil Code of 1827–29, in Raul Ortíz-Urquidi, *Oaxaca, cuna de la codificación iberoamericana* (Mexico City, 1974)
RCL   *Revista Científica y Literaria de Méjico*
SDN   *El Siglo Diez y Nueve*

SHU Semanario de Historia Urbana, Departamento de Investigaciones Históricas, Instituto Nacional de Antropología e Historia, Mexico City

SSM *Semanario de las Señoritas Mejicanas*

Zac. Code Zacatecas Civil Code of 1829, *Proyecto de código civil presentado al segundo congreso constitucional del estado libre de Zacatecas por la comisión encargada de redactarlo* (Zacatecas, 1829).

## Introduction

1. Calderón de la Barca, letters of Feb. 28, 1840, and Nov. 10, 1841, pp. 156, 533. See also her warning about first impressions, p. 614.

2. Fernández de Lizardi, *Quijotita*, p. 37.

3. *Cartas*, p. 8; *Nuevo Febrero*, 1: 63.

4. Fernández de Lizardi, *Quijotita*, p. 253.

5. García, *Leona Vicario*, p. 13.

6. Chris Camarano, "On Cuban Women," *Science and Society*, 35, 1 (Spring 1971): 50.

7. Andrés Molina Enríquez, *Los grandes problemas nacionales* (Mexico City, 1909), pp. 276, 321–22.

8. Presentation of Nov. 6, 1816, in Reyna y Vega vs. Martínez Calderón, C.17; Alamán, 1: 15; Payno, "Celibato femenino."

9. Gilberto Freyre's pioneering works contain superb statements of the stereotype of Latin American women. The "mere shreds" description is from his *The Mansions and the Shanties: The Making of Modern Brazil* (ed. and tr. Harriet de Onís, New York, 1963), p. 334.

10. Petitions for school licenses by Ana Josefa Caballero de Borda (Dec. 1823) and Guadalupe Silva (Nov. 1828) in AGN *Justicia e Instrucción Pública*, 7, no. 9., fol. 87, no. 23, fol. 203.

11. Mora, 1: 135.

12. Compare "Consejos," p. 22, with Nava, *Proclama de una americana*, p. 4.

13. In 1803, 49% of Mexico City's population was of Spanish descent as against 21% for the country as a whole; 24% was Indian as against 43% for the country as a whole; and 27% was Caste as against 36% for the country as a whole. Calculated from figures in Humboldt, 1: 109, 131, 209; 2: 62.

14. Brading, *Miners*, pp. 33–92; Florescano & Gil Sánchez, pp. 274–76.

15. On the causes of migration, see Cooper; Florescano; and Gibson. There is some evidence that the rural poor, like their social superiors,

were also attracted to Mexico City by possibilities of entertainment and the relaxation of village mores (Taylor, especially pp. 67, 160).

16. Villarroel, pp. 107, 110–11.

17. Otero, p. 37 (Mexico's "most distinguished citizens"); Alejandra Moreno Toscano and Carlos Aguirre, "Migraciones hacia la ciudad de México durante el siglo XIX: perspectivas de investigacíon," in SHU, *Investigaciones*, 1: 1–26; Florescano & Gil Sánchez.

18. According to Humboldt (2: 67–68), only London, Dublin, Paris, Madrid, and the Oriental cities of Calcutta and Damascus were larger. On U.S. and Latin American cities, see Richard M. Morse, "The Development of Urban Systems in the Americas in the Nineteenth Century," *Journal of Interamerican Studies and World Affairs*, 17, 1 (Feb. 1975): 6; and Morse, *Ciudades latinoamericanas*. On Mexican cities, see Davies; and Anna, pp. 4–5.

19. Davies, p. 501; Edward E. Calnek, "Conjunto urbano y modelo residencial en Tenochtitlan," in Moreno Toscano, *Ensayos*, p. 54.

20. Florescano & Gil Sánchez, pp. 272–75; Potash, pp. 11–24; Rosenzweig Hernández, pp. 477–91; McWatters.

21. Fernández de Lizardi (1820) and Mariano Otero (1841–42) analysis of social classes in Reyes Heroles, 2: 108–10; Angel Palerm Vich, "Factores históricos de la clase media en México (comentarios al estudio de Nathan L. Whetten)," in *Ensayos sobre las clases sociales*, pp. 99–104; López Cámara; "El populacho de México," *El Museo Mexicano*, 3 (1844): 450–51; Tella, p. 81; Poinsett, p. 49; Mayer, p. 42; Shaw, especially pp. 39–45.

22. Humboldt, 1: 235; "Moneda de cobre," *SDN*, Nov. 8, 1841; Ernest Vigneaux quoted in López Cámara, pp. 227–28. The figures on class sizes derived from the 1811 census sample agree with those of contemporary observers, who estimated the lower-class as four-fifths of the population. Mexico City's class ratios were apparently shared by the leading urban centers in Mexico. Tella (pp. 98–104) has calculated similar proportions of middle- and upper-class groups for Querétaro, as have Chance & Taylor (p. 472) for Oaxaca.

23. Ladd, pp. 133–50; Anna, 140–61.

24. Otero, pp. 24–27; Potash; Tenenbaum; Shaw, pp. 20–38; Poinsett, pp. 105–107; Coatsworth.

25. See, for example, Löwenstern, pp. 58–59; and Calderón de la Barca, p. 476.

26. Moreno Toscano, "México," in Morse, *Ciudades latinoamericanas*, pp. 172–88; Poinsett, pp. 62–63; Celia Maldonado, "La cólera en la ciudad de México," in SHU, *Investigaciones*, 1: 43; Shaw, p. 177.

Chapter One

1. Williams, p. 813. For a succinct liberal view of colonial women, see Castillo Negrete, 1: 334. These myths are embodied in Francisco Sosa's biographical sketch of Josefa Ortiz de Domínguez. Giving an illuminating twist to the legend of La Corregidora, Sosa noted that she patiently cut words out of her husband's books, pasting them together to form the famous message she sent Allende, because she knew how to read but not how to write, for "in those days it was illegal for women to learn to write so that they would not be able to compose love letters" (*Biografías*, p. 773). This account of her activities, which does not appear in the early biographies, contradicts available evidence on several counts. Not only was it legal for women to learn to write when Josefa Ortiz was a schoolgirl, but she attended Las Vizcaínas and her confident signature appears on surviving documents (see the facsimile reproduction of her letter to Viceroy Calleja of Feb. 28, 1814, in García, *Documentos*, 5: between pp. 362 and 363.

2. Benito Gerónimo Feijóo, *An Essay on Woman, or Physiological and Historical Defence of the Fair Sex*, tr. unknown (London, ca. 1770), especially pp. 28, 90–99; Pedro Rodríguez (Count of Campomanes), pp. 372–83; Josefa Amar y Borbón, *Discurso sobre la educación física y moral de las mujeres* (Madrid, 1790). For a discussion of the impact of these ideas in Mexico, see Tanck Estrada, *Educación*; Lavrin, "Religious Life," pp. 120–60, 261–62; and Johanna S. Mendelson, "The Feminine Press: The View of Women in the Colonial Journals of Spanish America, 1790–1810," in Lavrin, *Latin American Women*, pp. 198–218.

3. Caballero de Borda, pp. 3–4; *Cartas*, pp. 56–57. See also [Isidro Gondra], "Economía doméstica: obligaciones de una ama de casa . . .," *SSM*, 1 (1841): 353–59. Fernández de Lizardi recommended that, in addition, women should learn the basics of jurisprudence in order to protect themselves from those who would deceive them (*Quijotita*, pp. 101, 109).

4. F. M. del Castillo.

5. The Enseñanza Nueva, officially known as Nuestra Señora de Guadalupe de Indias, was originally founded under royal patronage and taken over by the Company of Mary in 1806. See Muriel, *Conventos*, pp. 460–64.

6. *Ibid.*, pp. 41–42; Obregón; Tanck Estrada, *Educación*; Kicza, p. 334; Humboldt, 4: 294.

7. "Cuestión interesante," p. 6. See also *SSM*, 2 (1841): 400.

8. Tanck Estrada, *Educación*, especially pp. 160–68, 217–20.

9. *Ibid.*, pp. 16, 168–73.

10. Obregón, pp. 95–104. See the description of Las Vizcaínas in 1840 in Calderón de la Barca, p. 171.

11. Muriel, *Recogimientos*, pp. 102, 144–46.

12. Tanck Estrada, *Educación*, p. 197.

13. *DM*, 5, 466 (Jan. 9, 1807): 34; "Cuestión interesante," pp. 4–5. See also "Variedades: reflexiones acerca del destino de las mujeres," *El Eco del Comercio*, Mar. 27, 1848; and *El Correo de los Niños* (1813), a weekly journal published by Juan Wenceslau Barquera for parents and teachers.

14. Caballero de Borda, pp. 1–2; *Cartas*, p. 5. For similar criticism of women, see "Sobre el luxo"; the account of Relumbrón's bankruptcy in Payno, *Bandidos*; "Carta de un padre a su hijo recién casado," *DM*, 3, 279 (June 28, 1806): 241–42; Payno, "Educación"; "Las dos hermanas: el decoro y el pudor," *SSM*, 1 (1841): 193–200; Guillermo Prieto, "Correspondencia sobre el matrimonio por Fidel," *RCL*, 1 (1845): 175–76; "Fragmento de balance de cuerpo y alma de Gil Fernández . . . ," *AM*, 1 (1849): 488–90; *Sermón de los hombres*; and Mendelson, "The Feminine Press" (cited in note 2, above), pp. 208–9.

15. Gondra, *Prospecto*, p. 4.

16. Mora, 1: 136–40.

17. Several foreign travelers praised Mexico City's public education, noting that it distinguished the capital from the provinces. See Poinsett, p. 83; Thompson, pp. 152–53; Calderón de la Barca, p. 287; and Robertson, 2: 329. See also "Consejos," p. 22; and Tanck Estrada, *Educación*, p. 215.

18. Tanck Estrada, *Educación*, especially p. 197. The doubling of enrollments in the 1850's is only an estimate, based on the founding of 28 new charity schools, as detailed in Shaw, pp. 211–12.

19. *La Semana de las Señoritas* 3, 20 (1852); *SSM*, 2 (1841): 369. For details on the growth of women's periodicals in the 19th century, see Herrick.

20. See Capca; Romero de Terreros; García, *Leona Vicario*; and Kentner, pp. 33–34.

21. On women's religious writings and entry into public contests, see Muriel, *Cultura femenina*, pp. 282–303, 500–506. For examples of their pamphlet production, see Nava's three works; Caballero de Borda; and *Cartas*.

22. This is an extremely rough estimate, calculated by applying the proportion of girls aged 5 to 14 in the 1811 census sample to the population of Mexico City in 1838 (Davies, p. 151).

23. Shaw, pp. 214–17.

24. Calderón de la Barca, pp. 171–72, 286–88. See also Robertson, 2: 146; and "La mujer," *La Semana de las Señoritas*, 1, 14 (Dec. 31, 1850).

25. The corresponding figures are 26 women and 5 men. However, since 21 men failed to respond to their wives' suits, the rate of male illiteracy could well be higher than 6%. For a description of these records, see Appendix C.

26. Calderón de la Barca, p. 288.

27. Diego Alvarez, 376–77.

28. Calderón de la Barca, p. 287.

29. "Consejos," p. 22. See also Mora, 1: 137–40; and Payno, *Fistol*, p. 715.

30. "Cuestión interesante," p. 5; Rivero, p. 136; Prieto, "Margaritas," p. 400; "Memorias de ultratumba de un marido viejo," *AM*, 1 (1849): 301. See also La Vizcaína Semi-erudita, "Sobre la confidencia de las mugeres," *DM*, 6, 692 (Aug. 22, 1807): 459–60.

31. Barquera quoted in María del Carmen Ruiz Castañeda's introduction to Fernández de Lizardi, *Quijotita*, p. xvi; *ibid.*, p. 105. See also "Educación," *SSM*, 3 (1842): 297–304.

32. [Isidro Gondra], "Introducción," *SSM*, 1 (1841): iv.

33. Comonfort supported their goal, but owing to the Wars of Reform, the long-promised secondary school did not open until 1869. Macías, pp. 9–12.

34. Fernández de Lizardi, *Quijotita*, p. 105.

35. Introduction to Lavrin, *Latin American Women*, p. 10.

36. Rodríguez, pp. 301–2, 357–84.

37. Reproduced in Viceroy Azanza's circular publicizing the decree: "Bando de don Miguel Joseph de Azanza," Apr. 22, 1799, AGN *Bandos*, 20, fols. 221–23. Some of the background to the case is also summarized in Konetzke, 3–2: 767–71.

38. Pedro Rodríguez, Conde de Campomanes, "Discurso sobre la legislación gremial de los artesanos," in *Apéndice a la educación popular* (Madrid, 1776), 2: iii-cclxx. See also Herr, pp. 123–27, 385–86.

39. Tanck de Estrada ("La abolición de los gremios," in *El trabajo y los trabajadores en la historia de Mexico*, ed. Elsa Frost et al., pp. 317–22) holds that guilds had been abolished by decrees of the Spanish Cortes in 1814 and 1820, but Carrera Stampa (*Gremios*, pp. 275–77) disagrees.

40. Obregón, pp. 86–87, 106; Tanck Estrada, *Educación*, p. 192; García Icazbalceta, pp. 15–16; Robertson, 2: 324–25. A Carmelite convent in Valladolid also operated a textile factory employing 145 young girls (Greenleaf, pp. 242–43).

41. Fernández de Lizardi, *Quijotita*, pp. 100–101. See also El Alferez Manteca, "Ocupaciones de mujeres," *DM*, 3, 247 (May 4, 1806): 143.

42. For a sympathetic view, see Lorenzo de Zavala's praise of Massachusetts factory girls in *Viage*, p. 294.

43. Decree of 1817 in Konetzke, 3–2: 770.

44. The deeds of royalist women are least evident in the historical record because, as the vanquished, they have been largely ignored by later generations of Mexicans. We know, however, that the royalist Patriotas Marianas alone organized over 2,000 women (Anna, p. 71). On the insurgent side, Miquel i Vergés lists about 100 heroines from Mexico City and several hundred from the provinces.

45. Kentner, p. 4.

46. Proceedings of Dec. 1811 against Carmen Camacho quoted in *ibid.*, pp. 125–33.

47. Calleja's report of Aug. 18, 1814, Iturbide's report of July 8, 1816, and the judicial ruling of Sept. 25, 1815, are quoted in *ibid.*, pp. 196, 255, 278.

48. *Ibid.*, pp. 12–15.

49. Rubio Siliceo, pp. 33–36; Kentner, pp. 40–43.

50. Anna, p. 71; Kentner, pp. 86–87; *Exhortación*; Nava, *Proclama*.

51. Robinson, p. 182; Kentner, pp. 164–65, 272–74, 323; Leal.

52. Kentner, pp. 58–79.

53. Quoted in *ibid.*, pp. 226–30.

54. "Llamada a las mujeres."

55. García, *Leona Vicario*, Echanove Trujillo, Carlos María de Bustamante, "Necrología de María Leona Vicario de Quintana Roo," *SDN*, Aug. 25, 1842; Kentner, pp. 166–217.

56. Fernández de Lizardi's *Calendario* of 1825 was reprinted in 1955 as *Heroínas mexicanas*; "Las republicanas de la América del Sur," *Panorama de las Señoritas*, 1 (1842): 478–85; *Ilustres americanas* (Paris, 1825); *Niles Register*, Sept. 11, 1819, p. 50.

57. Elsa Chaney, "Old and New Feminists in Latin America: The Case of Peru and Chile," *Journal of Marriage and the Family*, 35, 2 (May 1973): 332; Evelyn Cherpak, "The Participation of Women in the Independence Movement in Gran Colombia, 1780–1830," in Lavrin, *Latin American Women*, p. 230.

58. "De la influencia," p. 103; *Cartas*, p. 8.

59. Guillermo Prieto, "Un Novio," *SDN*, Mar. 28, 1843. See also "Las Doncellas," *El Museo Popular*, Jan. 15, 1840, pp. 74–79.

60. Bustamante, "Necrología" (cited in note 55, above).

61. García, *Leona Vicario*, pp. 187–89; also pp. 138–40, 179–86.

62. Echanove Trujillo, p. 37.

63. Asunción Lavrin advocates this wide definition of women's political activity in "Some Final Considerations on Trends and Issues in Latin American Women's History," in Lavrin, *Latin American Women*, p. 310.

64. Calderón de la Barca, p. 328.

65. Couturier, p. 143.

66. *Esposición;* Zamacois, 11: 707. Carlos María de Bustamante claims that he wrote the petition for the women (*Continuación del cuadro histórico de la revolución mexicana,* Mexico City, 1954, 3: 238).

67. "Representación que las señoras mejicanas elevaron al congreso constituyente, pidiendo no se establezca en la República la tolerancia de cultos," reproduced in Zamacois, 14: 1025–40.

68. *Representación que las señoras de Guadalajara.*

69. The petitions reinforced the image of women as conservative allies of the Church, already noted by Francisco Sánchez de Tagle in 1821 (Anna, p. 201). Thus during this period the idea was forged that women as a group shared similar political interests, even though they had so recently split on the issue of independence. For an excellent discussion of the concept of the "natural corporativeness" of women, see Michele Mattelart, "Chile: The Feminine Version of the Coup d'Etat," in Nash & Safa, pp. 287–91.

70. Calderón de la Barca, pp. 519–20, 531; Alessio Robles; Peza, p. 107.

71. Calderón de la Barca, pp. 532–33, 788 (note 9).

72. *Manifiesto.*

73. *Cartas,* p. 154; see also Aurora in Payno, *Fistol.*

74. Cynthia J. Little, "Education, Philanthropy, and Feminism: Components of Argentine Womanhood, 1860–1926," in Lavrin, *Latin American Women,* p. 236; Cherpak, "Participation of Women," in *ibid.,* pp. 223–34.

75. González, pp. 377–78; Shaw, pp. 25, 193.

76. See "Sociedad de Beneficencia . . .," AGN *Justicia e Instrucción Pública,* 9, no. 31, fol. 176; Peza, *passim;* and Alessio Robles, *passim.*

77. García Icazbalceta, pp. 33–34.

78. In 1874, 55 Sisters were French, bringing the total to 410. These figures represent nationwide membership (García Cubas, p. 52). See also González, pp. 406–10.

79. See Lavrin, "Women in Convents," pp. 254–58.

80. Muriel, *Recogimientos,* especially pp. 116, 217–19.

81. The first *montepíos* for the survivors of military employees were founded in 1761 (Lamas, pp. 207–44).

82. García Cubas, pp. 39–43. See also Muriel, *Conventos,* pp. 447–58; Capca; García Icazbalceta, pp. 37–63; and González, pp. 381–97, 406–10.

83. Indeed, in an attempt to expand individual freedom, the Gómez Farías government decreed in 1833 that monks and nuns were free to leave their convents if they wished. The law was revoked by the gov-

ernment that followed shortly thereafter. J. Lloyd Mecham, *Church and State in Latin America: A History of Politico-Ecclesiastical Relations* (rev. ed., Chapel Hill, N.C., 1966), pp. 351–53.

84. See Fernández de Lizardi, *Quijotita*, pp. 156–57; Mora, 1: 281–83; "Miscelánea," p. 259; *AM*, 1 (1849): 109; and "Felicidades." On the secularization of women's world, see also Muriel, *Cultura femenina*, especially pp. 318, 502–3.

85. Quoted in González, p. 408.

86. *SSM*, 3 (1842): 215. See also Francisco Zarco's statement, "The light of Christianity and Liberty have elevated her to the rank she deserves," in "Muger," p. 184; and Diego Alvarez, p. 376.

87. Nava, *Proclama*, p. 4.    88. "Consejos," p. 22.

89. Mora, 1: 135, 138–39.    90. "De la influencia," p. 102.

91. Petition from Caballero de Borda (1823) in AGN *Justicia e Instrucción Pública*, 7, no. 9, fol. 87.

92. Quoted in Tanck Estrada, *Educación*, p. 176.

93. Josefina Bachellerey's comment about French women (reprinted in "Educación de las mujeres," *Panorama de las Señoritas*, 1, 1842, p. 326) applies equally well to Mexico. See also p. 180 of that volume.

*Chapter Two*

1. See, for example, Rosa Signorelli de Martí, "Spanish America," in *Women in the Modern World*, ed. Rafael Patai (New York City, 1967), pp. 193–94; Ann Pescatello, *Power and Pawn: The Female in Iberian Families, Societies, and Cultures* (Westport, Conn., 1976), p. 176; Pescatello, "Latina Liberation: Tradition, Ideology, and Social Change in Iberian and Latin American Culture," in Carroll, ed., *Liberating Women's History*, pp. 168–69; and Charles Boxer, *Mary and Misogyny: Women in Iberian Expansion Overseas 1415–1815. Some Facts, Fancies, and Personalities* (London, 1975), p. 111. The most useful studies of Hispanic women's legal status are Bernal de Bugeda, "Situación jurídica;" Ots Capdequí, *Historia*, pp. 34–69, 214–25; and Ots Capdequí, "Sexo." However, even these studies contain some inaccuracies.

2. For an excellent historical treatment of Spanish law, see Jesús Lalinde Abadía, *Iniciación histórica al derecho español* (Barcelona, 1970), especially pp. 261, 583–635. The best history of Mexican law is Margadant. See also the introductions to Pérez y López and *Ilustración del derecho*.

3. Pascua, 1: 66–67. See also Pérez y López, 12: 398–99; and *Ilustración del derecho*, 1: 40.

4. Pérez y López, 20: 562. Compare P.4.23: 2.

5. P.7.33: 12. On entail, see Ladd, especially pp. 71–73.

6. On marriage, see P.4.1 and 4.2; *Nov. rec.*, 5 (10.2: 2, 9, 18); and *Ilustración del derecho*, 1: 79–90.

7. On guardianship, see P.1.1: 21, P.3.2: 7, P.6.1: 13, P.6.16: 12–21; *Nov. rec.*, 5 (10.1: 17); Pascua, 1: 67, 257; 2: 4; 3: 354; and *Ilustración del derecho*, 1: 162–63.

8. Lavrin, "In Search," p. 30; Ots Capdequí, "Sexo," p. 312; Ots Capdequí, *Historia*, p. 34, later cited by other authors.

9. Marriage empowered the minor husband to administer his own and his wife's property when he reached 18, but both he and his wife needed a *curador* (a type of guardian) to represent them in court until they turned 25. In addition, a son was automatically emancipated if he held an important government post. P.4.18: 1–18; *Nov. rec.*, 5 (10.1: 17, 10.2: 7, 10.5: 3); *Ilustración del derecho*, 1: 66–70, 106; *Nuevo Febrero*, 1: 125–26; *Sala mexicano*, 1: 365–71.

10. P.6.16: 13.

11. P.1.6: 26, P.3.4: 4, P.3.6: 3, P.3.16: 8, P.4.16: 2, P.6.1: 1, P.6.16: 4. For discussions of guardianship as a governmental function see Pascua, 1: 259; and José María Alvarez, 1: 178. González Castro (Art. 214) explains that women could not adopt children because they could not exercise the *patria potestas*, which is another way of saying that they could not rule. The wives of high Spanish functionaries in the Indies were also prohibited from engaging in activities that might conflict with their husbands' duties (Ots Capdequí, "Sexo," p. 337). The prohibition of a widow's remarrying within 300 days of her husband's death, often cited as a restriction against women, appeared in the Partidas but had been dropped (Pascua, 6: 273–74), only to be added again in Sierra's draft code (Art. 125) and in the 1870 Civil Code (Art. 311).

12. P.3.4: 4.

13. P.1.6: 26, P.3.6: 3.

14. P.3.5: 5, P.4.16: 2, P.6.16: 4; Pascua, 1: 236–37.

15. P.3.4: 4. Only one restriction in *derecho indiano* cited women's total inability to perform a given function, a royal decree of 1546 stating that women were "not competent or able to hold Indians in encomienda." This ruling was reversed in 1552 and had not been obeyed in any case, more because encomienda was considered a form of property guaranteeing a woman's livelihood than because it was seen as a form of female governance. See the discussion in Ots Capdequí, "Sexo," pp. 356–62.

16. "Bando de don Miguel Joseph de Azanza," Apr. 22, 1799, in AGN *Bandos*, 20, fols. 221–23. See also Dublán & Lozano, 1: 74–77; Konetzke, 3–2: 767–71; *Nov. rec.*, 5 (10.2: 9).

17. That 19th-century Mexicans understood these distinctions is evi-

dent in Pascua, 3: 354–56; *Nuevo Febrero*, 1: 582; and Fernández de Lizardi, *Periquillo*, p. 217. The decree of Mar. 13, 1863 (on the rights of excloistered nuns) is in Zamacois, 14: 363.

18. P.5.14: 31. Compare Bernal de Bugeda, p. 26. See Pascua, 3: 355, on the validity of women's contracts.

19. Minors (those under age 25) could revoke contracts by which they had been injured (P.1.1: 21, P.6.19: 2–3, P.3.5: 3).

20. P.4.1: 10, P.4.11: 8–9; *Nov. rec.*, 5 (10.3: 1–8). The arras had largely fallen into disuse by the 19th century.

21. Pascua, 1: 228.

22. *Ibid.*, 3: 358; Pérez y López, 20: 566; *Nov. rec.*, 5 (10.11: 3).

23. P.5.12: 2–3. See also the discussion in Pascua, 3: 356. Note that the Spanish term *fiadores* embraces two separate functions in U.S. law, not only that of providing guarantee or surety on property, but also that of being bondsman and fiduciary.

24. This is an extremely simplified presentation of the complicated Spanish inheritance laws. It neglects in particular *mejoras del quinto* and *mayorazgos* that allowed one child to inherit more than others. Children might also be disinherited if they defamed their parents, married against their father's wishes, and so on. For more detail on inheritance law, see *Ilustración del derecho*, 1: 286–394, 2: 1–62; P.6.4: 10–11, P.6.13: 1–7; Alvarez Posadilla, p. 124; and Rodríguez de San Miguel, 2: 678–81.

25. P.4.1: 7–8, P.5.11: 39. After 1776 esponsales were valid only with the consent of both sets of parents. Point clarified in later consultations about the Royal Pragmatic on Marriage in Konetzke, 3–2: 439, 465, 795; *Ilustración del derecho*, 1: 73.

26. The aim of this law was to protect the child, as was also the case in provisions that a pregnant woman could not be tortured or receive capital punishment until the baby was born: P.4.19: 5, P.7.30: 2, 10; *Nov. rec.*, 5 (10.5: 1).

27. P.7.9: 5, P.7.19: 1, P.7.20: 3.

28. P.7.8: 3; *Nov. rec.*, 5 (12.11: 1); *Sala mexicano*, 3: 468–69.

29. Women's sexual definition also led to dress restrictions. Thus, in an attempt to prevent unvirtuous sexual behavior, the law prohibited women from covering their faces, which supposedly facilitated secret rendezvous. *Nov. rec.*, 3 (6.13: 8). A regulation aimed at protecting public decorum was the Mexican archbishop's decree that women not wear low-cut dresses (Lizana y Beaumont, *Instrucción pastoral*).

30. Women who dressed like men also lost their right to protection (P.5.12: 3, P.7.19: 2, P.7.20: 3, P.7.22: 2). Note that the law regulated proper dress for men as well as women: *Nov. rec.*, 3 (6.13).

31. A man's "good reputation" was taken into account in qualifying

him to be a witness or hold public office, but it did not depend on his sexual behavior. For the definition of "bad reputation" in men and women, see P.3.16: 8, 10, 17. Another protective provision sometimes cited by writers on women's legal status is that women were not required to testify personally in court except in criminal cases. However, though women of good reputation could ask to be interrogated at home, the law granted men a similar privilege, allowing them to send their attorneys: P.3.7: 3.

32. *Nov. rec.*, 5 (10.11: 4). Despite this privilege, lower-class women were sometimes forced to work off debts in *atolerías* or cafés. The government attempted to terminate this practice in 1822 (see Muriel, *Recogimientos*, pp. 146–48).

33. P.7.8: 8, P.7.17: 16; *Nov. rec.*, 5 (12.29: 1, 12.30: 1–3). Legal commentators noted, however, that penalties for sexual crimes were milder in 19th-century Mexico than those prescribed by ancient laws (see, for example, Pascua, 3: 360; and Roa Bárcena, p. 739).

34. *Nov. rec.*, 5 (12.26: 7–8); *Ilustración del derecho*, 3: 280–82.

35. *Nov. rec.*, 5 (10.4: 11, 12.26–29); P.4.9: 7, P.7.8: 3, P.7.17: 1, 15; *Ilustración del derecho*, 3: 165–67, 257–63, 282–83. On 19th-century Mexican practice, see Fernández de Lizardi, *Periquillo*, p. 324; and the discussion in chap. 5.

36. Pascua, 6: 121; *Nov. rec.*, 5 (10.4: 5). The widow's share of the community property stayed in the family, being given to her heirs.

37. Alvarez Posadilla, pp. 122–23. Note that a wife was not required to reside with a husband who was imprisoned or went off on a military campaign or business trip (Pérez y López, 19: 348).

38. *Nuevo Febrero*, 1: 63–64; P.4.2: 1, 4, 7. See also the 20th-century formulation of canon law: *Código de derecho canónico* (7th ed., Madrid, 1962), canon 1013 (3.7: 5); canons 1110–13 (3.7: 9).

39. On annulment and separation, see P.4.4-P.4.10; Pascua, 1: 148–53, 232, 235; and *Sala mexicano*, 1: 296–97, 314–26, 329–30; 3: 62–63, 429.

40. *Sala mexicano*, 3: 428.

41. P.3.5: 10.

42. A wife needed her husband's permission to take religious vows, but so did a husband need his wife's, because canon law applied in this matter: P.1.8: 8, P.1.23: 12; *Nov. rec.*, 5 (10.1: 11–12, 10.18: 10); *Ilustración del derecho*, 1: 105; Pérez y López, 20: 566–67.

43. A wife also lost her share of the community property if she committed adultery. For a more complex presentation of the disposition of this property, see *Nov. rec.*, 5 (10.4: 1–9); Pascua, 1: 217–35; 6: 110–39; *Nuevo Febrero*, 2: 773; and *Sala mexicano*, 3: 62–63, 429.

44. Pérez y López, 11: 268.

45. *Nov. rec.*, 5 (10.3: 1–8); P.4.11: 19–32. For more detail, see Pascua, 1: 164–94; 3: 359–61.

46. Inheritances and donations made directly to a husband were also excluded from the community property (P.1.23: 12, P.4.11: 17); Pérez y López, 11: 275; *Sala mexicano*, 1: 344; González Castro, Arts. 132–37, 167–73. Entailed property was of a similar legal status to the *bienes parafernales* (Ladd, pp. 21–22).

47. *Nov. rec.*, 5 (10.11: 3); Pascua, 3: 359–62; P.4.11: 4–6.

48. Pérez y López, 11: 271–72.

49. P.4.11: 29; *Nov. rec.*, 5 (10.4: 5); *Sala mexicano*, 1: 343.

50. An additional privilege was that fathers, unlike guardians, did not need to draw up an inventory of their children's property (*Ilustración del derecho*, 1: 65). The father did not, however, enjoy the usufruct of his son's salary if it was earned in military service or public office (P.4.15: 4–8, P.4.17: 3–8, P.7.8: 9).

51. P.4.1: 8, 10; "Pragmática sanción para evitar el abuso de contraer matrimonios desiguales," Mar. 23, 1776, in *Nov. rec.*, 5 (10.2: 9) and Konetzke, 3–1: 406–13. The decree of Apr. 7, 1778 extending the Royal Pragmatic on Marriage to the Indies specified that parental consent was required only for whites and Indians, not in general for Blacks or those of mixed race unless they distinguished themselves in some way. In 1781 the requirement was extended to mestizos with 1 Spanish parent (Konetzke, 3–1: 439–40; 3–2: 476–82.

52. The only obligation not shared by the mother was the endowing of a daughter. A mother could do so voluntarily, however, and was required to if she was the girl's guardian (P.4.11: 8–9, P.4.19: 3). See also Pascua, 1: 101; and *Sala mexicano*, 1: 295.

53. José María Alvarez, 1: 124–25; *Ilustración del derecho*, 1: 61–62; Pascua, 1: 102.

54. Both sets of grandparents were also required to support and rear their legitimate grandchildren, but only the mother's parents had a legal obligation to illegitimate grandchildren: P.4.13: 2, P.4.15: 1,3, P.4.17: 12, P.4.19: 4–6, P.6.13: 8–11; *Nov. rec.*, 5 (10.5: 1, 10.20: 5–7); Pascua, 1: 102–3, 240; *Sala mexicano*, 1: 297; 3: 385; *Ilustración del derecho*, 1: 62; González Castro, Art. 200.

55. Royal Pragmatic on Marriage, in Konetzke, 3–1: 407; José María Alvarez, 1: 126.

56. Royal decree of Apr. 1803, in *Nov. rec.*, 5 (10.2: 18).

57. A widow could also appoint a guardian for children whom she left as heirs in her will (P.6.16: 2–6, 19, P.6.18: 1). See also Pascua, 2: 239.

58. P.4.2: 2, P.4.19: 3.

59. This is also the reason why the Partidas had forbidden widows to

remarry within a year of their husband's death. The restriction had been dropped by this time: *Nov. rec.*, 5 (10.2: 4); *Ilustración del derecho*, 1: 294–95.

60. *Sala mexicano*, 3: 427; P.7.17: 1. That women were the guardians of class endogamy is demonstrated in the distinctions made in the adultery laws. An upper-class woman's cross-class adultery was the most severely punished: in place of the normal penalty, the loss of the dowry and gananciales, and imprisonment (or death at the hands of her husband if he caught her in the act); the punishment for adultery with a slave was death by burning for both. In contrast, an upper-class man's adultery with a lower-class woman was not generally considered a crime, and where it was defined as such, was punished no more harshly (and sometimes less so) than his adultery within his social class. Indeed, the Partidas had prohibited lower-class men from killing their wives' upper-class lovers, but this provision, which denied lower-class men exclusive rights over their wives' sexual behavior, had been dropped: P.7.17: 15; Pérez y López, 2: 392; *Nov. rec.*, 5 (12.18: 1–5). For a discussion of honor, class, and property, see Martínez-Alier, pp. 120–23; and J. G. Peristiany, "Introduction," and Julian Pitt-Rivers, "Honor and Social Status," in Peristiany, ed., *Honor and Shame: The Values of Mediterranean Society* (Chicago, 1966), pp. 9–18, 21–77.

61. One 19th-century writer did indeed give a woman's physical debilitation from constant childbearing as a reason for her dependence on her husband. His article also reiterated the traditional view of woman's mental inferiority: Rivero, p. 134.

62. Women's status also bore some resemblance to that of nobles: neither could be imprisoned for debts, both were placed in separate prisons when incarcerated, and nobles, like pregnant women, could not be tortured: *Nov. rec.*, 3 (6.2: 1–20). During the colonial period, adult Indians were also subject to a form of guardianship: *Ilustración del derecho*, 3: 429.

63. *Ilustración del derecho*, 3: 180–81; P.4.18: 18.

64. P.7.8: 9. See also *Nov. rec.*, 5 (12.25: 4–5). A Mexican decree of 1830 reiterated that a servant's disobedience was a crime (Dublán & Lozano, 2: 718).

65. Pascua, 7: 146; Roa Bárcena, pp. 44–45, 698–99.

66. Pascua, 7: 59–60.

67. P.4.17: 3.

68. Minors above the ages of 12 and 14 could dispose of part, but not all, of their belongings without the father's permission (Pérez y López, 2: 4). The *Ilustración del derecho* even stated that minors did not need their father's permission to make a will (1: 272), but other legal handbooks disagreed.

69. Family members could not, as a general rule, bring suit or testify against each other (P.3.2: 2–7, P.3.7: 4, P.3.18: 105, P.4.7: 11, P.6.1: 13; *Ilustración del derecho*, 4: 8–10).

70. *Nov. rec.*, 5 (10.1: 12–15); Pascua, 3: 358, 361–62; González Castro, Art. 141; *Ilustración del derecho*, 2: 160.

71. The *Ilustración del derecho*, representing current opinion, stated that children could take their father to court if he failed to provide (4: 9), but the other legal handbooks disagreed. A minor daughter desiring to marry despite her father's objections was placed in *depósito* (deposit) by a judge in the home of a respected member of the community, where she could make up her mind free of pressure from both her father and her suitor: *Nov. rec.*, 5 (10.2: 2, 9, 16); *Sala mexicano*, 1: 311.

72. Introduction to P.4.5.

73. P.3.2: 8–9, P.3.7: 4, P.4.21: 6–7, P.6.1: 16; *Nov. rec.*, 5 (10.1: 16).

74. Pascua, 7: 66; *Sala mexicano*, 3: 429–30, 468; P.7.8: 3. The only other offense against a man's honor deemed serious enough to warrant murder was the rape of one of his female relatives, duels having been prohibited by royal decrees of 1716, 1723, and 1767: *Nov. rec.*, 5 (12.20: 2–3).

75. *Nov. rec.*, 5 (12.28: 1, 5); *Sala mexicano*, 3: 428–30; Pascua, 7: 65–66.

76. Roa Bárcena, 738–39; *Sala mexicano*, 3: 429.

77. Quoted in Lyle N. McAlister, "Social Structure and Social Change in New Spain," *HAHR*, 43, 3 (Aug. 1963): 364. Fernández de Lizardi explicitly described women in corporatist terms when he wrote that "each member of the State should be prepared to carry out the duties to which those of his category are destined," women's duties being the care of home and family (*Quijotita*, p. 101).

78. The applicability to Latin America of the corporate model, with its deep roots in medieval and Spanish Catholic thought, has attracted considerable attention in recent years. Yet the growing body of literature has ignored the relationship of women to this model. See Richard Morse, "The Heritage of Latin America," in Louis Hartz, ed., *The Founding of New Societies* (New York City, 1964), pp. 138–57; Howard Wiarda, "Toward a Framework for the Study of Political Change in the Iberic-Latin Tradition: The Corporate Model," *World Politics*, 25, 2 (Jan. 1973): 206–35; and *The Review of Politics* issue on "The New Corporatism: Social and Political Structures in the Iberian World," 36, 1 (Jan. 1974).

79. Royal Pragmatic of Mar. 23, 1776, in *Nov. rec.*, 5 (10.2: 9); Royal decree of May 26, 1783, in Pérez y López, 19: 243–46. See also *Sala mexicano*, 1: 295, which identified the "equilibrium" based on the paterfamilias's authority with "familial happiness."

80. P.1.23: 12, P.3.2: 5; Pérez y López, 19: 348; 22: 191; *Sala mexicano*, 1: 295.

81. An ambivalence toward female household heads is evident in the confusion over whether Indian and Black women paid tribute. Despite royal decrees prohibiting the practice, in New Spain these women customarily paid tribute from the ages of 18 to 50. Yet the doubt remained: witness the Audiencia's request to the Council of the Indies for guidance in the matter in 1786 (Ots Capdequí, "Sexo," pp. 346–49; Konetzke, 3–2: 605–6).

82. Pérez y López, 2: 400; 22: 190; *Sala mexicano*, 1: 299, 3: 428–30; *Nov. rec.*, 5 (12.21: 1, 12.28: 1); *Ilustración del derecho*, 1: 63; 3: 167; John Henry Merryman and David S. Clark, *Comparative Law: Western European and Latin American Legal Systems* (New York City, 1978), pp. 95–103, 129–32.

83. Pascua, 3: 360–62, and contracts in the AN.

84. See discussion in Goody, pp. 13–19, 62–64. There is indeed evidence for Latin America that the domination of wealth increased the paterfamilias' power over his family (see, for example, Carlos & Sellers, pp. 101–5).

85. Fernández de Lizardi, *Periquillo*, p. 217.

86. Pascua, 1: 66; 3: 360–62.

87. In 1832 the state of Jalisco also began work on a civil code, which was never completed or promulgated, and in 1852 Oaxaca drafted a new state civil code, which has been lost (see González Domínguez, "Notas"; and Clagett & Valderrama, pp. 63–64).

88. *Discurso sobre el derecho*, p. 19; Antonio Fernández de Córdoba, *Si ante la ley no hay igualdad no puede gozarse de libertad* (Mexico City, 1825). See also González Castro, p. v.

89. Fernández de Lizardi, *Quijotita*, pp. 32–33; Ignacio Ramírez, "La coqueta," in Frías y Soto et al., p. 139; *Nuevo Febrero*, 1: 64–65. See also A. Rodríguez, "Las mujeres: remitidos," *SSM*, 1 (1841): 244; Diego Alvarez, p. 376; and Zarco, "Muger," p. 184.

90. Legal changes introduced in the late 18th century and especially the Married Woman's Property Acts of the mid-19th century began to bring English and U.S. law more into line with Hispanic law on the rights of married women. A few wealthy women had in any case avoided some of the restrictions of common law by entering into prenuptial marriage settlements through the Courts of Equity. See "Special Report from the Select Committee on Married Woman's Property Bill; Together with the Proceedings of the Committee, Minutes of Evidence, Appendix, and Index," *Parliamentary Papers, Reports from Committee,* 1867–68 (London) 2: 339–466; Richard B. Morris, *Studies in the History of*

*American Law with Special Reference to the Seventeenth and Eighteenth Centuries* (2d ed., New York City, 1974), pp. 126–200; Eleanor M. Boatwright, "The Political and Civil Status of Women in Georgia, 1783–1860," *The Georgia Historical Quarterly*, 25, 4 (1941): 301–24; Marylynn Salmon, "Life, Liberty, and Dower: The Legal Status of Women After the American Revolution," in Carol R. Berkin and Clara M. Lovett, eds., *Women, War, and Revolution* (New York City, 1980), pp. 85–106; and Salmon, "Equality or Submersion? Feme Covert Status in Early Pennsylvania," in Berkin & Norton, pp. 92–111.

91. At the Constitutional Convention of 1856, Ramírez criticized his colleagues for ignoring women altogether in the 29 articles of the new constitution and urged his fellow lawmakers to guarantee women the same "privileges and prerogatives" conferred by colonial law. It was their protection of the "weak and needy," he argued, that made the ancient law codes last for centuries (speech of July 10, 1856, in Zarco, *Historia*, 1: 684–85; see also Fernández de Lizardi, *Quijotita*, p. 37).

92. *Nuevo Febrero*, 1: 44; González Castro, Art. 60; *Sala mexicano*, 1: 307; José María Alvarez, 1: 130; Oax. Code, Arts. 125–27; Sierra, Art. 47.

93. Oax. Code, Art. 114; Zac. Code, Art. 129; Sierra, Art. 86. The dowry is discussed in chap. 3.

94. L.M.R., the anonymous author of the 1841 *Discurso*, felt that the privileges of the dowry were "exorbitant," too often hurting a family's creditors, but even he believed that "women's dowries should be guaranteed" (pp. 20, 39).

95. Note that subsequent constitutions established literacy and property-owning requirements for male suffrage (Margadant, pp. 144–45; Marta Morineau, "Situación jurídica de la mujer en el México del siglo XIX," in *Condición jurídica*, pp. 41–43; Tena Ramírez, p. 206).

96. Ignacio Ramírez, speeches of July 10 and Sept. 17, 1856, in Zarco, *Historia*, 1: 684; 2: 321.

97. *Nuevo Febrero*, 1: 110–11, 139–40. The *Sala mexicano* gave similar arguments about a mother's "natural love and interest in her children's future" to explain why mothers were given the right of consent over children's marriages in 1776 (1: 301).

98. Zac. Code, Arts. 250–82, 325, 378; Oax. Code, Arts. 233–36, 242, 248–49, 254–55; Sierra, Arts. 180–85.

99. Sierra's code (Art. 186) gave single mothers this authority over their natural offspring once she had recognized them. It gave fathers of natural children the same rights. The Oaxaca and Zacatecas codes expanded a single mother's rights over her natural offspring also, but did not give them the full *patria potestas* given to the fathers of natural children (Oax. Code, Art. 239; Zac. Code, Arts. 272–74).

100. Oax. Code, Arts. 199, 220; Zac. Code, Arts. 216–24, 312; Sierra, Art. 220. Note that Sierra's code did include any provisions on adoption.

101. Sierra, p. iii.

102. Oax. Code, Arts. 80–81, 233; Zac. Code, Arts. 57, 252, 264, 291, 294; Sierra, Arts. 102, 159.

103. *Nuevo Febrero*, 1: 64–65.

104. *Ibid.*, pp. 63, 77–80, 94, 110.

105. *Sala mexicano*, 1: 344.

106. Oax. Code, Arts. 101–8; Zac. Code, Arts. 117–28; Sierra, Arts. 76–85.

107. Indeed Vicente González Castro, in his 1839 digest of existing law, presented the last two provisions as part of traditional Hispanic law, all the while insisting that he had simply codified the law as it was understood at the time, introducing no innovations (pp. vii, x, Arts. 135–41). Compare Pascua, 3: 358; and *Ilustración del derecho*, 2: 160.

108. Fernández de Lizardi, *Periquillo*, p. 324; *Sala mexicano*, 3: 429–30, 473; Roa Bárcena, pp. 738–43.

109. See Fernández de Lizardi, *Quijotita*, pp. 189–90; Fernández de Lizardi, *Periquillo*, p. 324; *Sala mexicano*, 3: 427–30; Pascua, 7: 67; *Nuevo Febrero*, 1: 63; and *Ilustración del derecho*, 3: 262.

110. As in so many other instances, the Oaxaca code was the most enlightened of the three: Arts. 100, 145. Compare Zac. Code, Arts. 116, 135–37; and Sierra, Arts. 76, 92. The first Mexican criminal code, drafted in 1871, incorporated the "softer" ideas about adultery. A husband was subject to 4 years' imprisonment if he killed his adulterous wife; his own adultery—defined equally for men and women—was in all cases punishable, though less harshly than his wife's (*Código penal*, Arts. 554, 816–17, 821).

111. González Domínguez, "Consideraciones," pp. 92, 128; González Domínguez, "Notas," pp. 115–19; *The Code Napoléon; or, The French Civil Code Literally Translated from the Original and Official Edition, Published in Paris, in 1804* [tr. George Spence] (London, 1824), especially pp. 62–63, 76, 107–9, 427–28.

112. Rafael Rogina Villegas, *Derecho civil mexicano* (Mexico City, 1959), 2: 98. Although the *bienes parafernales* could conceivably have been used to circumvent the community property laws, this possibility was not discussed in the legal literature of the time. A wealthy bride could protect her property by including it in the dowry, and a couple could enter into *capitulaciones matrimoniales* (a marriage contract), but the law specified that a written agreement in which the woman reserved the administration and usufruct of the dowry to herself could not be legally valid (Pérez y López, 11: 271; see also *Ilustración del derecho*, 1: 95, 102–3).

113. *Nuevo Febrero*, 1: 93; *Discurso sobre el derecho*, p. 20. Sierra allowed the separation of property when one spouse was absent, outlawed, or guilty in a divorce case (Arts. 1394–95, 1441–42). The Oaxaca code, following colonial law, permitted it only during a divorce (Arts. 109, 154). See also Zac. Code, Arts. 1379, 1416–18, 1425.

114. State of Mexico, decree of Aug. 16, 1826, in *Colección de decretos*, 1: 89; Zac. Code, Arts. 57, 67, 279, 284, 305; Oax. Code, Arts. 80, 232, 243, 358; Sierra, Arts. 53, 167–70, 176, 293–94.

115. Mexico City was also subject to the first book of the Civil Code of the Mexican Empire for a few brief months in 1867. The Emperor Maximilian had not yet promulgated the last 2 books when he was executed. See Clagett & Valderrama, p. 64.

116. Compare *Ilustración del derecho*, 1: 40, with *Sala mexicano*, 1: 258. See also Diego Alvarez, p. 376.

117. *Nuevo Febrero*, 1: 582. This reform was apparently widely accepted, since it was incorporated in the Zacatecas Civil Code (Arts. 1619–28) and Sierra's draft code (Arts. 1858–70). It would hardly have affected women's business activities in any case, since colonial law had explicitly given women the right to waive the provision against providing surety.

118. *Nuevo Febrero*, 1: 64–65.

119. *Ibid.*

120. *Ibid.*, pp. 65–66.

121. For the use of "El Sexo Débil," see Mora, 1: 283; for "El Sexo Flaco," see Pérez Gálvez vs. García Noriega, C.19.

122. In addition to revoking the remarried widow's *patria potestas* and guardianship rights, the 1870 code restricted the freedom of an unmarried daughter until she reached age 30 (5 more years than Sierra and 9 more than the Oaxaca code), did not allow women to be guardians of children other than their own descendants, and rejected the *Nuevo Febrero*'s suggestion that wives share the *patria potestas* with their husbands (see Arrom, "Cambios").

*Chapter Three*

1. See the discussion of censuses in Carlos Aguirre and Rosa María Sánchez de Tagle, "Padrones y censos de la ciudad de México," in SHU, *Fuentes*, pp. 5–33; Davies, pp. 502–4; and Anna, p. 229, note 5.

2. The summary totals of the 1811 census list sex ratios virtually identical to those in the sample: 44.4% male, 55.6% female, for the entire city, compared with 44.5% male, 55.5% female, for the sample ("Resumen de las operaciones de la nueva policía desde el día 26 de agosto último en que fue instalado," Jan. 6, 1812, AGN *Historia*, 454; Table

A.2). The proportion of the Spanish race in the sample (50.2%) is also similar to the 50.3% recorded in the 1790 census. In one respect the 1811 census sample appears biased: it shows a considerably higher proportion of Indians (32.5%) than in 1790 (24.4%; Humboldt, 1: 246; 2: 62; 4: 293; Table A.1). This difference may simply reflect undercounting of the Indian barrios in 1790. Or it may reflect the migration of Indian villagers to the capital in the two decades after 1790, as well as the fact that the peripheral area of the sample includes part of the old Indian barrio of San Antonio Tomatlan, which, though largely integrated into the city by this time, was still under the jurisdiction of the parcialidad of San Juan Tenochtitlan (see Lira-González, p. 560; and Alfonso Caso, "Los barrios antiguos de Tenochtitlan y Tlatelolco," *Memorias de la Academia Mexicana de Historia*, 15, 1 (Jan.-Mar. 1956): 7–63, map facing p. 63). The summary totals do not, unfortunately, include such variables as place of origin or employment, and only the 1790 totals include marital status and age.

3. Although the Treaty of Guadalupe Hidalgo ended the Mexican-American War in Feb. 1848, U.S. troops remained in Mexico City until September. On the goals of the census, see Lira-González, pp. 152, 211.

4. See Fernández de Lizardi, *Periquillo*, p. 315; Poinsett, p. 160; and Calderón de la Barca, p. 194. Humboldt used a 7-race scheme, dividing the population into Spaniards, Creoles, Mestizos, Mulattoes, Zambos, Indians, and Negroes; however, as he himself noted, there were almost no Mulattoes, Zambos, or Negroes in Mexico City (1: 130, 170, 190, 236, 245–46).

5. Fernández de Lizardi and Mora cited in Reyes Heroles, 2: 102, 108–9; Abad y Queipo cited in *Ensayos sobre las clases sociales*, p. 21; Otero, pp. 54–57.

6. Borah, "Race," pp. 331–42; McAlister, pp. 349–70; Brading, *Miners*, pp. 19–24; Brading, "Government," pp. 389–90; Chance & Taylor, pp. 457–87; McCaa et al.; Seed; Mörner.

7. Edgar Love, "Marriage Patterns of Persons of African Descent in a Colonial Mexico City Parish," *HAHR*, 51, 1 (Feb. 1971): 79–91; Brading, *Miners*, pp. 258–60; Brading & Wu, pp. 7–9; Marcelo Carmagnani, "Demografía y sociedad: la estructura social de los centros mineros del norte de México, 1600–1720," *Historia Mexicana*, 21, 3 (1972): 419–59; Borah & Cook, *Essays*, 2: 251–67; Chance & Taylor, pp. 477–81; McCaa et al., pp. 424–29.

8. Lira-González, pp. 115, 189, 215, 227, etc.

9. Indeed, Lombardi (pp. 75–82) found that in Venezuela, the larger the city the greater the excess of women over men. See also Borah & Cook, *Essays*, 1: 210–12; Poinsett, p. 163; Ramos, "Marriage," p. 215; and Hajnal, "European Marriage," p. 107.

10. 1790 summary totals in Humboldt, 1: 254; 1811 summary totals in "Resumen de las operaciones" (cited above, note 2); 1842 summary totals in Shaw, p. 170; 1848 figures from my census sample.

11. Quoted in Archer, *Army*, p. 225. On the problem of census evasion and the steps authorities took to prevent it, see *ibid.*, pp. 85, 226; and also Orozco y Berra, p. 72; Borah & Cook, *Essays*, 1: 207–27.

12. Only these Indians living in the *parcialidades de Indios*, or Indian republics within the city boundaries, were required to pay tribute. On the parcialidades and tribute collection in the first half of the nineteenth century, see Lira-González, p. 40 and *passim*.

13. In addition to married men and widowers with children, those of any marital status were exempt if they were their parents' or siblings' sole source of support. So were nobles, government officials, clergymen, doctors, lawyers, students, merchants and their assistants, muleteers who owned their mules, servants of illustrious persons, the sick, those under five feet tall, and those who had already served six years (Archer, *Army*, p. 231; and Rodríguez de San Miguel, 2: 136–37). According to Archer (*Army*, pp. 226–37; "To Serve the King: Military Recruitment in Late Colonial Mexico," *HAHR*, 55, 4, May 1975, pp. 230–38), these exemptions were sometimes honored in the breach, at least for lower-class men.

14. It is true that some older men might have tried to avoid taxation, but the affluent were too well known in their communities to escape enumeration or taxation (as, indeed, the Indians in parcialidades were too well-known to the indigenous tax collector to escape tribute payment). Moreover, taxes dependent on censuses, such as those on windows or (as projected in 1848) on real estate, applied to both sexes and could not easily be evaded.

15. Humboldt, 1: 250, 253; sex ratio for Mexico City calculated from Table 3, in *ibid.*, 4: 292; Navarro y Noriega, p. 16.

16. Owing to the out-migration and undercounting of city-born men, male migrants constitute a slightly higher share of the male population: 41%.

17. Over two-thirds of the female migrants came from central Mexico: 34.8% from the state of Mexico, 17.7% from Hidalgo, and 15.9% from Puebla. But some females came from as far away as Sonora, Chihuahua, Veracruz, and Oaxaca. Migrants from abroad were overwhelmingly male: of the 61 foreigners in the census sample, 53 were from Spain (including 3 women), 5 from the U.S. (including 4 women), 2 from Cuba, and 1 from Guatemala (the last 3 male).

18. Villarroel, p. 108.

19. Scardaville ("Crime," pp. 56, 82) has found a similar age distribution for female migrants in late colonial criminal records, not suscep-

tible to the same biases as the census. He also found that they were younger on the whole than their male counterparts.

20. See Elinor C. Burkett, "Indian Women and White Society: The Case of Sixteenth-Century Peru," in Lavrin, *Latin American Women*, pp. 101–28.

21. Because a similar sexual imbalance was already recorded in the 1753 census, which listed 55.7% of the population as female (Vázquez Valle, p. 95), it seems dangerous to emphasize the newness of migratory patterns. Furthermore, the 1790 data suggest a comparable age distribution to that of 1811, with a preponderance of women in the 16–40 age group (Humboldt, 4: 292), although the summary statistics are too aggregated to construct a population pyramid by 5- or even 10-year brackets.

22. Orozco y Berra, p. 74.

23. The increased ratio of female migrants in 1848 may be partially due to rural dislocations caused by the Mexican-American War, for men who normally would have gone to the capital may have gone off to fight instead. But the migrant women recorded in the 1848 census were not wartime refugees, since the peace treaty had already been signed by the time the count was made. A sample of the 1849 municipal census, taken a full year later, also reveals heavy migration (Shaw, pp. 169, 401–2). Shaw's data, though not directly comparable to mine, reveal similar age and sex characteristics as the previous counts.

24. Gustavo Cabrera, "Selectividad por edad y sexo de los migrantes en México," in *Conferencia regional latinoamericana de población: Actas*, ed. Susana Lerner and Raúl de la Peña (Mexico City, 1972), 1: 517–19; Jelin; Dora Orlansky and Silvia Dubrovsky, *The Effects of Rural-Urban Migration on Women's Role and Status in Latin America* (Paris, 1978; UNESCO).

25. Demographers commonly use the age group 45–49 to represent the proportion of a population that never married (Hajnal, "European Marriage," p. 102). I have used the 10-year age group 45–54, however, because the extreme heaping at age 50 in the 1811 census leaves too few people in the 45–49 bracket for analysis.

26. Mora (1: 118) attributed the prevalence of consensual unions to the high cost of obtaining legal marriages. Records of policemen's daily rounds show that many lower-class couples were apprehended for incontinence and concubinage in the colonial period (see AP, "Libro de reos de la vara del alcalde ordinario de 2° voto, don Pedro González de Noriega, para el año . . . 1807"). The prevalence of informal unions, often stable over 2 or 3 decades, is also referred to in such ecclesiastical records as "Los curas del Sagrario sobre generalización de casamientos en artículo de muerte, 1824," AGN *Bienes Nacionales*, 102; and in peti-

tions to amend baptismal records in *ibid.*, 75, no. 8; 76, nos. 9, 20, 23–25; 470, no. 33. See also Shaw, pp. 172, 220, 243; and Borah & Cook, "Marriage," pp. 960–62, 976–77.

27. William Folan and Phil Weigand found that widowhood was widely claimed by single mothers and separated women in contemporary Mexico for these reasons ("Fictive Widowhood in Rural and Urban Mexico," *Anthropologica*, 10, 1, 1968, pp. 119–27).

28. The census sample suggests that "teen pregnancy" was unusual (or very well hidden), since the 5 girls listed as widows from the ages of 12 16 represent only 2% of the females in that age group. The 2 12-year-old widows are not included in the discussion of marriage ages on pp. 116–17.

29. The exclusion of the 20 nuns (6.7% of the female testators) hardly alters the proportion of single females, since all but 2 were minors when they professed and made their wills; the removal of 29 priests (9.7% of the men), all of them adults and 2 of them widowers, reduces the proportions of single males from 36.9% to 30.8%.

30. Indeed, 60.3% of the wills open with some variation of the phrase "being sick in bed with the illness that God our Father has chosen to send me," and 49 testators (8%) were already too infirm to sign their names. It is my impression that it was rare for healthy people to make wills unless they were very old or about to embark on a journey, exposing themselves to the risk of shipwreck or death in a foreign land.

31. J. H. Hajnal, "Age at Marriage and Proportions Marrying," *Population Studies*, 7, 2 (Nov. 1953): 130. The age thus calculated, based on the proportions single from the ages of 10 to 54, applies only to first marriages contracted below the age of 50.

32. See Fernández de Lizardi, *Quijotita*, chap. 23; Emilio de Girardin, "Educación de las niñas," *SSM*, 1 (1841): 124; and Payno, *Bandidos*, Mariana's story, especially pp. 309–15. Furthermore, the move to raise the minimum marriage age for girls from 12 to 14 (discussed in *Nuevo Febrero*, 1: 54, but enacted only in the Zacatecas Civil Code, Art. 56) would have strengthened women's freedom of choice in marriage.

33. A cursory examination of petitions for *licencias matrimoniales* (permits to marry) among the military and *dispensas de impedimentos* (dispensations of impediments to marriage) even suggests that the bride was as often older than the groom as she was younger (see, for example, AGN *Matrimonios*, 75, no. 5, and 76, no. 3).

34. Life expectancies cannot be determined from the census alone because it does not represent a closed population. It is likely, for example, that part of the dramatic decrease in Mexico City's over-30 female population (Fig. 1) was caused by migrant women returning to their native

villages on marriage, rather than by mortality. Furthermore, it is probable that many elderly people exaggerated their age when interviewed by the census taker.

35. Ots Capdequí, "Sexo," p. 312.

36. The proportions of single adults were also nearly identical for both sexes (Table 5), but the addition of draft evaders would increase the numbers of single men in the 25–39 age group. A larger proportion of single adult men than women is reasonable if men married a year and a half later, on average, than women. The male proportion single from the ages of 45 to 54 is more reliable, since those men were no longer eligible for military recruitment.

37. There were 519 married women and 510 married men, minor and adult, in the census sample. The 9 extra women may have been abandoned or separated from their husbands. It is also possible that the missing married men were merely away on business trips, though in such cases the husband was usually listed as *ausente* (absent) and all information for him given. It is unlikely, however, that the missing men were evading military recruitment, for in that case their wives would have declared themselves widowed so as not to provoke questions from the census taker (and, in any case, most married men were theoretically exempt from the draft).

38. Of the 300 women, 27 had married twice and 3 thrice; of the 300 men, 27 had married twice and 2 thrice. I doubt whether these figures indicate the same rate of remarriage for both sexes. Rather, I suspect that a woman who had previously been married and had children from that union was more likely to draw up a will because of her complicated legal situation than a woman who had only married once, whose estate could easily be divided without such a document. Men's more complex investments may have made those married only once just as likely to dictate a will as those with more than one wife.

39. Figures for 1790 calculated from Humboldt, 4: 291–92, 297. The number of religious has been added to the secular population in Humboldt's Table 3 (p. 292), giving 40,809 women and 30,695 men age 16 and over. The 1850 calculation applies the same proportions single to population figures in Davies, p. 501. The number of nuns in 1850 is taken from Bazant, p. 218. The single men in the census samples do include a few priests: 7 in 1811 and 3 in 1848.

40. The differences between mean ages at first marriage in 1790 and 1811 are difficult to explain until we know whether 1811 ages were typical of the 18th century, with the 1790 pattern representing a temporary decline in response to new prosperity that supported larger families, or whether the lower marriage age was typical, with the higher 1811 ages

representing a response to population pressure and people's perception that the city's growth was outstripping available resources, especially given the insecurity caused by recurring harvest failures and epidemics, as well as Spain's forced loans. A high marriage age in 1811 might also reflect the decline of the dowry, as discussed below.

41. The connections among members of a household often have to be inferred from shared last names or the order of the listing. I followed the decisions of the Seminario de Historia Urbana's coders in assigning motherhood to women in the 1811 census sample, which I took from their data bank. When coding the 1848 census myself, I kept those women about whose status I was unsure in a separate category. They accounted for 2.7% of all wives and widows, and 1 single woman. I included them in the statistics on mothers presented here in order to make the 1848 data comparable to those of 1811, for it is my impression that the Seminario's coders assigned the status of mother to women rather liberally.

42. Shaw, pp. 156–72. Petitions that baptismal records be amended (cited above, note 26) show the difficulty of using parish registers to study legitimacy: many illegitimate children had originally been listed as the legitimate children of the maternal grandparents or as *expósitos* (abandoned children).

43. Decree of Sept. 7, 1803, and "Prospectus for Addition to the Poor House," July 1, 1806, in Dublán & Lozano, 1: 300, 307–11; Calderón de la Barca, p. 532.

44. The following statistics exclude 7 children born to 4 single mothers, but include 5 children born to 3 women before they were married.

45. Celia Maldonado found that although the average age of death in Mexico City was 24.1, reflecting uniformly high infant mortality, the age was considerably lower in parishes with high concentrations of poor people than in those where the elites lived ("Edad promedio a la muerte, ciudad de México, 1840–49," in SHU, *Investigaciones*, 3: 157–58). Studies of other areas of Mexico have found high infant mortality for all groups, with the highest among Indians (Brading & Wu, pp. 20–21; Morin, pp. 77–79; Shaw, pp. 161–66). The rate of infant death was entirely in keeping with contemporary Europe. See, for example, Peter Laslett, *Family Life and Illicit Love in Earlier Generations: Essays in Historical Sociology* (Cambridge, Eng., 1977), p. 69; and Wrigley, *Population*, pp. 100, 169–71.

46. Humboldt, 2: 65. His remark on the high Mexican birthrate relative to Europe (1: 105–6) referred to New Spain in general, which he noted had a higher fertility rate than the capital.

47. AN, Not. 155, 1803, fols. 379–87; Not. 715, 1827, fols. 91–95v;

Not. 417, 1802, fols. 547v-57; Not. 426, 1854, fols. 403v-6; Not. 711, 1803, fols. 1–3v.

48. Although 76 wills list children's ages, 47 could not be used to calculate birth intervals because they listed only surviving children, making vague references to "others that died" without telling us when they were born. In the other 29 cases either all children survived or information about deceased children was given. Yet the information is still rather rough, because the wills do not give exact birth dates; children born anywhere from 12 to 23 months apart could, for example, be listed as one year apart in age. Although the number of longer intervals may cancel out the shorter ones, the averages given here should be treated with caution, especially since they are based on so few cases. I have nonetheless deduced the practice of breastfeeding both from birth intervals (the French demographer Louis Henry, in his pioneering family reconstitution study, found the normal interval between births when mothers breastfed their children was 2.5 years: E. Gautier and L. Henry, *La Population de Crulai*, Paris, 1958, p. 151) and from the silence in the Mexican literature on the subject. (Fanny Calderón mentions wet nurses only in relation to the orphans in the Foundling Home and only Fernández de Lizardi makes an issue of breastfeeding in *La Quijotita*.) I read this silence as evidence that mothers breastfed their infants whenever possible, for if wet nursing had been as common as in contemporary Europe, reformers would undoubtedly have condemned it as often as they did abroad.

49. E. A. Wrigley posits that for Europe unusually long intervals between the last 2 births show attempts to limit fertility, probably achieved by means of *coitus interruptus* ("Family Limitation in Pre-Industrial England," *Economic History Review*, 2d series, 19, Apr. 1966, p. 123). But it is also possible that the larger gap merely reflects women's declining fertility as they age. There is no evidence in the Mexican literature that contraception was used, and given the large size of families where couples were fertile and lived together over the woman's childbearing years, its use could not have been widespread (or effective) even among the Mexican elites. I found only one reference to contraception: in 1758 the countess of Regla wrote her mother that, because of her poor health, she was looking for the skin of an animal "so that it would not be so easy to have children." Her attempts to prevent conception did not succeed, however, since she died in 1766, a month after giving birth to her 7th child in 10 years (Couturier, pp. 131, 133–34). The resort to abortives dated back at least to the time of the Siete Partidas, which prohibited their use. According to colonial authorities, abortion was used to prevent illegitimate children (Dublán & Lozano, 1: 307–11).

50. AN, Not. 426, 1827, fols. 826–29v; Not. 158, 1803, fols. 126–32v.

51. Two of her children perished as infants, the other 3 as adults. See Valle Arizpe; and "La Güera's" will in AN, Not. 426, 1850, fols. 596v-601v.

52. Although these single women may have been unwed mothers, they may also have been unmarried women who took in orphans to raise. This practice may have been widespread in Mexico City at the time (see Payno, *Bandidos*, p. 47; and Prieto, *Memorias*, p. 74), but there was no such instance in the will sample; however, 5 married couples and 4 widows had taken in orphans.

53. Mayer, pp. 41–42, 294; Calderón de la Barca, pp. 264–65.

54. AN, Not. 417, 1803, fols. 238v-41; Not. 426, 1828, fols. 676–78v; Not. 531, 1827, fols. 31v-33v.

55. Some problems in the definition of household heads are suggested by the 30 married women so designated (see Table 8). Nine of the husbands were recorded as absent; the other 21 women may have been abandoned or separated, or they may have been hiding their husbands from the census-takers (but see discussion in note 37 above). But it is also possible that the census taker simply made a mistake in recording the information. Fortunately, these only represent 5% of all households in the sample. Nonetheless, they demonstrate the ambiguous nature of the census as a historical source.

56. Lavrin, "Women in Convents," p. 269.

57. Prieto, "Las Margaritas," p. 401. See also Gondra, p. 5; and "Estudios morales: la flor marchita," *RCL*, 2 (1846): 63–67. Contrast Fernández de Lizardi, *Quijotita*, p. 275; Payno, "Celibato femenino"; Prieto, *Memorias*, p. 294; and "El mundo," p. 201.

58. On the Fagoaga sisters, see Calderón de la Barca, pp. 506, 531; on the countess of Regla, see Couturier, pp. 141–43; and Romero de Terreros. See also Tutino on the "matriarchal" countess of Santiago. Tutino emphasizes, however (p. 366), that "only a minority of unmarried or widowed heiresses ever escaped male patriarchal rule over their economic affairs," and then under limited conditions.

59. AN, Not. 169, 1853, vol. 1, fols. 126v-27.

60. See depiction in Payno, "Celibato femenino"; Prieto, *Memorias*, pp. 16–17, 327, 332, 341–42.

61. Lavrin, "Women in Convents," p. 253; Williams, pp. 233–34.

62. Although the low marriage rate of Spanish women meant that as a group they had fewer children than Indian women, the 1811 census sample shows that Indian women were only slightly more likely to have children living at home at the time of the census enumeration (41% of all Spanish women compared with 47% of all Indian women). The un-

expectedly low number of Indian households with children probably reflects the higher infant mortality among Indians as well as the death of husbands at a relatively young age. Indian children may also have left home at an earlier age than Spanish children, either to work or to establish their own families.

63. "Sobre la necesidad"; El Sustentante, untitled piece, *DM* 2, 126, (Feb. 3, 1806): 135.

64. "Sobre el luxo," p. 125; Payno, "Celibato femenino."

65. Among men making wills, 44.1% of those born in Spain were single compared with 23.9% of those born in Mexico. Further, peninsular Spaniards decreased from 47% of testators in 1802–3 to 24% after independence. See note 83 below for a discussion of the marriage patterns of Spanish immigrants in Mexico.

66. Fernández de Lizardi, *Quijotita*, p. 275; "Representación humilde que hace la muy noble y leal ciudad de México . . .," May 2, 1972, quoted in Hamill, p. 29.

67. The justification given for establishing the Mexico City Foundling Home and the Poor House's Section for Unwed Mothers was similarly to increase the population by preventing infanticide "prejudicial to the State" (decree of July 30, 1794, on legitimizing expósitos, in Dublán & Lozano, 1: 34; decree prohibiting prostitution, in *Sala mexicano*, 3: 384). See also "Bando de la Real Audiencia con nuevas resoluciones acerca de la pragmática de matrimonios," June 3, 1782, in AGN *Bandos*, 12, exp. 38, fols. 126–40; "Sobre la necesidad," p. 305; Humboldt, 2: 65; Navarro y Noriega, p. 18; and manifesto of Benito Juárez, July 7, 1859, in Zamacois, 15: 928.

68. Pascua, 3: 356.

69. Lira-González (pp. 256, 307–8, etc.) develops this idea with respect to the attack on Indian corporations.

70. Fernández de Lizardi, *Quijotita*, p. 105; "Sobre el luxo," p. 126; Guillermo Prieto, "Estudios morales: la joven sin amor," *El Museo Mexicano*, 2 (1843): 430–31; Payno, "Celibato femenino."

71. Calderón de la Barca, p. 230.

72. See, for example, Carlos & Sellers; and Ramos, "Marriage," pp. 218–20.

73. See Tutino, p. 372.

74. Payno, "Celibato femenino"; Prieto, *Memorias*, p. 327.

75. Hamill, p. 29; Navarro y Noriega, p. 22, note 14. On the popularity of ecclesiastical careers for men, see also Brading, *Miners*, pp. 213–14.

76. The 1790 figures were calculated from Humboldt, 4: 197, 291–93. The number of eligible women in 1828 and 1850 was calculated by ap-

plying the proportion of Spanish women 16 and over in the 1811 census sample (19%) to population data provided by Davies (p. 501). Nuns in the convent for Indian women were excluded from these calculations. Note that the decline in male religious was apparently even more dramatic than among women, since the number of regular clergy in all of Mexico decreased by almost half from 1826 to 1850, compared with a reduction of approximately a quarter for nuns (Bazant, p. 38).

77. Prieto, *Memorias*, p. 327. On the 16th-century writers, see Lavrin, "In Search," pp. 25–27.

78. Brading, *Miners*, p. 102.

79. For a discussion of inheritance strategies, see Goody, pp. 95–110. Nuns did not inherit beyond the dowry required for their entrance in a convent, and priests usually returned their inheritances to their kin. The Mexico City cabildo, in discussing ecclesiastical celibacy in 1792, attributed the popularity of the religious life to financial problems, apparently because it was cheaper to set up a son in the priesthood than in other careers (Hamill, p. 29).

80. Presentation of Mar. 1, 1856, in Pasarán vs. Rosales, C.72. The 1811 and 1848 census schedules show that, though the poor lived with whomever they could (in rooms, corners of houses, even renting space on stairwells), it was exceedingly rare among the upper classes for married couples to live with their parents, except occasionally with a widowed mother. Indeed, in 1819 the countess of Regla opposed her son's marriage on the grounds that the family's financial crisis prevented the establishment of a new household. In the end she lost her legal battle and moved out of her house to give the young couple a home of their own (Couturier, pp. 142–43). The countess of Rul similarly protested that she was "too ruined" to permit her son to marry (Ladd, p. 150).

81. "Sobre el luxo," pp. 124–25. See also Payno, "Celibato femenino."

82. The author of "On the Necessity of Marriage" considered it deplorable that so many merchants not only remained single themselves, but insisted on celibacy in their employees ("Sobre la necesidad," p. 307). See also S.C., "Preocupaciones sobre matrimonios," *DM*, 3, 329 (Aug. 25, 1806): 475; and Archer, *Army*, p. 258. Jorge González Angulo (p. 130) found that artisans did not wait to become masters to marry, but did so as journeymen.

83. The extraordinarily late age of marriage and tendency to remain single among Spanish immigrants to Mexico, documented by Brading for Guanajuato (*Miners*, p. 252) and Vázquez Valle for Mexico City ("Habitantes," p. 118), are an extreme example of this broader trend. Although peninsular men arrived penniless on Mexican shores, they had a good chance of economic and social success because of their racial

purity and the prejudice in favor of hard-working foreigners. Consequently, they waited to marry until they could attract a well-to-do creole woman. The average immigrant reached that position late in life, marrying a woman much younger than himself. But many never married: 38% of peninsular Spaniards in Guanajuato over 50, 47% of the 15 male Spaniards age 45–54 in the 1811 census sample, and 43% of the 7 Spaniards of that age in the 1848 sample were single.

84. This was even the case in the second marriage of "La Güera" Rodríguez. See her will in AN, Not. 426, 1850, fols. 596v-601v. See also the wills of doña María Josefa Norzagaray, Not. 155, 1803, fols. 91–94, and don Juan Monasterio, Not. 417, 1803, fols. 413v-45v.

85. See AGN *Bienes Nacionales*, 74.

86. This requirement was dropped after independence. It was, in any case, waived for the daughters of other military officers (Royal order of June 30, 1789, Konetzke, 3–2: 652–53. See such post-independence legislation as the decree of Feb. 19, 1849, in Dublán & Lozano, 5: 532).

87. Ladd, pp. 21–23.

88. "Sobre la necesidad," pp. 305–6.

89. Calderón de la Barca, p. 230. In contrast, the *Diario de México* complained of "excessive liberty in the relations between sexes": 5, *466* (Jan. 9, 1807): 34.

90. Verena Martínez-Alier's findings for 19th-century Cuba suggest that caution is warranted in accepting this explanation of lower-class behavior. According to her evidence, in Cuba the free Blacks at the bottom of the social scale were intensely preoccupied with status and were highly selective in choosing marriage partners ("Elopement and Seduction in Nineteenth-Century Cuba," *Past and Present*, 55, 1972, pp. 91–129). There is some evidence, though, that Black lower classes behaved differently from those of Indian descent. See Carlos & Sellers; and Ramos, "Marriage," p. 209. Use of a more strictly legal definition of the term marriage in Ramos's Brazilian data, however, might invalidate these comparisons.

91. *Nov. rec.*, 5 (10.2: 9 and 19); Konetzke, 3–1: 214–15, 294–99, 401–13, 438–42; 3–2: 476–82, 794–96. At first the parental consent requirement applied only to whites and Indians, not in general to Negroes or Mulattoes and other Castes. It became a requirement for all marriages without racial distinction by a royal decree of 1803. For a detailed discussion of some of these decrees, see Martínez-Alier, *Marriage*, pp. 11–13.

92. Archer (*Army*, p. 206) found that the process of obtaining a license might delay the marriage of military officers up to 3 years.

93. Hajnal, "European Marriage," pp. 101–43. Note that by the late

18th century the U.S. also followed Western European marriage patterns: Robert V. Wells, "Quaker Marriage Patterns in a Colonial Perspective," in Cott & Pleck, pp. 81–106.

94. Mean ages at marriage have been taken from Katharine Gaskin, "Age of First Marriage in Europe Before 1850: A Summary of Family Reconstitution Data," *Journal of Family History*, 3, 1 (Spring 1978): 34–35. In presenting the Western European range I have excluded an isolated French case where the female marriage age was 18.3 and the male 21.3. If this case is included in the "European" range, then Mexico City's marriage age was not unlike Europe's even in 1848.

95. Jean-Louis Flandrin, *Families in Former Times: Kinship, Household and Sexuality*, tr. Richard Southern (Cambridge, Eng., 1979), pp. 58–59; Thomas McKeown and R. G. Brown, "Medical Evidence Related to English Population Changes in the Eighteenth Century," in *Population and Industrialization*, ed. M. Drake (London, 1969), pp. 56–57; Wrigley, *Population*, pp. 101–5.

96. Morin, pp. 67–70; Cecilia A. Rabell, "El patrón de nupcialidad en una parroquia rural novohispana: San Luis de la Paz, Guanajuato. Siglo XVIII," in *Memorias*, pp. 120–26. Borah & Cook (*Essays*, 2: 278) also examine marriage ages, but their findings for rural Oaxaca are artificially low because they are based only on those who married before the age of 25. The low marriage ages for New Spain as a whole given by Navarro y Noriega (p. 18) and Humboldt (1: 106) reflect the country's largely rural character.

97. See Lombardi, pp. 82–86; Donald Ramos, "City and Country: The Family in Minas Gerais, 1804–1838," *Journal of Family History*, 3, 4 (Winter 1978): 375, 369; and Ramos, "Marriage," pp. 207–11. Studies restricted to elite groups in Latin America confirm the overall patterns of marriage and fertility found for the Spanish population in Mexico City. For example, Carmen Arretx et al., in their analysis of Chilean genealogical records, found similar mean ages at first marriage for well-to-do families (21.8 for women, 26.6 for men) and even higher proportions who never married (33% for women, 24% for men). Their calculations of marital fertility, based on women who lived to the age of 50 along with their spouses, were also similar to Mexico City women in that situation ("Preliminary Report on Nuptiality, Fertility, and Mortality, Based on Histories of Chilean Families," mimeograph, Centro Latinoamericano de Demografía, Santiago, 1977, pp. 16–19, 23, 27). In late-18th-century Buenos Aires, though all but 10% of the merchants studied eventually married, 18% of their daughters never did. The women's marriage age was also lower than the men's there, more in keeping with Mexico City in 1790 and 1848 (Susan M. Socolow, *The Merchants of*

Buenos Aires, 1778–1810: Family and Commerce, Cambridge, Eng., 1978, pp. 37–44). The women in A. J. R. Russell-Wood's study of Brazilian wills in the 17th century had approximately the same number of children as the women in Mexico City wills ("Female and Family in the Economy and Society of Colonial Brazil," in Lavrin, Latin American Women, pp. 80–82). Because Mexico City women married later than Buenos Aires merchants' wives, they had somewhat smaller families (Susan Socolow, "Marriage, Birth, and Inheritance: The Merchants of Eighteenth-Century Buenos Aires," HAHR, 60, 3, Aug. 1980, pp. 392–94). But the proportion of infertile couples in Mexico City was nearly identical to that found in the Argentine and Brazilian studies.

98. John Knodell and Mary Jo Maynes, "Urban and Rural Marriage Patterns in Imperial Germany," Journal of Family History, 1, 2 (Winter 1976): 129–61; Michael Anderson, "Marriage Patterns in Victorian Britain: An Analysis Based on Registration Data for England and Wales 1861," ibid., 1, 1 (Autumn 1976): 55–78.

99. The aspects of "traditional" marriage patterns that persisted were undoubtedly those that proved adaptive for each group. There is evidence, for example, that the Spanish population in America temporarily departed from its characteristic customs in response to unusual demographic circumstances; because of a severe shortage of Spanish women in the New World immediately after the Conquest, Spanish women were pressured to wed, and a property-holding widow's duty to remarry even came to be enforced by officials representing the Crown (Ots Capdequí, "Sexo," p. 328). Furthermore, contact with Spaniards may have reinforced some indigenous traditions while Europeanizing others. For example, rural priests may have encouraged matrimony to increase tribute payments (ibid., p. 334; Borah & Cook, "Marriage," p. 963). Perhaps it is for this reason that Morin (pp. 26, 73–74) finds that Indians had the lowest rate of consensual marriage and illegitimate births.

100. Eric Wolf, Sons of the Shaking Earth (Chicago, 1959), pp. 220–21.

101. Scardaville, "Crime," pp. 148, 192; Gilmore, p. 223; Alejandra Moreno Toscano, "Algunas características de la población urbana: ciudad de México, siglos XVIII y XIX," in Memorias, p. 409; Morin, pp. 66, 71–73; Borah & Cook, "Marriage," pp. 962–65; Borah & Cook, Essays, 1: 253, 2: 282. Brading and Wu (pp. 12–14) confirm these differences for the town of León, though their marriage ages are too low because they present the median only (often lower than the mean) and base it on declarations of intent to marry rather than on actual marriage ages. Rabell found higher marriage ages, but not lower marriage rates, among the Spanish population of San Luis de la Paz (Memorias, p. 426).

102. Robert McCaa ("New Approach") attempted to disentangle the effects of race and class for men in the northern Mexican mining town of Parral in 1788 by using a sophisticated statistical method. He found marital propensities to be more strongly associated with occupation than with race in the Spanish and Caste population that he studied. However, he was unable to explore the behavior of Indians, the crucial group to compare with the Spanish, because only 7% of the men in his sample were Indian. I do not doubt that differences *within* the population largely following European patterns are influenced by occupation and other related measures of status (such as numbers of servants, as noted above), and I would never argue that Mestizos, Mulattoes, etc. had distinct marital customs correlated with race (which is the hypothesis he tests). It is only the marked differences between the Spanish and Indian groups that concern me. These are evident even in the Parral sample, where none of the few Indian men were single by the age of 45, compared with 7% of the Caste and 10% of the Spanish men.

103. Less than 10% of the Mexican population lived in centers of more than 10,000 inhabitants, and the capital itself had only 2% of the national population during the first half of the 19th century. Percentages calculated on the basis of data for 1803–55 provided by Alejandra Moreno Toscano, "México," in Morse, *Ciudades latinoamericanas*, p. 174.

104. Payno, *Bandidos*, p. 388.

105. Although 20th-century marriage patterns have not been sufficiently studied for Mexico, it appears that the marriage rate rose, and the marriage age may have fallen for most women as well. The 1960 Mexican census shows that 29% of the women 15 and over were single —much lower than the 37% for that age group in 1811, and equivalent to the 27% in 1848. The 8.7% of single women aged 45–54 in 1960 is smaller than both the 16.2% in 1811 and the 12.5% in 1848. Since many in consensual unions were probably included among the never-married in 1960, the "marriage" rate, defined as in 1811, may thus have risen even more than suggested by these figures. The mean age at first marriage for women of 22, which I calculated from 1960 census data, was only slightly younger than in 1811 and higher than in 1848 (see summaries of the 1960 census in Nadia Youssef, "Cultural Ideals, Feminine Behavior and Family Control," *Comparative Studies in Society and History* 15, 3 (June 1973): 331–32). For solid conclusions about changing trends, however, we need to compare the 19th-century data with modern statistics for Mexico City alone, rather than with those for Mexico as a whole. A study of Mexico City marriage ages, broken down by educational levels that roughly correlate with class (David Yaukey et al., "Marriage at an Earlier Than Ideal Age in Six Latin American Capital

Cities," *Population Studies*, 26, 2 (July 1972): 265), suggests that the mean marriage age has remained relatively high for upper-class women but dropped for those of the lower classes. Women who completed secondary school in 1970 (roughly upper class) married at 23.9 years, compared with 21.2 and 19.2, respectively, for women who completed only primary school or failed to complete primary school (roughly lower class). On 20th-century marriage patterns, see also Wrigley, *Population*; and Robert E. McCaa, Jr., *Marriage and Fertility in Chile: Demographic Turning Points in the Petorca Valley, 1840–1976* (Boulder, Colo., 1983).

### Chapter Four

1. See James Lockhart, *Spanish Peru, 1532–1560: A Colonial Society* (Madison, Wis., 1968), chap. 9; Elinor Burkett, "Early Colonial Peru: The Urban Female Experience" (Ph.D. dissertation, University of Pittsburgh, 1975), pp. 124–246; Edith Couturier, "Micaela Angela Carrillo: Widow and Pulque Dealer," in *Struggle and Survival in Colonial America*, ed. Gary B. Nash and David G. Sweet (Berkeley, Calif., 1981), pp. 362–75; Donna J. Guy, "Women, Peonage, and Industrialization: Argentina, 1810–1914," *Latin American Research Review*, 16, 3 (1981): 65–89; and Asunción Lavrin, "In Search," pp. 40–47. Two analyses of the 1753 census of Mexico City provide information on working women: Vázquez Valle, "Habitantes," and Seed, "Social Dimensions."

2. See Hannah Papanek, "Family Status Production: The 'Work' and 'Non-Work' of Women," *Signs*, 4, 4 (Summer 1979): 775–81; and Larissa Adler Lomnitz and Marisol Pérez Lizaur, "The History of a Mexican Urban Family," *Journal of Marriage and the Family*, 3, 4 (Winter 1978): 398, 404.

3. Prostitution was legalized in 1867, with the government licensing prostitutes who submitted to medical examinations and were found free of venereal diseases. From June to November between 581 and 872 women applied and were examined each month, some of them under 18 years of age ("Memoria"). See also "Proyecto de decreto y reglamento sobre prostitución, 1851," reproduced in *Boletín del Archivo General de la Nación*, 3d series, 3 (July-Sept. 1979): 10–12. On illegal taverns, see Scardaville, "Alcohol Abuse," p. 653.

4. Jorge González Angulo (pp. 138–41) believes that independent artisans must have relied on family labor in order to compete with the larger shops funded by merchant capitalists or prosperous master artisans who owned several shops—increasingly common practices, although they violated guild regulations. However, he has no firm evidence on this point. The large number of cases of *riveateras* married to *zapateros* may be found in Cuartel No. 2 of the 1811 census (AGN *Padrones*, 77), an area not included in the sample.

5. González Angulo, p. 17. I have calculated the proportions by assuming that the total female work force in the entire city was 20,500, a figure based on the proportion of female workers in the sample. The proportion of spinners in the sample (2.9%) is very close to the estimate for the entire city (3.1%), but the proportion of seamstresses in the sample (2.7%) is somewhat lower than in the city as a whole (4.9%), perhaps because many were concentrated in the northern part of the city that was not covered by the sample. In any case, a difference of only 2 percentage points would not change any of my conclusions. Unfortunately, González Angulo does not provide information on the age or marital status of these female workers. He does, however, provide a very useful analysis of the geographical specialization of production, in his chap. 4.

6. Doña María del Carmen Andrade vs. don Felipe Reyna (alimentos), 1845, AJ *Pleitos Civiles entre Cónyuges*, 1800–1879.

7. Mayer, p. 43. See, for example, Calderón de la Barca, pp. 109–10; and Arróniz, pp. 131–33.

8. In her analysis of the same census, Seed finds that 30% of all women worked (pp. 585–86), but she does not tell us what age group she bases this figure on. Moreover, her totals are smaller than Vázquez Valle's, as though she did not have access to the complete census. Her other statistics on working women are nonetheless similar to Vázquez Valle's.

9. In 1753, 54% of Indian women, 44% of Mestizas, 21% of Castizas, 14% of Spanish women, 60% of Mulattas, and all female slaves listed an occupation (Vázquez Valle, pp. 134, 153–54, 180–81, 196, 204–5, 236, 271, 295, 363, 394, 398, 400). Although the women with the highest rate of employment were thus Blacks and Mulattas, not Indians, by 1811 there were few slaves, and Blacks were a neglible part of Mexico City's population, having largely melded in with the Castes. Indeed, Poinsett (p. 185) found so few Blacks in Mexico City in 1822 that he thought the race "nearly extinct in Mexico."

10. Vázquez Valle, pp. 398, 400. The predominance of servants in 1753 may in part reflect the omission of some working women who lived on the outskirts of the city, and who would have been more likely to enter other trades, assuming the 1811 pattern holds for the earlier year. But the decline of servants is still evident in the central neighborhood from 1811 to 1848.

11. *Gazeta de México*, 12, *28* (Feb. 26, 1805): 248; Carrera Stampa, p. 77; Kicza, p. 496.

12. Carrera Stampa, p. 76.

13. González Angulo, pp. 139, 195. On the decline of the guilds, see also *ibid.*, pp. 121, 186, 215–16, 227.

14. *Ibid.*, pp. 53–55, 59, 160–61, 163.

15. See *Relación de los gremios, artes y oficios* . . ., 1788, reproduced in Kicza, p. 475; Carrera Stampa, pp. 207, 299–319; and González Angulo, pp. 28, 53.

16. Bullock, 1: 207. See also Galván Rivera, *Calendario*, pp. 91–92.

17. These 6 types of female workers were included along with 25 male; 2 more female "types" were the elegant coquette and the *china*, or working-class belle (Frías y Soto et al.).

18. Male and female servants together had decreased from 34% of those listing an occupation in 1753 (Vázquez Valle, pp. 396–400) to 24% in 1811 and 15% in 1848. When the category of servants in 1811 and 1848 is expanded to include coachmen, cooks, porters, laundresses, and *mozos* (errand runners) who may or may not have served as domestic servants, the proportion is 26% and 19%, respectively. (Although Vázquez Valle used the narrower definition of servant, it is possible that the declarations to the census taker were not consistent in the three censuses.) In the central section of the sample, where the data are more reliable for 1848, servants declined from 42% of the employed population in 1811 to 25% in 1848, or from 45% to 32% if the wider definition is used.

19. There is some evidence, however, that a few women moved into bread baking. One of the 41 bakers in the 1848 census sample was female, and Reyna (pp. 436–37) has found some women working in bread bakeries in 1849, though they may merely have performed domestic chores for the male bakers. Even if they were baking bread this would not constitute an entry into a classic artisan craft, since only the bakery owners were guild members (González Angulo, pp. 46–47). The bakers themselves were either salaried employees or convict labor.

20. See González Angulo, pp. 122–24.

21. Most of the increase in seamstresses occurred in the central section of the sample, where they rose from 3% to 18% of all working women. It is possible that some of the seamstresses were domestic servants, though the literature of the time does not portray them as such. If they were, the number of domestic servants would not have fallen off so steeply from 1811 to 1848.

22. See Table A.5. Because so many of the female workers in the center were young maids, women's share of the labor force is much lower, as shown in Table 14, when only workers 18 years or over are considered.

23. Scardaville, "Alcohol Abuse," p. 653. See also Kicza, p. 140.

24. See AN, Not. 542, 1827, fol. 83v; and the 1841 case against doña R. Iriarte (for rent owed on mesón), AJ *Tocas Civiles*, 1839–42.

25. Segault vs. Ouvrard, C.47. In 1854 the *Guía* (p. 371) listed a shop under the name of Eugenia Ouvrard, probably her daughter.

26. Calderón de la Barca, p. 133.

27. Doña María's advertisement in *Gazeta de México*, 12, 40 (Sept. 17, 1805): 347; doña María Fernández de Jáuregui published the *Diario de México* and the *Semanario Económico de México* in the first decade of the century and was active at least until 1815, the "Imp. de Doña Herculona del Villar y Socios" is known for 1823, and the "Imp. de la Vda. de Romero" for 1825 (compare *Guía*, pp. 318–19, 325); Mayer, p. 49.

28. See Felipe Díaz de Ortega to Viceroy Azanza, report on textile production, Jan. 6, 1800, AGN *Historia*, 122, no. 2.

29. Pérez vs. Rodríguez, C.34; Herrera vs. Carrillo, C.4; Vinsoneo vs. Rolero, C.12. See also Ortega vs. Moreno, C.44.

30. See, for example, AGN *Justicia e Instrucción Pública*, 8, no. 33 (1842).

31. Statement dating from 1804 quoted in Tanck Estrada, *Educación*, p. 163.

32. According to Tanck Estrada (*Educación*, pp. 160–68), amigas earned anywhere from 200 to 700 pesos a year in 1820. (Compare with salary ranges in chap. 5, pp. 198, 200.) Furthermore, as Lira-González suggests (pp. 61 note 42, 138, 286), their salaries were probably augmented by gifts from students.

33. On Mexico City in 1753, see Vázquez Valle, p. 313. On 1802, see Tanck Estrada, *Educación*, p. 197. On New England, see Kathryn Kish Sklar, "The Founding of Mount Holyoke College," in Berkin & Norton, p. 181.

34. *Guía*, pp. 166–67; Tanck Estrada, *Educación*, p. 166.

35. See AGN *Justicia e Instrucción Pública*, 8 (1842); *SDN*, Nov. 24, 1844; *La Semana de las Señoritas*, 10, 4 (1852); and García Cubas, p. 411.

36. Gilberto Freyre, "Social Life in the Middle of the Nineteenth Century," *HAHR*, 5, 4 (Nov. 1922): 609.

37. Morales, "Estructura urbana," pp. 368, 386.

38. See Ladd, pp. 21–22, 29, 136; Kizca, especially pp. 22–23; and Aída Castilleja, "Abastecimiento de carne en la ciudad de México, 1714–1811," in SHU, *Investigaciones*, 3: 92, 106.

39. Romero de Terreros, pp. 459–60; Couturier, "Women in a Noble Family."

40. Juan Nepomuceno Almonte, *Guía de forasteros y repertorio de conocimientos útiles* . . . (Mexico City, 1852), p. 464. See also señora Adalid's contract with doña Guadalupe Sánchez to deliver 44–45 *cargas* of pulque a week from the Adalids' hacienda in San Juan Teotihuacan, AN, Not. 426, 1850, fol. 184.

41. Robert Potash, in his index to Mexico City notarial records for 1829, found that women signed a slightly lower, but still substantial, proportion of the instruments. Although women were 28% of those en-

gaging in notarial transactions, they signed only 19% of the instruments. The discrepancy between his figures and mine may reflect the inclusion of convent business in his list, since attorneys for convents were always male. Potash's list of women's transactions shows the variety of activities in which they were involved (*Guide to the Notarial Records of the Archivo General de Notarías Mexico City for the Year 1829*, in collaboration with Jan Bazant and Josefina Z. Vázquez, Amherst, Mass., 1982, pp. 197, 199–234).

42. Morales, "Cambios"; Barbara A. Tenenbaum, "Mexico in the Age of the Moneylenders 1821–1857," unpublished manuscript, pp. 96–97 (forthcoming, University of New Mexico Press). On the business climate in general, see Cardoso.

43. It was not possible to obtain a random sample of the civil court cases because of the peculiar organization of the Archivo Judicial (see Arrom & Gibson). I examined both stacks of unsorted papers and approximately 40 legajos from the following courts: *Comandancia General Civil, Juzgado de Cuartel, Juzgado de Letras, Juzgado Mercantil,* and *Tocas Civiles.*

44. Charges were brought against women in approximately one-fifth of 400 criminal cases examined for the first half of the 19th century. I chose the cases arbitrarily from stacked documents in the Archivo General de los Juzgados Unitarios Penales (AP) and Vols. 9 and 12, Archivo Judicial (AJ). The most useful of the criminal court documents is the book of records of the policemen's daily rounds: AP, "Libro de reos de la vara del alcalde ordinario de 2° voto don Pedro González de Noriega, para el año . . . 1807." A particularly interesting case is that of a slave against her master, "Expediente que sigue María Bárbara, esclava . . .," 1809, AJ *Cuaderno*, 7. On women and crime, see also Humboldt, 4: 296; Muriel, *Recogimientos*, pp. 123–28; and Shaw, pp. 266–95, 416–17.

45. Capca, p. 6; testament of doña María Ignacia Rodríguez de Elizalde, AN, Not. 426, 1850, fol. 600.

46. Margarita Urías Hermosillo, "Manuel Escandón: de las diligencias al ferrocarril, 1833–1862," in Cardoso, p. 47; Guillermo Beato, "La Casa Martínez del Río: del comercio colonial a la industria fabril, 1829–1864," in *ibid.*, p. 62.

47. Segault vs. Ouvrard, C.47; doña Josefa Escalona and don Pedro Padilla (reunion compact), 1854–55, AGN *Bienes Nacionales*, 513, no. 140; Gómez vs. Mercado, C.42. See also López vs. Trejo, C.74.

48. Tanck Estrada, *Educación*, pp. 163–64. Lira-González (p. 469) finds that couples taught together mainly in Indian barrios.

49. In Cuartel Menor 30, Manzana 230, 1848 census, AAA *Padrones*, 3409.

50. Shaw, pp. 113–17.

51. Petition of Josefa Vitorero, 1815, AGN *Tabaco*, 242.

52. María Amparo Ros, in her study of Indian and Caste cigar makers who lived in the Parcialidad de San Juan in 1800, found the majority of the women were married ("Serie de mapas: tributarios de la Fábrica de Puros y Cigarros de México," in SHU, *Investigaciones*, 3: 147). See also "Prevenciones de la Dirección General que deben observarse exactamente en la Fábrica de Puros y Cigarros de esta capital . . .," Mar. 20, 1792, AGN *Tabaco*, 432; McWatters, pp. 151, 155, 196, 243; and Robertson, 2: 307.

53. Theresa M. McBride, "The Long Road Home: Women's Work and Industrialization," in *Becoming Visible: Women in European History*, ed. Renate Bridenthal and Claudia Koonz (Boston, 1977), p. 282.

54. Lira-González, pp. 168–69.

55. Humboldt, 1: 253.

56. See, for example, AN, Not. 155, 1827, fol. 748; Not. 169, 1853, vol. 1, fols. 348–48v; and Not. 169, 1853, vol. 2, fol. 659. But a wife did occasionally make a legal transaction without her husband's permission; see doña Cecilia Ortiz (petition for back salary), 1826, AJ *Juzgado de Letras*, Q (1807–27).

57. Lamas, pp. 210–63; "Circular," July 21, 1806, AGN *Montepíos y Pensiones*, 18, no. 29.

58. Vargas vs. Contreras, C.38.

59. *Representación que las maestras*, p. 7.

60. Konetzke, 3–2: 768.

61. As early as 1785 Villarroel (p. 109) noted "the repugnance of most of the people to serving as *criados* and *criadas* in houses," as did Joaquín García Icazbalceta (p. 130) in 1864. See also the description of a chambermaid in Pantaleón Tovar, "La recamarera," in Frías y Soto et al., pp. 99–101.

62. See, for example, Sartorius, p. 61; and Reyna y Vega vs. Martínez Calderón, C.17.

63. On the servants' legal obligations to their masters, see law of Aug. 8, 1834, in Dublán & Lozano, 2: 718. On the sexual implications of this obligation, see Vincenco vs. Rolero, C.12, Urrutia vs. Gil, C.22; and Ortega vs. Moreno, C.44. See also doña Alejandra Zamorano (petition to have the baptismal certificate of her husband's illegitimate child corrected), 1833, AGN *Bienes Nacionales*, 509.

64. Calderón de la Barca, pp. 252–54. See also Flora Salazar, "Los sirvientes domésticos," in SHU, *Ciudad*, pp. 124–32. On a woman's begging being less degrading than working, see Payno, *Fistol*, p. 543.

65. Theresa M. McBride, *The Domestic Revolution: The Modernization of Household Service in England and France, 1820–1920* (London, 1976), espe-

cially pp. 57, 62–63, 97. Furthermore, the respectable middle-class job of governess did not exist in Mexico.

66. Margo L. Smith, "Domestic Service as a Channel of Upward Mobility for the Lower-Class Woman: The Lima Case," in Pescatello, pp. 191–207; Jelin.

67. Doña Dolores Cecilia Valiente vs. Lt. Magdaleno Ortiz (alimentos), 1845, AJ *Comandancia General Civil*, 1844–46. For a description of women's handiwork, see *Revista Mensual de la Sociedad Promovedora de Mejoras Materiales*, 1 (1852): 337.

68. Prieto, *Memorias*, pp. 41, 44.

69. 37% of the 30 spinners were Indian, compared with 16% of the 19 other women, and 42% were widowed, compared with 28% of the others. The spinners also had a higher median age (39) than the 19 other women (30), but both groups tended to have been born in Mexico City: 73% of the spinners versus 68% for the others. Although these numbers alone are too few for conclusive generalizations, González Angulo (pp. 53–55, 154) also found spinners to be of lower rank than seamstresses. Still, the 1753 census provides evidence that seamstresses and spinners as a group were better off than other female workers, since Spanish women dominated those two trades in 1753 as well (Seed, p. 587; Vázquez Valle, pp. 271–72).

70. Fernández de Lizardi, *Quijotita*, pp. 100–101. See also Hilarión Frías y Soto, "La costurera," and Niceto de Zamacois, "La casera," in Frías y Soto et al., pp. 49–56, 231, respectively.

71. González Angulo, pp. 53–55, 111.

72. Manuela Gaitán de Vergés (petition for dowry), June 4, 1857, AGN *Bienes Nacionales*, 74, no. 80. See also "Cuestión interesante," p. 6; "Memoria;" and García Icazbalceta, pp. 127–28.

73. "Reservadísimo sobre fábricas y telares de manufacturas del Reino," and follow-up reports, 1799–1800, AGN *Historia*, 122, nos. 1–2; Rosenzweig Hernández, pp. 484–85; Potash, *Banco*, especially pp. 20–23.

74. Chávez Orozco; Gilmore, p. 218; Potash, *Banco*; Jan Bazant, "The Evolution of the Textile Industry in Puebla: 1544–1845," *Comparative Studies in Society and History*, 7, 1 (1964): 56–69.

75. María Dolores Rondero (petition for dowry), 1853, AGN *Bienes Nacionales*, 74, no. 80.

76. See Keremetsis, p. 209; Zavala, p. 294; Beato, "Casa Martínez del Río," in Cardoso, pp. 82–83; and Potash, *Banco*, p. 236.

77. Dolores Morales, "La expansíon de la ciudad de México en el siglo XIX: el caso de los fraccionamientos," in SHU, *Investigaciones*, 1: 73–74; Robertson, 2: 349.

78. Manuel Payno, "La hilandera," *RCL*, 2 (1846), p. 346.

79. On mechanization, see Potash, *Banco*; Beato, "Casa Martínez del Río," in Cardoso, especially pp. 99–100; and Carrera Stampa, p. 289.

80. McWatters, p. 108.

81. Robertson, 2: 306.

82. *Ibid.*, pp. 305–6; McWatters, pp. 149, 231, 252; María Amparo Ros, "La Real Fábrica de Puros y Cigarros: organización del trabajo y estructura urbana," in SHU, *Ciudad*, pp. 47–66; and Ros, "La Fábrica de Puros y Cigarros de México," paper given at Simposio sobre la organización de la producción y relaciones de trabajo en el siglo XIX en México, Veracruz, Feb. 1978.

83. McWatters, pp. 190–91, 195.

84. *Ibid.*, pp. 177, 189, 203; Villarroel, p. 107. Villarroel noted that migrants did not often find the jobs they sought, however, since the factory mostly hired city-born workers.

85. McWatters, pp. 102, 142; "Prevenciones" (cited in note 52, above).

86. Law of Feb. 20, 1830, in Dublán & Lozano, 2: 227; McWatters, pp. 154–55.

87. Robertson, 2: 306–7.

88. See, for example, AGN *Tabaco*, 242.

89. Circular of Aug. 22, 1794, *ibid.*, 432.

90. Robertson, 2: 306–7; McWatters, pp. 156–58, 182–85; "Prevenciones" (cited in note 52, above); Shaw, pp. 111–12.

91. McWatters, pp. 142, 202, 206, 243, 256; Poinsett, p. 86; Robertson, 2: 305.

92. McWatters, pp. 179, 186, 191, 196, 199, 202–3, 213, 216.

93. *Ibid.*, pp. 189–207.

94. It was in fact the government's policy to grant the concession for an estanquillo instead of a pension whenever possible in order to save money, as stated in the reply to doña Josefa Acevedo de Arce's petition, Aug. 31, 1815, AGN *Tabaco*, 242. See petitions throughout this volume and vol. 104. See also Ignacio Ramírez, "La estanquillera," in Frías y Soto et al., pp. 177–82.

95. Quoted in Tanck Estrada, *Educación*, pp. 166–67.

96. Petition, 1829, AGN *Justicia e Instrucción Pública*, 7, no. 23, fol. 206.

97. Petition, 1823–24, *ibid.*, no. 9, fol. 87, and accompanying pamphlet, *Sobre la necesidad*. See also *Cartas*, p. 3.

98. *Panorama de las Señoritas*, 1 (1842): 517; statement dating from 1817 quoted in Anna, p. 176.

99. The first decree I located requiring midwives to be licensed dates from Dec. 23, 1840 (chap. 2, art. 55, in *Colección de decretos*, 1: 443), but it is likely that licenses were already issued when the obstetrical school

opened ("Oficio de la Junta Superior de Sanidad," AAA *Actas de Cabildo*, 1822, fols. 463, 480, 520–26, 669).

100. María Montaño's advertisement in *El Monitor Republicano*, Nov. 16, 1855; listings in *Guía*, pp. 352–53. See also Juan de Dios Arias, "La partera," in Frías y Soto et al., pp. 267–72. Parteras had long been recognized as part of the medical profession, along with doctors, surgeons, and apothecaries, in decrees requiring that they treat the injured at any hour of the day or night (Dublán & Lozano, 2: 769–70).

101. "Doña Dorotea López," *AM*, 1 (1849): 357–59; "Doña María de Jesús Moctezuma," *AM*, 2 (1849): 1–5; Arróniz, pp. 109, 114; García Cubas, pp. 162, 260–67, 521–22; Kicza, p. 434; Pulido, pp. 72–76; Wright de Kleinhans, pp. 356–58.

102. 1849 industrial census, reproduced in Shaw, pp. 366–68.

103. See the critique of these programs in García Icazbalceta, pp. 127–28.

104. Shaw, p. 366; Calderón de la Barca, p. 257.

105. Record of salaries paid in 1803, AGN *Montepíos y Pensiones*, 18. On women's lower productivity, see McWatters, pp. 148, 184.

106. See, for example, Fernández de Lizardi, *Quijotita*, pp. 100–101; El Alferez Manteca, "Ocupaciones de mujeres," *DM*, 3, 247 (May 4, 1806), 143; Antuñano, pp. 3, 5; "Memoria"; Shaw, p. 119; and Zamacois, "La casera," in Frías y Soto et al., pp. 227–36.

107. Lamas, pp. 10–11, 236, 242, 262; Rodríguez de San Miguel, 2: 136–37.

108. Testament of doña Manuela de Roa, AN, Not. 155, 1803, fols. 430–32. See also testament of doña María Antonia Galicia, *ibid.*, fols. 393–95.

109. Since there was no longer a scarcity of white women, as there had been in the 16th century, marriages between social unequals were exceedingly rare. Tantalizing bits of evidence in novels and travel accounts suggest that widowers occasionally married below their station in second marriages, providing one avenue of upward mobility for women (see, for example, Calderón de la Barca, pp. 290–91, 473). A far more likely avenue was through marriage to a soldier who worked his way up the ranks.

110. Testament of Antonio Meneses, AN, Not. 41, 1855, fol. 87.

111. Employment not only mirrored class divisions, then, but also established the relationship of women of different classes to each other. Elite women were insulated from unpleasant tasks and the intrusion of the outside world by servants. Mistresses gained power by having maids to command within their household. Thus, as Leonore Davidoff noted for Europe, maids performed a symbolic as well as real function,

their presence defining ladies' gentility just as it branded the maids inferior ("Mastered for Life: Servant, Wife, and Mother in Victorian and Edwardian Britain," *Journal of Social History*, 7, 4, 1974, pp. 406-28).

112. Helen I. Safa, "The Changing Class Composition of the Female Labor Force in Latin America," *Latin American Perspectives*, 4, 4 (Fall 1977): 126-36.

113. This statement, made by Ada Heather-Bigg in 1894, neatly summarizes the argument of Louise Tilly and Joan Scott, *Women, Work, and Family* (New York City, 1978). It is reproduced in their frontispiece.

114. Ester Boserup, *Women's Role in Economic Development* (New York City, 1970), pp. 187-93.

115. On contemporary Latin American working women, see Lourdes Arizpe, "Women in the Informal Labor Sector: The Case of Mexico City," *Signs*, 3, 1 (Autumn 1977): 25-37; Gloria González Salazar, "Participation of Women in the Mexican Labor Force," in Nash & Safa, pp. 183-201; and Catalina H. Wainerman et al., "The Participation of Women in Economic Activity in Argentina, Bolivia, and Paraguay," *Latin American Research Review*, 15, 2 (1980): 143-51.

*Chapter Five*

1. Couples appearing before the divorce court represented somewhere on the order of 1% of all legally contracted marriages, and an even smaller proportion of unions if the large number of consensual marriages is taken into account. The 1% figure was arrived at by comparing the average of 15 divorce cases filed per year from 1800 to 1818 with an average of 1,266 marriages contracted annually in all Mexico City parishes, as cited in "Noticia de los matrimonios, nacidos y muertos que ha habido en la ciudad de México en los años que se designan (1790-1825)," *La Línea de Vulcano*, Dec. 14, [1826?], (Colección Lafragua, Biblioteca Nacional).

2. This figure is an estimate, because the notebooks are incomplete (I found divorce cases that were not recorded there) and also contain cases that do not seem to involve divorce petitions. The notebooks do indicate, however, that there was little yearly fluctuation in the number of divorces sought. "Cuaderno de Divorcio," 2 vols., in Filmoteca de la Sociedad Genealógica Mexicana, *Mexico, D.F.*, roll 1116.

3. The court entrusted the writs of the case only to a procurator, who was usually, but not always, a lawyer. One litigant, an official of the ecclesiastical court, was considered trustworthy enough to be allowed to represent himself (Pérez vs. Rodríguez, C.34).

4. Third Mexican Provincial Council in Galván Rivera, *Concilio*, p. 350.

5. Pérez vs. Nuñez, C.73. See also Soberanis vs. Rivera, C.45.

6. Marriages might be invalidated by a number of circumstances—for instance, because they had not been consummated or because of a prior impediment arising from consanguinity or affinity (P.4.4–P.4.10). I located only 7 requests for annulments in the late colonial and early republican period, in AGN *Judicial*, 32, and AGN *Bienes Nacionales*, 75, 470, 609, 655, 1187.

7. See opinions of the *promotores fiscales* in Segault vs. Ouvrard, C.47, and Reyna y Vega vs. Martínez Calderón, C.17.

8. If a woman was raped or deceived, or if the husband had consented to her adultery, it did not provide grounds for a divorce. On the grounds for ecclesiastical divorce, see Pascua, 1: 148–53, 232, 235; *Ilustración del derecho*, 1: 91–93, 3: 180–81; *Nuevo Febrero*, 1: 46–52, 3: 726–30; *Sala mexicano*, 1: 296–97, 314–26, 329–30, 3: 62–63, 429; and P. 7.17: 1.

9. Recognizing the difficulty of producing eyewitnesses in cases involving intimate family matters, the court allowed the testimony of servants and relatives, normally inadmissible in a Mexican court, in divorce suits (Pascua, 5: 83). On the inadmissibility of confessions, see opinion of the *promotor fiscal* in María Trinidad Martínez vs. Aniceto Ocaña (annulment), 1834–37, AGN *Bienes Nacionales*, 470, no. 28. On acceptable proofs of adultery, see Pascua, 1: 151–52, 232; Roa Bárcena, p. 735; and Pérez y López, 6: 157.

10. Drunkenness, for example, was considered "the root of all vices. The drunkard is liable to be lascivious, adulterous, corrupt. [He is given to] homicide and the other evils that women and children perpetually lament" (Pascua, 1: 150). Such acts as the denial of medicine and medical care during sickness were considered evidence of implacable hatred. For discussions of the philosophy of granting ecclesiastical divorce, see the opinions of the *promotores fiscales* in Segault vs. Ouvrard, C.47, and Soberanis vs. Rivera, C.45. See also Román Punzalán Zapata vs. Ana María Zendejas (divorce appeal), 1809, AGN *Judicial*, 32; and "Jurisdicción eclesiástica," *Gaceta de los Tribunales de la República Mexicana*, Dec. 1, 1860.

11. The laws on the effects of divorce are somewhat ambiguous. In theory, but not in practice, a wealthy woman who was found guilty was supposed to pay her husband a pension during their separation. The legal commentator Anastasio de la Pascua stated that the guilty party "took nothing" from the community property, implying that he lost his share (*Febrero mejicano*, 1: 232). But other legal texts explained that the community property was divided unless the woman committed adultery, an interpretation shared by the litigants in Mexican divorce cases. It is clear, though, that once a divorce was declared, the community

property was abolished and a regime of separate property established for the duration of the separation (*Sala mexicano*, 3: 62–63, 429; *Ilustración del derecho*, 1: 95; González Castro, Art. 120).

12. Flores Alatorre vs. Izedo, C.29.

13. This type of separation was granted automatically without the need of a formal trial. Also, a woman who considered herself to be in immediate danger could leave her husband on her own accord, but she was then supposed to file for divorce. The separation of bed alone was considered a private matter to be decided on by the spouses without the intervention of ecclesiastical authorities (Pascua, 1: 148–52).

14. A divorced woman's status was not explicitly covered by the law. Because the marital bond was not broken, Pascua (3: 362–63) concluded that she had the legal status of a married woman whose husband was absent, and so needed a judge's validation of her contracts. Pascua's discussion suggests, however, that in practice she was on her own. Notarial records and secular court cases of the first half of the 19th century indicate that divorced women often recovered their full juridical capacity. See, for example, don José María Recio vs. doña María Josefa de Villar y Villamil, 1827 (concerning debts), AJ *Comandancia General Civil*, 1823–27; AN, Not. 210, 1803, fol. 7. But see also the 2 cases where divorced women obtained a judge's authorization for their legal acts: doña Vicenta González vs. don Benito Ortiz (concerning debts), 1832, AJ *Juzgado de Letras* G, 1830–33; AN, Not. 170, 1853, fol. 96v. The Oaxaca Civil Code, Art. 109, explicitly states that divorce restored a woman's full juridical capacity; the other civil codes did not mention her status.

15. Presentation of June 8, 1816, in Mijares vs. García, C.18.

16. Presentations of April 18 and May 9, 1816, in Reyna y Vega vs. Martínez Calderón, C.17.

17. María Balderas vs. José María Espino (annulment), 1855, AGN *Bienes Nacionales*, 76, no. 17.

18. See, for example, Soberanis vs. Rivera, C.45, where a *fianza* was paid to a guarantor.

19. The procedure followed in *juicios de conciliaciones* became more standardized after independence. A series of laws issued in 1821, 1837, and 1846 defined which judge should preside over the juicio, how it should be recorded, and so on (see Dublán & Lozano, 3: 402–3, 5: 178). In 1836 couples were given 8 days after the juicio to reconsider their action and a second one was then held. This procedure was later dropped. The secular authorities' greater involvement after independence, reflecting the increased control of State over Church, had little effect on the divorce process itself.

20. For a description of the juicio in Leiva vs. Iturria, C.66, see Arrom, *Mujer mexicana*, p. 20. See also Ortega vs. Moreno, C.44.

21. The depósito took place either immediately after the *juicio de conciliación* or when the divorce petition was filed, whichever came first. However, the depósito was considered temporary until the divorce was filed. During the republican period it was usually the secular authority conducting the *juicio de conciliación* who ordered the temporary depósito. The permanent depósito was then assigned by the provisor.

22. Galván Rivera, *Concilio*, p. 351.

23. Although ordered by the ecclesiastical judge, the depósito derived its legal force from the cooperation of secular authorities. A municipal constable or, if the husband enjoyed military fueros, a soldier under his commander accompanied the ecclesiastical sheriff (*alguacil*) and the woman to her depósito. Thereafter, if the husband violated that house he was prosecuted under the appropriate secular jurisdiction.

24. See Manzano vs. Camacho, C.25; López vs. López, C.39; Riofrío vs. González, C.43; and Villar vs. Velásquez, C.57.

25. After lengthy litigation a woman might be able to force her husband to pay her expenses either by obtaining a lien on his salary (usually one-third) or having his property embargoed. See, for examples, Sotomayor vs. Tovar de Zárate, C.9; Manzano vs. Camacho, C.25; and Villar vs. Velásquez, C.57. However, court action was not always successful, especially if a man had no salary or stable place of residence. On the ensuing problems of depositarios, see Villar vs. Velásquez, C.57; and Córdoba vs. Morales, C.59.

26. Decree of Dec. 19, 1836, in Soberanis vs. Rivera, C.45. The depósito was lifted in 6 cases.

27. The language used to describe the process of depósito treated the woman like a passive entity, "extracted" from one house and "delivered" to another, and accepted by a depositario who pledged "to maintain her in his house and in the company of his family . . . guarding and safekeeping her person, and not releasing her until the *provisor* orders it, for she is at his disposal" (Carrero vs. Castañares, C.81). The standard phrases used to record the transaction of the depósito varied little during the half century under consideration.

28. Ramírez vs. Hernández, C.8; Rosel vs. Imhoff, C.70.

29. A general point of law held that mothers received the custody of children under 3 years of age, and fathers the custody of the older ones (Pascua, 1: 102–3). But since the innocent spouse received custody in divorce cases, this occasionally led to controversies over who should keep the children during the trial. See, for example, Gutiérrez de Rosas vs. Enciso, C.1, in particular doña Apolonia's presentation of Mar. 15,

1803, in which she alleges that her husband kidnapped their daughter on the city streets.

30. Information on the depósito is available for 50 women; 29 were placed in a home identified as a relative's for at least 1 depósito.

31. Medina vs. Ramírez, C.41; Segault vs. Ouvrard, C.47.

32. See the discussion in the presentation of Oct. 21, 1802, in Villamil y Primo vs. Rodríguez, C.3; and Rosel vs. Imhoff, C.70.

33. Carrero vs. Castañares, C.81; Villamil y Primo vs. Rodríguez, C.3; Pasarán vs. Rosales, C.72. For more details on depósito, see Arrom, *Mujer mexicana*, pp. 38–42.

34. Zac. Code, Art. 142; Sierra, Art. 98.

35. Rosel vs. Imhoff, C.70; Segault vs. Ouvrard, C.47. It is intriguing that 2 of the most extreme statements came from foreigners. The prominence of foreigners among accused husbands (7 had non-Hispanic surnames, and at least 2 were from Spain) suggests that Mexican women may have found it easier to divorce foreigners than Mexicans, perhaps because the men were viewed as outsiders or lacked families to back them up. But the number of cases is too small to support such generalizations.

36. Galván Rivera, *Concilio*, p. 351; Segault vs. Ouvrard, C.47.

37. The ecclesiastical courts were nearly paralyzed in the conduct of much of their business from 1821 until 1836, when the Vatican recognized the Mexican republic (see Staples), but whether or not this accounted for the slowness of divorce cases is unclear, since secular justice was apparently equally slow (see Otero, p. 69, and Manuel Payno, "Los Ministerios," *SDN*, Feb. 25, 1842), and the number of divorce petitions that were approved in the 1820's and 1830's (1 of 4 and 2 of 25, respectively) was not too different from the proportion approved in the previous decades (1 of 9 in 1800–1809 and 2 of 10 in 1810–19). Furthermore, one can hardly make any judgment on so few a number of cases; the discovery of some new documents in Mexican archives might easily change the proportions.

38. The court could declare contumacious a party who abused these procedures or refused to cooperate in the case. It could then levy a fine to cover the costs of all unnecessary transactions and could continue the trial without waiting for the contumacious party to be notified. However, the court rarely took these extreme actions. One case where it did was Soberanis vs. Rivera, C.45. Excommunication, requested by the plaintiff in only 1 divorce case, was denied (Villamil y Primo vs. Rodríguez, C.3). On the passivity of the court, see the testimony of don Mariano Icara, Jan. 1855, in Medina vs. Pintado, C.63.

39. However, many of the initial petitions in the divorce cases asked

the provisor to formalize a depósito to which the woman had already moved of her own accord. See, for example, Ortega vs. Moreno, C.44. This was even so in the case of doña Josefa Mijares (C.18), who moved into the Convent of Santa Isabel, where she had friends among the nuns. Such a depósito would not have been permitted by the provisor had he been previously consulted, but faced with a fait accompli, he formalized it.

40. Rosel vs. Imhoff, C.70; Raso vs. Martínez, C.23; presentation of Jan. 21, 1836, in Pérez vs. Rodríguez, C.34; Morales vs. Martínez, C.71. See also Reyna y Vega vs. Martínez Calderón, C.17.

41. Salazar vs. Galván, C.55. See also Ortega vs. Moreno, C.44.

42. Doña Ignacia León vs. don Pedro Estrada (concerning cruelty and abuse), 1802, AJ *Penal*, 9, no. 7. See also María Cresencia Rojas vs. Feliciano Basurto (concerning cruelty and abuse), 1804, AJ *Penal*, 1801–4.

43. Numerous records of such marital litigation may be found throughout the Archivo General de los Juzgados Unitarios Penales and the Archivo Judicial's *Juzgados de Cuartel, Juzgados de Letras, Comandancia General Civil, Penal,* and *Pleitos Civiles entre Cónyuges.* Copies of some *juicios de conciliación* may also be found in ecclesiastical records; see, for instance, doña Victoriana del Espíritu Santo vs. don Modesto Dayo, 1856, AGN *Bienes Nacionales*, 76, no. 41. For an example of a juicio that had the desired effect, see doña Josefa Escalona vs. don Pedro Padilla (reunion compact), 1854–55, AGN *Bienes Nacionales*, 513, no. 140. For an analysis of some late colonial criminal records, see Scardaville, "Crime," especially chap. 4 on family life.

44. Raso vs. Martínez, C.23.

45. For example, a 1-page petition cost 6 pesos in 1854, including the price of the stamped paper; the recording of a *juicio de conciliación* was 4 reales in 1854, and of a depósito 2 pesos 6 reales in 1849. The *promotor fiscal* charged 5 pesos to read and advise on a case in 1836. See the complete bill for an unfinished case in Morales vs. Noriega, C.52. Voluminous cases, frequent among the elites in the colonial period, cost much more. See, for instance, the 1,000-page record of the litigation between Pérez Gálvez and García Noriega, C.19.

46. Royal decree of 1808 in Rodríguez de San Miguel, 3: 201. Scardaville maintains that the decree was not received in Mexico until 1818 ("Crime," p. 142), but the first request for *ayuda por pobre* I encountered among divorce litigants came in 1809, and another was made in 1816. Although it is true that most requests came in the later periods, this issue needs more investigation, since research in colonial divorces may show that the Church already waived the costs of the trial on a case-by-case basis. After all, the tradition of assigning *abogados de pobres* and

waiving judicial fees for indigents was an old one in Spanish civil law (Woodrow Borah, "Social Welfare and Social Obligation in New Spain: A Tentative Assessment," in *XXXVI Congreso Internacional de Americanistas, España, 1964: Actas y Memorias*, Seville, 1966, 4: 50).

47. Marginal note of Dec. 2, 1836, in Soberanis vs. Rivera, C.45.

48. Where information was sketchy, the placement in either of 2 adjacent categories was somewhat arbitrary. The most frequent problems arose in distinguishing the 2 lower groups, where cases were often abandoned and therefore incomplete. When in doubt, I categorized people as lower-middle class rather than lower class. Salaries have been calculated on the basis of information in the census of 1850, AAA, 3406; *Ordenanza militar para el régimen, disciplina, subordinación y servicio del ejército aumentada con las disposiciones relativas, anteriores y posteriores a la independencia con las tarifas de haberes* (Mexico City, 1842), pp. 317–53; and decree of May 24, 1838, in Dublán & Lozano, 3: 402.

49. These documents do not indicate race. It is possible that the colonial cases analyzed here do not include Indians, for Indians may have been tried by a separate tribunal whose records have not surfaced: the case of Román Punzalán Zapata vs. Ana María Zendejas (divorce appeal, 1809, AGN *Judicial*, 32) refers to a "Provisorato de Indios y Chinos," but this may mean Orientals exclusively, since Punzalán was from the Philippines. We cannot conclude, however, that the republican cases do not include Indians because racial designations were dropped from legal documents in 1822. I have found some evidence in other sources of Indian participation in divorce litigation: on June 3, 1803, the Indian María Ignacia de la Luz, with the help of an interpreter, gave her power of attorney to a procurator in order to petition for divorce (AN, Not. 210).

50. Social categories in the divorce cases and census population are roughly comparable to the extent that the number of servants was used as a selection criterion (see Table A.4). I have added a second middle-class category for the divorces because the detailed information permitted me to make distinctions that could not be drawn with the census data.

51. See, for example, the exemplary consideration of evidence by the *promotor fiscal* in the presentation of June 20, 1840, in Segault vs. Ouvrard, C.47; and Villar vs. Velásquez, C.57. Moreover, the litigants usually accepted the decision of the judge in divorce cases. 16% of the final verdicts were appealed, but only 2 complaints are known to have been filed against the judge accusing him of prejudice, both of these by members of the gentry: Villamil y Primo vs. Rodríguez, C.3; Pérez Gálvez vs. García Noriega, C.19. The first of these cases involved the only

jurisdictional quarrel I found between secular and ecclesiastical authorities. It was finally sent to the king for resolution.

52. Valdivieso vs. Valdivieso (counts of San Pedro de Alamo), C.11; Pérez Gálvez vs. García Noriega, C.19. The other three divorce actions filed by nobles were abandoned: Villamil y Primo vs. Rodríguez, C.3; Bienpica and Ovando, C.6; Alcázar vs. Ampucho, C.10.

53. It is possible, though not very likely, that some of the cases I have designated as abandoned were actually incomplete. Because the records were sturdily sewn together, it is more likely for an entire case to have disappeared than for a few final pages to have been lost. Moreover, since the final pages usually contained notarial formulas attesting to the fact that each party had heard the decree and accepted it, the loss of a final page would not have obliterated a verdict. The high rate of abandoned divorce suits is also noted by Pedro Grenón in his description of the ecclesiastical divorce records in Buenos Aires ("Nuestros divorcios históricos," *Historia*, 3, 11 [Jan.-Mar. 1958])—the only mention I have found of these records for Latin America.

54. See, for example, Hernández vs. Morales, C.48; doña María Rafaela Berruecos vs. don Anastacio Gómez (alimentos), 1823, AJ *Juzgado de Letras B*, 1813–25; and testament of don Benigno Fernández, AN, Not. 611, 1854, fol. 104. The suit against "La Güera" Rodríguez (C.3), the only woman for whom we have a detailed biography (Valle Arizpe), was eventually resolved by the death of her husband in 1805. But by then it had lain dormant for over 2 years, during which time the couple had remained separated.

55. Third Mexican Provincial Council in Galván Rivera, *Concilio*, p. 351.

56. See, for instance, Gómez vs. Mercado, C.42. Some couples may have reunited after abandoning their suits, but it was customary to inform the provisor when this occurred.

57. Leiva vs. Iturria, C.66.

58. Punzalán Zapata vs. Zendejas (divorce appeal), 1809, AGN *Judicial*, 32.

59. This use of the certificate is revealed in such requests for certificates as the petition of Jan. 29, 1811, in Sotomayor vs. Tovar de Zárate, C.9; and in doña María Candelaria Alvarez (inheritance), 1809, AJ *Penal*, 12, no. 48.

60. Soberanis vs. Rivera, C.45; Hernández vs. Morales, C.48.

61. These were still sealed to be used as evidence, never presented, when I found them in the National Archive. See presentation of Dec. 11, 1854, in Medina vs. Pintado, C.63. 2 of the love letters are reproduced in Arrom, *Mujer mexicana*, pp. 214–16.

62. See petition from José María Pabón, June 1856, AGN *Bienes Nacionales*, 75, no. 7; Inocencio Corona vs. Mariana Jiménez (annulment), 1856, *ibid.*, no. 8; and doña Cecilia Valiente vs. don Magdaleno Ortiz (alimentos), 1845, AJ *Comandancia General Civil*, 1844–46.

63. Petition from Alvarez (cited in note 59, above).

64. Granados vs. Avila, C.61.

65. See presentations of Sept. 12 and Dec. 6, 1802, in Villamil y Primo vs. Rodríguez, C.3; Reyna y Vega vs. Martínez Calderón, C.17; Manzano vs. Camacho, C.25; and Villar vs. Velásquez, C.57.

66. See Larios vs. Montesinos de Lara, C.5; Reyna y Vega vs. Martínez Calderón, C.17; Mijares vs. García, C.18; Estrada vs. Yoldi, C.26; and Segault vs. Ouvrard, C.47.

67. Doña Josefa Escalona vs. don Pedro Padilla (reunion compact), 1854–55, AGN *Bienes Nacionales*, 513, no. 140; Gutiérrez vs. Enciso, C.1; Villamil y Primo vs. Rodríguez, C.3; Reyna y Vega vs. Martínez Calderón, C.17. See also Domínguez Sotomayor vs. Tovar de Zárate, C.9; Molina vs. Ibáñez, C.14; and Granados vs. Avila, C.61.

68. See Herrera vs. Carrillo, C.4; Gómez vs. Mercado, C.42; Ortega vs. Moreno, C.44; and López vs. Trejo, C.74.

69. Reyna y Vega vs. Martínez Calderón, C.17; Manzano vs. Camacho, C.25; Pasarán vs. Rosales, C.72. See also Villamil y Primo vs. Rodríguez, C.3; and Soriano vs. Carrera, C.37.

70. Omaña vs. Barroso, C.36; Escalona vs. Padilla (cited in note 67, above); Salazar vs. Galván, C.55. See also Carrero vs. Castañares, C.81.

71. See descriptions of the marriage ceremony in depositions of Aug. 7, 1837, in Soberanis vs. Rivera, C.45; and Mar. 1, 1856, in Pasarán vs. Rosales, C.72.

72. Presentation of July 8, 1816, in Mijares vs. García, C.18; presentation of May 31, 1816, in Reyna y Vega vs. Martínez Calderón, C.17; Segault vs. Ouvrard, C.47. See also Pasarán vs. Rosales, C.72.

73. Presentation of Sept. 28, 1816, in Reyna y Vega vs. Martínez Calderón, C.17; Arellano and Ochoa, C.50. Both of these husbands had fueros because of their occupations as merchant and soldier, but here they were extending the term to include their rights over their wives.

74. See, for example, Manzano vs. Camacho, C.25; Ortega vs. Moreno, C.44; presentation of Aug. 7, 1837, in Soberanis vs. Rivera, C.45.

75. Esteves vs. Lozano, C.67; Hernández vs. Morales, C.48.

76. Escalona vs. Padilla (cited in note 67, above); Zavala vs. Leiva, C.33. Compare presentations of Sept. 12 and Oct. 21, 1802, in Villamil y Primo vs. Rodríguez, C.3.

77. Pérez vs. Rodríguez, C.34. See also Morales vs. Rodríguez, C.52.

78. Omaña vs. Barroso, C.36.

79. Bullock, 1: 198; Fernández de Lizardi, *Quijotita*, p. 36; Pascua, 7: 60, 146.

80. See especially the testimony given on Dec. 1 and Dec. 4, 1802, by the vicar Manuel Arévalo and Francisco Beye Cisneros in Villamil y Primo vs. Rodríguez, C.3.

81. See, for example, Pérez Gálvez vs. García Noriega, C.19; and Omaña vs. Barroso, C.36.

82. The growing research on wife abuse indicates that it is a universal phenomenon. Without better comparative statistics one cannot conclude that it was more widespread in 19th-century Mexico than in other countries and centuries. For a summary of contemporary research, see Del Martin, *Battered Wives* (San Francisco, 1976); and Wini Breines and Linda Gordon, "The New Scholarship on Family Violence," *Signs*, 8, 3 (Spring 1983): 490–531. For historical studies, see Roderick Phillips, "Women and Family Breakdown in Eighteenth-century France: Rouen, 1780–1800," *Social History*, 2 (May 1976): 197–218; Elizabeth Pleck, "Wifebeating in Nineteenth Century America," *Victimology* 4, 1 (Fall 1979): 62–74; and Nancy Tomes, "A 'Torrent of Abuse': Working-Class Men and Women in London, 1840–1875," *Journal of Social History*, 11, 3 (Spring 1978): 328–45. See also R. H. Helmholtz, *Marriage Litigation in Medieval England* (London, 1975); Alain Lottin, ed., *La Désunion du couple sous l'ancien régime: L'Exemple du Nord* (Paris, 1975); Nancy F. Cott, "Divorce and the Changing Status of Women in Eighteenth-Century Massachusetts," *William and Mary Quarterly*, 33 (Oct. 1976): 586–614; and Jane F. Collier, *Law and Social Change in Zinacantan* (Stanford, Calif., 1973), pp. 183–89.

83. See, for example, Calderón de la Barca, p. 750.

84. Urrutia vs. Giral, C.22.

85. Mijares vs. García, C.18.

86. Pasarán vs. Rosales, C.72.

87. Presentation of Nov. 8, 1836, in Pérez vs. Rodríguez, C.34.

88. "Ejecución de justicia," *DM*, 2, *176* (Mar. 25, 1806): 334–36; Fernández de Lizardi, *Quijotita*, pp. 36–37; Ignacio Ramírez, speech of July 10, 1856, in Zarco, *Historia*, 1: 684. See also *DM*, 5 (Jan. 2, 1807): 459.

89. Compare Art. 3, Vagrancy Code, Mar. 2, 1845, in AAA *Vagos*, 4778, no. 334 (reproduced in Shaw, p. 414) with decree of Mar. 3, 1828 (Dublán & Lozano, 2: 61–62). See also Pascua, 7: 146; and Roa Bárcena, pp. 44–45, 698–99. A petition like Francisco Oliver's to the Vagrant's Tribunal demonstrates that the law was at least occasionally enforced: having been imprisoned on Sept. 17, 1845, on his wife's accusation of abuse, he was still being held without trial a month later (AAA *Vagos*, 4778).

90. Reyna y Vega vs. Martínez Calderón, C.17.

91. Testimony of Friar José Herrera and don Alejandro Jove, presentation of Dec. 2, 1802, in Villamil y Primo vs. Rodríguez, C.3. Note that only 1 of "La Güera's" 3 confessors, Manuel Arévalo, finally advised her to seek a divorce.

92. Pérez vs. Rodríguez (loose sheet 1836 or 1837), C.34; García vs. Hajo, C.77.

93. Hernández vs. Morales, C.48. See also Larios vs. Montesinos de Lara, C.5; Vinsoneo vs. Rolero, C.12; Córdoba vs. Morales, C.59; and Jiménez vs. Nápoles, C.62.

94. Mijares vs. García, C.18.

95. Doña Josefa Escalona vs. don Pedro Padilla (reunion compact), 1854–55, AGN *Bienes Nacionales*, 513, no. 140.

96. 23 of the 25 women also charged their husbands with cruelty and abuse, and 13 charged them with failure to provide.

97. See presentation of June 8, in Mijares vs. García, C.18. Note that 1 woman, apparently under her lawyer's influence, gave primary emphasis to her husband's adultery in her second deposition, a complaint that had not figured importantly in the initial petition (Hernández vs. Morales, C.48).

98. Presentation of Aug. 25, 1832, in Manzano vs. Camacho, C.25; testimony of Dec. 4 and Dec. 6, 1802, in Villamil y Primo vs. Rodríguez, C.3; presentation of July 8, 1816, in Mijares vs. García, C.18.

99. Presentation of Dec. 16, 1837, in Soberanis vs. Rivera, C.45.

100. See, for example, Soberanis vs. Rivera, C.45; and such secular court cases as doña Ana María García against her husband and María Francisca (incontinence), 1828, AJ *Juzgado de Letras G*, 1827–29; and Feliciana Ortega vs. José Timoteo Alvarez (adultery), 1802, AJ *Pleitos Civiles entre Cónyuges*, 1801–79. See also Fernández de Lizardi, *Periquillo*, p. 34.

101. Reyna y Vega vs. Martínez Calderón, C.17.

102. Presentation of July 14, 1818, and *passim* in Pérez Gálvez vs. García Noriega, C.19.

103. Don Francisco Tavoada vs. doña María Josefa Arriaga (adultery), 1809, AJ *Penal*, 12, no. 21.

104. Poinsett, p. 160; Sartorius, p. 55; Calderón de la Barca, p. 290. See also *Lettres*, pp. 61–62.

105. Letter from Manuel Blanco of Oct. 14, 1854, in Medina vs. Pintado, C.63. See also testimony of don Celestino Porras, Oct. 2, 1816, in Reyna y Vega vs. Martínez Calderón, C.17.

106. Chávez vs. Solórzano, C.56. On women's attempts to hide their affairs, see Pérez Gálvez vs. García Noriega, C.19; and Medina vs. Pintado, C.63.

107. Presentation of Apr. 18, 1816, in Reyna y Vega vs. Martínez Calderón, C.17; Hernández vs. Morales, C.48. Note that even in the 3 cases where a husband brought his lover into the home to torment his wife, this was not the principal reason given for her divorce suit.

108. Reform law of July 23, 1859, in Dublán & Lozano, 8: 691–95; Sierra, Art. 92; 1870 Civil Code, Arts. 241–42; 1884 Civil Code, Arts. 227–28; Art. 27, *Ley sobre relaciones familiares, expedida por el c. Venustiano Carranza* (Mexico City, 1917). Of the earlier codes, Zacatecas adopted the more discriminatory definition of adultery as grounds for divorce, following the Code Napoléon (Art. 136); the Oaxaca Civil Code did not (Art. 145).

109. Soberanis vs. Rivera, C.45. Doña María Antonia Reyna accused her husband of causing a daughter's death by taking her out on a cold night (Reyna y Vega vs. Martínez Calderón, C.17), and Paula Pasarán attributed a miscarriage to her husband's beatings (Pasarán vs. Rosales, C.72). The relative silence about children in the divorce records contrasts sharply with the findings for the U.S. later in the century. See Elaine T. May, "The Pursuit of Domestic Perfection: Marriage and Divorce in Los Angeles, 1890–1920" (Ph.D. dissertation, University of California, Los Angeles, 1975), p. 238.

110. Gutiérrez de Rosas vs. Enciso, C.1; Pasarán vs. Rosales, C.72. See also doña Rafaela Camposanto vs. don José Antonio Castañeda, 1837, AJ *Tocas Civiles*, 1838–42; presentation of Aug. 6, 1802, in Villamil y Primo vs. Rodríguez, C.3; and Segault vs. Ouvrard, C.47.

111. See, for example, Esteves vs. Lozano, C.67; Pasarán vs. Rosales, C.72; and Escalona vs. Padilla (cited in note 94, above).

112. For example, doña Dolores Cecilia y Valiente went to live with her mother after being abandoned by her husband, don Magdaleno Ortiz, in 1839. Only 6 years later, after her mother died, did doña Dolores sue her husband for alimentos (AJ *Comandancia General Civil*, 1844–45). See also Estrada vs. Yoldi, C.26; and Soberanis vs. Rivera, C.45. Note that several women convicted of sexual offenses were entrusted to their parents' care, as in Pérez Gálvez vs. García Noriega, C.19.

113. Villamil y Primo vs. Rodríguez, C.3; Ortega vs. Moreno, C.44; Pasarán vs. Rosales, C.72.

114. Testimony of Dec. 2, 1802, in Villamil y Primo vs. Rodríguez, C.3.

115. Escalona vs. Padilla (cited in note 95, above).

116. 4 lived with the wife's parents, 1 with the husband's. Citations are from presentation of Mar. 1, 1856, in Pasarán vs. Rosales, C.72; Rosel vs. Imhoff, C.70; Díaz vs. Espinosa, C.69; and Salazar vs. Galván, C.55. See also Escalona vs. Padilla (cited in note 95, above).

117. Nancy F. Cott, "Eighteenth-Century Family and Social Life Re-

vealed in Massachusetts Divorce Records," *Journal of Social History*, 10, 1 (Fall 1976): 28, 32.

118. Arrieta and Neira, C.32; Vásquez vs. Bastida, C.79; Esteves vs. Lozano, C.67; Omaña vs. Barroso, C.36. Because the new attitudes were voiced by well-to-do litigants it is tempting to speculate that these ideas originated in that class, but there are too few cases to draw such a conclusion.

119. Medina vs. Pintado, C.63; Villar vs. Velásquez, C.57.

120. Pascua, 1: 154–55; "Convenio entre doña Francisca Javiera Saenz de Santa María y el Capitán Retirado don Francisco Durán," AN, Not. 426, 1827, fol. 14v. Further evidence that such separations may have occurred among the elites, at least by the 1840's, comes from a satirical newspaper article depicting a wealthy couple who separated "by common accord" to "avoid public scandal" ("Anécdotas: el matrimonio," *AM*, 1, 1849, p. 92).

121. *Nuevo Febrero*, 1: 42, 46–52.

122. *Ibid.*, 1: 47.

123. Zac. Code, Art. 139; Oax. Code, Arts. 145, 162; Sierra, Art. 93; law of July 23, 1859, in Dublán & Lozano, 8: 691–95. On the 1870 Civil Code, see Arrom, "Cambios," pp. 506–11.

124. Omaña vs. Barroso, C.36; Rodríguez vs. Desés, C.58. See also Esteves vs. Lozano, C.67. At no time during this period was an entirely instrumental view of marriage accepted, however. Society frowned on the man who married a woman for her money or the parents who arranged marriages in the family interest. See presentation of Apr. 18, 1816, in Reyna y Vega vs. Martínez Calderón, C.17; and Manzano vs. Camacho, C.25. See also Mariana's arranged match in Payno, *Bandidos*.

125. *Nuevo Febrero*, 1: 64; *Cartas*, p. 17; Diego Alvarez, p. 376; Ignacio Ramírez, speech of July 10, 1856, in Zarco, *Historia*, 1: 684.

126. Presentation of Nov. 8, 1836, in Pérez vs. Rodríguez, C.34; Morales vs. Rodríguez, C.52.

127. Information on the number of years married before filing for divorce is available in 47 cases. No marital crisis years are evident in these data. Likewise, no discernible pattern emerges from the ages of the litigants. 5 of the women involved were minors (under 25), and the oldest woman, married 42 years, was 57.

128. See, for example, Aguilera vs. Quijano, C.64; Arellano vs. Canizo, C.65; Manzano vs. Camacho, C.25; and García vs. Alvarado, C.35.

129. Such transactions are only a minimal indicator, however, since some separated people whose spouses died listed themselves as widowed rather than divorced, as did doña Francisca Pérez Gálvez 33 years after her divorce was granted (loan agreement, AN, Not. 169, 1853, vol. 1, fol. 57).

130. Leiva vs. Iturria, C.66; Luna and Gávito, C.68; Segura vs. Tangassi, C.75; Pérez vs. Núñez, C.73. Divorce compacts were used in 2 cases dating from the 1840's, but only after the couple had gone through the lengthy judicial process and presented formal proofs (Espíndola vs. Martínez, C.49; Chávez vs. Solórzano, C.56). Compacts signed by both spouses and containing provisions to resolve earlier differences were also used for reunions effected in the 1850's (Escalona vs. Padilla, cited in note 94 above, who reunited before formally filing for divorce; Díaz vs. Espinosa, C.69).

131. Vásquez vs. Bastida, C.79; Esteves vs. Lozano, C.67. Compare Arrieta and Neira, C.32.

132. Carrero vs. Castañares, C.81.

## Conclusion

1. Evelyn Stevens, "Marianismo: The Other Face of Machismo in Latin America," in Pescatello, pp. 89–101; Jane Jacquette, "Literary Archetypes and Female Role Alternatives: The Woman and the Novel in Latin America," in ibid., pp. 18–20.

2. Daniel Scott Smith, "Family Limitation, Sexual Control, and Domestic Feminism in Victorian America," Feminist Studies, 1, 3–4 (Winter-Spring 1973): 40–57; Glenda Riley, "The Subtle Subversion: Changes in the Traditionalist Image of the American Woman," The Historian, 32 (1970): 210–27; Michelle Z. Rosaldo, "Women, Culture, and Society: A Theoretical Overview," in Rosaldo & Lamphere, pp. 37–38. Barbara Welter, who coined the term "cult of true womanhood," disagrees with this interpretation, arguing that women suffered, rather than gained power, from their restricted domestic roles: "The Cult of True Womanhood: 1820–1860," American Quarterly, 18, 2 (Summer 1966): 151–74.

3. Anthropologists, who find the Cult of Mary most pronounced in patriarchal societies where women command little respect, have not observed that it gives women power. See Eric Wolf, "The Virgin of Guadalupe: A Mexican National Symbol," Journal of American Folklore, 71 (1978): 34–39; Gilberto Freyre, Order and Progress: Brazil from Monarchy to Republic, tr. and ed. Rod Horton (New York City, 1970), p. 18; and Lawrence Stone, "The Rise of the Nuclear Family in Early Modern England: The Patriarchal Stage," in The Family in History, ed. Charles Rosenberg (Philadelphia, 1975), p. 34. Furthermore, the anthropological literature suggests that, as Michelle Rosaldo puts it, "insofar as woman is defined in terms of a largely maternal and domestic role, we can account for her universal subordination," and conversely, that the most egalitarian societies are those where men and women participate equally

in the domestic and public spheres (Rosaldo, "Introduction," p. 7, and Karen Sacks, "Engels Revisited: Woman, the Organization of Production, and Private Property," in Rosaldo & Lamphere, pp. 206–22).

4. In *La Quijotita*, Fernández de Lizardi toyed with the idea of women's spiritual superiority "in some cases" (p. 37), but could not bring himself to accept it. Indeed, his discussions of women's subordination reveal considerable ambiguities in his thought. Although at one point (pp. 34–35) he stated that women were equal to men in all but physical strength, he immediately qualified that statement by noting the interrelationship of body and soul—and in other places he explicitly termed women inferior (as on pp. 28–29). Despite his lip service to Enlightenment ideas of natural equality, the plot of the novel reveals his belief in women's weakness of character. In it, he has two malleable sisters, identically raised, take the shape of the contrasting men they married. Several other characters brought up without "the defects commonly associated with the Sex" (p. 64) also become spoiled by corrupt and libertine men. Thus even the best education could not alter female weakness, since Fernández de Lizardi did not credit women with the strength to uphold their convictions.

5. Although Fernández de Lizardi already referred to women as the Devout Sex (*Quijotita*, p. 34), intense religiosity and participation in charity organizations seem to have been as characteristic of men as women: *Cartas*, pp. 4–5; Roa Bárcena, p. 743; "Influencia de la muger en la educación popular," *SSM*, 3 (1842): 68; "Fragmento de balance de cuerpo y alma de Gil Fernández," *AM*, 1 (1849): 489; Calderón de la Barca, p. 523; Alessio Robles; Peza. By 1821, however, women were coming to be viewed as conservative allies of the Church because of their alleged opposition to the liberal constitution of the Spanish Cortes (Anna, p. 201).

6. For examples of later views, see García Cubas, p. 139; and Alessio Robles, p. 65.

7. Payno, "Educación"; Emilio de Girardin, "Educación de las niñas," *SSM*, 1 (1841): 127–28; *Cartas*, p. 8; *Nuevo Febrero*, 1: 110–11; "Consejos," p. 17; Francisco Zarco, "Una madre," *Presente Amistoso Dedicado a las Señoritas Mexicanas*, 3 (1852): 1–7; "Misión de la abuela en la familia," *Panorama de las Señoritas*, 1 (1842): 477; F. M. del Castillo. Compare Fernández de Lizardi, *Quijotita*, p. 29.

8. Alamán, 1: 15; *SSM*, 3 (1842): 215; Zarco, "Muger," p. 183. See also "Felicidad conyugal," *AM*, 1 (1849): 108; and *SSM*, 2 (1842): 109.

9. *Cartas*, especially pp. 4, 16–20, 55, 163. See also Jouy, "Influencia del Bello Sexo" (translated from the French), *SSM*, 1 (1841): 213–15.

10. Adelina Zendejas (*La mujer en la intervención francesa*, Mexico City,

1962, p. 13) contends that 81 women petitioned Juárez to grant them suffrage when the Constitutional Convention met in 1856. Although she gives Zamacois as her source, I have been unable to substantiate this citation after a careful review of his works. The literature I have found clearly advocates changes only in women's status in the family. See the preamble to the Reform law of July 23, 1859, and the civil marriage vow that was supposed to rehabilitate women, in Dublán & Lozano, 8: 690, 693; Diego Alvarez, p. 376; and Zarco, "Muger," p. 184.

11. "De la influencia," p. 102; "Diferencia entre el entendimiento del hombre y de la muger" (translated from the English), AM, 2 (1849): 5. A more timorous Mexican view was that "in our times . . . women are confined to an excessively narrow circle": "Las mugeres: remitido," SSM, 1 (1841): 246.

12. Cott, Bonds, p. 197. For this use of the term equality in Mexico, see Ignacio Ramírez' speech of July 10, 1856 (Zarco, Historia, 1: 684), often misread by 20th-century readers.

13. Payno "Celibato femenino." See also the Nuevo Febrero's caution against an "excess" of liberty for the Fair Sex (1: 65–66).

14. Nuevo Febrero, 1: 41; "Felicidades," p. 109; "Miscelánea," p. 259; AM, 1 (1849): 109. See also note 7, above, for articles extolling motherhood.

15. Marcelino Castañeda quoted in Richard Sinkin, "The Mexican Constitutional Congress, 1856–57: A Statistical Analysis," HAHR, 53, 1 (Feb. 1973): 7. See also the advice to husbands from Guillermo Prieto, a liberal himself, that they not be so "democratic" as to allow their wives to talk with "liberals who affirm that there is no soul, no religion, nothing" ("Dos palabras," SDN, Dec. 17, 1844).

16. Fernández de Lizardi, Quijotita, p. 105; "Educación," SSM, 3 (1842): 300; Cartas, p. 45. Indeed, strident antifeminist tracts began appearing when women's rights became an issue abroad; see "El mundo," pp. 201–2; and Rivero, especially p. 133.

17. Lerner Sigal. See also Payno, "Educación," p. 470.

18. I have been unable to locate any biographies of heroines published during the second half of the 19th century, although Francisco Sosa's Biografías (1884) includes portraits of 10 women. Genaro García published his outstanding biography of Leona Vicario in 1910, and collections of laudatory sketches of independence heroines, usually devoting only a few paragraphs to each woman and recycling well-known information, have appeared regularly ever since. See, for example, Wright de Kleinhans (1910); Hernández (1918); Rubio Siliceo (1929); and Aurora Fernández y Fernández, Mujeres que honran a la patria (Mexico City, 1958).

19. See Philippe Ariès, *Centuries of Childhood: A Social History of Family Life*, tr. Robert Baldick (New York City, 1962); Ruth H. Bloch, "American Feminine Ideals in Transition: The Rise of the Moral Mother, 1785–1815," *Feminist Studies*, 4, 2 (June 1978): 101–26; Cott; Mary Beth Norton, "The Paradox of 'Women's Sphere,'" in Berkin & Norton, pp. 139–49; and Stone, *Family*.

# Bibliography

# Bibliography

*Manuscript Sources*

Archivo del ex-Ayuntamiento de la Ciudad de México, Mexico City:
  Actas de Cabildo
  Padrones
  Vagos
Archivo General de la Nación, Mexico City:
  Bandos                   Justicia e Instrucción
  Bienes Nacionales        Pública
  Criminal                 Matrimonios
  Historia                 Montepíos y Pensiones
  Judicial                 Padrones
  Justicia Eclesiástica    Tabaco
Archivo General de Notarías, Mexico City: 1790–1857
Archivo General de los Juzgados Unitarios Penales, Mexico City:
  1806–1844
Archivo Judicial del Tribunal Superior de Justicia del D.F.,
  Mexico City:
  Alimentos                Juzgado de Cuartel
  Comandancia General      Juzgado de Letras
  Civil                    Juzgado Mercantil
  Cuadernos                Penal
  Divorcios                Pleitos Civiles entre
  Familiares                 Cónyuges
  Libros de Reos           Tocas Civiles
Departamento de Investigaciones Históricas, Instituto Nacional
  de Antropología e Historia, Mexico City: Banco de Datos,
  Padrón de 1811
Filmoteca de la Sociedad Genealógica Mexicana, Mexico City:
  Mexico, D.F., Roll 1116

### Nineteenth-Century Periodicals

These periodicals were published in Mexico City and are housed at the Hemeroteca Nacional de México, Mexico City.

*El Album de la Familia,* 1839
*El Album Mexicano,* 1849
*El Correo de los Niños,* 1813
*El Diario de México,* 1805–10
*Diario de los Niños,* 1839–40
*El Eco del Comercio,* 1848
*Gaceta de los Tribunales de la República Mexicana,* 1860
*Gazeta de México,* 1800–1820
*El Monitor Republicano,* 1848–56
*El Museo Mexicano,* 1843–49
*El Museo Popular,* 1840
*Panorama de las Señoritas,* 1842
*Presente Amistoso Dedicado a las Señoritas Mexicanas,* 1847–52
*El Recreo de las Familias,* 1838
*Revista Científica y Literaria de Méjico,* 1845–46
*Revista Mensual de la Sociedad Promovedora de Mejoras Materiales,* 1852
*La Semana de las Señoritas,* 1850–52
*La Semana de las Señoritas Mexicanas,* 1851–52
*Semanario Económico de México,* 1808–10
*Semanario de las Señoritas Mejicanas,* 1841–42
*El Siglo Diez y Nueve,* 1841–57

### Printed Works

The following list includes only the books and articles that are cited in the Notes in short form. Unless otherwise noted, pamphlets are in the Colección Lafragua, Biblioteca Nacional, Mexico City.

Alamán, Lucas. *Historia de Méjico, desde los primeros movimientos que prepararon su independencia en el año de 1808 hasta la época presente.* 5 vols., Mexico City, 1849–52.

Alessio Robles, Miguel. *La filantropía en México.* Mexico City, 1944.

Almonte, Juan Nepomuceno. *Guía de forasteros y repertorio de conocimientos útiles.* . . . Mexico City, 1852.

———. *Plano general de la ciudad de México, formado según los datos mas recientemente adquiridos para servir a la guía de forasteros.* . . . Mexico City, 1852.

Alvarez, Diego. "Discurso sobre la influencia de la instrucción publica en la felicidad de las naciones," *Revista Mensual de la Sociedad Promovedora de Mejoras Materiales,* 1 (1852): 370–80.

Alvarez, José María. *Instituciones de derecho real de Castilla y de Indias*. 4 vols., 1818–20; 2d ed., New York City, 1827. [A concise presentation of laws pertaining to Latin America, revised specifically for Mexico in this edition.]

Alvarez Posadilla, Juan. *Comentarios a las leyes de Toro según su espíritu y el de la legislación de España*. Madrid, 1833.

Anna, Timothy E. *The Fall of the Royal Government in Mexico City*. Lincoln, Neb., 1978.

Antuñano, Esteban de. *Ventajas políticas, civiles, fabriles, y domésticas, que por dar ocupación también a las mujeres en las fábricas de maquinaria moderna que se están levantando en México, deben recibirse*. Puebla, 1837 (pamphlet, Bancroft Collection, University of California, Berkeley).

Archer, Christon. *The Army in Bourbon Mexico, 1760–1810*. Albuquerque, N.M., 1977.

Arechederreta, Juan Bautista. *Estado general de los conventos de religiosas y de los colegios para educación de niñas . . . en el arzobispado de México. . . .* Mexico City, 1828 (broadside, Archivo General de la Nación *Justicia Eclesiástica*, vol. 50).

Arrom, Silvia M. "Cambios en la condición jurídica de la mujer mexicana en el siglo XIX," in *Memoria del II Congreso de Historia del Derecho Mexicano*, pp. 493–518. Mexico City, 1981.

———. *La mujer mexicana ante el divorcio eclesiástico (1800–1857)*. Mexico City, 1976.

Arrom, Silvia M., and Anne L. Gibson "Mexico City's Tribunales and Penitencia Archives: New Sources for Mexican History," *The Americas: A Quarterly Review*, 35, 3 (Oct. 1978): 249–52.

Arróniz, Marcos. *Manual del viajero en México o compendio de la historia de la ciudad de México*. Paris, 1858.

[Barreda de Trigueros, Petra]. *Manifiesto que la junta de beneficencia del hospital del Divino Salvador da al público sobre el estado en que encontró dicho hospital, y en el que lo deja*. Mexico City, 1844 (pamphlet).

Bazant, Jan. *Alienation of Church Wealth in Mexico: Social and Economic Aspects of the Liberal Revolution, 1856–1875*. Ed. and tr. Michael Costeloe. Cambridge, Eng., 1971.

Berkin, Carol R., and Mary Beth Norton, eds. *Women of America: A History*. Boston, 1979.

Bernal de Bugeda, Beatríz. "Situación jurídica de la mujer en las Indias occidentales." In *Condición jurídica de la mujer en México*, ed. Facultad de Derecho, Universidad Autónoma de México, pp. 21–40. Mexico City, 1975.

Borah, Woodrow. "Race and Class in Mexico," *Pacific Historical Review*, 23, 4 (Nov. 1954): 331–42.

Borah, Woodrow, and Sherburne Cook. *Essays in Population History: Mexico and the Caribbean.* 3 vols., Berkeley, Calif., 1971–79.

———. "Marriage and Legitimacy in Mexican Culture: Mexico and California," *California Law Review,* 54 (1966): 946–1008.

Brading, David. "Government and Elite in Late Colonial Mexico," *Hispanic American Historical Review,* 53, *3* (Aug. 1973): 389–414.

———. *Miners and Merchants in Bourbon Mexico, 1763–1810.* Cambridge, Eng., 1971.

Brading, David, and Celia Wu. "Population Growth and Crisis: León, 1720–1860," *Journal of Latin American Studies,* 5, *1* (May 1973): 1–36.

Bullock, W. *Six Months' Residence and Travels in Mexico.* 2 vols. 1824; reprint New York City, 1971.

Bustamante, Carlos María de. *Cuadro histórico de la revolución mexicana, comenzada el 15 de septiembre 1810.* . . . 3 vols., Mexico City, 1961.

[Caballero de Borda, Ana Josefa]. *Necesidad de un establecimiento de educación para las jóvenes mexicanas.* Mexico City, 1823 (pamphlet; signed A.J.C.B.).

Calderón de la Barca, Frances. *Life in Mexico: The Letters of Fanny Calderón de la Barca with New Material from the Author's Private Journals.* Ed. Howard T. Fisher and Marion Hall Fisher. New York City, 1966.

Campomanes, *see* Rodríguez.

Capca, Bernardo. *Apuntes biográficos de la señora doña María Ana Gómez de la Cortina, condesa de la Cortina.* Mexico City, 1853.

Cardoso, Ciro F. S., ed. *Formación y desarrollo de la burguesía en México: siglo XIX.* Mexico City, 1978.

Carlos, Manuel L., and Lois Sellers. "Family, Kinship Structure, and Modernization in Latin America," *Latin American Research Review,* 7, 2 (Summer 1972): 95–124.

Carrera Stampa, Manuel. *Los gremios mexicanos: la organización gremial en Nueva España, 1521–1861.* Mexico City, 1954.

Carroll, Berenice A., ed. *Liberating Women's History: Theoretical and Critical Essays.* Urbana, Ill., 1976.

*Cartas sobre la educación del bello sexo, por una señora americana.* Mexico City, 1851 (pamphlet).

Castillo, Florencio M. del. "Educación de la mujer," *Monitor Republicano,* April 14, 1856.

Castillo Negrete, Emilio de. *México en el siglo XIX: o sea, su historia desde 1800 hasta la época presente.* 25 vols., Mexico City, 1875–91.

Chance, John K., and William B. Taylor. "Estate and Class in a Colonial City: Oaxaca in 1792," *Comparative Studies in Society and History,* 19 (Oct. 1977): 454–87.

Chávez Orozco, Luis. *El comercio exterior y el artesanado mexicano (1825–1830)*. Mexico City, 1965.

Clagett, Helen L., and David M. Valderrama. *A Revised Guide to the Law and Legal Literature of Mexico*. Washington, D.C., 1973.

Coatsworth, John H. "Obstacles to Economic Growth in Nineteenth-Century Mexico," *American Historical Review*, 83, 1 (Feb. 1978): 80–100.

*Código penal para el Distrito Federal y territorio de la Baja-California sobre delitos del fuero común*. . . .

*Colección de decretos del congreso constituyente de México*. . . . Toluca, 1850. [Decrees of the State of Mexico during the federalist interlude, 1824–35.]

*Condición jurídica de la mujer mexicana*. Ed. Facultad de Derecho, Universidad Nacional Autónoma de México. Mexico City, 1975.

"Consejos a las señoritas," *Presente Amistoso Dedicado a las Señoritas Mexicanas*, 2 (1850): 17–22 (signed J.J.P.).

Cooper, Donald. *Epidemic Disease in Mexico City, 1761-1813*. Austin, Tex., 1965.

Cott, Nancy. *The Bonds of Womanhood: "Woman's Sphere" in New England, 1780–1835*. New Haven, Conn., 1977.

Cott, Nancy, and Elizabeth Pleck, eds. *A Heritage of Her Own: Toward a New Social History of American Women*. New York City, 1979.

Couturier, Edith. "Women in a Noble Family: The Mexican Counts of Regla, 1750–1830." In *Latin American Women: Historical Perspectives*, ed. Asunción Lavrin, pp. 129–49. Westport, Conn., 1978.

"Cuestión interesante: si a las mujeres conviene la ilustración ¿En que grado debe ser esta, y en que circunstancias?" *Semanario Económico de México*, 2, 1 (Jan. 4, 1810): 4–6.

Davies, Keith. "Tendencias demográficas urbanas durante el siglo XIX en México," *Historia Mexicana*, 83 (Jan.-Mar. 1972): 481–524.

"De la influencia de las mugeres en la política," *Panorama de las Señoritas*, 1 (1842): 99–102.

*Discurso sobre el derecho con algunas observaciones acerca de las reformas que deben hacerse en nuestra legislación*. Mexico City, 1841 (pamphlet; signed I. M. R.).

Dublán, Manuel, and José María Lozano, ed. *Legislación mexicana o colección completa de las disposiciones legislativas expedidas desde la independencia de la República*. 34 vols., Mexico City, 1876–1904. [Highly selective, despite its title.]

Echanove Trujillo, Carlos A. *Leona Vicario: la mujer fuerte de la independencia*. Mexico City, 1945.

*Ensayos sobre las clases sociales en México*, ed. Editorial Nuestro Tiempo. 4th ed., Mexico City, 1974.

*Esposición que varias señoras mexicanas presentaron al Exmo. señor General D. Vicente Guerrero, electo presidente de los Estados Unidos Mexicanos, sobre la ley general de espulsión de españoles, la noche del 24 de marzo de 1829.* Mexico City, 1829 (pamphlet).

*Exhortación de una patriota mariana a las señoras sus compañeras con motivos de la festividad de nuestra señora de los Remedios hoy 1° de septiembre de 1815.* Mexico City, [1815] (pamphlet).

"Felicidades del matrimonio: idilio," *Semanario Económico de México,* 2, 46 (Nov. 15, 1810): 378–81.

Fernández de Lizardi, José Joaquín. *Heroínas mexicanas: María Leona Vicario, María Rodríguez Lazarín, María Fermina Rivera, Manuela Herrera y otras.* 1825; reprint Mexico City, 1955.

———. *El Periquillo Sarniento.* 1816; reprint Mexico City, 1974.

———. *La Quijotita y su prima: historia muy cierta con apariencias de novela.* 1818–19; rev. ed. María del Carmen Ruiz Castañeda. Mexico City, 1973.

Florescano, Enrique. *Precios del maíz y crisis agrícolas en México, 1708–1810.* Mexico City, 1969.

Florescano, Enrique, and Elena Gil Sánchez. "La época de las reformas borbónicas y el crecimiento económico, 1750–1808." In *Historia general de México,* ed. Centro de Estudios Históricos, El Colegio de México, vol. 2: 185–301. Mexico City, 1976.

Frías y Soto, Hilarión, et al. *Los mexicanos pintados por sí mismos: tipos y costumbres nacionales.* 1854–55; reprint Mexico City, 1974.

Galván Rivera, Mariano. *Calendario manual y guía de la ciudad de Méjico para el año de 1832.* Mexico City, 1832.

———, ed. *Concilio III Provincial Mexicano.* 1585; reprint Mexico City, 1859.

García, Genaro. *Leona Vicario: heroína insurgente.* Mexico City, 1910.

———, ed. *Documentos históricos mexicanos.* 5 vols., Mexico City, 1910.

García Cubas, Antonio. *El libro de mis recuerdos: narraciones históricas, anecdóticas y de costumbres mexicanas anteriores al actual orden social.* Mexico City, 1904.

García Icazbalceta, Joaquín. *Informe sobre los establecimientos de beneficencia y corrección de esta capital . . . en 1864.* Mexico City, 1907.

Gibson, Charles. *The Aztecs Under Spanish Rule: A History of the Indians of the Valley of Mexico, 1519–1810.* Stanford, Calif., 1964.

Gilmore, Nancy Ray. "The Condition of the Poor in Mexico, 1834," *Hispanic American Historical Review,* 37, 2 (May 1957): 213–26.

Gondra, Isidro Rafael. *Prospecto. Semanario de las Señoritas Mejicanas.* Mexico City, 1841 (pamphlet).

González, Armida de. "Los ceros sociales." In *Historia moderna de Mé-*

*xico III. La República Restaurada: la vida social*, ed. Daniel Cosío Villegas, pp. 369–410. 2d ed., Mexico City, 1974.

González Angulo Aguirre, Jorge. *Artesanado y ciudad a finales del siglo XVIII*. Mexico City, 1983.

González Castro, Vicente. *Redacción del código civil de México, que se contiene en las leyes españolas, y demás vigentes en nuestra república*. Guadalajara, 1839. [A compilation of the principal laws used in independent Mexico, arranged in the form of a civil code.]

González Domínguez, María del Refugio. "Consideraciones en torno a la aplicación del derecho civil en México de la independencia al II Imperio," thesis, Facultad de Derecho, Universidad Nacional Autónoma de México, 1973.

————. "Notas para el estudio del proceso de la codificación civil en México (1821–1928)." In *Libro del cincuentenario del Código Civil*, pp. 95–136. Mexico City, 1978.

Goody, Jack. *Production and Reproduction: A Comparative Study of the Domestic Domain*. Cambridge, Eng., 1976.

Greenleaf, Richard E. "The Obraje in the Late Mexican Colony," *The Americas: A Quarterly Review*, 23 (Jan. 1967): 227–50.

*Guía de forasteros de la ciudad de Mégico*. Mexico City, 1854 (Biblioteca Nacional, Mexico City).

Hajnal, J. H. "European Marriage Patterns in Perspective." In *Population in History: Essays in Historical Demography*, ed. D. V. Glass and D. E. C. Eversley, pp. 100–143.

Hale, Charles A. *Mexican Liberalism in the Age of Mora, 1821–1853*. New Haven, Conn., 1968.

Hamill, Hugh M., Jr. *The Hidalgo Revolt: Prelude to Mexican Independence*. Gainesville, Fla., 1966.

Hernández, Carlos. *Mujeres célebres de México*. San Antonio, Tex., 1918.

Herr, Richard. *The Eighteenth-Century Revolution in Spain*. Princeton, N.J., 1958.

Herrick, Jane. "Periodicals for Women in Mexico During the Nineteenth Century," *The Americas: A Quarterly Review*, 14, 2 (1957): 135–44.

Humboldt, Alexander von. *Political Essay on the Kingdom of New Spain*. 1811; tr. John Black, 4 vols., 2d ed., London, 1814.

*Ilustración del derecho real de España . . . reformada y añadida con varias doctrinas y disposiciones del derecho novísimo y del patrio*. 5 vols., Mexico City, 1831–33. [A revised Mexican edition of Juan Sala's *Ilustración del derecho real de España*; Valencia, 1803.]

Jelin, Elizabeth. "Migration and Labor Force Participation of Latin American Women: The Domestic Servants in the Cities," *Signs*, 3, 1 (Autumn 1977): 129–41.

Kentner, Janet R. "The Socio-Political Role of Women in the Mexican Wars of Independence," Ph.D. dissertation, Loyola University, Chicago, 1975.

Keremetsis, Dawn. *La industria textil mexicana en el siglo XIX*. Mexico City, 1973.

Kicza, John E. "Business and Society in Late Colonial Mexico City," Ph.D. dissertation, University of California, Los Angeles, 1979.

Konetzke, Richard, ed. *Colección de documentos para la historia de la formación social de Hispanoamérica, 1493–1810*. 4 vols., Madrid, 1953–58.

Ladd, Doris M. *The Mexican Nobility at Independence, 1780–1826*. Austin, Tex., 1976.

Lamas, Adolpho. *Seguridad social en la Nueva España*. Mexico City, 1964.

Lavrin, Asunción. "In Search of the Colonial Woman in Mexico: The Seventeenth and Eighteenth Centuries." In *Latin American Women*, ed. Lavrin (below), pp. 23–59.

———. "Religious Life of Mexican Women in the Eighteenth Century," Ph.D. dissertation, Harvard University, 1962.

———. "Women in Convents: Their Economic and Social Role in Colonial Mexico." In *Liberating Women's History: Theoretical and Critical Essays*, ed. Berenice A. Carroll, pp. 250–77. Chicago, 1976.

———, ed. *Latin American Women: Historical Perspectives*. Westport, Conn., 1978.

Lavrin, Asunción, and Edith Couturier. "Dowries and Wills: A View of Women's Socioeconomic Role in Colonial Guadalajara and Puebla, 1640–1790," *Hispanic American Historical Review*, 59, 2 (May 1979): 280–304.

Leal, María Luisa. "Mujeres insurgentes," *Boletín del Archivo General de la Nación*, 20, 4 (1949): 543–604.

Lerner Sigal, Victoria. "La idea de los Estados Unidos a través de los viajeros mexicanos, 1830–1945," M.A. thesis, El Colegio de México, 1971.

*Lettres sur le Mexique, ou guide du voyageurs*. . . . New Orleans, La., 1827 (pamphlet).

Lira-González, Andrés. "Indian Communities in Mexico City: The Parcialidades of Tenochtitlan and Tlatelolco (1812–1919)," Ph.D. dissertation, State University of New York, Stony Brook, 1982.

Lizana y Beaumont, Francisco Javier. *Instrucción pastoral . . . sobre la costumbre de llevar las señoras el pecho y brazos desnudos*. Mexico City, 1808 (pamphlet).

"Llamada a las mujeres a luchar por la independencia, 1812," *Boletín del Archivo General de la Nación*, 3d ser., 3, 3 (July-Sep. 1979): 13.

Llamas y Molina, Sancho. *Comentario crítico, jurídico, literal a las ochenta y tres leyes de Toro*. 3d ed., Madrid, 1853.

Lombardi, John. *People and Places in Colonial Venezuela.* Bloomington, Ind., 1976.

López Cámara, Francisco. *La estructura económica y social de México en la época de la Reforma.* 2d ed., Mexico City, 1973.

Löwenstern, Isidore. *Le Mexique: Souvenirs d'un voyageur.* Paris, 1843.

McAlister, Lyle N. "Social Structure and Social Change in New Spain," *Hispanic American Historical Review,* 43, 3 (Aug. 1963): 349–70.

McCaa, Robert. "A New Approach for Analyzing Population Data: Log Linear Models of Tables of Counts," *Latin American Population Newsletter,* 2, 4 (Fall 1981): 39–46.

McCaa, Robert, Stuart B. Schwartz, and Arturo Grubessich. "Race and Class in Colonial Latin America: A Critique," *Comparative Studies in Society and History,* 21, 3 (July 1979): 421–33.

McWatters, David L. "The Royal Tobacco Monopoly in Bourbon Mexico, 1764–1810," Ph.D. dissertation, University of Florida, Gainesville, 1979.

Macías, Anna. *Against All Odds: The Feminist Movement in Mexico to 1940.* Westport, Conn., 1982.

Margadant, Guillermo Floris. *Introducción a la historia del derecho mexicano.* Mexico City, 1971.

Martínez-Alier, Verena. *Marriage, Class, and Colour in Nineteenth-Century Cuba: A Study of Racial Attitudes and Sexual Values in a Slave Society.* London, 1974.

Mayer, Brantz. *Mexico As It Was and As It Is.* New York City, 1844.

"Memoria del primer semestre, que conforme al reglamento de prostitución en México, presenta al C. Gobernador del Distrito y Consejo Superior de Salubridad, el médico en gefe de la sección respectiva," *La Gaceta de Policía,* Dec. 17, 1868, pp. 2–4.

*Memorias de la 1ª reunión nacional sobre investigación demográfica en México,* ed. Consejo Nacional de Ciencia y Tecnología. Mexico City, 1978.

Mendieta Alatorre, Angeles. *Margarita Maza de Juárez: epistolario, antología, iconografía y efemérides.* Mexico City, 1972.

Miquel i Vergés, Josep María. *Diccionario de insurgentes.* Mexico City, 1969.

"Miscelánea: a las madres de familia," *La Semana de las Señoritas Mexicanas,* 1 (1851): 259.

Mora, José María Luis. *Méjico y sus revoluciones.* 2 vols., Paris, 1836.

Morales, María Dolores. "Cambios en la estructura de la propiedad en la cd. de México, 1813–1848," paper presented at the meeting of the Latin American Studies Association, held in Washington, D.C., Mar. 1982.

———. "Estructura urbana y distribución de la propiedad en la cd. de México en 1813," *Historia Mexicana,* 25, 3 (Jan.-Mar. 1976): 363–402.

Moreno Toscano, Alejandra, ed. *Ensayos sobre el desarrollo urbano de México.* Mexico City, 1974.

Morin, Claude. *Santa Inés Zacatelco (1646–1812): contribución a la demografía histórica del México colonial.* Mexico City, 1973.

Mörner, Magnus. "Economic Factors and Stratification in Colonial Spanish America with Special Regard to Elites," *Hispanic American Historical Review,* 63, 2 (May 1983): 335–69.

Morse, Richard M., ed. *Las ciudades latinoamericanas II: desarrollo histórico.* Mexico City, 1973.

"El mundo el año de 3.000," *El Album Mexicano,* 1 (1849): 198–202 (signed J.I).

Muriel, Josefina. *Conventos de monjas en la Nueva España.* Mexico City, 1946.

———. *Cultura femenina novohispana.* Mexico City, 1982.

———. *Los recogimientos de mujeres: respuesta a una problemática social novohispana.* Mexico City, 1974.

Nash, June, and Helen I. Safa, eds. *Sex and Class in Latin America.* New York City, 1976.

Nava, María Francisca de. *Proclama de doña María Francisca de Nava, mexicana llena de entusiasmo y de amor acia su soberano el señor don Fernando VII (Q.D.C.).* Mexico City, [ca. 1808] (pamphlet).

———. *Proclama de una americana a sus compatricias, sobre la obligación y modo de hacer a los nuevos enemigos de la religión y del estado.* Mexico City, 1810 (pamphlet).

———. *Sueño alegórico dedicado a la religión, objeto amable de la antigua y nueva España.* Mexico City, n.d. (pamphlet).

Navarro y Noriega, Fernando. *Memoria sobre la población del reino de Nueva España.* Rev. ed., Mexico City, 1820 (pamphlet; Archivo General de la Nación *Impresos Oficiales,* vol. 60, no. 48).

*Novísima recopilación de las leyes de España.* . . . 6 vols., Madrid, 1805–29. [Official compilation of Spanish legislation updating earlier versions of the *Nueva recopilación de las leyes de Castilla.* . . . Excludes laws from the Siete Partidas.]

*Nuevo Febrero mexicano: obra completa de jurisprudencia teórico-práctica.* . . . 4 vols., Mexico City, 1850–52. [An updated and considerably revised version of Pascua's popular handbook, with extensive commentary on the law.]

Obregón, Gonzalo, Jr. *El Real Colegio de San Ignacio de México.* Mexico City, 1949.

Orozco y Berra, Manuel. *Historia de la ciudad de México desde su fundación hasta 1854,* ed. Seminario de Historia Urbana, Departamento de Investigaciones Históricas, Instituto Nacional de Antropología e Historia. Mexico City, 1973.

Ortiz-Urquidi, Raul. *Oaxaca, cuna de la codificación iberoamericana.* Mexico City, 1974.

Otero, Mariano. "Ensayo sobre el verdadero estado de la cuestión social y política que se agita en la república mexicana." 1842; reprinted in *Obras,* ed. Jesús Reyes Heroles, vol. 1: 1–94. Mexico City, 1967.

Ots Capdequí, José María. "El sexo como circunstancia modificativa de la capacidad jurídica en nuestra legislación de Indias," *Anuario de Historia del Derecho Español,* 7 (1930): 311–80.

————— *Historia del derecho español en América y del derecho indiano.* 2d ed., Madrid, 1967.

Pascua, Anastasio de la. *Febrero mejicano, o sea la librería de jueces, abogados y escribanos . . . nuevamente adicionado. . . .* 9 vols., Mexico City, 1834–35. [A Mexican adaptation of Eugenio Tapia's *Febrero novísimo. . . .* (Valencia, 1828–31), which was itself a revised version of José Febrero's *Librería de escribanos. . . .* (Madrid, 1769).]

Payno, Manuel. *Los bandidos de Río Frío.* 1889–91; reprint Mexico City, 1975.

—————. "Celibato femenino," *El Siglo Diez y Nueve,* Dec. 9, 1843.

—————. "Educación maternal," *Revista Científica y Literaria de Méjico,* 1 (1845): 470–71.

—————. *El fistol del diablo: novela de costumbres mexicanas.* 1845–46; rev. ed. Antonio Castro Leal, Mexico City, 1967.

Pérez y López, Antonio. *Teatro de la legislación universal de España e Indias. . . .* 28 vols., Madrid, 1791–98. [An annotated collection of laws, arranged in alphabetical order. The most complete reference work available in the first half of the nineteenth century.]

Pescatello, Ann, ed. *Female and Male in Latin America: Essays.* Pittsburgh, Pa., 1973.

Peza, Juan de Dios. *La beneficencia en México.* Mexico City, 1881.

Poinsett, Joel R. *Notes on Mexico Made in the Autumn of 1822. . . .* Philadelphia, 1824.

Potash, Robert A. *El Banco de Avío de México: el fomento de la industria.* Mexico City, 1959.

Prieto, Guillermo. "Las Margaritas," *El Album Mexicano,* 2 (1849): 399–402 (signed Fidel).

—————. *Memorias de mis tiempos, 1828–1853.* Mexico City, 1906.

*Proyecto de código civil presentado al segundo congreso constitucional del estado libre de Zacatecas por la comisión encargada de redactarlo.* Zacatecas, 1829.

Pulido, Esperanza. *La mujer mexicana en la música (hasta la tercera década del siglo XX).* Mexico City, 1958.

Ramos, Donald. "Marriage and the Family in Colonial Vila Rica," *Hispanic American Historical Review,* 55, 2 (May 1975): 200–225.

*Representación que las maestras, oficiales y demás empleadas de la Fábrica de Tabacos de esta ciudad dirigen al Supremo Gobierno, pidiendo no se adopte el proyecto de elaborar los puros y cigarros por medio de una máquina.* Mexico City, 1846 (pamphlet, Biblioteca del Departamento de Investigaciones Históricas, Instituto Nacional de Antropología e Historia).

*Representación que las señoras de Guadalajara dirigen al Soberano Congreso Constituyente sobre que en la carta fundamental que se discute, no quede consignada la tolerancia de cultos en la República.* Guadalajara, 1856 (pamphlet).

Reyes Heroles, Jesús. *El liberalismo mexicano.* 3 vols., 2d ed., Mexico City, 1974.

Reyna, María del Carmen. "Las condiciones del trabajo en las panaderías de la ciudad de México durante la segunda mitad del siglo XIX," *Historia Mexicana,* 31, 3 (Jan.-Mar. 1982): 431–48.

Rivero, A. "El destino de la muger," *Revista Científica y Literaria de Méjico,* 1 (1845): 129–37.

Roa Bárcena, Rafael. *Manual razonado de práctica criminal y médico-legal forense mexicana.* Mexico City, 1859.

Robertson, William P. *A Visit to Mexico by the West India Islands.* 2 vols., London, 1853.

Robinson, William Davis. *Memoirs of the Mexican Revolution.* . . . Philadelphia, 1820.

Rodríguez, Pedro (Count of Campomanes). *Discurso sobre la educación popular de los artesanos, y su fomento.* Madrid, 1775.

Rodríguez de San Miguel, Juan N. *Pandectas Hispano-Mejicanas, o sea código general comprensivo de las leyes generales, útiles y vivas de las Siete Partidas, Recopilación Novísima de las Indias, autos y providencias.* . . . 3 vols., Mexico City, 1839. [A compilation of selected Spanish laws used in independent Mexico.]

Romero de Terreros, Manuel. "La condesa escribe," *Historia Mexicana,* 1, 3 (Jan.-Mar. 1952): 456–67.

Rosaldo, Michelle Z., and Louise Lamphere, eds. *Woman, Culture, and Society.* Stanford, Calif., 1974.

Rosenzweig Hernández, Fernando. "La economía novo-hispana al comenzar el siglo XIX," *Ciencias Políticas y Sociales,* 9, 33 (1963): 455–94.

Rubio Siliceo, Luis. *Mujeres célebres en la independencia de México.* Mexico City, 1929.

*Sala mexicano, o sea: la ilustración al derecho real de España* . . . *y las leyes y principios que actualmente rigen en la república mexicana.* 4 vols., Mexico City, 1845–49. [An expanded version of the Mexican *Ilustración* . . . *reformada.*]

Sartorius, Carl. *Mexico About 1850.* 1858; reprint Stuttgart, 1961.

Scardaville, Michael C. "Alcohol Abuse and Tavern Reform in Late Co-
lonial Mexico City," *Hispanic American Historical Review*, 60, 4 (Nov.
1980): 643–71.
———. "Crime and the Urban Poor: Mexico City in the Late Colonial
Period," Ph.D. dissertation, University of Florida, Gainesville, 1977.
Scott, Samuel, tr. *Las Siete Partidas*. New York City, 1931.
Seed, Patricia. "Social Dimensions of Race: Mexico City, 1753," *Hispanic
American Historical Review*, 62, 4 (Nov. 1982): 569–606.
Seminario de Historia Urbana, Departamento de Investigaciones His-
tóricas, Instituto Nacional de Antropología e Historia, ed. *Ciudad de
México: ensayo de construcción de una historia*. Mexico City, 1978.
———. *Fuentes para la historia de la ciudad de México*. Mexico City, 1972.
———. *Investigaciones sobre la historia de la ciudad de México*, 3 vols. Mex-
ico City, 1974–78.
*Sermón de los hombres contra las mujeres*. Mexico City, 1850 (pamphlet).
Shaw, Frederick J., Jr. "Poverty and Politics in Mexico City, 1824–54,"
Ph.D. dissertation, University of Florida, Gainesville, 1975.
Sierra, Justo. *Proyecto de un código civil mexicano formado de orden del su-
premo gobierno. . . .* Mexico City, 1861.
"Sobre el luxo de las mugeres," *Semanario Económico de México*, 2, 16
(Apr. 19, 1810): 123–26.
"Sobre la necesidad del matrimonio," *Semanario Económico de México*, 2,
16 (Apr. 19, 1810): 305–8.
Sosa, Francisco. *Biografías de mexicanos distinguidos*. Mexico City, 1884.
Staples, Ann. "Ecclesiastical Affairs in the First Mexican Federal Repub-
lic, 1821–1835." M.A. thesis, University of Texas, Austin, 1967.
Stone, Lawrence. *The Family, Sex and Marriage in England, 1500–1800*.
London, 1977.
Tanck Estrada, Dorothy. *La educación ilustrada 1786–1836: educación pri-
maria en la ciudad de México*. Mexico City, 1977.
Taylor, William B. *Drinking, Homicide, and Rebellion in Colonial Mexican
Villages*. Stanford, Calif., 1979.
Tella, Torcuato di. "The Dangerous Classes in Early Nineteenth-Century
Mexico," *Journal of Latin American Studies*, 5, 1 (May 1973): 79–105.
Tempsky, G. F. von. *Mitla: A Narrative of Incidents and Personal Adventures
on a Journey in Mexico, Guatemala, and Salvador in the Years 1853 to 1855.
. . .* London, 1858.
Tena Ramírez, Felipe. *Leyes fundamentales de México, 1808–1973*. 5th
ed., Mexico City, 1973. [Texts of Mexican constitutions and related
documents.]
Tenenbaum, Barbara A. "Straightening Out Some of the Lumpen in the
Development," *Latin American Perspectives*, 2, 2 (1975): 3–16.

Thompson, Waddy. *Recollections of Mexico*. New York City, 1846.

Tutino, John. "Power, Class, and Family: Men and Women in the Mexican Elite, 1750–1810," *The Americas: A Quarterly Review*, 39, 3 (Jan. 1983): 359–81.

Valle Arizpe, Artemio del. *La Güera Rodríguez*. 9th ed. rev., Mexico City, 1960.

Vázquez Valle, Irene. "Los habitantes de la ciudad de México vistos a través del censo del año de 1753," M.A. thesis, El Colegio de México, 1975.

[Villarroel, Hipólito]. *México por dentro y fuera bajo el gobierno de los virreyes, o sea, enfermedades políticas que padece la capital de la Nueva España . . . y remedios que se deben aplicar para su curación*. Written in 1785; ed. Carlos María de Bustamante, Mexico City, 1831.

Williams, Mary Wilhemine. *The People and Politics of Latin America*. Rev. ed., New York City, 1945.

Wright de Kleinhans, Laureana. *Mujeres notables mexicanas*. Mexico City, 1910.

Wrigley, E. A. *Population and History*. New York City, 1969.

Zamacois, Niceto de. *Historia de Méjico, desde sus tiempos mas remotos hasta nuestros días*. . . . 22 vols., Mexico City, 1876–1903.

Zarco, Francisco. *Historia del Congreso estraordinario constituyente de 1856 y 1857*. . . . 2 vols., Mexico City, 1857.

———. "La muger," *Presente Amistoso Dedicado a las Señoritas Mexicanas*, 3 (1852): 181–84.

Zavala, Lorenzo de. *Viage a los Estados Unidos del Norte de América*. Paris, 1834.

# Sources of Illustrations

Book title page: "Las cadenas en una noche de luna," drawing by C. Castro, in *Mexico y sus alrededores: colección de vistas monumentales, paisajes, y trajes del país,* rev. ed. (Mexico City, 1869). Beinecke Rare Book Library, Yale University.

1. Title page: *Semanario de las Señoritas Mejicanas,* vol. 1, 1841.

2. "Call to the Women to Fight": Anon. pen and ink, 1812. Archivo General de la Nación, Mexico City, ramo *Operaciones de Guerra,* vol. 406, fol. 195.

3. Leona Vicario: Anon. 19th c. oil. Museo Nacional de Historia, Instituto Nacional de Antropología e Historia, Mexico City.

4. Public scribe: Claudio Linati, *Costumes et Moeurs de Mexique* (London, 1830), plate 29. Beinecke Rare Book Library, Yale University.

5. Fruit and vegetable vendor: "Trajes Mexicanos," drawing by C. Castro, in *México y sus alrededores: colección de vistas, trajes, y monumentos* (Mexico City, 1855–56), plate 18. Beinecke Rare Book Library, Yale University.

6. Families by racial type: "De Castiza y Español, Español"; "De Lobo e India, Sambaioo"; "De Coyote Mestizo y Mulata, Ahí te estás," anon. early 19th c. oils from the Colección de Castas series. Museo Nacional de Historia, Instituto Nacional de Antropología e Historia, Mexico City.

7. Apartment manager: "La Casera," drawing by H. Iriarte, in Hilarión Frías y Soto et al., *Los mexicanos pintados por si mismos: tipos y costumbres nacionales* (Mexico City, 1854–55), facing p. 208. Library of Congress, Washington, D.C.

8. Domestic servant: "La Cocina Poblana," oil by Manuel Serrano, ca. 1855. Museo Nacional de Historia, Instituto Nacional de Antropología e Historia, Mexico City.

9. Tobacconist: "La Estanquillera," drawing by H. Iriarte, in Hilarión Frías y Soto et al., *Los mexicanos pintados por si mismos: tipos y costumbres nacionales* (Mexico City, 1854–55), facing p. 168. Library of Congress, Washington, D.C.

10. Midwife: "La Partera," drawing (artist unknown), in Hilarión Frías y Soto et al., *Los mexicanos pintados por si mismos: tipos y costumbres nacionales*, facsimile ed. (Mexico City, 1974), facing p. 268.

11. Divorce diagram: Archivo General de la Nación, Mexico City, ramo *Bienes Nacionales*, leg. 898.

12. Mother and child: "Los esposos felices," illustration in *Diario de los Niños*, vol. 3, 1840.

# Index

# Index